Legal Documents as Sources for the History of Muslim Societies

Studies in Islamic Law and Society

VOLUME 42

The titles published in this series are listed at *brill.com/sils*

Legal Documents as Sources for the History of Muslim Societies

Studies in Honour of Rudolph Peters

Edited by

Maaike van Berkel

Léon Buskens

Petra M. Sijpesteijn

BRILL

LEIDEN | BOSTON

Library of Congress Cataloging-in-Publication Data

Names: Peters, Rudolph, honouree. | Berkel, Maaike van, editor. | Buskens, Leon, 1962–, editor. | Sijpesteijn, Petra, editor.
Title: Legal documents as sources for the history of Muslim societies : studies in honour of Rudolph Peters / Edited by Maaike van Berkel, Leon Buskens, Petra M. Sijpesteijn.
Description: Leiden : Brill, 2017. | Series: Studies in islamic law and society ; 42 | Includes bibliographical references and index.
Identifiers: LCCN 2017022411 (print) | LCCN 2017022712 (ebook) | ISBN 9789004343733 (E-book) | ISBN 9789004343726 (hardback : alk. paper)
Subjects: LCSH: Legal documents (Islamic law) | Islamic law—History. | Law—Islamic countries—History. | Sociological jurisprudence.
Classification: LCC KBP173.25 (ebook) | LCC KBP173.25.L44 2017 (print) | DDC 909/.097670072—dc23
LC record available at https://lccn.loc.gov/2017022411

Typeface for the Latin, Greek, and Cyrillic scripts: "Brill". See and download: brill.com/brill-typeface.

ISSN 1384-1130
ISBN 978-90-04-34372-6 (hardback)
ISBN 978-90-04-34373-3 (e-book)

This book is printed on acid-free paper and produced in a sustainable manner.

Contents

List of Figures and Tables

Figures

Tables

Notes on Contributors

Maaike van Berkel
is professor of Medieval History at Radboud University in Nijmegen. Her research focuses on the social and cultural history of Muslim societies, with a particular interest in literacy, court culture, and urban organization.

Maurits H. van den Boogert
(PhD Leiden University, 2001) is a historian of the Ottoman Empire. He has published two monographs, *The Capitulations and the Ottoman Legal System* (Leiden: Brill, 2005) and *Aleppo Observed: Ottoman Syria Through the Eyes of Two Scottish Doctors, Alexander and Patrick Russell* (Oxford: OUP, 2010), and (co)edited several collective volumes. He has also published a dozen articles on aspects of Ottoman history and the history of Oriental studies in Europe. He works for Brill.

Léon Buskens
holds a chair for Law and Culture in Muslim societies at Leiden University and is director of the Netherlands Institute in Morocco (NIMAR). His research is about Islamic law and society, and the anthropology of Muslim societies, with a particular interest in Morocco and Indonesia. He focuses at present on the multiple relations between scholarship on Islamic law and the practices of colonial and post-colonial administration. In this framework he works on a study on the life and work of the Dutch Orientalist Christiaan Snouck Hurgronje (1857–1936).

Khaled Fahmy
is professor of History at the American University in Cairo, and currently the Shawwaf visiting professor at the Center for Middle Eastern Studies at Harvard University. His research interests lie in the social and cultural history of modern Egypt. Specifically, he has written on military history, history of law (shariʿa), history of medicine and of public hygiene – all with an emphasis on nineteenth-century Egypt.

Aharon Layish
(PhD 1973) is professor emeritus of the Hebrew University of Jerusalem. He has published extensively on modern trends in Islamic law with special reference to Israel, Islamization of tribal customary law in Libya and the Judean desert,

the family waqf as a means of circumventing Islamic inheritance law and as a prop for the social and political order, marriage, divorce, succession and testamentary waqf in the Druze family, and reinstatement of Islamic law in Sudan. His recent publications are *Sharīʿa and Custom in Libyan Tribal Society. An Annotated Translation of Decisions from the Sharīʿa Courts of Ajdābiya and Kufra*, (Leiden: Brill, 2005); *Legal Documents from the Judean Desert. The Impact of the Shariʿa on Bedouin Customary Law* (Leiden: Brill, 2011). Forthcoming: *Revival of Islamic Law in Late 19th Century Sudan. The Mahdī's Legal Methodology and its Application*. Layish was executive editor of Islamic Law and Society from 1994 until 2011 and president of the Israel Oriental Society from 2004 until 2006.

Sergio Carro Martín
studied Arabic and Islamic History at the Universidad de Salamanca (2007) and defended his master's thesis at the Universidad Autónoma de Madrid (2011). He worked as a research assistant in the research team "Manuscript Heritage and the History of Texts" (Consejo Superior de Investigaciones Científicas [CSIC] – Centro de Ciencias Humanas y Sociales [CCHS], Madrid), where he began his research in Arabic paleography and legal documents. Since 2011 he has participated in the "DVCTVS National Papyrological Funds" project, managing the databases of the Spanish papyrological collections, and the Mummy Labels database of the "Death on the Nile" project. He is currently a PhD candidate in the field of Arabic codicology at the Universitat Pompeu Fabra in Barcelona, focusing on the bureaucracy of pilgrimage during the first centuries of Islam.

Brinkley Messick
is professor of Anthropology and of Middle Eastern, South Asian, and African studies at Columbia University in New York. He was the chair of the anthropology department (2004–2011) and was founding co-director of the Center for Palestine Studies (2010–2015). Currently, he is director of the Middle East Institute. In 2009, he received the Outstanding Senior Scholar Award from the Middle East section of the American Anthropological Association. He has conducted research in Yemen and Morocco, and is the author of *The Calligraphic State. Textual Domination and History in a Muslim Society* (University of California Press, 1993), which was awarded the Albert Hourani Prize of the Middle Eastern Studies Association, and has been translated into Turkish (2016). He is co-editor of *Islamic Legal Interpretation: Muftis and Their Fatwas* (Harvard University Press, 1996). His historical anthropology of a textual tradition, *Sharīʿa Scripts*, is forthcoming from Columbia University Press.

Toru Miura
is professor of Comparative History at Ochanomizu University in Tokyo, Japan, and head of the West Asian Studies Department at the Toyo Bunko (Oriental library). He is the author of *Dynamism in the Urban Society of Damascus: The Sāliḥiyya Quarter from the Twelfth to the Twentieth Centuries* (Leiden: Brill, 2016) and co-editor of *The Vellum Contract Documents in Morocco in the Sixteenth to Nineteenth Centuries* (Tokyo: Toyo Bunko, 2015) as well as of *Islamic Urban Studies: Historical Review and Perspectives* (London: Routledge, 1994).

Christian Müller
(PhD Freie Universität Berlin, 1997) is directeur de recherche (research professor) at the Centre national de la recherche scientifique (CNRS) in Paris. Since 2004, he has acted as head of the Arabic section of the Institut de recherche et d'histoire des textes. He has taught undergraduate and postgraduate courses in many institutions in France and Germany. In 2015–2016 he taught at the Ludwig-Maximilians-Universität München where he was visiting professor. His research interests center on the practice of Islamic law in the pre-modern period with a special focus on fatwa literatures and legal documents. He is mainly interested in the doctrinal evolution of juridical casuistry within the framework of Islamic legal systems. From 2009 until 2013, he acted as principal investigator of the ERC project "Islamic Law Materialized" which focuses on the edition, categorization and analysis of Arabic legal documents dated from the eighth to the sixteenth centuries and gave rise to the online data base Corpus of Arabic Legal Documents (CALD). Among Christian Müller's recent publications are *Der Kadi und seine Zeugen. Studie der mamlukischen Ḥaram-Dokumente in Jerusalem* (Wiesbaden: Harrassowitz, 2013) and "Recht I: vormodern," in *Islam. Einheit und Vielfalt einer Weltreligion*, ed. R. Brunner (Stuttgart: Kohlhammer, 2016), 237–257.

Petra M. Sijpesteijn
holds the chair of Arabic at Leiden University and is chargée de recherche at the Institut de recherche et d'histoire des textes at the Centre national de la recherche scientifique (CNRS) in Paris. She obtained her PhD in Near Eastern Studies from Princeton University and was a junior research fellow at Christ Church, Oxford. She is the author of *Shaping a Muslim State: The World of a Mid-Eighth-Century Egyptian Official* (Oxford University Press, 2013). Sijpesteijn is the principal investigator on a five-year ERC project to study the social foundations of the early Islamic Empire.

Mathieu Tillier
is currently professor of Medieval Islamic History at the University of Paris-Sorbonne and a member of the research unit "Orient et Méditerranée" (UMR 8167) at the Centre national de la recherche scientifique (CNRS) in Paris. Previously, he was associate professor at Aix-Marseille Université (2005–2014). He spent two years in Oxford as a Marie Curie research fellow (2008–2010) and four years in the Middle East (Damascus, Beirut) at the Institut français du Proche-Orient (Ifpo, 2010–2014). His research focuses on justice, on the formation of Islamic law, and on the institutions of Christian communities in the first centuries of Islam. He is the author of *Les cadis d'Iraq et l'État abbasside (132/750–334/945)* (Damascus: Presses de l'Ifpo Press, 2009), and translated into French the works of Ibn Hajar al-ʿAsqalani and al-Kindi devoted to Egyptian qadis: *Vies des cadis de Miṣr, 237/851–366/976. Extrait du* Rafʿ al-iṣr ʿan quḍāt Miṣr *d'Ibn Ḥağar al-ʿAsqalānī* (Cairo: Institut français d'archéologie orientale/ [Ifao], 2002); al-Kindi, *Histoire des cadis égyptiens* (Cairo: Ifao, 2012). He is the editor of Abu Hilal al-ʿAskari's book *Le Livre des califes qui s'en remirent au jugement d'un cadi* (Cairo: Ifao, 2011) and has recently began editing documents on papyrus and paper related to judicial institutions in medieval Egypt.

Amalia Zomeño
is a tenured researcher at the Instituto de Lenguas y Culturas del Mediterráneo y Oriente Próximo (Consejo Superior de Investigaciones Científicas [CSIC] – Centro de Ciencias Humanas y Sociales [CCHS], Madrid). She holds a PhD in Arabic philology from the University of Barcelona. The main topic of her research is Islamic law. She is the author of *Dote y matrimonio en al-Andalus y el norte de África. Estudio sobre la jurisprudencia Islámica medieval* (Madrid: CSIC, 2000). She is currently studying the collections of Arabic legal documents preserved in the archives of Granada in order to analyze family and gender in fifteenth century Granada, and has written several papers on the subject. She is also the author of two catalogues of Arabic manuscripts preserved at Montserrat Abbey.

Bibliography of Rudolph Peters

Books

1976

With G.J.H. van Gelder. *A Bibliography of Dutch Publications on the Middle East and Islam, 1945–1975*. Amsterdam: University of Amsterdam, Institute of Modern Near Eastern Studies.

1977

Jihad in Mediaeval and Modern Islam: The Chapter on Jihad from Averroes' Legal Handbook 'Bidayat al-Mudjtahid' *and the Treatise* 'Koran and Fighting' *by the Late Shaykh al-Azhar, Mahmud Shaltut.* Translated and annotated by Rudolph Peters. Leiden: Brill.

- Translated into Spanish as *La yihad en el islam medieval y moderno*. Sevilla: Universidad de Sevilla, 1998.

Oemm Saad: Palestijnse verhalen. Translation of Ghassan Kanafani's *Umm Sa'd*. Translated from Arabic into Dutch and introduced by Ruud Peters. Amsterdam: Stichting Palestina Publicaties.

1979

Islam and Colonialism: The Doctrine of Jihad in Modern History. Religion and Society 20. The Hague: Mouton and Berlin.

- Translated into Arabic as *Al-Islam wa-l-Isti'mar: 'Aqidat al-Jihad fi l-Tarikh al-Hadith*. Al-Qahira: Dar Shuhdi li-l-nashr bi-l-ta'awun ma' al-Ma'had al-Hulandi li-l-athar al-Misriyya wa-l-dirasat al-'Arabiyya, 1985.
- Translated into Turkish by Süleyman Gündüz as *İslam ve Sömürgecilik: Modern Zamanlarda Cihad Öğretisi*. Istanbul: Nehir Yayınları, 1989.

1981

With A.H. de Groot and M. Bernards. *A Bibliography of Dutch Publications on the Middle East and Islam, 1945–1981*. Nijmegen: MOI publicaties.

1994

With Laila Al-Zwaini. *A Bibliography of Islamic Law, 1980–1993*. Handbuch der Orientalistik, 1/19. Leiden: Brill.

1996

Jihad in Classical and Modern Islam. A Reader. Princeton Series on the Middle East. Princeton: Markus Wiener Publishers.

- Translated into Arabic as *Al-jihad fi al-Islam qadiman wa-hadithan.* Cairo: Markaz Al-Ahram li-l-tarjama wa-l-nashr, 1996.
- Translated into Danish as *Jihad i klassisk og moderne islam.* Oversat til dansk af Sune Haugbølle. With a new chapter "The notion of jihad at the turn of the 21st century." København: Forlaget Vandkunsten, 2004.
- Second and updated edition published as *Jihad in Classical and Modern Islam.* Princeton Series on the Middle East. Princeton: Markus Wiener Publishers, 2005.
- Chapter of the book (2005 edition) translated in Spanish as "El concepto de *yihad* a comienzos del siglo XXI." In *Activismo político y religioso en el mundo islámico contemporáneo*, edited by Cristina de la Puente and Delfina Serrano, 45–62. Madrid: Siglo XXI, 2007.
- Third and updated edition published as *Jihad: A History in Documents.* Princeton Series on the Middle East. Princeton: Markus Wiener Publishers, 2015.

2003

With the assistance of Maarten Barends. *Islamic Criminal Law in Nigeria.* Spectrum Books.

2005

Crime and Punishment in Islamic Law: Theory and Practice from the Sixteenth to the Twenty-First Century. Themes in Islamic Law 2. Cambridge: Cambridge University Press.

2011

Watha'iq madinat al-Qasr fi al-Wahat al-Dakhila masdaran li-tarikh Misr fi al-ʿasr al-ʿUthmani (The documents of the town of al-Qasr in the Dakhla oasis as a source for the history of Egypt in the Ottoman period). Silsilat Dirasat Watha'iqiyya, 1. Cairo: Dar al-Watha'iq al-Qawmiyya (National Archive).

Edited Works

1981

Proceedings of the Ninth Congress of the Union Européenne des Arabisants et Islamisants. Amsterdam, 1–7 September 1978. Leiden: Brill.

1982

With A.H. de Groot and C.A. van de Koppel. *Van vreemde herkomst: achtergronden van Turkse en Marokkaanse landgenoten.* Bussum: Het Wereldvenster, 1982. Second revised edition: Houten: Het Wereldvenster, 1987.

With Ibrahim El-Sheikh and C.A. van de Koppel. *The Challenge of the Middle East: Middle Eastern Studies at the University of Amsterdam*. Amsterdam: University of Amsterdam, Institute of Modern Near Eastern Studies.

1992

With Roel Meijer. *Inspiratie en kritiek: moslimse intellectuelen over de islam.* MOI publicaties, nieuwe reeks, 11. Muiderberg: Coutinho.

1994

With J.M. Bremer and Th.P.J. van den Hout. *Hidden Futures: Death and Immortality in Ancient Egypt, Anatolia, the Classical, Biblical and Arabic-Islamic World.* Amsterdam: Amsterdam University Press.

1999

Guest editor of *The Legal History of Ottoman Egypt*, theme issue of *Islamic Law And Society* no. 6: 129–271.

Guest editor of *State Law and Society in Nineteenth-century Egypt*, special issue of *Die Welt des Islams* 39, no. 3: 267–397.

2005

With Muhammad Khalid Masud and David S. Powers. *Dispensing Justice in Islam: Qadis and their Judgements*. Studies in Islamic Law and Society 22. Leiden: Brill.

With Peri Bearman and Frank E. Vogel. *The Islamic School of Law: Evolution, Devolution, and Progress.* Harvard Series in Islamic Law 2. Cambridge, MA: Harvard University Press, 2005.

2014

With Peri Bearman. *The Ashgate Research Companion to Islamic Law*. Farnham, UK: Ashgate.

Reports

2001

With the assistance of Maarten Barends. *The Reintroduction of Islamic Criminal Law in Northern Nigeria: A study Conducted on Behalf of the European Commission*. Lagos.

2005

De ideologische en religieuze ontwikkeling van Mohammed B. Deskundigenrapport in de strafzaak tegen Mohammed B. in opdracht van het Openbaar Ministerie voor de arrondissementsrechtbank Amsterdam.

2016

With Daan Weggemans, Edwin Bakker, and Roel de Bont. *Bestemming Syrië: een exploratieve studie naar de leefsituatie van Nederlandse 'uitreizigers' in Syrië*. Report commissioned by the District Court of Rotterdam, The Netherlands.

- Translated into English as *Destination Syria: An Exploratory Study into the Daily Lives of Dutch 'Syria travellers'*. Leiden: Leiden University, Institute of Security and Global Affairs.

Articles

1969

"Recente discussies rond de islamitische vastenmaand Ramadan." *Internationale Spectator* 23: 1813–25.

1976

"Djihad: War of Aggression or Defense?" In *Akten des VII, Kongresses für Arabistik und Islamwissenschaft (Göttingen, Aug. 1974)*, edited by A. Dietrich, 282–289. Göttingen: Vandenhoeck & Ruprecht.

With G.J.J. de Vries. "Apostasy in Islam." *Die Welt des Islams* 17, no. 1/4: 1–26.

1977

"Dar al-Harb, Dar al-Islam und der Kolonialismus." In *XIX. Deutscher Orientalistentag (Freiburg i.B., Sept.–Okt. 1975). Vorträge*, edited by Wolfgang Voigt, ZDMG, Suppl. III, 1, 579–88. Wiesbaden.

1978
"De studie van het Midden-Oosten en de islam in Nederland." In *Wij en het Midden-Oosten: Midden-Oosten- en islamstudies in ander perspectief*, edited by Rudolph Peters, 1–9. Nijmegen: MOI publicaties.

"Abendländische islamkunde aus morgenländischer Sicht." In *Wij en het Midden-Oosten: Midden-Oosten- en islamstudies in ander perspectief*, edited by Rudolph Peters, 61–72. Nijmegen: MOI publicaties.

"Islam and the Palestinian National Movement During the Mandate Period." In *La signification du bas moyen age dans l'histoire et la culture du monde musulman. Actes du 8e Congrès de l'Union Européenne des Arabisants et Islamisants (Aix-en-Provence, sept. 1976)*, 185–96. Aix-en-Provence: Edisud.

1980
"*Idjtihād* and *Taqlīd* in 18th and 19th Century Islam." *Die Welt des Islams* 20: 131–46.

1982
"Mysteries of the Oriental Mind: Some Remarks on the Development of Western Stereotypes of Arabs." In *The Challenge of the Middle East: Middle Eastern Studies at the University of Amsterdam*, edited by I.A. El-Sheikh, C.A. van den Koppel, and R. Peters, 73–91. Amsterdam: Institute of Modern Near Eastern Studies.

"Islam en imperialisme." In *De Arabische uitdaging: Europa oog in oog met een nieuwe realiteit*, edited by P. Aarts and B. van Heijningen, 86–100. Rotterdam: Ordeman.

1983
"Islam and the Legitimation of Power: The Mahdi-Revolt in the Sudan." In *XXI. Deutscher Orientalistentag (Berlin, März 1980): Ausgewählte Vorträge*, edited by F. Steppat, ZDMG, Suppl. V, 409–20. Wiesbaden: Steiner.

1984
"Erneuerungsbewegungen im Islam vom 18. bis 20. Jahrhundert und die Rolle des Islams in der neueren Geschichte: Anti-kolonialismus und Nationalismus." In *Der Islam in der Gegenwart*, edited by W. Ende and U. Steinbach, 91–131. München: Beck.

"Fikh (rechtswetenschap)" and "Het recht – recente ontwikkelingen." In *Islam: Norm, ideaal en werkelijkheid*, edited by Jacques Waardenburg and J.T.P. de Bruijn, 167–77, 292–311. Weesp-Antwerpen: Het Wereldvenster-Standaard Uitgeverij. Second revised edition: Houten: Het Wereldvenster, 1987, 171–81, 296–313.

1986

"Religous Attitudes Towards Modernization in the Ottoman Empire: A Nineteenth Century Pious Text on Steamships, Factories, and the Telegraph." *Die Welt des Islams* 26, no. 1/4: 76–105.

"Calvinisme, islamitisch fundamentalisme en Weber." In *Islamitisch Fundamentalisme*, edited by K. Wagtendonk and P. Aarts, 41–52. Muiderberg: Coutinho.

"The Political Relevance of Jihad Doctrine in Sadat's Egypt." In *National and International Politics in the Middle East. Essays in Honour of Elie Kedourie*, edited by E. Ingram, 252–271. London: Frank Cass.

1987

"The Battered Derwishes of Bab Zuwayla: A Religious Riot in Eighteenth-Century Cairo." In *Eighteenth-Century Renewal and Reform in Islam*, edited by N. Levtzion and J.O. Voll, 93–111. Syracuse: Syracuse University Press.

"Jihad." In *The Encyclopaedia of Religion*, edited by Mircea Eliade, vol. 7, 88–91. New York: Macmillan.

"Islamischer Fundamentalismus: Glauben, Handeln, Führung." In *Max Webers Sicht des Islams: Interpretation und Kritik*, edited by Wolfgang Schluchter, 217–242. Frankfurt a.M.: Suhrkamp Verlag.

"Gods wet of 's mensen wet: de Egyptische politiek en de toepassing van het islamitisch recht." In *Recht van de islam* 5 (teksten van het op 20 mei 1987 gehouden 5e RIMO symposium), 20–49. Maastricht: RIMO.

1988

"Divine Law or Man-Made Law? Egypt and the Application of the Shari'a." *Arab Law Quarterly* 3, no. 3: 231–253.

1989

"'De Duivelsverzen' in de islamitische wereld." In *Rushdie-effecten: afwijzing van moslim-identiteit in Nederland?*, edited by R. Haleber, 33–41. Amsterdam: SUA.

1990

"Het islamitisch strafrecht." *Justitiële Verkenningen* 16, no. 6: 67–87.

"Who Killed 'Abd Allah al-Ghazza: A Murder Trial Before a Nineteenth Century Egyptian Qadi." In *Amsterdam Middle Eastern Studies*, edited by M. Woidich, 84–98. Wiesbaden: Reichert Verlag.

"Schulze's Quest for an Islamic Enlightenment." *Die Welt des Islams* 30, no. 1: 160–2.

"Murder on the Nile: Homicide Trials in 19th Century Egyptian Shari'a Courts." *Die Welt des Islams* 30: 98–116.

1991
"Djihaad tussen wettig gezag en revolutie. De heilige oorlog in de hedendaagse islam." In *Heilige oorlogen: een onderzoek naar historische en hedendaagse vormen van collectief religieus geweld*, edited by Martin Gosman and Hans Bakker, 176–192. Kampen-Kapellen: Kok Agora-Pelckmans.

"The Codification of Criminal Law in 19th Century Egypt: Tradition or Modernization?" In *Law, Society, and National Identity in Africa*, edited by J.M. Abun-Nasr, Ulrich Spellenberg, and Ulrike Wanitzek, 211–225. Hamburg: Buske.

1992
"Inleiding." In *Inspiratie en kritiek: moslimse intellectuelen over de islam*, edited by Ruud Peters and Roel Meijer (MOI publicaties, nieuwe reeks, 11), 7–17. Muiderberg: Coutinho, 1992.

"Whisky in de Nijl: islamitische regimes en de islamisering van het recht." Rede uitgesproken bij de aanvaarding van het ambt van bijzonder hoogleraar in het recht van de islam en het Midden-Oosten vanwege de Vereniging voor de Studie van het Recht van de Islam en het Midden-Oosten (RIMO), aan de Universiteit van Amsterdam, op 7 december 1992. Amsterdam: Instituut voor het Moderne Nabije Oosten.

1993
"Hoe koranisch is het islamitische recht? " In *De Koran: ontstaan, interpretatie en praktijk*, edited by M. Buitelaar and H. Motzki (MOI publicaties, nieuwe reeks, 12), 45–55. Muiderberg: Coutinho.

1994
"Resurrection, Revelation and Reason: Husayn al-Jisr (d. 1909) and Islamic Eschatology." In *Hidden Futures: Death and Immortality in Ancient Egypt, Anatolia, the Classical, Biblical and Arabic-Islamic World*, edited by J.M. Bremer, Th.P.J. van den Hout, and R. Peters, 221–231. Amsterdam: Amsterdam University Press.

"The Islamization of Criminal Law: A Comparative Analysis." *Die Welt des Islams* 34, no. 2: 246–274.

"Rukhṣa." In *Encyclopaedia of Islam*, 2nd edition, vol. VIII, edited by P. Bearman, Th. Bianquis, C.E. Bosworth, E. van Donzel, and W.P. Heinrichs, 598. Leiden: Brill.

"Safar." In *Encyclopaedia of Islam*, 2nd edition, vol. VIII, edited by P. Bearman, Th. Bianquis, C.E. Bosworth, E. van Donzel, and W.P. Heinrichs, 764. Leiden: Brill.

"Muhammad al-ʿAbbasi al-Mahdi (d. 1897), Grand Mufti of Egypt, and his *al-Fatawa al-Mahdiyya.*" *Islamic Law and Society* 1, no. 1: 66–82.

1995

"Introduction." In *Law and the Islamic World: Past and Present. Papers Presented to the Joint Seminar at the Universities of Copenhagen and Lund, March 26th–27th, 1993*, edited by Chr. Toll and J. Skovgaard-Petersen (Historisk-filosofiske Meddelser, 68), 7–13. Copenhagen: Det Kongeliges Danske Videnskabernes Selskab.

"Ṣaḥīḥ (in law)." In *Encyclopaedia of Islam*, 2nd edition, vol. VIII, edited by P. Bearman, Th. Bianquis, C.E. Bosworth, E. van Donzel, and W.P. Heinrichs, 836. Leiden: Brill.

"Jihad." In *The Oxford Encyclopedia of the Modern Islamic World*, edited by J. Esposito, vol. II, 369–373. New York: Oxford University Press.

"Dar al-Islam." In *The Oxford Encyclopedia of the Modern Islamic World*, edited by J. Esposito, vol. I, 338. New York: Oxford University Press.

"Dar al-sulh." In *The Oxford Encyclopedia of the Modern Islamic World*, edited by J. Esposito, vol. II, 339. New York: Oxford University Press.

"Pays Bas: de l'intégration multiculturelle à l'intégration sociale: Statut juridique de l'islam." In *Islams de l'Europe: Intégration ou insertion communautaire*, edited by R. Bistolfi and François Zabbal, 184–188. La Tour d'Aigues: Eds de l'Aube.

"Moord, verkrachting en misbruik van macht in het negentiende-eeuwse Egypte of hoe een schurk uiteindelijk zijn verdiende loon kreeg." In *Schurken en schelmen: cultuurhistorische verkenningen rond de Middellandse Zee*, edited by I. de Jong and A.M. van Erp Taalman Kip, 161–173. Amsterdam: Amsterdam University Press.

"Sharia and the State: Criminal Law in Nineteenth Century Egypt." In *State and Islam*, edited by C. van Dijk and A.H. de Groot, 152–177. Leiden: CNWS.

1996

"L'Islam et le système de droit en Egypte." In *Familles – Islam – Europe: le droit confronté au changement*, edited by Marie-Claire Foblets, 195–208. Paris: l'Harmattan.

"S̲h̲āhid." In *Encyclopaedia of Islam*, 2nd edition, vol. IX, edited by P. Bearman, Th. Bianquis, C.E. Bosworth, E. van Donzel, and W.P. Heinrichs, 207–8. Leiden: Brill.

"The Lions of Qasr al-Nil Bridge: The Islamic Prohibition of Images as an Issue in the 'Urabi Revolt." In *Islamic Legal Interpretation: Muftis and their Fatwas*, edited by M.K. Masud, B. Messick, and D. Powers, 214–220. Cambridge, MA: Harvard University Press.

1997

"Islamic and Secular Criminal Law in 19th Century Egypt: The Role and Function of the Qadi." *Islamic Law and Society* 4, no. 1: 70–90.

"De hedendaagse toepassing van het islamitische recht." In *In het huis van de islam*, edited by Henk Driessen, 259–277. Nijmegen: SUN.

1998

"Islamitisch recht en mensenrechten: een bijdrage aan een voortdurend debat." In *Mensen, rechten en islam*, edited by Katja Noordam, Roemer van Oordt, and Coşkun Çörüz, 81–98. Amsterdam: Bulaaq.

– Translated into Turkish as "İslam Hukuku ve İnsan Hakları: Süregelen Bir Tartışmaya Katkı." *Tabula rasa* yıl:1, sayı:2 (2001): 203–218.

"The Infatuated Greek: Social and Legal Boundaries in Nineteenth-century Egypt." *Egypte/Monde arabe* 34: 53–65.

1999

"An Administrator's Nightmare: Feuding Families in Nineteenth Century Bahariya Oasis." In *Legal Pluralism in the Arab World*, edited by B. Dupret, M. Berger, and Laila al-Zwaini, 135–145. Den Haag: Kluwer Law International.

"Islamic Law and Human Rights: A Contribution to an Ongoing Debate." *Islam and Christian-Muslim Relations* 10, no. 1: 5–14.

With Khaled M. Fahmy. "Introduction: The Legal History of Ottoman Egypt." *Islamic Law and Society* 6: 129–135.

"'For his Correction and as a Deterrent Example to Others': Mehmed 'Ali's First Criminal Legislation (1829–1830)." *Islamic Law and Society* 6, no. 2: 164–193.

"State, Law and Society in Nineteenth Century Egypt: Introduction." *Die Welt des Islams* 39, no. 3: 267–272.

"Administrators and Magistrates: The Development of a Secular Judiciary in Egypt, 1842–1871." *Die Welt des Islams* 39, no. 3: 378–397.

2000

"Waḳf (in classical Islamic law)." In *Encyclopaedia of Islam*, 2nd edition, vol. XI, edited by P. Bearman, Th. Bianquis, C.E. Bosworth, E. van Donzel, and W.P. Heinrichs, 59–63. Leiden: Brill.

"Petitions and Marginal Voices in Nineteenth Century Egypt: The Case of the Fisherman's Daughter." In *Marginal Voices in Literature and Society*, edited by Robin Ostle, 119–133. Strasbourg: European Science Foundation, 2000.

"Zinā or Zināʾ." In *Encyclopaedia of Islam*, 2nd edition, vol. XI, edited by P. Bearman, Th. Bianquis, C.E. Bosworth, E. van Donzel, and W.P. Heinrichs, 509–510. Leiden: Brill.

2001

"Booty." In *Encyclopaedia of the Qurʾān*, edited by Jane D. McAuliffe, vol. 1, 252. Leiden: Brill.

2002

"Murder in Khaybar: Some Thoughts on the Origin of the *qasama* Procedure in Islamic Law." *Islamic Law and Society* 9, no. 2: 132–167.

"Prisons and Marginalisation in Nineteenth Century Egypt." In *Outside In: On the Margins of the Modern Middle East*, edited by Eugene Rogan, 31–53. London: I.B. Tauris.

"Egypt and the Age of the Triumphant Prison: Legal Punishment in Nineteenth Century Egypt." *Annales Islamologiques* 36: 253–285.

"From Jurists' Law to Statute Law or What Happens When the Shariʿa is Codified." *Mediterranean Politics* 7, no. 3: 82–95. Special issue on Shaping the Current Islamic Reformation, edited by B.A. Roberson.

"Waṣiyya." In *Encyclopaedia of Islam*, 2nd edition, vol. XI, edited by P. Bearman, Th. Bianquis, C.E. Bosworth, E. van Donzel, and W.P. Heinrichs, 171–172. Leiden: Brill.

2003

"'Regerende bij de gratie gods en gebonden aan zijn wetten?' Godsdienst en politiek in islam en christendom." In *Vreemde verwanten: overeenkomsten tussen islam en christendom*, edited by Paul van Tongeren and Gerrit Steunebrink, 129–151. Annalen van het Thijmgenootschap 91/3. Nijmegen: Valkhof Pers.

2004

"Controlled Suffering: Mortality and Living Conditions in Nineteenth Century Egyptian Prisons." *International Journal of Middle Eastern Studies* 36, no. 3: 387–407.

"The Reintroduction of Sharia Criminal Law in Nigeria: New Challenges to the Muslims of the North." In *Beiträge zum Islamischen Recht IV*, edited by S. Tellenbach and Th. Hanstein, 9–23. Leipziger Beiträge zur Orientforschung 15. Frankfurt a.M.: Peter Lang.

"Sharīʿa strafrecht in Noord-Nigeria en de mensenrechten." *Recht van de islam* 21 (2004): 72–87.

"Hidjra." In *Encyclopaedia of Islam. Supplement*, 2nd edition, vol XII, edited by P. Bearman, Th. Bianquis, C.E. Bosworth, E. van Donzel, and W.P. Heinrichs, 368. Leiden: Brill.

"Nafaḳa." In *Encyclopaedia of Islam. Supplement*, 2nd edition, vol. XII, edited by P. Bearman, Th. Bianquis, C.E. Bosworth, E. van Donzel, and W.P. Heinrichs, 643–644. Leiden: Brill.

2005

"'The Enforcement of God's Law': The shariʿa in the Present World of Islam." In *Comparative Perspectives on Shariʿa in Nigeria*, edited by Ph. Ostien, Jamila M. Nasir, and F. Kogelmann, 107–134. Ibadan: Spectrum Books.

With M.K. Masud and D.S. Powers. "Qāḍīs and Their Courts: An Historical Survey." In *Dispensing Justice in Islam: Qadis and Their Judgments*, edited by M.K. Masud, R. Peters, and D. Powers. Studies in Islamic Law and Society 15, 1–44. Leiden: Brill.

"The Re-Islamization of Criminal Law in Northern Nigeria and the Judiciary: The Safiyyatu Hussaini Case." In *Dispensing Justice in Islam: Qadis and Their Courts*, edited by M.K. Masud, R. Peters, and D. Powers, Studies in Islamic Law and Society 15, 219–41. Leiden: Brill.

"What Does it Mean to be an Official Madhhab: Hanafism and the Ottoman Empire." In *The Islamic School of Law: Evolution, Devolution, and Progress*, edited by P. Bearman, R. Peters, and F. Vogel, 147–158. Cambridge, MA: Harvard University Press.

2006

"Islam-bashing en jihad: de radicalisering van jonge moslims in Nederland." In *Straatkwaad en jeugdcriminaliteit: naar een algemene of een etnisch specifieke aanpak?*, edited by Mieke Komen, 84–97. Apeldoorn-Antwerpen: Het Spinhuis.

" 'A Dangerous Book.' Dutch Public Intellectuals and the Koran." European University Institute Working (EUI) Papers / Robert Schuman Centre for Advanced Studies (RSCS), no. 39.

2007

With S. Vellenga. "Contested Tolerance: Public Discourse in the Netherlands on Muslim Migrants." In *Konfliktfeld Islam in Europa*, Soziale Welt, Sonderband 17, edited by Monika Wohlrab-Sahr and Levent Tezcan, 221–40. Baden-Baden: Nomos.

With S. Vellenga. "Homoseksualiteit in orthodox-religieuze kring: islam en protestantisme." *Justitiële Verkenningen* 1: 70–82.

"Between Paris, Istanbul, and Cairo: The Origins of Criminal Legislation in Late Ottoman Egypt." In *Studies in Islamic law: A Festschrift for Colin Imber*, edited by A. Christmann and R. Gleave, 211–232. Oxford: Oxford University Press.

"De koran in het Nederlandse islamdebat." *ZemZem* 3, no. 3: 14–20.

2008

"The Poldermujahidin: The Radicalization of Young Dutch Muslims." In *Islam & Europe: Challenges and Opportunities*, edited by Marie-Claire Foblets, 47–62. Leuven: Leuven University Press.

"Dutch Extremist Islamism: Van Gogh's Murderer and His Ideas." In *Jihadi Terrorism and the Radicalisation Challenge in Europe*, edited by Rik Coolsaet, 115–130. London: Ashgate.

"Sharecropping in the Dakhla Oasis: Shari'a and Customary Law in Ottoman Egypt." In *The Law Applied: Contextualizing the Islamic Shari'a. A Volume in Honor of Frank Vogel*, edited by P. Bearman, W. Heinrichs and B. Weiss, 79–89. London: I.B. Tauris.

"The Violent Schoolmaster: The 'Normalisation' of the Dossier of a Nineteenth-Century Egyptian Legal Case." In *Narratives of Truth in Islamic law*, edited by B. Dupret, B. Drieskens, and A. Moors, 69–85. London: MacMillan.

"Waar zijn we in godsnaam mee bezig? Over de loopgraven en de valkuilen van de islamwetenschap." *ZemZem* 3: 98–105 (short version of his farewell lecture on 22 October 2008).

2009

"Islam en geloofsafval in de diaspora." *Recht van de islam* 23: 141–146.

"*Sharīʿa* and 'Natural Justice': The Implementation of Islamic Criminal Law in British India and Colonial Nigeria." In *Islamica: Studies in the Memory of Holger Preißler (1943–2006)*. *Journal of Semitic Studies*, supplement 26, 127–150 . Oxford: Oxford University Press.

2010

"New Sources for the History of the Dakhla Oasis in the Ottoman Period." In *Proceedings of the International Conference on Egypt during the Ottoman Era, 26–30 November 2007, Cairo*, 307–324. Istanbul: IRCICA/Supreme Council of Culture, Ministry of Culture, A.R.E.

"Sharia in de polder? Islamitische rechtspraak in Nederland." *Kleio* 51, no. 5: 30–34.

2011

"Geschillenbeslechting in de sharia: het proces voor de *qadi*." *Recht van de islam* 25: 11–16.

"Dutch Extremism Islamism: Van Gogh's Murderer and His Ideas." In *Jihadi Terrorism and the Radicalisation Challenge: European and American Challenges*, second edition, edited by Rik Coolsaet, 145–161. Aldershot, UK: Ashgate.

2013

"(In)compatibility of Religion and Human Rights: The Case of Islam." In *Human Rights and the Impact of Religion*, edited by J.A. van der Ven and H.G. Ziebertz, 75–96. Leiden: Brill.

2014

"Body and Spirit of Islamic Law: *Madhhab* Diversity in Ottoman Documents from the Dakhla Oasis, Egypt." In *Islamic Law in Theory: Studies on Jurisprudence in Honor of Bernard Weiss*, edited by A.K. Reinhart and R. Gleave, 317–331. Leiden: Brill.

With Peri Bearman. "Introduction: The Nature of the Sharia." In *The Ashgate Research Companion to Islamic Law*, edited by Rudolph Peters and Peri Bearman, 1–12. Farnham, UK: Ashgate.

2015

"'Het huwelijk is de ruil van seks voor een goed': voorstellingen van premoderne oelema over het huwelijk." *Recht van de Islam* 29: 11–20.

2016

"Highway robbery." In *Encyclopaedia of Islam THREE*, edited by Kate Fleet, Gudrun Krämer, Denis Matringe, John Nawas, and Everett Rowson. Leiden: Brill.

"Homicide and murder." In *Encyclopaedia of Islam THREE*, edited by Kate Fleet, Gudrun Krämer, Denis Matringe, John Nawas, and Everett Rowson. Leiden: Brill.

2017

"ʿĀqila." In *Encyclopaedia of Islam THREE*, edited by Kate Fleet, Gudrun Krämer, Denis Matringe, John Nawas, and Everett Rowson. Leiden: Brill.

"Guarantee." In *Encyclopaedia of Islam THREE*, edited by Kate Fleet, Gudrun Krämer, Denis Matringe, John Nawas, and Everett Rowson. Leiden: Brill.

"Booty." In *Encyclopaedia of Islam THREE*, edited by Kate Fleet, Gudrun Krämer, Denis Matringe, John Nawas, and Everett Rowson. Leiden: Brill.

"Amputation." In *Encyclopaedia of Islam THREE*, edited by Kate Fleet, Gudrun Krämer, Denis Matringe, John Nawas, and Everett Rowson. Leiden: Brill.

Book Reviews

1982

Review of *Studies on Islam*, by Merlin L. Swartz. *Die Welt des Islams* 22: 143.

1983

Review of *Islam: Continuity and Change in the Modern World*, by J.O. Voll. *The Muslim World* 73: 142–3.

1984

Review of *Arabic Studies in the Netherlands*, by J. Brugman and F. Schröder. *Bibliotheca Orientalis* 41: 246–249.

Review of *Challenging Colonialism: Bank Misr and Egyptian Industrialization, 1920–1941*, by E. Davis. *Die Welt des Islams* 23–24: 508–509.

1986

Review of *European Dialogue: The Relations Between the Two Cultures: Acts of the Hamburg Symposium, April 11th to 15th, 1983*, English version edited by D. Hopwood. *MESA Bulletin* 20: 231–232.

Review of *Studies in Islamic Society: Contributions in Memory of Gabriel Baer*, edited by G.L. Warburg and G.G. Gilbar. *MESA Bulletin* 20: 242–243.

1989

Review of *Inleiding tot de islam*, by J.J.G. Jansen. In *Midden-Oosten en Islam Publicaties, Witte Reeks*, no. 14. Nijmegen: 63–67.

Review of *The Neglected Duty: The Creed of Sadat's Assassins and the Islamic Resurgence in the Middle East*, by J.J.G. Jansen. In *Midden-Oosten en Islam Publicaties, Witte Reeks*, no. 14. Nijmegen: 67–70.

Review of *Du statut inférieur de la femme musulmane*, by Ghassan Ascha. *Sharqiyyat* 2: 151–157.

1990

Review of *Islam and Revolution in the Middle East*, by Henry Munson Jr. *The International History Review* 12: 601–602.

Review of *The Islamic Law on Land Tax and Rent*, by Baber Johansen. *Die Welt des Islams* 30: 245–247.

1992

Review of *Die Anfänge der Islamischen Jurisprudenz: ihre Entwicklung in Mekka bis zur Mitte des 2./8. Jahrhunderts*, by H. Motzki. *Sharqiyyat* 4: 161–164.

Review of *Das Bild des Richters in der "Adab al-Qāḍī"-Literatur*, by I. Schneider. *Bibliotheca Orientalis* 49: 276–278.

Review of *The Enigmatic Saint: Ahmad Ibn Idris and the Idrisi Tradition*, by R.S. O'Fahey. *The International History Review* 14: 792–794.

1994

Review of *Der Nahe Osten in der Zwischenkriegszeit 1919–1939: die Interdependenz von Politik, Wirtschaft und Ideologie.* Edited by L. Schatkowski Schilcher and C. Scharf. *Der Islam* 71: 382.

Review of *Westliche Islamwissenschaft im Spiegel muslimischer Kritik: Grundzüge und Merkmale einer innerislamischen Diskussion*, by Ekkehard Rudolph. *Die Welt des Islams* 34: 157–159.

Review of *Studies in Early Muslim Jurisprudence*, by Norman Calder. *International Journal of Middle Eastern Studies* 26: 699–701.

1996

Review of *Toward and Islamic Reformation: Civil Liberties, Human Rights, and International Law*, by Abdullahi Ahmed An-Naʿim. *Bibliotheca Orientalis* 53: 260–263.

Review of *The Concept of Islamic International Criminal Law: A Comparative Study*, by Farhad Malekian. *Islamic Law and Society* 3 (1996): 380–383.

1997

Review of *Der Handel im mālikitischen Recht. Am Beispiel des k. al-buyūʿ im Kitāb al-Muwaṭṭaʾ des Mālik b. Anas und des salam aus der Mudawwana al-kubrā von Saḥnūn*, by Rüdiger Lohlker. *Bibliotheca Orientalis* 54: 804–806.

1998

Review of *The Dual Nature of Islamic Fundamentalism*, by J.J.G. Jansen. *Internationale Spectator* 52, no. 1: 50–52.

1999

Review of "A History of Islamic Legal Theories: An Introduction to Sunnī Uṣūl al-Fiqh," by W. Hallaq. *Islamic Law and Society* 6: 281–284.

2001

Review of "Die zeitgenössische Diskussion um den islamischen Beratungsgedanken (Shura) unter dem besonderen Aspekt ideeengeschichlicher Kontinuitäten und Diskontinuitäten," by Roswitha Badry. *Die Welt des islams* 41: 114–115.

2002

Review of *The Rule of Law in the Arab World: Courts in Egypt and the Gulf*, by Nathan Brown. *Islamic Law and Society* 9: 122–124.

Review of *Authochthone islamische Aufklärung im 18. Jahrhundert: Theoretische und filologische Bemerkungen; Fortführung einer Debatte*, by Bernd Radtke. *Die Welt des Islams* 42: 135–137.

Review of *Jihad: The Origin of Holy War in Islam*, by Reuven Firestone. *International Journal of Middle East Studies* 34: 738–740.

2007

Review of *Family and Court: Legal Culture and Modernity in Late Ottoman Palestine*, by Iris Agmon. *American Historical Review*: 965.

Review of *Land, Law and Islam. Property and Human Rights in the Muslim World*, by Hilary Lim and Siraj Sait. *Bibliotheca Orientalis* 64.

2009

Review of *Islamic Imperial Law: Harun-al-Rashid's Codification Project*, by Benjamin Jokisch. *Journal of the American Oriental Society* 129, no. 3: 10–11.

2011

Review of *The Expert Witness in Islamic Courts: Medicine and Crafts in the Service of the Law*, by Ron Shaham. *Journal of the American Oriental Society* 131, no. 3.

2012

Review of *Crime and Punishment in Istanbul, 1700–1800*, by Fariba Zarinebaf. *American Historical Review* 117: 640–641.

2015

Review of *Muslimische Positionen zur Berechtigung von Gewalt. Einzelstimmen, Revisionen, Kontroversen*, by Mariella Ourghi. *Die Welt des Islam* 55: 128–129.

2016

Review of *Doubt in Islamic Law: A History of Legal Maxims, Interpretation, and Islamic Criminal Law*, by Intisar A. Rabb. *Law and History Review* 34, no. 1: 233–235.

Review of *Starke Reformer oder schwache Revolutionäre? Ländliche Notabeln und das ägyptische Parlament in der ʾUrabi-Bewegung, 1866–1892*, by Irene Weipert-Fenner. *Zeitschrift der Deutschen Morgenländische Gesellschaft* 166, no. 2: 486–487.

2017

Review of *Zeitgenössische islamische Positionen zu Koexistenz und Gewalt*, edited by Tilman Seidensticker. *Bibliotheca Orientalis* 74, no. 1–2: 212–214.

Introduction

Maaike van Berkel, Léon Buskens and Petra M. Sijpesteijn

A couple of years ago professor Ruud Peters gave a presentation at Leiden University on the nineteenth-century documents from the Dakhla oasis that he recently edited and published in an impressive volume.[1] As images of the precious paper objects started to appear on the screen and Ruud began to decipher their contents, he posed us a question: "Why would divers be listed amongst the inhabitants of this late Ottoman Egyptian oasis community? What possible function could they have fulfilled in the middle of the desert?" The answer, he told us, lay in one of the documents from the collection. This document, a list of expenses for the repair of a well, dated 1187–1188 AH, contained the payment of a diver for dredging the silted well, bringing up surplus sand that was obstructing the free flow of water.[2] Using information from labour agreements, rental and sale contracts and other Dakhla documents, Ruud continued to paint a lively image of the jobs these divers undertook: they were paid per diem with a maximal number of dives; they used a rod and a basket on their dives which lasted several minutes each; and they worked their way up and down the shaft via a line connected to the top of the well. In the course of his presentation, Ruud connected the information from the documents to environmental and economic-historical developments in the oasis that had an impact on the water system, society, and, ultimately, on the livelihood of the divers. Using the images of the documents, he also showed us how legal witnesses sometimes travelled together with legal parties to the court in Cairo, where the transactions were registered in front of a judge. He connected this information to developments in the law of late Ottoman Egypt, the organization of the judiciary in this period, and the ways in which this had an impact on the inhabitants of Dakhla. Finally, while examining the witnesses' signatures he drew our attention to practices peculiar to particular witnesses, such as the usage of individualized phrases or signs after their name and the traces left by the court clerks on the document.

1 Rudolph Peters, *Watha'iq Madinat al-Qasr bi-l-Wahat al-Dakhila Masdaran li-Tarikh Misr fi al-'Asr al-'Uthmani* (The Documents of al-Qasr in the Dakhla Oasis as a Source for the History of Egypt in the Ottoman Period), Silsilat Dirasat Watha'iqiyya (Cairo: Dar al-Kutub wa-l-Watha'iq al-Qawmiyya, 2011).

2 D.05.016 verso, lines 4, 7 and 13. Peters, *Watha'iq*, 567–568.

 | DOI 10.1163/9789004343733_002

Ruud's talk on water management in Dakhla as expressed in the documents found in the oasis closely engaged with the most recent developments in documentary studies and the historiography of the practice of Islamic law that we want to highlight in this volume published in his honour. Even a cursory look at the list of Ruud's publications shows the contributions that he has made in this field and how far back his interest goes in the use of documents as a source of Islamic law and history. Contrary to what previous scholarship often argued, Ruud's repeatedly expressed observation that the (documentary and narrative) sources show no dichotomy between, on the one hand, a theory, and on the other, a practice of Islamic law, underlies all the papers in this book that use documentary sources in tandem with narrative texts to reconstruct different aspects of Islamic law and history throughout the Muslim world from its earliest history to the contemporary period. The dialectical relations between social practices and legal theory of the law and the embeddedness in society of legal institutions are also expressed in the definition of legal documents that the contributors apply. From letters appointing legal officials and the correspondence between legal authorities to the contracts and court documents recording legal transactions and the documentation produced in the course of the treatment of a legal case in court, the documents presented in this publication are extremely diverse. As the different contributions to the volume show, these documents have, however, one thing in common: they are all expressions of and instruments in the social relations that the actors involved maintained.

The initiative for this publication was taken at the one-day symposium entitled "Legal Documents as Sources for the History of Muslim Societies" that was held in honour of professor Ruud Peters on 27 May 2011 in Amsterdam, organized by the Netherlands Interuniversity School for Islamic Studies (NISIS), together with the University of Amsterdam (UvA), the Amsterdam School for Cultural Analysis (ASCA), and the Dutch association for the Study of Islamic law and the law of the Middle East (RIMO). Several speakers of that symposium have contributed to the volume to which additional contributors were invited.

For several years now, scholars of Islamic law, historians and anthropologists of the Muslim world have devoted considerable attention to the study of legal documents. Inspired by the insights of so-called "new philology" and developments in book studies, scholars more recently started to read documents not only for the contents of the texts they contain, but to involve the many material and historical layers of the documents.[3] Among anthropologists,

3 Sheldon Pollock, "Future Philology? The Fate of a Soft Science in a Hard World," *Critical Enquiry* 35 (2009): 931–961.

similar trends are present, resulting in a strong interest in texts as social phenomena and reading and writing as culturally diverse practices. The concomitant interests in "the social life of things," an expression made famous by Arjun Appadurai, and in materiality furthered the gradual emergence of a social codicology.[4] These kindred developments in philology, history and anthropology have resulted in important new insights in the manifold uses of legal documents in Muslim societies. Documents have also proven to be valuable sources for social history in the broadest sense. From tracing developments in legal practices and legal institutions and constituencies to changing social constellations and interactions in different historical contexts, documents have shown to be a hugely potential source for historians and anthropologists studying the Muslim world.

This is exactly what Ruud showed us when he used the legal documents from the Dakhla oasis as a source of legal practice and the functioning of legal institutions and their impact on society. His lecture built on his extensive and important work examining the practice of Islamic law through court records and documents, and its relation to theoretical legal discussions, especially in nineteenth-century Egypt. Khaled Fahmy discusses the contributions that Ruud made in this field in the introductory chapter in this volume.

What Do Documents Do?

The use of legal documents to examine the practice of Islamic law and their shaping of social relations has obvious advantages. As Toru Miura demonstrates, legal documents, despite obvious regional and cultural differences, can in all their differences be well compared across linguistic, religious and geographical boundaries. Such comparison offers interesting insights into common and particular legal expressions and usages. Several papers show how documentary sources complement, and, often, correct the narrative sources. Mathieu Tillier warns us that most reconstructions of the Umayyad and early Abbasid qadi's office are based on narrative sources of the ninth- and tenth-centuries. Besides being composed much later, these texts are part of a literary discourse on the judiciary in which descriptions of qadis function as *exempla* of early Islamic law and have been accordingly directed. Maurits van den Boogert presents an eighteenth-century document of sale from Aleppo that

4 For the Muslim world, the publications of Brinkley Messick and Ghislaine Lydon have served as major sources of inspiration.

contradicts or at least questions the accepted knowledge that Western residents could not own property in the Ottoman Empire.

The documents – recording, formalizing, shaping, and to a certain extent even producing every-day, actual events and procedures – give us insights into incidents and practices that for whatever reason did not make it into the legal treatises. Brinkley Messick's examples of witness statements as recorded in twentieth-century Yemeni court records show the practicalities of giving evidence in court in a way that no legal handbook does, including the deliberations amongst the parties in the streets on the way to and from the court. The personal practices that fifteenth-century notaries from Granada applied to their signatures allows Amalia Zomeño to reconstruct the relations that could develop between "customers" and the legal clerks. The legal advisory role that the notaries fulfilled in this relationship as reconstructed on the basis of their appearance in the documents is not the subject of legal discussions recorded in narrative sources.

The papers in this volume also show the great variety of documents produced by legal institutions and practices. Letters appointing legal officials and the correspondence and documentation generated by these officials are not necessarily the outcome of their professional activities in court, but nevertheless offer very important information on the functioning of the law and legal apparatus as Petra Sijpesteijn and Mathieu Tillier show. Documents produced in the context of legal transactions and claims brought to court are also very diverse in form, function and legal status, from noting and even constructing facts and statements relevant to a case, notarized or not, to documents authenticated by a judge or other legal officers. Zomeño and Christian Müller discovered, for fifteenth-century Granada and Jerusalem respectively, the prevalence of notarized documents that lacked the authorization by the qadi and were therefore not accepted as legal evidence in court. These documents obviously functioned at a different level of legal practice, but – and this is the important observation – constitute fully functioning and relevant elements of the legal system.

The cases described in the documents, moreover, might be too mundane to be recorded in the narrative sources, lacking the spectacular or exemplary aspects that chroniclers favor. As Müller shows in his contribution, non-dramatic and less serious cases of homicide and bodily harm that were brought to court in Mamluk Jerusalem differ significantly from the cases discussed in the legal treatises. They provide us with important information on the role of the judge in the Islamic legal decision making process. Maaike van Berkel shows how a waqf deed on the founding of a *sabīl* (a public water fountain) provides us with information on the everyday practice of the distribution of drinking water – the jar and mugs that were needed, the cleaning of the place, the staff involved in the distribution – that is lacking in narrative sources.

At the same time, the actual court cases as recorded in the documents present, even more so than the narrative sources do, the specific cultural and historical context of judgements and verdicts and the functioning of legal practices. The decisions of the court – referring to a system of divine law – are always made in response to a specific incident involving particular individuals and offer first of all an immediate solution to an acute problem. The court's decisions can thus be considered temporal solutions to pressing "temporary" issues. The ephemerality of the cases is reflected by the scarcity of the documents recording them, which were mostly thrown out when the individuals involved were no longer present and are thus lost for the modern historian. Yet, it is from these real-life cases as recorded in court documents and papers produced by the institutions, officers and clerks that the functioning of the Islamic judicial system in practice can be reconstructed in a particular place and time.

Finally, the study of documents as physical objects, including the ways in which they were stored and used – and not only for the texts they contain – has opened up important new venues for research. Léon Buskens does this most explicitly in this volume. Understanding the changing categories and labels ascribed to documents in different contexts shows how social attitudes towards the written word develop and are formed. Understanding how our sources are identified and constructed makes us reconsider the theoretical framework we apply to our field and our epistemological presuppositions.

Four main themes that the papers of this book present are discussed here. The first theme is how the documents can enlighten us on the every-day functioning of legal institutions, including the interaction between the authorities and the representatives of the law, but also the quotidian concerns of the officers, litigants, criminals, witnesses and others in their dealings with the court. Next some cases are presented that show how political change affects legal documentary practice. When was impact felt directly? When did the effect take longer to present itself? What legal documents can tell us about daily life and how they can be used as a source for social history at large are dealt with as well. Finally, the study of the physical features of the documents and what they tell us about their use in society but also about their value as a source are discussed.

The Daily Life of Islamic Legal Systems

A number of papers in this volume use documentary sources to reconstruct the functioning of Islamic legal systems and courts in the different regions and periods of Muslim history. For the earliest period of Islam's history much contemporary documentary evidence has been lost in most areas of the Muslim world. A wealth of documents have survived, however, in the Egyptian deserts in the form of papyri and papers now scattered throughout museums and library collections around the world. Tillier uses papyri from Umayyad and Abbasid Egypt to examine the position and functions of the qadi in Egypt. He argues that in this early period political and judicial functions clearly interacted in the qadi's position. With the emigration of the Arab population into Egypt's countryside and the increased interaction between indigenous population and rulers, Muslim legal offices that were thoroughly integrated into the provincial administration were established. This changed from the ninth century onwards, when a judicial power operating independently of the authorities and more in sync with the developments in jurisprudence as expressed by the *fuqahāʾ* can be observed to have operated in Egypt. The Egyptian papyrus that Sijpesteijn presents here picks up from this point and shows how this more developed and extensive legal apparatus functioned. The document offers evidence of the office of delegates of the qadi's court in Fustat in remote areas of the province. The document also traces the imposition of stronger centralized structures by caliph al-Maʾmun's (r. 198/813–218/833) representatives.

In the study of the early history of Islamic law, documents, although important correctives, are ultimately much less voluminous than the narrative sources. For later periods, the documentary record becomes denser, and several substantial archives have been preserved. The Mamluk court records from the Haram al-Sharif in Jerusalem discussed here by Müller record in meticulous detail the injuries that victims suffered and in some cases died of. The differing circumstances surrounding the observation and recording of the physical inflictions determined the kind of document produced in court, with inspections, declarations and questioning all playing a role. It shows the wide range of documents, each following separate prescribed linguistic elements, that legal cases could produce. The dealings of bodily harm and homicide cases in the qadi's court also allow Müller to make some important observations concerning the interaction between politics and the law. While such cases would generally have been dealt with by the administration, the appearance of the low-level cases in the qadi's court show that the authorities had a shared responsibility over these cases with the judge's court.

Eighteenth and twentieth-century examples are provided by Van den Boogert and Messick. Transcripts of statements by witnesses and litigants made in mid-twentieth-century Yemen give access to the realities of the giving of testimony, including reports of pressure and intimidation, accusations of falsehood as well as discussions amongst witnesses outside the court. Rather than using these records to reconstruct doctrine, Messick aims to access the logic of court practice, including the strategies of litigants and the discourses of the witnesses who testify on their behalf.

On the basis of legal documents from Aleppo and decrees and surveys preserved in the archives in Istanbul, Van den Boogert shows how Western residents in Ottoman Syria organized the practicalities of handling their economic affairs in court: appointing representatives and appealing to foreign contacts. The records also show the flexibility and malleability of the pluralistic Ottoman legal system that was well equipped to also serve political aims. As the documents show, this flexibility made it possible for Western residents of the Empire to register their properties in spite of Islamic legal complications related to or even prohibitions on such ownership. When this century-long practice became the object of a political discussion over the privileges of European citizens inside the Ottoman Empire, that same legal system functioned as an appeal court for Western residents.

Regime Change as Reflected in Legal Documentation

As Miura states in his chapter, contracts are not exclusively defined by the law, but also reflect social and political realities. The documents presented by Müller from Mamluk Jerusalem and by Van den Boogert from eighteenth-century Aleppo clearly show how politics and the courts interacted. While definitely referring to Islamic law, qadis were very much part of the world in which they lived. In other words, society and law were closely connected and in constant conversation through the actions of legal scholars, rulers, officials of the court and litigants. With rulers and their representatives in the administration and government regularly involved in the execution and organization of the law, it is expected that regime change will have a direct and visible effect on judicial practice. The installment of a new regime will eventually lead to the creation of new offices and systems and demand new linguistic, material, formalistic forms and expressions also in the legal realm. When exactly political changes appear in the legal records depends on the incoming regime and its ambitions, as well as its relationship to the local population and the offices in place. Whether or not changes are clearly visible is also related to the kind of documents under examination. As normativity and legal practices are always political phenomena, changes in the political framework are often visible in the specific form that writers impose on documents. Buskens demonstrates this, for example, in his discussion of changes in the material appearance of Moroccan legal documents during the French protectorate period. In fact, the production of legal documents and their further use can directly contribute to the function of the polity, for example in relation to the levying of taxes through the obligation to use specific kinds of paper.

The most direct impact on legal rules and rulings can be found when rulers take, for whatever reason, a hands-on approach. The Mahdi who took power in nineteenth-century Sudan, for example, proposed substantial legal reforms that he supported by extensive legal reasoning. Aharon Layish discusses how the Mahdi's visions as expressed in his legal opinions were applied to cases of divorce, inheritance, false accusation of unlawful intercourse and homicide. The Mahdi's claim of infallibility on the basis of his descend from and direct communication with the prophet Muhammad allowed him to put the traditional interpreters of the law, the 'ulama', to the side and added force to his own statements. As Layish shows, the Mahdi's legal opinions impacted legal practice in these fields directly, albeit limited to the period covered by his political rule.

Similarly, the political reorganization of the Abbasid Empire by caliph al-Ma'mun had a direct effect on the organization of the judiciary and the position and function of individual legal officials. The resulting greater centralization of the office of the qadi and the judicial apparatus are reflected in a papyrus from Egypt discussed by Sijpesteijn. She shows that new offices tied the lowest legal officials operating in the province's oases with the chief judge in the capital Fustat. These new relations were expressed through the use of titles and the mentioning of named officials in documents.

Zomeño and Tillier, on the other hand, show that regime change does not always have an immediate effect on legal practice and organization. Tillier argues that the Abbasid take-over in 133/750 only gradually effected the organization of the judicial system in Egypt. While changes in the way chief judges were appointed to Egypt and their background eventually show a clear pattern of change, initially most judicial practices continued unaltered, including the office of appointed officials.

Zomeño, in her turn, shows that the same officials who served the replaced regime continued the judicial practices they were familiar with. Thus, the witnesses endorsing legal transactions in Granada after the take-over by the Nasrid Christian rulers continued to design and sign their documents in Arabic using the same expressions as they did in the Muslim period. Arabic continued to be used for several decades longer, while Islamic legal rules similarly continued to influence legal documentary practice in Christian Spain.

Sources for Daily Life

As stated above, legal documents encompass much more than the authenticated, notarized documents that constitute legal proof in a Muslim court, including the whole documentary production related to the Law and its institutions. Besides their function in the legal system, such documents contain priceless information on social history. As in Ruud's contract on the reparation of a well in late Ottoman Dakhla, these legal documents of transaction offer important information on daily-life experiences and circumstances of the societies that produced them. Documents are never a plain record of what happened, but rather a construction of facts and stories in a peculiar language wielded by specialists. In order to access the information on everyday life scholars should study these processes of construing facts and narratives, the ways in which these specialists select materials to be included or excluded in their reports, and the relation between the colloquial languages and the technical terminology of the trade. The writing of a legal document and the multiple ways in which people might use such an instrument in daily life are important objects of study in themselves.

Exemplary is the document discussed by Van Berkel – the foundation deed of the *sabīl* of sultan Faraj b. Barquq from early fifteenth-century Cairo. The document contains detailed descriptions of the services provided by the public fountain, the opening hours, and the rights and obligations of the staff working there. It also describes the architectural features of the building and the basin as well as the tools in use. Together this information allows Van Berkel not only to present a detailed picture of the organization of transport and distribution of water in the city, but also to discuss the character and configuration of public services in Mamluk Cairo.

Beyond social conditions and interactions, legal documents can also be used to study the history of mentalities. Van Berkel discusses how the waqf institution organised urban public responsibilities and commitments following religious and social recommendations. The motives behind the foundation of the fountain extended to the instructions on how it had to function. The *sabīl*'s staff is prescribed in the document to treat drinkers well, make them feel at ease and facilitate their drinking from the fountain. Zomeño uses legal documents to offer insights into the organization of financial and legal services in fifteenth-century Granada. She is able to show how clerks operated in and outside the court as legal professionals, but also how they offered services to their clients that suggest long-standing commitments and fruitful relationships. Similarly, Messick, focusing on claims and recorded instances of false testimony, describes the practical logic of falsehood in operation in twentieth-century Yemen. In all these instances, the observations based on legal documents have relevance for the world outside the legal context, widening the conclusions to society at large.

Likewise Miura compares contracts in eighteenth- to twentieth-century Syria, Iran, Central Asia, China and Japan to examine how concepts of ownership and contract differed in these cultures. By examining how contracts were drawn up (the lay-out, formula, and language used) and how such records were preserved and transmitted to establish ownership in new contexts, Miura reconstructs the socio-economic needs of recording and filing property ownership. While certain elements can be found in documents produced in all examined legal cultures, additional components reflect, as Miura shows, particular socio-economic historical circumstances that differed over time in the same cultural-regional context or in unconnected regions.

Materiality of Legal Documents

The study of texts as material objects has witnessed important new developments under influence of recent advances in book studies, philology, anthropology and heritage studies. Moving beyond the contents of the documents, the texts are approached as historical and social phenomena in themselves. The physical features of a text, the writing materials used, the material context in which they appear, but also the writings surrounding or intertwining with the text offer insights into the scholarly, social, and religious attitude towards writing(s). In this vein studies on the production and transmission of scholarship, on literacy, and the economy of written and literary productions also appeared. More specifically, questions about the relation between the text and the material on which it is written, the inks, paper size and shape, the lay-out and script of the text, and any written and material additions in the form of stamps, seals, and notes related to archival practices, legal procedure, but also re-use and even modern cataloguing efforts are taken into account. In this way the material turn in documentary studies has made scholars much more aware of the relation between documents and their environment. Legal documents, often produced and used in different stages and various institutional and private environments, are especially fruitful sources for such an approach, as is shown in several papers in this volume.

Miura observes that the increased length of documents filed in nineteenth-century Ottoman Syrian law courts points to the extended verification process applied to records of property ownership. Contents were no longer solely summarized, but quoted verbatim. In addition, extra steps in the verification process were entered, including officials adding their comments. The results were longer documents. By examining the hand writing, the script size and style as well as any other identifying features of the notaries and other court officials who produced the documents, Müller and Zomeño were able to trace individuals and their professional activities in different documents from fifteenth-century Iberia and Mamluk Jerusalem respectively. Zomeño, for example, focuses on the legal validations of documents, and she shows how the divergences from the general conventions in this make it possible to discern individual notaries. Müller discusses the attitude towards writing, and specifically towards written proof, when analyzing the various levels of authentication and their meaning or judicial consequences.

In his contribution, Buskens points at how the use and meaning of legal documents differs over time and place, resulting in various treatments of documents, especially concerning their preservation, archiving, and re-use. Focusing on the discovery and gathering of legal documents for research purposes, Buskens shows how the imbedding of legal documents in private and public collections constitutes but one phase in the documents' social history. The selection and compilation of documents for private and public collections produced new constellations and relations between texts that did not exist before and with specific meanings ascribed to the writings in the researcher's collection. By examining the motives behind the formation of these new groupings and corpora, Buskens not only shows how the production of legal documents and the way people deal with papers differed in different settings, but he also aims to return to the documents a history of use and meaning before contemporary scholars started using them.

We are grateful to the Leiden University Centre for the Study of Islam and Society (LUCIS) for its support in making this volume possible. We are extremely grateful to Annemarie van Sandwijk's incessant support to bring this volume into being. We would like to thank Nazreen Sahebali for her help in the editorial process.

June 2017

CHAPTER 1

Rudolph Peters and the History of Modern Egyptian Law

Khaled Fahmy

For nearly thirty years, Ruud Peters has been publishing pioneering work that has considerably enriched our understanding of Islamic law. In addition to path-breaking books, scholarly articles and book chapters on such diverse topics as jihad,[1] *qasāma* (a principle in Islamic law attempting to determine who is liable for a murder if the perpetrator is unknown or the legal evidence against him or her is inadequate),[2] the development of *madhāhib* (schools of thought),[3] Ottoman criminal law and the application of Islamic criminal law in modern times,[4] he has also produced ground-breaking work on nineteenth-century Egyptian criminal law. The significance of Peters' work on the history of Egyptian criminal law lies not only in revolutionizing our understandings of the origins of the modern Egyptian legal system or in his unique ability to combine thorough knowledge of *fiqh* with a deep command of archival material, but also in painting a detailed picture of the complex ways in which Islamic law was applied in a modern state context.

This chapter analyzes Ruud Peters' copious scholarship on nineteenth-century Egyptian criminal law with an attempt to stress the originality and significance of his research on *siyāsa*. *Siyāsa* is a system of public law that has its origins in the *fiqhī* principle of *taʿzīr*, i.e. the right of the qadi to pass discretionary punishment, and which can therefore be traced to the very beginnings of Islamic law, but which the Ottomans embellished over the centuries and

1 Rudolph Peters, *Islam and Colonialism: The Doctrine of Jihad in Modern History* (The Hague, New York: Mouton, 1979) and Peters, *The Jihad in Classical and Modern* (Princeton: Markus Wiener, 1996).

2 Rudolph Peters, "Murder in Khaybar: Some Thoughts on the Origins of the Qasāma Procedure in Islamic Law," *Islamic Law and Society* 9, no. 2 (2002): 132–67.

3 Rudolph Peters, "What Does it Mean to Be an Official Madhhab? Hanafism and the Ottoman Empire," in *The Islamic School of Law: Evolution, Devolution, and Progress*, ed. Peri Bearman, Rudolph Peters, and Frank Vogel (Cambridge, MA: Harvard University Press, 2005), 147–158.

4 Rudolph Peters, *Crime and Punishment in Islamic Law: Theory and Practice from the Sixteenth to the Twenty-First Century* (Cambridge: Cambridge University Press, 2005).

 DOI 10.1163/9789004343733_003

which the khedives in Egypt took to unprecedented heights. To highlight the significance of Peters' contribution in this field, the chapter offers, first, a short historiographical account of how *siyāsa* has been conspicuously absent from most scholarly works on the history of modern Egyptian law. The chapter then offers a brief survey of Peters' work on different aspects of nineteenth-century Egyptian criminal law before concluding with a few notes on the significance of Peters' pioneering oeuvre.

The Historiography of the Origins of Modern Egyptian Law

When discerning what might have prompted the khedives to pass new legislations,[5] analyzing the logic that might have informed judicial practice[6] or describing the changes undergone in legal education and training,[7] the standard narrative of Egyptian law has been primarily concerned with detecting European influences ostensibly affecting these changes in nineteenth-century Egyptian legal environment. This standard narrative of legal reform (as with other stories affecting various aspects of social, political and economic life) typically starts with Bonaparte's invasion of 1798. Ahmad Fathi Zaghlul, who in 1900 published a book that, as will be shown below, was destined to play a canonical role in shaping historical consciousness about nineteenth-century Egyptian law, flatly asserted that before the advent of the French "Egypt lacked a judicial system."[8] Farhat Ziadeh, for his part, takes Bonaparte's establishment of a commercial court, *Mahkamat al-Qadaya*, as "a complete innovation [... that] set the pattern for later reforms by Muhammad ʿAli and his successors in the field of judicial organization."[9] According to Ziadeh, the significance of the French innovations stemmed from there being "very little in the Islamic background of Egypt that was conducive to the rise of constitutionality or the rule of law."[10]

5 For example, Gabriel Baer, "Tanzimat in Egypt – The Panel Code," *Bulletin of the School of Oriental and African Studies* 26 (1963): 29–49.

6 Latifa Salim, *Tarikh al-qada' al-misri al-hadith* (*History of the Modern Egyptian Judiciary*) (Cairo: al-Hay'a al-Misriyya al-ʿAmma li-l-Kitab, 2001).

7 Byron Cannon, "Social Tension and the Teaching of European Law in Egypt before 1900," *History of Education Quarterly* 15, no. 3 (1975): 299–315.

8 Ahmad Fathi Zaghlul, *al-Muhamah* (Cairo, 1900), 158.

9 Farhat Ziadeh, *Lawyers, the Rule of Law and Liberalism in Modern Egypt* (Stanford: Hoover Institution, 1968), 10.

10 Ziadeh, *Lawyers*, vii.

According to this standard narrative, European influence is seen to have continued unabated during the long reign of Muhammad ʿAli (r. 1805–1848). The Pasha is described as sending student missions to Europe to acquire various skills, and although law is not usually mentioned as one of these skills, accounts usually highlight the role subsequently played by Rifaʿa al-Tahtawi, the imam of one of the early student missions, in founding a School of Translation and in translating, together with many of the graduates of this school, numerous legal codes from French into Arabic.[11] More significantly, Muhammad ʿAli is often described as being deeply inspired by European legal systems. Latifa Salim, for example, in her comprehensive history of the modern Egyptian legal system, argues that when the Pasha established Jamʿiyyat al-Haqqaniyya[12] in 1842 as the capstone of his legal institutions, the Pasha "had finally achieved his goal of following in Europe's footsteps in the legal field."[13] Furthermore, both ʿAziz Khanki and Ahmad Fathi Zaghlul, in their influential works on nineteenth-century Egyptian law, quote the Pasha as saying that "we are bound to take Europe as a model in legal matters."[14]

Under Muhammad ʿAli's successors, Europe's imprint on Egyptian law is seen in this standard narrative to have become deeper and irreversible. It is no longer only the khedive and a few men around him who are seen to have been lured by the West; rather, wider segments of the Egyptian elite are described as looking to Europe for inspiration. In the words of a prominent legal scholar, "given the fundamental social changes that [Muhammad ʿAli] had implemented, [European legal principles] were adopted by middle class intellectuals who had recently returned from their educational missions to Europe, thus providing the budding Egyptian capitalism with its intellectual support and enlightened culture."[15] The decisive turning point that sealed the future of Egyptian law is seen to be the founding in 1876 of the Mixed Courts. Anxious to find a way to limit the jurisdiction of consular courts that adjudicated disputes among Europeans in Egypt and between Europeans and Egyptian subjects thus causing an environment of legal chaos and seriously curtailing the

---

11 Jacques Tagher, *Harakat al-tarjamah bi-Misr khilal al-qarn al-tasiʿ ʿashar* (*The Translation Movement in Egypt During the Nineteenth Century*) (Cairo: Dar al-Maʿarif, 1945), 99.

12 On Jamʿiyyat al-Haqqaniyya, see below.

13 Salim, *Tarikh al-qadaʾ*, vol. 1, 28.

14 ʿAziz Khanki, "Legislation and the Judiciary before the Inauguration of the National Courts," in *al-Kitab al-dhahabi li-l-mahakim al-ahliyya* (*The Golden Book of the National Courts*) (Cairo: Bulaq, 1937), v.1, 92–93. See also Zaghlul, *al-Muhamah*, 172, 183.

15 Muhammad Nur Farahat, *al-Mujtamaʿ wa-l-shariʿa wa-l-qanun* (*Society, Shariʿa and Law*) (Cairo: Dar al-Hilal, 1986), 128–129, 137, 141.

sovereignty of the Egyptian state, Nubar Pasha, the chief minister of Khedive Ismail (r. 1863–1879), worked tediously for ten years to convince European consuls to renounce their consular courts and to replace them with a single court. The resulting compromise was the foundation of the Mixed Courts that appointed European judges, applied French codes and firmly upheld the principle of the separation of the judiciary from the executive.[16] Seven years later, in 1883, the final step in the complete triumph of European law in Egypt was accomplished by extending the principles of the Mixed Courts to the newly founded National Courts that adjudicated disputes among Egyptians. These new courts are seen to have seriously marginalized shariʿa and to have encroached on the jurisdiction of the traditional shariʿa courts, with the latter dealing with little more than personal status disputes.

While rich in polemics, this standard narrative of the history of Egyptian law is not based on any serious work on how the legal system actually worked. For example, we lack any detailed research on how the shariʿa courts functioned, how qadi rulings were carried out, how muftis interacted with qadis, or how the *siyāsa* councils (about which more below) operated alongside the shariʿa courts. In the few occasions when these *siyāsa* councils are mentioned, it is usually to describe them as representing a muddled attempt to Westernize Egyptian law. Alternatively, they are often dismissed outright as part of a corrupt, inefficient, slow and inherently unjust legal system. Two historical studies written by lawyers during the first half of the twentieth century have decisively shaped our understanding of the pre-1883 legal system. The first is Ahmad Fathi Zaghlul's *al-Muhamah* (*Advocacy*) that contains a long section on the history of the Egyptian legal system in the nineteenth century, with an extensive appendix that reproduces more than twenty original Khedival orders pertaining to various legal aspects. The book, therefore, has been taken to be a primary source and there is hardly a study on the history of modern Egyptian law that does not take it to be an indispensable guide. Throughout his book, Zaghlul does not spare any effort in depicting the legal system before the founding of the National Courts in 1883 as corrupt and inefficient. He cites some examples of legal cases reviewed by the councils to argue that the detailed records they kept were clear signs of inefficiency and cluttered bureaucracy. It was this

16 The scholarship on the Mixed Courts is extensive, but see the following important works: Jasper Y. Brinton, *The Mixed Courts of Egypt* (New Haven: Yale University Press, 1968); Byron Cannon, *Politics of Law and the Courts in Nineteenth-Century Egypt* (Salt Lake City: University of Utah Press, 1988); and the excellent dissertation by Will Hanley which, for the first time, uses records from these Mixed Courts: Will Hanley, "Foreignness and Localness in Alexandria, 1880–1914," PhD Dissertation, Princeton University, 2007.

inefficiency, he further argues, that accounts for the fact that the councils often took an inordinately long period to look into some cases, sometime even more than a decade,[17] leading the public to lose their confidence in the whole legal system. All in all, the book is a damning indictment of the entire legal system, which is consistently described as despotic and inherently unjust. While he recounts the story of the establishment of the councils by reproducing the original Khedival orders that founded them, Zaghlul failed to uncover the logic that informed their activity, and he could not help but reproduce his modernist thinking of them as failing to live up to Western legal principles. Specifically, he blamed the legal system for not upholding the principle of separation of powers and criticized the many councils that were founded in the 1850s, 1860s and 1870s for being presided over by provincial governors and for thus blurring the distinction between the executive and the judiciary.[18] He also wondered how a legal system could ever claim to be just if it did not uphold the principle of equality before the law; if it lacked any clear notion of procedural law and its differentiation from substantive law; and, finally, if it denied litigants the right not only of legal counsel but also of appearing in front of the legal tribunal reviewing their case. Given the positive law perspective of these arguments, it is no wonder his book still appeals to many a scholar of Egyptian legal history.

The second study that is of comparable significance for the historiography of modern Egyptian law is the elegant two-volume *al-Kitab al-Dhahabi l-il-Mahakim al-Ahliyya* (*The Golden Book of the National Courts*), which was issued on the occasion of the semi-centennial of the National Courts and which was mimicking the *Livre d'Or: Les Jurisdictions d'Egypte, 1876–1926* that had been published on the occasion of the semi-centennial of the Mixed Courts a few years earlier. *Al-Kitab al-Dhahabi* contains a number of original essays pertaining to different aspects of Egyptian legal history, e.g. the history of the office of the public prosecutor (*al-niyāba al-ʿumūmiyya*), the prisons' department (*maṣlaḥat al-sujūn*), the law school (*kuliyyat al-ḥuqūq*), and advocacy (*al-muḥāmāh*). Regardless of their topic, all essays have two things in common: the assumption that the beginning of legal history, strictly defined, could only be traced back to the opening of the National Courts in 1883 and the idea that whatever existed before then could be described as legal chaos at best, and as outright despotism, at worst. This unambiguous conflation of Westernization with civilization can most clearly be detected in ʿAziz Khanki's

17 Zaghlul, *Al-Muhamah*, 222. See also 240ff.
18 See, for example, *al-Muhamah*, 169–170.

essay "Legislation and adjudication before the opening of the National Courts."[19] Providing a scathing assessment of the pre-1883 legal system, Khanki's essay proved nearly as influential as Zaghlul's tome. Khanki enumerates five features that rendered the entire legal system inherently unjust: the domination of the Pasha, i.e. the governor of Egypt, over judicial and legal matters; the control of the judiciary by the executive branch; the domination of the military over civilian aspects of administration; the overlap of sovereignty between the Ottoman sultan and the pasha of Egypt in applying the shari'a in Egypt; and the linguistic incompetence of judges and administrators. He concludes by stating that:

> Legislative powers during Mehmed Ali's time, and then during the rules of 'Abbas, Sa'id and Isma'il emanated from the governor and from him alone; executive powers were also monopolized by him. Justice in these times was not consistent, for maintaining the courts or removing them depended on the whims of the ruler. Laws were passed to protect the rights of the state not the individual. Laws back then were a mixture of backwardness and barbarism, on the one hand, and refinement and civilization, on the other.[20]

The standard narrative of the development of Egyptian law in the nineteenth century, therefore, is informed by an explicit Eurocentric assumption that sees the adoption of western (and specifically French) laws and Western-style courts to be the teleological end to which any process of legal reform should aspire. Accordingly, any legal system in which shari'a played even a small role, and which did not respect the principle of separation of powers, was, by definition, considered unfit for a modern state. These were precisely the reasons why the legal system that was applied in Egypt for most of the nineteenth century was ignored by historians in their incessant quest for modernity. And they were also the same reasons why judges and lawyers trained in a positive-law tradition could easily characterize this legal system by a series of lacks: lack of the principle of separation of powers, lack of distinction between substantive and procedural law, lack of justice, etc. Rather than deconstruct this history of absences on a theoretical level, Ruud Peters set out to find out first what *was* present in the Egyptian legal system and then to offer a comprehensive explanatory account of its development throughout the nineteenth century.

---

19 'Aziz Khanki, "Legislation and Adjudication before the Opening of the National Courts," in *al-Kitab al-dhahabi*, v.1, 62–96.

20 Khanki, "Legislation and Adjudication," 95–96.

Rudolph Peters' Scholarship on Egyptian Law

One of Rudolph Peters' earliest articles on Egyptian criminal law appeared in 1988 and dealt with the thorny question of how to apply shari'a in modern-day Egypt.[21] The article closely followed different legislative proposals dating from the 1970s and 1980s that aimed at enforcing shari'a by amending existing laws and drafting new ones. In this article, Peters manages to track key legislative proposals, identifies their main MP drafters and follows the rugged path they took in parliamentary committees and on the floor of Parliament at large. The article also explains why and when the government appeared to change course and to withdraw its tacit backing to enact these proposals. In addition to tracing the course taken by the judiciary (as opposed to the legislature) regarding this very contentious issue – implementing shari'a – Peters then offers a brief survey of public debate as depicted in the press surrounding the different legislative proposals in the 1970s and 1980s. Finally, the article includes an appendix that summarized the most salient features of the different proposals put forward to enforce *ḥadd* punishments for theft (*sariqa*), highway robbery (*ḥirāba*), illicit sexual intercourse (*zinā*), false accusations of illicit sexual intercourse (*qadhf*) drinking wine (*shurb al-khamr*) and apostasy (*ridda*).

Two years later and apparently deciding that the best way to study the position of shari'a in Egyptian law is by going back in time and analyzing the origins of the modern Egyptian legal system, Peters published a landmark article that launched his decades-long interest in the history of nineteenth-century Egyptian criminal law.[22] Titled "Murder on the Nile: Homicide trials in 19th century Egyptian shari'a courts," the article ostensibly describes the manner in which homicide cases were adjudicated in shari'a courts. Written in the wake of path-breaking studies that used sharī'a court registers to write the social history of Egypt in the 17th–19th centuries,[23] and attempting to fill the gap left by the few studies that dealt specifically with eighteenth- and nineteenth-century Egyptian criminal law,[24] this article, although dealing with homicide

21 Rudolph Peters, "Divine Law or Man-Made Law? Egypt and the Application of Shari'a," *Arab Law Quarterly* 3, no. 3 (1988): 231–253.

22 Rudolph Peters, "Murder on the Nile: Homicide Trials in 19th Century Shari'a Courts," *Die Welt des Islams* 3, no. 1/4 (1990), 98–116.

23 André Raymond, *Artisans et commerçants au Caire au XVIIIe siècle* (Damascus: Institut français de Damas, 1973–1974); Judith Tucker, *Women in Nineteenth Century Egypt* (Cambridge: Cambridge University Press, 1985).

24 Galal H. El-Nahal, *The Judicial Administration of Ottoman Egypt in the Seventeenth Century* (Minneapolis: Bibliotheca Islamica, 1979); Gabriel Baer, "Tanzimat in Egypt-The Penal Code," *Bulletin of the School of Oriental and African Studies* 26, no. 1 (1963): 29–49; Ehud R.

cases only, sets out to describe the contours of the entire criminal law system for much of the nineteenth century.

Crucially, Peters does not rely in this article on the shari'a court registers that historians had been using for at least two decades; rather, he relied on the little consulted fatwas of Egypt's Grand Mufti, Muhammad al-'Abbasi al-Mahdi (1827–1897). Published in seven volumes under the title *al-Fatawa al-Mahdiyya fi al-Waqa'i' al-Misriyya*,[25] the fatawas included in al-Mahdi's encyclopedic work "offer vivid pictures of the fights and quarrels that were and sometimes still are typical of Egyptian social life in the countryside. [Accordingly,] they are worth being studied as contributions to Egyptian social history."[26] But instead of using the record of these trials to paint a vivid picture of social and cultural life in nineteenth-century Egypt, Peters prefers to focus on the legal aspects of these trials.

By relying on this very rich source as well as other published compendia of nineteenth-century Egyptian laws,[27] Peters is able to shed light on many aspects of the history of Egyptian criminal law that had not been known before. For example, he cites contemporary legislation that determined the value of the *diyya* (bloodmoney) for a free man (15,093.75 piasters) which, he also manages to calculate, amounted to "200 times the monthly wage of a coffee man, 20 times that of a High Court mufti, and 14 times that of the head clerk (*bāshkātib*)."[28] He also explains intricate details about the application of shari'a in criminal cases, e.g., how despite the fact that there is no office of public prosecution in *fiqh*, nineteenth-century Egyptian state authorities succeeded in creating such an office; how state law managed to find ways to deal with complicated cases of complicity in homicide despite the fact that shari'a does not recognize collective liability;[29] and how the practice of *qasāma* (an oath repeated fifty times by the inhabitants of the place in which a murder had occurred asserting their innocence of the murder in question) and the concept of *'aqīla* (a group whose members would help each other "in the sense that if for some reason one's house was destroyed, the others would help him

Toledano, "Law, Practice, and Social Reality: A Theft Case in Cairo, 1854," *Asian and African Studies* 17 (1983): 153–173.

25 Muhammad al-'Abbasi al-Mahdi, *al-Fatawa al-Mahdiyya fī al-Waqa'i' al-Misriyya* (Cairo: al-Matba'a al-Azhariyya, 1883–85).

26 Peters, "Murder on the Nile," 100.

27 Zaghlul, *al-Muhamah*; Filib Jallad, *al-Qamus al-'Amm li-l-Idara wa-l-Qada'* (Matba'at Bani Laghudaki, 1899–1908).

28 Peters, "Murder on the Nile," 105.

29 Ibid., 106.

to restore it") were often applied.[30] All in all, in this article Peters makes an important correction to the standard narrative of nineteenth-century Egyptian law by insisting that, far from being marginalized, shariʿa played a crucial role in trying homicide cases.

In the same year, 1990, Peters published an article that was based on the records of a single lawsuit in order to explain in detail how the legal system handled homicide cases.[31] The lawsuit dated from August 1877 and was referred to the Grand Mufti, Muhammad al-ʿAbbasi al-Mahdi, to get his opinion about many intricate details that the case raised. The Grand Mufti, in turn, recorded the full transcript of the case in his *al-Fatawa al-Mahdiyya*[32] before giving his fatwa, and it is this full transcript that Peters reads critically, explaining and elaborating on many legal intricacies with regards to both *fiqh* and state law. Peters starts by giving a brief summary of the case. He then gives a succinct summary of the Islamic law of homicide stressing the Hanafi school's interpretation of the law, given that al-ʿAbbasi al-Mahdi was Hanafite and that the Hanafite *madhhab* was the official *madhhab* in Egypt at the time. Among the issues that he explains and that are pertinent to homicide cases are procedural rules of proof, the differences between intentional and unintentional killing, the conditions for asking for *qiṣāṣ*, i.e. a death sentence, the conditions of paying *diyya*, i.e. bloodmoney, the conditions of asking for a *qasāma* oath and the rules governing cases when the plaintiffs are minors and had a guardian representing them.

After summarizing these *fiqhī* rules regarding homicide, Peters then gives an equally clear and succinct summary of the *siyāsī* laws, i.e. state-enacted laws and regulations governing the same matter, *viz.* homicide. The logic of coupling *fiqh* with *siyāsa* is so lucidly explained that it is worth quoting at some length:

> It is obvious that, from the point of view of public security, the Sharīʿa's laws of homicide were not satisfactory for the State. Too much depended on the will of the plaintiffs and too often the strict Sharīʿa rules of evidence protected the culprit whose guilt was beyond doubt.... Therefore, the State had to intervene and to punish those murderers who, for some

30 Ibid., 108–09.

31 Rudolph Peters, "Who Killed ʿAbd Allah al-Ghazza? A Murder Trial before a Nineteenth Century Egyptian Qadi," in *Amsterdam Middle Eastern Studies*, ed. Manfred Woidich (Wiesbaden: Verlag, 1990), 84–98.

32 al-ʿAbbasi al-Mahdi, *al-Fatawa al-Mahdiyya*, vol. 4, 440–45 (fatwa dated 1 Ṣafar 1295 / 3 February 1878).

> reason or another, had escaped punishment by the qadi or whose punishment was not considered sufficiently severe. This was not opposed to the principles of Islamic law, since on the basis of *ta'zīr*, the State had the right to make punishable any undesirable and sinful act.[33]

What follows is a full translated transcript of the case as was recorded in al-'Abbasi al-Mahdi, *al-Fatawa al-Mahdiyya* with complete annotations and explanations of every legal twist in this long case.[34]

In 1994, Peters probed more deeply in *al-Fatawa al-Mahdiyya*. In an article published in the very first issue of *Islamic Law and Society*, he combed through the approximately 13,500 fatwas that al-'Abbasi had selected for inclusion in his *al-Fatawa al-Mahdiyya*.[35] Peters' interest was not only to shed light on the character of al-'Abbasi as Egypt's chief mufti, but also to explain the increasingly important role that the office of Grand Mufti, an office al-'Abbasi occupied from 1848 till his death in 1897, played in Egyptian political and legal life. One of the important signs of this office's enhanced role was overseeing the bureaucratization and standardization of the jobs of the numerous muftis appointed to such state agencies as the Bayt al-Mal (an agency which, among other things, dealt with orphans and legacies of people who died without heirs), the Waqf administration (which dealt with religious endowments), the Majlis al-Ahkam (which is described in more details below) and the Cairo Police Department (the *Ḍabṭiyya*). By placing the Grand Mufti on top of the muftis working in all these state agencies and imposing a uniform interpretation of the Hanafi *madhhab* on them, the office of the Grand Mufti appeared as a crucial tool to streamline shari'a and to ensure its uniform application. Most importantly, by closely reading different ordinances that were passed to regulate the functioning of the shari'a courts, Peters showed how the Grand Mufti handled complaints and petitions to the verdicts issued by these courts. The result of these statutes and ordinances, Peters concluded, was the introduction of an intricate system of judicial oversight whereby "the function of the Grand Muftī came to resemble that of the Court of Cassation in French and Dutch Law. The task of such courts was to ensure the correct application of the law."[36]

In 1997 Peters deepened his pioneering analysis of the origins of modern Egyptian law by having a close look at the role the qadi played in adjudicating

33 Peters, "Who Killed 'Abd Allah al-Ghazza?," 86.

34 Ibid., 90–98.

35 Rudolph Peters, "Muhammad al-'Abbasi al-Mahdi (d. 1897), Grand Mufti of Egypt and his "*al-Fatawa al-Mahdiyya*," *Islamic Law and Society* 1, no. 1 (1994): 66–82.

36 Peters, "Muhammad al-'Abbāsī al-Mahdi," 78.

different kinds of criminal cases.[37] In an article titled "Islamic and Secular Criminal Law in Nineteenth Century Egypt: The Role and Function of the Qadi," he set out to explain in detail the relationship between shariʿa courts and other judicial bodies in dealing with criminal cases. For the first time, we are given a comprehensive list of criminal codes passed from the late 1820s, when Muhammad ʿAli passed his first criminal legislation, to the early 1880s, when the entire legal system witnessed a radical overhaul. We are also given a clear chronology of the establishment throughout Egypt of councils which enforced these criminal legislations and which were called *siyāsa majālis* instead of *maḥākim*, the latter term being reserved exclusively for the shariʿa courts. "These councils did not form an independent judiciary and were staffed by administrators."[38] Peters also gives detailed information on how the shariʿa courts were reformed, first in 1856 as a result of Egypt's ruler Saʿid Pasha (r. 1854–1863), snatching from the Ottoman sultan the right to appoint Egyptian qadis (with the exception of the qadi of Cairo), and then by establishing a hierarchical system in which these councils were enmeshed and which set down clear procedures for appealing the sentences of any given qadi.

Most significantly, Peters gives a lucid explanation of how a dual judiciary, composed of shariʿa courts and *siyāsa* councils, came into existence with respect to criminal law. After noting the important distinction that courts and councils held between the criminal and the civil aspects of any given case, and after enumerating the different crimes in which the *maḥākim* and the *majālis* ruled jointly (homicide, wounding and grievous bodily harm, offenses against one's honor, offenses against one's property and offenses against public order), Peters then quotes from records of actual cases in order to show how both sides of the dual judiciary dealt with such cases.

Among the many conclusions that Peters reached in this ground-breaking article, two stand out for their significance. The first is that contrary to the standard narrative that sees nineteenth-century Egyptian law developing along Western secular lines, Peters argued that the Egyptian legal system saw "no tendency to restrict the application of Islamic law."[39] The second is a point that appears, at first glance, to be contradictory to this conclusion, namely that there is no evidence that retribution (*qiṣāṣ*) as a punitive punishment for murder and wounding was applied in practice. "Mutilating penalties and death sentences by stoning or in combination with crucifixion were not carried out,"

---

37 Rudolph Peters, "Islamic and Secular Criminal Law in Nineteenth Century Egypt: The Role and Function of the Qadi," *Islamic Law and Society* 4, no. 1 (1997): 70–90.

38 Peters, "Islamic and Secular Criminal Law," 75.

39 Peters, "Islamic and Secular Criminal Law," 78.

he asserts.[40] In cases that involved bodily injury (short of homicide), he found "no evidence that *qiṣāṣ* ... was applied in practice."[41] Furthermore, a sample of 100 homicide cases that he studied revealed that "only five percent ended in a conviction to pay blood money (*diya*) and a mere two percent resulted in a death sentence."[42] While the full meaning of these two apparently contradictory conclusions is teased out in Peters' subsequent publications, in this 1997 article he convincingly shows how nineteenth-century Egypt presents us with a remarkable example of how shariʿa was applied by coupling *fiqh* with *qānūn* and *maḥākim* with *majālis*.

The following year, 1998, Peters published an article that shed further light on the nineteenth-century Egyptian legal system, specifically concentrating on how that system's dual tracks, shariʿa and *siyāsa*, handled criminal cases. Titled "The infatuated Greek: Social and Legal Boundaries in Nineteenth-Century Egypt," the article was a departure from Peters' emphasis so far on homicide and dealt instead with a case of injuring honor (*hatk ʿirḍ*).[43] The case that Peters analyzes in this article is a fascinating one involving a young girl from Alexandria, Siteta, who fell in love with a Greek man, Filippo, who was a tobacconist living in Cairo. The couple met when Filioppo lived for a short while in a tenement house in Alexandria where Siteta's father was the *bawwāb*, or doorman. Determined to live together, the girl took the train to Cairo, and the couple lived together in an apartment that Filippo had rented in al-Muski quarter in Cairo. Siteta's brother then went to the police station in Alexandria and notified them that a *dhimmī*, i.e. non-Muslim, man had seduced his sister and requested that the police find her and her seducer.

As tantalizing as the case record can be as a source for social history, Peters uses this record to explain in detail the intricate nature of the legal system and how it handled the case. Noting that what was at stake in this case is the crossing of legal boundaries about marriage (the couple lived together without being married) and religion (Filippo was Christian while Siteta was Muslim), Peters first discusses the concept of legal capacity in classical Islamic law in order to clarify legal boundaries between different capacities of legal persons. He then builds on important insights he had already elaborated upon in his earlier publications, namely, that nineteenth-century Egyptian law did not witness a waning of shariʿa as had earlier been believed, but its exact opposite:

---

40 Ibid., 86.

41 Ibid., 84.

42 Ibid., 90.

43 Rudolph Peters, "The Infatuated Greek: Social and Legal Boundaries in Nineteenth-Century Egypt," *Égypte/Monde arabe*, no. 34 (1998): 53–65.

"At the time of this case," he reminds us, "Islamic law was still the law of the land in Egypt. The Penal Code enforced at that time must be regarded as codified *taʿzīr*," referring to the *fiqhī* principle of the right of the qadi to pass discretionary punishment.[44]

Among the many important features of this article, two stand out. The first is methodological and pertains to the kind of archival source used. For unlike his previous articles that relied on transcripts of criminal cases as recorded in *al-Fatawa al-Mahdiyya*, Peters here relies squarely on a case transcript that is recorded in the registers of the budding legal system itself. These were, to be more specific the records of Majlis al-Ahkam to which the case was eventually forwarded after having been tried first in the Police Council (Majlis al-Ḍabṭiyya) and then in the Cairo council. Using the case's thorough record, Peters is able to illustrate in detail how the councils handled cases of injured honor and specifically how they paid close attention both to precepts of the *qānūn* and the principles of *fiqh*. Secondly, and as in earlier publications, Peters adds a short appendix in which he reproduces an English translation of the sections in the Penal Code that were relevant to the case.[45]

This marked an important turn in Peters' scholarship, and for the following few years he shifted his interest from reading fatwas and case records to studying legislation. For a long time, it was commonly believed that Muhammad ʿAli's first act of legislation was *Qanun al-Filaha*, a code of fifty-five articles. Enacted in Shaʿban 1245 / January-February 1830, it deals with rural crimes and has been printed several times in its Arabic version. In 1999, however, Peters published an article shedding light on an earlier law that also deals with rural crime and that was enacted on 21 Rabiʿ I 1245/ 20 September 1829.[46] Although this *qānūn* was published in Arabic twice during the nineteenth century, Peters showed that these translations were inaccurate. Relying on two texts that he discovered in the Egyptian National Archives, he transcribed the Ottoman Turkish original version in addition to providing a complete English translation.

44 Peters, "The Infatuated Greek," 60.

45 These are Chapter two, Sections 1, 2, 6 and 7; Peters, "The Infatuated Greek," 64–5.

46 Rudolph Peters, "'For His Correction and as a Deterrent Example for Others': Meḥmed Alī's First Criminal Legislation (1829–1830)," *Islamic Law and Society* 6, no. 2 (1999): 164–92. In a recent article, ʿImad Hilal argued that while searching in the Egyptian National Archives, he found many decrees that pre-date 1829. While his article does refer to numerous earlier ordinances by Muhammad ʿAli and some of his assistants, none of these earlier ordinances could be described as a code; rather, they were orders dealing with specific instances in which the Pasha intended to punish certain individuals for particular offences. ʿImad Hilal, "Irhasat la'ihat ziraʿat al-fallah: al-tashriʿ al-jinai'i fi Misr, 1805–1830," *al-Ruznamah*, 4 (2006): 249–303.

Peters starts this important article by drawing attention to the main conclusion reached by his research so far, namely, that contrary to received wisdom, most famously propagated by Gabriel Baer in an influential 1969 article,[47] in Egypt it is not true that "the enactment of statute laws dealing with homicide, theft and robbery implied a restriction on the shariʿa, or even its abolition in criminal matters."[48] After summarizing his earlier work that explained how the qadi abided strictly by *fiqh* principles in his shariʿa court while at the same time working in conjunction with the *siyāsa majālis* that applied state enacted laws, *qānūns*, Peters makes the important observation that coupling *fiqh* with *qānūn* was consistent with older Ottoman practice and was not something that the khedives applied *ex nihilo*. However, he draws our attention to important differences between Egyptian and Ottoman *qawānīn*, the most important of which was that Egyptian *qawānīn* clearly specified penalties for each offense, whereas Ottoman ones merely stated that certain offences deserved punishment without specifying what these punishments should be. Another difference, he adds, was that when they did specify punishment, e.g. flogging, Ottoman *qawānīn* hardly ever specified the quantity, i.e. the number of lashes. Equally important is the fact that whereas Ottoman *qānūn*s referred to a wide range of corporal punishments that included the amputation of parts of the body (nose, ears, hands, male organ) as well as impaling and branding, Egyptian *qawānīn* showed a remarkably lesser propensity to inflict corporal punishment, so much so that by the 1830s hanging became the normal way of execution and the other forms of corporal punishments were hardly ever resorted to. Finally, Peters also points to the increased prominence that Egyptian penal codes gave to imprisonment, a feature that he picks up in later articles analyzed below.[49]

Most significantly, having studied the 1829 penal code closely and compared it to subsequent *qawānīn*, Peters reflects on the motives that might have been behind Muhammad ʿAli enacting these penal codes. Although many European influences could be detected in the ideas and phraseologies of some of these codes, and even though these codes, like their European counterparts, show a tendency of relying less on physical punishment and more on imprisonment, Peters cautions against seeing these laws as granting Egyptian subjects rights against the state. "The idea that law limits the powers of the sovereign by granting rights to subjects or citizens is totally alien to these codes as evidenced by

47 Gabriel Baer, "Tanzimat in Egypt," in *Studies in the Social History of Modern Egypt*, ed. Gabriel Baer (Chicago: The University of Chicago Press, 1969), 109–133.

48 Peters, "For His Correction," 167.

49 Peters, "For His Correction," 167–168.

the fact that they were not promulgated, and that copies were sent only to officials without any instruction to make them public."[50] Rather, Peters attributes the dwindling reliance on physical punishment and the corresponding rise of the importance of imprisonment to three principal reasons. The first was Muhammad 'Ali's "ambition to impose a centralized and rational order in his realm ... The idea of centralization was very much vested in his person. Muhammad 'Ali wanted to be the ultimate authority in criminal justice and the new laws expressed the notion that all punishment derived from his omnipresent authority, even if it was in fact imposed by his agents."[51] Secondly, the spread of public security in the realm meant that there was no need to resort to physical punishment. "As Foucault has mentioned with respect to Europe, the greater the chance for a criminal to be apprehended, the less the authorities feel the need for spectacles of cruel punishments in order to discourage crime."[52] Thirdly, Peters mentions an economic factor that might have also influenced the shift away from corporal punishments in the form of maiming, crippling or executing culprits. The shortage of manpower and the state's insatiable need for labor meant that "maiming and crippling able-bodied men could affect the availability of labor and soldiers. [At the same time,] forced labor as punishment was much more profitable for the state than the destruction of the human labor force and potential military recruits."[53]

While Peters was thus charting out the process of enacting laws and statutes and explaining the rationale behind the penal codes in particular, he also published an article that described in detail another aspect of the evolving legal system, namely, the establishment of council bodies that had important judicial roles, the *siyāsa majālis*. In an article published in 1999, Peters combed through the myriad of published decrees that founded these councilor bodies, appointed their members and specified their duties.[54] We thus learn that an important milestone in the evolving legal system was the establishment of the *Cemʿiyet-i Ḥaḳḳāniye* (Ar. Jamʿiyyat al-Haqqaniyya) in 1842 as a specialized judicial council whose president and six members had no other duty but to deal with criminal cases. Peters then follows the evolution of this council till it was replaced by Majlis al-Ahkam in 1849. This council was to preside over the entire legal system till it was replaced by the National Courts in 1883. Peters managed

50 Ibid., 172.

51 Ibid., 173.

52 Ibid., 174–175.

53 Peters, "For His Correction," 175.

54 Rudolph Peters, "Administrators and Magistrates: The Development of a Secular Judiciary in Egypt, 1842–1871," *Die Welt des Islams* 39, no. 3 (1999): 378–397.

to locate the founding decree of this important council and the subsequent decrees that amended and expanded its jurisdiction. He then completes the picture by following the slow process of establishing councils of first instance throughout the provinces (hence their name: "provincial councils"), so that by 1871 there were a total of fifteen councils. He also describes the logic and dates of formation of different appeal councils. Presiding above all these councils and supervising their activities, and overseeing their verdicts was Majlis al-Ahkam. All in all, the article gives us a clear chronology of the formation by the 1870s of a multi-tiered legal system in which these *majālis* dealt with criminal, civil suits and disputes over land.

Peters singles out three features that are crucial for understanding the true nature of this budding legal system. The first he had already touched upon in his earlier publications, namely, how these councils worked in tandem with the shari'a courts. "These new councils," he is quick to remind us, "were not regarded as an encroachment on the sharīʿa.... Islamic rules continued to play a role in the councils, witness the fact that the muftis were appointed to them and that the higher ones counted important 'ulama' among their members. Homicide cases were tried in one session by a qāḍī and secular council."[55] Secondly, he points out a peculiar feature of how these councils went about their business: "the examination of the cases was to take place on the basis of documents."[56] In these "trials", the council would act both as prosecutor and judge while "the defendant was not party of the trial, but rather the object of an investigation."[57] Thirdly, Peters also reminds us that while these councils were manned by administrators who were governed by statute law and who were constantly reminded of the importance of impartial analysis of the cases in front of them, they were not judges who had been trained in the letter of the law. Rather, they were administrators whose membership to these councils "was part of [their] normal bureaucratic career."[58]

Having studied the twin processes of enacting penal laws and establishing councilor bodies, Peters then directed his attention to describing in detail the prison system. In a series of three articles, he undertook to analyze a number of central questions about nineteenth-century Egyptian prisons and the role imprisonment played in the budding penal system. First, in an article published in 2002, he laid down the main characteristics of the prison system as could

55 Peters, "Administrators and Magistrates," 391–392.
56 Peters, "Administrators and Magistrates," 382.
57 Ibid., 394.
58 Ibid., 393.

be gleaned from archival sources.[59] We learn, for example, that there was no national authority in charge of all prisons throughout the country, and that prisons fell under the authority of several departments; that the prison population included, in addition to convicts, debtors and people awaiting trial; and that there were many places to which people were sent to serve their prison sentences: factories, fortresses, as well as the army. Most significantly, Peters remarks that there were no "indications of the existence of an explicit philosophy of punishment – other than the general notions of retribution and deterrence – that resulted in a specific penal policy. Prisons were located in normal houses, bought or rented for the purpose, in wards for example in the Cairo citadel, and in sheds and barracks." Equally significant is his observation that imprisonment did not seem to have had a stigmatizing effect and that prisoners did not feel marginalized in society. The reason he gives for this important remark is that there was "widespread mistrust of the government ... [with] most Egyptians [seeing] ... that the state mainly served the interests of the Turkish elite. This awareness affected the way they looked at criminal justice.... [As a result, those] sentenced for tax evasion, draft-dodging, desertion, sheltering deserters, escaping corvée, and official negligence, were certainly not seen as criminals, but rather as victims of the arbitrariness and oppression of the state."[60]

Also in 2002, Peters published what can only be described as a magisterial study on the history and nature of Egyptian prisons in the nineteenth century. Titled "Egypt and the age of the triumphant prison: Legal punishment in nineteenth century Egypt," this article attempted to analyze the philosophy of imprisonment.[61] Having argued that there was no explicit policy ever formulated by the ruling elite, Peters attempts to discover the general principles that might have informed the policy of incarceration by reading between the lines, so to speak, a large number of Khedival ordinances and decrees as well as prison sentences passed by the *majālis*.

Building on his earlier studies in which he had established that rather than capital or corporal punishment, prisons appeared in the nineteenth century as *the* central element of the penal system, Peters remarks that this was similar to contemporaneous European developments. He then engages with both

59 Rudolph Peters, "Prisons and Marginalisation in Nineteenth-Century Egypt," in *Outside In: On the Margins of the Modern Middle East*, ed. Eugene Rogan (London: IB Tauris, 2002), 31–52.

60 Peters, "Prisons and Marginalisation," 36–37.

61 Rudolph Peters, "Egypt and the Age of the Triumphant Prison: Legal Punishment in Nineteenth Century Egypt," *Annales Islamologiques* 36 (2002): 253–285.

Foucault's and Spierenburg's studies on European prisons[62] to ask if the reasons behind the twin process of the gradual aversion to spectacular punishment and the increased preference to imprisonment in Egypt were similar to those in Europe. Interestingly, he remarks that "contrary to Western Europe, the Egyptian prisons were not transformed into instruments of discipline. Imprisonment, like corporal punishment, was a mode of repression aimed at subjecting, not at disciplining the population. Disciplining activities of the State ... were directed at the State servants ... and not the population at large."[63] Given that "there was no public debate in nineteenth century Egypt about penal policies," and given that he found no "express official statements laying down e.g. a philosophy of legal punishment of the principles of legal reform,"[64] Peters nevertheless sought to tease out what this penal philosophy might have been. By reading penal laws, khedival decrees, sentences of the *majālis* as well as case records, he concludes that the aim of imprisonment was mainly retribution as well as to deploy the prison population in hard labor. "Almost all prisoners had to work," he observes. "Prison labor had essentially an economic function as a means to provide manpower for necessary but arduous, dirty or unhealthy work."[65]

Two years later, Peters published his third and last article on nineteenth-century prisons.[66] In this article, he attempted to get inside the prisons, so to speak, to find out what the living conditions were. Relying on five registers listing entries of prisoners in Egypt's principal national prison, the one housed in the Alexandria Arsenal and usually called *līmān Iskandariyya*, he was able to calculate the mortality rates of this central prison. The five registers cover two periods, one in the late 1840s and the other in the 1860s, and because these registers list the date of entry, release or death of the inmates, Peters was able to compare mortality figures for these two periods and to conclude that whereas the early period witnessed a mortality rate among prison inmates of 13 percent, this figure came down sixteen years later to 4.5 percent.[67] He then gives vivid descriptions of the living conditions of Egyptian prisons with respect

62 Michel Foucault, *Surveiller et punir: naissance de la prison* (Paris: Gallimard, 1975); Pieter Spierenburg, *The Prison Experience: Disciplinary Institutions and the Their Inmates in Early Modern Europe* (New Brunswick: Rutgers University Press, 1991).

63 Peters, "Egypt and the Age of the Triumphant Prison," 255.

64 Ibid., 256.

65 Peters, "Egypt and the Age of the Triumphant Prison," 265.

66 Rudolph Peters, "Controlled Suffering: Mortality and Living Conditions in 19th-Century Egyptian Prisons," *International Journal of Middle East Studies* 36 (2004): 387–407.

67 Peters, "Controlled Suffering," 391.

to accommodation, food, and labor conditions. Most interestingly, he raises the important question of how to explain the significant decline in mortality figures and the overall improvement of health conditions of prison inmates. In answer, he argues that there were three factors behind the amelioration of prison conditions between roughly 1850 and 1865. The first was the significant improvement of public health and the growing involvement of public health services with prisons. Secondly, there was a general increased sophistication of the Egyptian state administration. Thirdly, Peters draws on his previous work on Egyptian legal history and on his earlier articles on the history of nineteenth-century prisons to argue that improving health conditions was made necessary by the evolving philosophy informing penal law.

> Reforms to improve the living conditions in prisons were supported by the administration as a result of the spread of new ideas about crime and punishment that informed the penal system that emerged in Egypt after 1829. One of the characteristics was the notion of quantification of penalties to avoid arbitrariness in criminal justice. After 1829, penal codes listed the punishment for each offense, and criminal sentences specified the penalties imposed. However, such a system can work only if prison conditions do not expose the inmates to serious health risks. In that case, imprisonment might result in excessive and gratuitous suffering of death, which would be in conflict with the idea of precisely quantified penalties. Control of suffering was therefore necessary so that a "just measure of main" would be inflicted on every convict: convicts sentenced to the same type of imprisonment must be imprisoned under the same conditions.[68]

Conclusion

The above brief summary of Ruud Peters' articles on nineteenth-century Egyptian law shows how pioneering and significant his scholarship is. With very few exceptions,[69] the standard narrative of the history of modern Egyptian law

---

68 Peters, "Controlled suffering," 401.

69 ʿImad Hilal, "Irhasat"; Hilal, *al-Fallah wa-l-Sulta wa-l-Qanun* (Cairo: Dar al-watha'iq wa-l-kutub al-qawmiyya), 2007); Hilal, "al-Siyasatnama al-Thaniyya: Safha Majhula min Tarikh al-Tashriʿ al-Jina'i fi ʿAss Muhammad ʿAli, *al-Ruznama* 8 (2010): 41–74; Khaled Fahmy, "Law, Medicine and Society in Nineteenth-Century Egypt," *Egypte/Monde arabe*, no. 34

has dismissed this entire system as essentially flawed and despotic, viewed it from a Eurocentric angle and judged it to be lacking some fundamental characteristics of "proper" law. Thanks to Ruud Peters' meticulous research and copious publications, we now have a proper history of nineteenth century Egyptian law, one that is interested not in measuring it against some other legal system but rather in studying it on its own terms, explaining its internal dynamics and underlying the inherent logic that informed its historical development.

Peters' pioneering oeuvre on nineteenth-century Egyptian law exhibits three central features whose importance cannot be overestimated. The first, on a simple empirical level, is the way in which Peters has supplied us with information that was simply unavailable to us before. Not only do we now know the value of blood money for free, male Muslims; the different kinds of prisons that existed with a detailed description of daily life of prisoners; and the number, dates and nature of the general amnesties that Egypt's rulers had issued on different occasions throughout the nineteenth century; but we also have a complete list of the penal codes drafted from the late 1820s to the early 1880s as well as the different *siyāsa* councils that had been established to deal with criminal, administrative and land disputes.

Secondly, on a methodological level, unlike the overwhelming majority of scholars of Islamic law, Peters' scholarship is not solely based on mastery of *fiqh* sources whether they are the *mutūn*, the *shurūḥ*, the *fatāwā*, or the *rasāʾil*.[70] He is also not content with relying on the shariʿa court records which for the past thirty odd years have been used extensively by Middle East historians as

---

(1998): 17–51; Fahmy, "The Anatomy of Justice: Forensic Medicine and Criminal Law in Nineteenth-Century Egypt," *Islamic Law and Society* 6 (1999): 224–271; Fahmy, "The Police and the People in Nineteenth-Century Egypt," *Die Welt des Islams* 39 (1999): 1–38; Fahmy, "Medical Conditions in Egyptian Prisons in the Nineteenth Century," in *Marginal Voices in Literature and Society: Individual and Society in the Mediterranean Muslim World*, ed. Robin Ostle (Strasbourg: European Science Foundation, 2000), 135–153; Fahmy, "Justice, Law and Pain in Khedival Egypt," in *Standing Trial: Law and the Person in the Modern Middle East*, ed. Baudouin Dupret (London: I.B. Tauris, 2004), 85–116; and Fahmy, "The Birth of the Secular Individual: Medical and Legal Methods of Identification in 19th-Century Egypt," in *Registration and Recognition: Documenting the Person in World History*, ed. Keith Breckenridge and Simon Szerter (Oxford: Oxford University Press, 2012), 335–356.

70 On the distinction between these sources, see Baber Johansen, "How the Norms Change: Legal Literature and the Problem of Change in the Case of the Land Rent," in his *Contingency in a Sacred law: Legal and Ethical Norms in the Muslim Fiqh* (Leiden: Brill, 1999), 446–464.

sources for economic,[71] social,[72] cultural[73] and legal history.[74] Rather, and in addition to mastering all of these "traditional" sources, Peters brings to light two bodies of legal sources that so far have been used by only a handful of scholars, namely, the voluminous records of the *siyāsa* councils and the texts of Egyptian *qawānīn*.

Thirdly, on a more substantial level, using these hitherto seldom used sources, Peters provides us with a detailed description of the inner workings of the nineteenth-century Egyptian legal system. Instead of the earlier Eurocentric accounts of Egyptian law that saw it as lacking in some fundamental characteristics, Peters presents us with a detailed picture of how this system worked. Most importantly, he stressed the Ottoman origins of the modern Egyptian penal system, elaborated on the significant innovations that the khedives introduced and convincingly argued that contrary to received wisdom, shariʿa played an important role in this system. However, the shariʿa that was applied in the nineteenth-century Egyptian system was not only based on *fiqh*, but also deployed *qawānīn*, and it was practiced not only in the shariʿa courts, but also in the *siyāsa* councils.

Prior to Peters' scholarship, modern Egyptian law was believed to have its origins either in the brief efforts introduced by the French under Bonaparte at the end of the eighteenth century, or in Muhammad ʿAli's reforms that were seen as mimicking Europe. By concentrating on criminal law and by relying on new documentary evidence, Peters paints an alternative picture of a complex legal system in which *fiqh* plays an important role and one which builds on centuries of Ottoman legal practice. In this picture, Muhammad ʿAli and his successors are seen as repeatedly enacting laws that are neither derived from *fiqh* nor are they copied from French legal codes, but are inspired by the age-old precedent of the Ottoman sultans issuing *qawānīn*. Despite the fact that these Egyptian legislations were also called *qawānīn*, and despite the fact that they might have had Ottoman influences, they reflected Egyptian realities and

---

71 See, for example, Cuno, *The Pasha's Peasants.*

72 Dror Ze'evi, "The Use of Ottoman Shariʿa Court Records as a Source for Middle Eastern Social History: A Reappraisal," *Islamic Law and Society* 5, no. 1 (1998): 35–56.

73 Nelly Hanna, *In Praise of Books: A Cultural History of Cairo's Middle Class, Sixteenth to the Eighteenth Century* (Syracuse: Syracuse University Press, 2003).

74 See for example, Leslie Peirce, *Morality Tales: Law and Gender in the Ottoman Court of Aintab* (Berkeley: University of California Press, 2003); Iris Agmon, *Family and Court: Legal Culture and Modernity in Late Ottoman Palestine* (Syracuse, N.Y.: Syracuse University Press, 2006).

expressed the wish of the Khedives. These laws were implemented in newly established judicial councils called *siyāsa majālis* which dealt with criminal, administrative and land disputes. The result of this detailed picture is that we now have a much better understanding of the workings of the Egyptian criminal system in the nineteenth century. Indeed, we can say that thanks to Rudolph Peters, we now have an alternative history of modern Egyptian law.

Bibliography

Agmon, Iris. *Family and Court: Legal Culture and Modernity in Late Ottoman Palestine.* Syracuse, N.Y.: Syracuse University Press, 2006.

Baer, Gabriel. "Tanzimat in Egypt – The Panel Code." *Bulletin of the School of Oriental and African Studies* 26 (1963): 29–49.

Baer, Gabriel. "Tanzimat in Egypt." In *Studies in the Social History of Modern Egypt*, edited by Gabriel Baer, 109–133. Chicago: The University of Chicago Press, 1969.

Cannon, Byron. "Social Tension and the Teaching of European Law in Egypt before 1900." *History of Education Quarterly* 15, no. 3 (1975): 299–315.

Fahmy, Khaled. "Law, Medicine and Society in Nineteenth-Century Egypt." *Egypte/Monde arabe* 34 (1998): 17–51.

Fahmy, Khaled. "The Anatomy of Justice: Forensic Medicine and Criminal Law in Nineteenth-Century Egypt." *Islamic Law and Society* 6 (1999): 224–271.

Fahmy, Khaled. "The Police and the People in Nineteenth-Century Egypt." *Die Welt des Islams* 39 (1999): 1–38.

Fahmy, Khaled. "Medical Conditions in Egyptian Prisons in the Nineteenth Century." In *Marginal Voices in Literature and Society: Individual and Society in the Mediterranean Muslim World*, edited by Robin Ostle, 135–153. Strasbourg: European Science Foundation, 2000.

Fahmy, Khaled. "Justice, Law and Pain in Khedival Egypt." In *Standing Trial: Law and the Person in the Modern Middle East*, edited by Baudouin Dupret, 85–116. London: I.B. Tauris, 2004.

Fahmy, Khaled. "The Birth of the Secular Individual: Medical and Legal Methods of Identification in 19th-Century Egypt." In *Registration and Recognition: Documenting the Person in World History*, edited by Keith Breckenridge and Simon Szerter, 335–356. Oxford: Oxford University Press, 2012.

Faraḥat, Muhammad N. *al-Mujtamaʿ wa-l-Shariʿa wa-l-Qanun* (*Society, Shariʿa and Law*). Cairo: Dar al-Hilal, 1986.

Foucault, Michel. *Surveiller et punir: naissance de la prison*. Paris: Gallimard, 1975.

Hanna, Nelly. *In Praise of Books: A Cultural History of Cairo's Middle Class, Sixteenth to the Eighteenth Century.* Syracuse: Syracuse University Press, 2003.

Hilal, ʿImad. "Irhasat La'ihht Ziraʿat al-Fallah: al-Tashriʿ al-Jinai'ī fi Misr, 1805–1830." *al-Ruznamah* 4 (2006): 249–303.
Hilal, ʿImad. *al-Fallah wa-l-Sulta wa-l-Qanun*. Cairo: Dar al-Watha'iq wa-l-kutub al-qawmiyya, 2007.
Hilal, ʿImad. "al-Siyasatnama al-Thaniyya: Safha Majhula min Tarikh al-Tashriʿ al-Jina'i fi ʿAsr Muhammad ʿAli." *Al-Ruznamah* 8 (2010): 41–74.
Jallad, Filib. *al-Qamus al-ʿAmm li-l-Idara wa-l-Qada'*. Matbaʿat Bani Laghudaki, 1899–1908.
Khanki, ʿAziz. "Legislation and the Judiciary before the Inauguration of the National Courts." In *al-Kitab al-dhahabi li-l-maahkim al-ahliyya* (*The Golden Book of the National Courts*), vol. 1, 62–96. Cairo: Bulaq, 1937.
Mahdi, Muhammad al-ʿAbbasi al-. *al-Fatawa al-mahdiyya fī al-waqa'iʿ al-misriyya*. Cairo: al-Matbaʿa al-Azhariyya, 1883–85.
Nahal, Galal H. El-. *The Judicial Administration of Ottoman Egypt in the Seventeenth Century*. Minneapolis: Bibliotheca Islamica, 1979.
Peirce, Leslie. *Morality Tales: Law and Gender in the Ottoman Court of Aintab*. Berkeley: University of California Press, 2003.
Peters, Rudolph. *Islam and Colonialism: The Doctrine of Jihad in Modern History*. The Hague, New York: Mouton, 1979.
Peters, Rudolph. "Divine Law or Man-Made Law? Egypt and the Application of Shariʿa." *Arab Law Quarterly* 3, no. 3 (1988): 231–53.
Peters, Rudolph. "Murder on the Nile: Homicide Trials in 19th Century Shariʿa Courts." *Die Welt des Islams* 3, no. 1 (1990): 98–116.
Peters, Rudolph. "Who Killed ʿAbd Allah al-Ghazza? A Murder Trial before a Nineteenth Century Egyptian Qadi." In *Amsterdam Middle Eastern Studies*, edited by Manfred Woidich, 84–98. Wiesbaden: Reichert Verlag, 1990.
Peters, Rudolph. "Muḥammad al-ʿAbbasi al-Mahdi (d. 1897), Grand Mufti of Egypt and his '*al-Fatawa al-Mahdiyya*.'" *Islamic Law and Society* 1, no. 1 (1994): 66–82.
Peters, Rudolph. *Jihad in Classical and Modern Islam*. Princeton: Markus Wiener, 1996.
Peters, Rudolph. "Islamic and Secular Criminal Law in Nineteenth Century Egypt: The Role and Function of the Qadi." *Islamic Law and Society* 4, no. 1 (1997): 70–90.
Peters, Rudolph. "The Infatuated Greek: Social and Legal Boundaries in Nineteenth-Century Egypt." *Égypte/Monde arabe*, no. 34 (1998): 53–65.
Peters, Rudolph. "Administrators and Magistrates: The Development of a Secular Judiciary in Egypt, 1842–1871." *Die Welt des Islams* 39, no. 3 (1999): 378–97.
Peters, Rudolph. "'For His Correction and as a Deterrent Example for Others': Mehmed ʿAli's First Criminal Legislation (1829–1830)." *Islamic Law and Society* 6, no. 2 (1999): 164–92.
Peters, Rudolph. "Egypt and the Age of the Triumphant Prison: Legal Punishment in Nineteenth Century Egypt." *Annales Islamologiques* 36 (2002): 253–85.

Peters, Rudolph. "Murder in Khaybar: Some Thoughts on the Origins of the Qasāma Procedure in Islamic Law." *Islamic Law and Society* 9, no. 2 (2002): 132–167.

Peters, Rudolph. "Prisons and Marginalisation in Nineteenth-Century Egypt." In *Outside In: On the Margins of the Modern Middle East*, edited by Eugene Rogan, 31–52. London: IB Tauris, 2002.

Peters, Rudolph. "Controlled Suffering: Mortality and Living Conditions in 19th-Century Egyptian Prisons." *International Journal of Middle East Studies* 36 (2004): 387–407.

Peters, Rudolph. *Crime and Punishment in Islamic Law: Theory and Practice from the Sixteenth to the Twenty-First Century*. Cambridge: Cambridge University Press, 2005.

Peters, Rudolph. "What Does it Mean to be an Official Madhhab? Hanafism and the Ottoman Empire." In *The Islamic School of Law: Evolution, Devolution, and Progress*, edited by Peri Bearman, Rudolph Peters and Frank Vogel, 147–158. Cambridge, MA: Harvard University Press, 2005.

Raymond, André. *Artisans et commerçants au Caire au XVIIIe siècle*. Damascus: Institut français de Damas, 1973–1974.

Salim, Latifa. *Tarīkh al-Qada' al-Misri al-Hadith* (*History of the Modern Egyptian Judiciary*). Cairo: al-Hay'a al-misriyya al-ʿamma li-l-kitab, 2001.

Spierenburg, Pieter. *The Prison Experience: Disciplinary Institutions and the Their Inmates in Early Modern Europe*. New Brunswick: Rutgers University press, 1991.

Tagher, Jacques. *Harakat al-Tarjamah bi-Misr khilal al-Qarn al-Tasiʿ ʿAshar* (*The Translation Movement in Egypt During the Nineteenth Century*). Cairo: Dar al-Maʿarif, 1945.

Toledano, Ehud R. "Law, Practice, and Social Reality: A Theft Case in Cairo, 1854." *Asian and African Studies* 17 (1983): 153–173.

Tucker, Judith. *Women in Nineteenth Century Egypt*. Cambridge: Cambridge University Press, 1985.

Zaghlul, Ahmad F. *al-Muhamah*. Cairo, 1900.

Ze'evi, Dror. "The Use of Ottoman Shariʿa Court Records as a Source for Middle Eastern Social History: A Reappraisal." *Islamic Law and Society* 5, no. 1 (1998): 35–56.

Ziadeh, Farhat. *Lawyers, the Rule of Law and Liberalism in Modern Egypt*. Stanford: Hoover Institution, 1968.

PART 1

Regime Change and Legal Institutions

CHAPTER 2

The Qadis' Justice according to Papyrological Sources (Seventh–Tenth Centuries CE)

Mathieu Tillier

Introduction*

Narrative sources provide a vivid and colorful picture of the history of the judiciary. Since the edition of al-Kindi's *Akhbar al-qudat* in the early twentieth century,[1] followed forty years later by the publication of Waki''s *Akhbar al-qudat*,[2] historians have relied almost exclusively on this type of biographical literature to reconstruct the history of early Islamic judgeship. Documentary evidence was not taken into account by either Émile Tyan in his seminal study of judicial organization in Islam[3] nor Wael Hallaq half a century later.[4] Documentary sources are indeed lacking for most of the Islamic empire in its formative period, and narrative sources are undeniably useful to recreate the image of the judiciary as it was seen by Muslim scholars of the ninth and tenth centuries CE. Furthermore, this image contains real evidence about the early period. As Fred Donner argued, Muslims appear to have kept early records of their officials and administrators, including qadis.[5] The genealogy of al-Kindi's

* I am thankful to Maaike van Berkel, Petra Sijpesteijn and Naïm Vanthieghem for their useful comments on a previous version of this paper.

1 al-Kindi, *The Governors and Judges of Egypt*, ed. Rhuvon Guest (Leiden: E.J. Brill, 1912). Another edition had been proposed a few years earlier by Richard J.H. Gottheil: *The History of the Egyptian Cadis as Compiled by Abu Omar Muhammad ibn Yusuf ibn Ya'qub al-Kindi/ Kitab al-Qudat alladhina walu Qada' Misr* (Paris-Madinat al-Rumiyya al-'uzma [Istanbul]: Paul Geuthner, 1908). Guest's edition has since then been regarded as the standard one.

2 Waki', *Akhbar al-Qudat*, ed. 'Abd al-'Aziz Mustafa al-Maraghi (Cairo: Matba'at al-sa'ada, 1947–1950).

3 Émile Tyan, *Histoire de l'organisation judiciaire en pays d'Islam*, 2nd edition (Leiden: E.J. Brill, 1960).

4 Wael B. Hallaq, *The Origins and Evolution of Islamic Law* (Cambridge: Cambridge University Press, 2005).

5 Fred M. Donner, *Narratives of Islamic Origins. The Beginnings of Islamic Historical Writing* (Princeton: The Darwin Press, 1998), 167–168.

 | DOI 10.1163/9789004343733_004

book confirms that his chronicle of Egyptian judgeship is basically an expansion of a list that formed the bulk of a chapter on qadis in Ibn ʿAbd al-Hakam's *Futuh Misr*.[6] Problems in the interpretation of these narrative sources have long been raised, however, especially for the seventh century. Apparent contradictions in Wakiʿ's text led historians to disqualify his reports concerning the pre-Umayyad period.[7] Moreover, al-Kindi himself is unsure of the chronology of early Egyptian judgeship, and provides two different versions of its history before 60 A.H. (679–80 CE).[8] The exact duties of the first "qadis" are usually omitted from literary sources, and it is uncertain whether they were actual judges who adjudicated and issued binding decisions, or rather some kind of religious advisers and mediators.[9]

The way in which ninth- and tenth-century authors managed their lack of confirmed knowledge about the early period is linked to a wider problem, which is that their narratives constitute a literary discourse on the judiciary. Narratives about the Umayyad qadis were not designed to describe judges' lives or practices, but rather to record *exempla* within the broader context of the early formation of Islamic law. One of the main materials they drew upon was non-prophetic hadith recording authoritative deeds or opinions of the generations of the Companions and the Successors. Therefore, the content and scope of early biographies of qadis do not fundamentally differ from non-canonical hadith collections such as the *Musannaf*s by ʿAbd al-Razzaq al-Sanʿani (d. 211/827) and Ibn Abi Shayba (d. 235/849). The quest for authoritative judicial precedents explains why a biography such as Shurayh's, in Wakiʿ's *Akhbar al-qudat*, is nearly two hundred pages, and contains repetitions and contradictory statements.[10] Furthermore, one of the obvious purposes of this biographical literature is to show the continuity of Islamic judgeship since the early conquest, as well as to provide a historical basis for its relationship with the government and the law. The reconstruction of qadis' history in the form it reached us dates from the second Abbasid period, after a new political and religious order was established following the end of the *miḥna*, the inquisition through which the caliphate tried to impose the doctrine of the created Qur'an

6 Mathieu Tillier, "Introduction," in al-Kindi, *Histoire des cadis égyptiens*, trans. Mathieu Tillier (Cairo: Institut Français d'Archéologie Orientale, 2012), 10.

7 Mathieu Tillier, *Les cadis d'Iraq et l'État abbasside (132/750–334/945)* (Damascus: Presses de l'Ifpo, 2009), 68–69.

8 al-Kindi, *The Governors and Judges of Egypt*, 300–311.

9 Wael B. Hallaq, *The Origins and Evolution of Islamic Law*, 34ff.; Tillier, *Les cadis d'Iraq et l'État abbasside*, 74–75.

10 Wakiʿ, *Akhbar al-Qudat*, 2: 189–400.

on scholars (between 218/833 and 234/848 or 237/852). Relationships between scholars (including qadis) and rulers had been subjected to tremendous ordeal, and the process leading to this new order had to be explained, understood and justified.[11]

Documentary sources directly relating to Islamic judgeship are scarce, and biographical dictionaries will certainly remain essential. It is nevertheless necessary to compare the picture they provide with the scattered documentary evidence of Arabic papyri that have come to light especially (but not only) in Egypt. This documentation only provides a partial image of the judiciary. Its availability depends on accidental discoveries, and covers only a few areas, mainly in Upper Egypt.[12] As a matter of fact, narrative and documentary evidence appear to mirror different realities. Whereas biographies of qadis depict (retrospectively, and to a certain extent only) the judicial situation in a large city like Fustat, papyri usually provide an account of day-to-day reality in small Egyptian towns.

In this paper, I shall attempt to piece together what information can be gathered about the institution of the qadi in Egyptian papyri until the tenth century CE. Due to the scattered and fragmented nature of these papyri, the picture reconstructed from such evidence should complement – rather than replace – narrative sources. However, these Egyptian papyri offer a vision of the judiciary that may reveal historical tendencies not always apparent in literary sources.

The Qadi, Absent from Umayyad Papyri?

Judicial institutions represented in the Umayyad papyri are different from the qadis' courts as described by the literary sources. During the Sufyānid period (41–64/661–684), Greek papyri found in Edfu (the so-called dossier of Papas) show that justice in the Thebaid district was still being dispensed by either the Christian *dux* (Ar. amir) residing in Antinoe or his representative, the *topoteretes*. At a local level, Christian pagarchs (Ar. *ṣāḥib al-kūra*, head of a rural

11 On this issue, Mathieu Tillier, *L'invention du cadi. La justice des musulmans, des juifs et des chrétiens aux premiers siècles de l'Islam* (Paris: Publications de la Sorbonne, 2017), 157–159.

12 More generally, see Roger S. Bagnall, *Reading Papyri, Writting Ancient History* (London: Routledge, 1995), 8–11; Petra M. Sijpesteijn, *Shaping a Muslim State. The World of a Mid-Eighth-Century Egyptian Official* (Oxford: Oxford University Press, 2013), 2.

district or *kūra*) were the main judicial authority.[13] During the Marwanid period (64–132/684–750), the main judicial officials attested in the papyri are local pagarchs and governors of Fustat as documented by the famous dossier of Qurra b. Sharik (r. 90–96/709–714).[14] Until the last two decades of the Umayyad period, pagarchs mentioned in judicial documentation are all Christians and therefore cannot be assimilated to qadis. From the 720s CE. onwards, Muslim pagarchs begin to appear in Coptic papyri, having the same legal responsibilities as their Christian predecessors.[15] At the level of a village like Jeme, in Upper Egypt, litigants more often solicited their representative (Muslims as well) for adjudication of their disputes. Both the pagarch and his representative bear the title of amir in Coptic sources, however, and that of qadi is never attested.[16] Likewise in Palestine, the only local judge who appears to be a Muslim, in the late seventh century CE, is an official from Khirbet el-Mird called ʿUmar b. ʿUbayd Allah (*P.Mird* 18).[17] His title does not appear in the papyrus, however, and his assimilation to a qadi would be speculative.[18]

No qadi appears nominally in the Umayyad papyri, and no document dating from this period can be identified as having been issued by a qadi's court. Is this absence of mention of any qadi in Umayyad documents purely accidental? Or could we suppose that documents issued by/for qadis have been kept less diligently than those issued by governors and pagachs? Should we believe that literary sources, which consider the office of qadi as a creation of the Medinese caliphate – or, for the most critical traditions, of the caliph

---

13 Mathieu Tillier, "Du pagarque au cadi: ruptures et continuités dans l'administration judiciaire de la Haute-Égypte (Ier-IIIe/VIIe-IXe siècle)," *Médiévales* 64, no. 1 (2013): 21.

14 On Qurra b. Sharīk, see Nabbia Abbott, *The Ḳurrah Papyri from Aphrodito in the Oriental Institute* (Chicago: The University of Chicago Press, 1938), 66ff; Jasir b. Khalid Abu Safiya, *Bardiyyat Qurra b. Sharik al-ʿAbsi. Dirasa wa-Tahqiq* (Riyad: Markaz al-Malik Faysal li-l-buhuth wa-l-dirasat al-islamiyya, 2004), 27–57; C.E. Bosworth, "Ḳurra b. Sharīk", in *The Encyclopaedia of Islam, Second edition*, 5: 500; al-Kindi, *The Governors and Judges of Egypt*, 63–66; Henri Lammens, "Un gouverneur omaiyade d'Égypte. Qorra ibn Šarîk d'après les papyrus arabes," *Bulletin de l'Institut d'Égypte*, 5e série, tome II (1908): 99–115.

15 See for example Terry G. Wilfong, *Women of Jeme. Lives in a Coptic Town in Late Antique Egypt* (Ann Arbor: University of Michigan Press, 2002), 127.

16 See *P.KRU* 42 in Leslie S.B. MacCoull (trans.), *Coptic Legal Documents. Law as Vernacular Text and Experience in Late Antique Egypt* (Tempe: Arizona Center for Medieval and Renaissance Studies, 2009), 128; A. Arthur Schiller, "A Family Archive from Jeme," in *Studi in honore di Vincenzo Arangio-Ruiz* (Napoli: Jovene, 1953), 344–45.

17 *P.Mird* = Adolf Grohmann, *Arabic Papyri from Ḫirbet el-Mird* (Louvain: Bibliothèque du Muséon, 1963).

18 See Tillier, *L'invention du cadi*, 81–83.

Muʿawiya (r. 41–60/661–680)[19] – projected on the early period an institution that actually developed later?

This last hypothesis was recently favored by Fred Donner. Drawing on the absence of any occurrence of the term qadi in first/seventh-century papyri, Donner argues that its emergence is typical of a wider "qur'anization" of the politico-religious terminology which occurred in the second/eighth century. "The ruler seems to have initiated a new position or office, designated by the term qadi, to handle judicial procedures that heretofore had been part of the duties of a governor."[20] In other words, the qadi was an institutional innovation from the eighth century CE. Donner is certainly correct when he argues that the title of qadi reflects qur'anic rhetoric, and we may doubt that the term was adopted as early as literary sources claim. However, it should be noticed that early Arabic papyri were reluctant to use official titles, and individuals were usually called by their names only. Arabic letters from Qurra b. Sharik never mention that the sender is the provincial governor, and his official title is only given in Greek and Coptic papyri.[21] Furthermore, would the (relatively) late invention of this title rule out the possibility that the *function* of qadi existed previously?

No papyrus or any literary source refers to a qadi in Upper Egypt before the Abbasid period; presumably no qadi was appointed in secondary towns of the Egyptian landscape under the Umayyads, which could be related to the absence of large groups of Muslims. What was the situation in Umayyad main cities? Should we imagine that dispensing justice was a prerogative of the sole governor? Or should we abide by later literary sources that claim that the judiciary was already partly delegated to lower judges (whether they were referred to as qadis, as mentioned above, is another question) in the second half of the seventh century? Literary sources state that qadis were operating in Fustat since 23/643[22] and in Alexandria since the end of the seventh century CE.[23] However, edited documents are still silent about this issue. None of them bear any mention of "qadis" in both cities during the Umayyad

19 Tillier, *Les cadis d'Iraq et l'État abbasside*, 68–69.

20 Fred M. Donner, "Qur'anicization of Religio-Political Discourse in the Umayyad Period," *Revue des Mondes Musulmans et de la Méditerranée* 129 (2011): 86.

21 See *P.Lond.* IV. I am thankful to Petra Sijpesteijn, who first drew my attention to this phenomenon. On the titles of early Islamic provincial governors, see Federico Morelli, "Consiglieri e comandanti: i titoli del governatore arabo d'Egitto *symboulos* e *amîr*," *Zeitschrift für Papyrologie und Epigraphik* 173 (2010): 158–166.

22 Mathieu Tillier, "Introduction," in al-Kindi, *Histoire des cadis égyptiens*, 24.

23 Ibid., 23.

period. The significance of this absence should not be overestimated, for two reasons. Firstly, very few papyri discovered in Fustat have been edited to date.[24] Secondly, the absence of judiciary documents issued by Fustat's court does not mean that no such court existed, and this is the reason why we must look at what literary sources tell about the use of documents by Fustat's qadis.

In his *Akhbar Qudat Misr*, al-Kindi (d. 350/961) says little about the qadis' use of written documents during the Umayyad period. However, he systematically mentions the names of scribes (*kuttāb*) working at Fustat's court when he happens to know them. The earliest scribe he names was employed by qadi Tawba b. Namir al-Hadrami (in office 115–120/733–738).[25] Later, Ibn Hajar al-ʿAsqalani (d. 852/1449), who probably had access to other sources, finds mention of earlier scribes. The earliest, ʿAbd al-Malik b. Abi l-ʿAwwam, served qadi ʿAbd al-Rahman b. Hujayra al-Khawlani (in office 97–98/716–717).[26] Al-Kindi heard also about Yahya b. Maymun al-Hadrami's scribes (105–114/724–732), who had been the subject of complaints,[27] but he does not mention their names. No single scribe is named during the period between 98/717 and 114/732.[28] No scribe has been attested in Fustat before 97/716, and literary evidence suggests that this legal profession did not develop systematically before the 720s, or even the 730s.

Could the absence of judicial staff specializing in preparing documents until a relatively later period – at least later than Qurra b. Sharik – explain why no qadi is ever mentioned in the Umayyad papyri? This hypothesis deserves closer examination. If the qadis of Fustat did not feel the need for scribes during the Sufyanid and early Marwanid periods, could it be because the amount of documents issued by them did not require any assistance from scribes? The first qadi's *dīwān* (a word that should probably be understood as "archives"[29]) known from literary sources was founded in 118/736 in order to administrate pious foundations.[30] According to al-Kindi, the turning-point in the qadis' use

24 About 500 papyri, among which a few ones can be dated to the Umayyad period, were discovered during the excavations of Istabl ʿAntar carried on by Roland-Pierre Gayraud in the 1980s and the 1990s. Their edition is currently prepared by Sobhi Bouderbala at IFAO.

25 al-Kindi, *The Governors and Judges of Egypt*, 343.

26 Ibn Hajar al-ʿAsqalani, *Rafʿ al-Isr ʿan Qudat Misr*, ed. ʿAlī Muhammad ʿUmar (Cairo: Maktabat al-Khanji, 1998), 215.

27 al-Kindi, *The Governors and Judges of Egypt*, 340.

28 Mathieu Tillier, "Scribes et enquêteurs. Note sur le personnel judiciaire en Égypte aux quatre premiers siècles de l'hégire," *Journal of the Economic and Social History of the Orient* 54, no. 3 (2011): 373–379.

29 Wael B. Hallaq, "The *qāḍī*'s *dīwān* (*sijill*) before the Ottomans," *Bulletin of the School of Oriental and African Studies* 61, no. 3 (1998): 415–436.

30 al-Kindi, *The Governors and Judges of Egypt*, 346.

of documents should be placed not before the end of the eighth century CE. Faithful to the *awāʾil* tradition,[31] al-Kindi follows the "inventors" of new practices, and here is what he remarks about qadi al-Mufaddal b. Fadala (in office 168–169/785–786, then 174–177/790–793):

> Al-Mufaḍḍal b. Faḍāla is the first qadi who extended the registers (*sijillāt*), and copied in them parchments (*kutub al-siḥāʾ*),[32] testaments (*waṣāyā*) and [acknowledgements of] debts (*duyūn*). Before him it did not happen that way.[33]

Of course individuals had been recording their transactions or wills well before that date.[34] They certainly presented them in court – even though written documents were not considered as evidence in theory – and the tribunal's scribes probably issued written decisions. According to this extract, however, *administrative* use and record keeping of written documents was limited. Qadis did not systematically register documents that were submitted by litigants. It is likely that the use of written documents developed progressively in Fustat's court. Only under the Abbasids did the qadi's court achieve its transformation into a judicial organization founded upon written practices. This does not mean that qadis did not play a significant role before that. The qadi's decisions could be binding without multiplying documents, and even without written judgments. However, it shows that the Umayyad qadis of Fustat – whatever their original title and their actual prerogatives – were at the head of a modest judicial structure that could not be compared with the much more developed administration of the governor.

The Documentary Birth of the Qadi

First Documentary Traces of the Qadi

The first known occurrence of the word qadi in a papyrus supposedly dates from the end of the Umayyad period. A letter regarding a debt, written in the 730s or 740s and edited by Petra Sijpesteijn, apparently mentions a qadi (*sic*)

---

31 Annliese Nef and Mathieu Tillier, "Introduction: Les voies de l'innovation dans un empire polycentrique," *Annales Islamologiques* 45 (2011): 9–10.

32 "The documents of the pious foundations (*kutub al-aḥbās*)" in Ibn Hajar, *Rafʿ al-Isr ʿan Qudat Misr*, 438.

33 al-Kindi, *The Governors and Judges of Egypt*, 379.

34 Petra M. Sijpesteijn, "Landholding Patterns in Early Islamic Egypt," *Journal of Agrarian Change* 9, no. 1 (2009): 125.

(*P.MuslimState* 26).[35] According to this letter, he is involved in a commercial network and does not seem to play any judicial role regarding the debt.[36] Despite numerous spelling "mistakes"[37] that give an air of uncertainty about the reading and interpretation of the papyrus, it might indeed be a qadi who held office in Fustat.[38] This papyrus is one potential source containing the use of the title "qadi" at the end of the Umayyad period. However, it does not allow us to draw any other conclusion than the simple existence of commercial relationships between a qadi of Fustat and a private individual in the Fayyum.

Apart from this single mention, the interpretation of which is difficult, the appearance of the term "qadi" in papyri dates only from the Abbasid period. Several papyri give account of growing scriptural activities of Fustat's qadis. A short summons, issued by Ghawth b. Sulayman, refers to a qadi of the same name (in office 135–144/753–761, then 167–168/783–785).[39] Ghawth b. Sulayman is also mentioned in an official letter, written by governor Musa b. Kaʿb (r. 141/758–759), which also attests to the historical existence of the *baqṭ*, an early treaty between Egypt and Nubia.[40] Another document registers a testimony presented before his immediate successor, al-Mufaddal b. Fadala[41] – this is precisely the same qadi whom al-Kindi regards as being responsible for the development of scriptural administration in Fustat (see above). Finally, a document, found in an early ninth-century stratum during the excavations of Istabl ʿAntar in Fustat, mentions twice the "[*qā*]*ḍī* ʿĪsā b. al-Munkadir" (in office 212–214/827–829).[42]

35 I am grateful to Petra Sijpesteijn for sending me her thesis before its final publication.

36 Sijpesteijn, *Shaping a Muslim State*, 204.

37 It is also necessary to mention that in the context of a debt issue, the root *q.ḍ.y.* could mean "settle" the debt.

38 Ibid., 403.

39 al-Kindi, *The Governors and Judges of Egypt*, 356ff.; Mathieu Tillier, "Deux papyrus judiciaires de Fusṭāṭ (IIᵉ/VIIIᵉ siècle)," *Chronique d'Égypte* 89 (2014): 414.

40 Martin Hinds and Hamdi Sakkout, "A Letter from the Governor of Egypt to the King of Nubia and Muqurra Concerning Egyptian-Nubian Relations in 141/758," in *Studia Arabica et Islamica. Festschrift for Ihsan ʿAbbas on his Sixtieth Birthday*, ed. Wadad al-Qadi (Beirut: American University of Beirut, 1981), 222. See also J. Martin Plumley, "An Eighth Century Arabic Letter to the King of Nubia," *The Journal of Egyptian Archaeology* 61 (1975): 246. However, Plumley reads by mistake "ʿAwn b. Sulaymān."

41 Mathieu Tillier, "Deux papyrus," 423.

42 This is *P.Fustat* nº 4182. Sobhi Bouderbala, who was so kind to show me this papyrus, is currently editing it.

Fustat versus Upper Egypt

As we have already seen, during the Marwanid period (i.e. end of the seventh–first half of the eighth century), justice in Upper Egypt was mainly in the hands of pagarchs. However, Qurra b. Sharik's papyri reveal that in a number of cases, especially in litigations with high financial stakes, litigants brought their complaints directly to the governor of Fustat, who in turn sent a judicial rescript to the litigants' pagarchs including conditional judgments. Even far away in his capital, the governor appeared to non-Muslim litigants as holding higher judicial authority than the pagarch – an opinion the governor himself would not have refuted.[43] Rare documentary evidence from the early Abbasid period suggests that the situation was not very different in Fustat.

The relationship between the governor of Fustat and his qadi appears through Musa b. Kaʿb's letter mentioning Ghawth b. Sulayman (see above). It reveals a judicial structure in which the governor continues to appear as the highest authority within the province, with the qadi as his assistant. Let us examine more closely the context and content of this letter. A complaint was lodged before the sub-governor (*ʿāmil*) of Aswan, Salm b. Sulayman, accusing the king of Nubia of imprisoning and mistreating two Muslim merchants (one of whom, at least, was of servile status). Salm b. Sulayman asked Muhammad b. Zayd – one of the captive merchants' masters – to produce testimonial evidence (*bayyina*) to prove his case. The claimant brought to the sub-governor's court several honorable Muslims (*ʿudūl*) who testified that the merchant had come to Nubia where he had been abused. The sub-governor of Aswan wrote then to the governor of Fustat to inform him about the case, and sent him the claimant, Muhammad b. Zayd. In his letter, the governor Musa b. Kaʿb explains that he summoned Muḥammad b. Zayd at his arrival in Fustat and heard him together with the king of Nubia's emissary, a man called Bitreh (Peter). The governor did not judge the case himself, however. He states that he ordered the "qadi of Misr's inhabitants" (*qāḍī ahl Miṣr*), Ghawth b. Sulayman, to consider the case (*an yanẓura fī amri-him*), and that the latter rendered a judgment. The qadi ordered Bitreh to release the merchant and his goods were he still alive, and if he was not, to pay a financial compensation (*diya*) of one thousand dinars.[44]

43 Mathieu Tillier, "Dispensing Justice in a Minority Context: The Judicial Administration of Upper Egypt under Muslim Rule (Early Eighth Century CE)," in *The Late Antique World of Early Islam: Muslims among Jews and Christians in the East Mediterranean*, ed. Robert Hoyland (Princeton: The Darwin Press, 2015).

44 Hinds and Sakkout, "A Letter from the Governor," 222.

This letter dating from the beginning of caliph al-Mansur's reign reveals some of the characteristics of legal administration in Upper Egypt and in Fustat. In Upper Egypt, the claimant does not lodge his complaint before a qadi but before a sub-governor who bears the title of *ʿāmil*. The latter gathers evidence provided by the claimant before writing to the governor of Fustat. There was apparently no qadi in Aswan at that time, and as during the Umayyad period, sub-governors were responsible for dispensing justice in their districts. The main difference is that such sub-governors no longer assumed the title of *ṣāḥib al-kūra* (the term in use in Qurra b. Sharik's letters to designate the pagarch).[45] The governor of Fustat was still regarded as the highest judicial authority of the province. Owing to the political nature of the case involving the king of Nubia, the *ʿāmil* of Aswan informs the governor and the latter decides to proceed with the case at a higher level. Although the governor begins by hearing the litigants, he subsequently decides to delegate the case to his qadi. According to al-Kindi, Ghawth b. Sulayman had been appointed by the Egyptian governor Abu ʿAwn (r. 133–136/751–753).[46] The qadi of Fustat was not yet considered a prominent figure appointed by the Abbasid caliph as a legal equivalent to the governor. He appears here as a mere assistant to the governor – what Schacht called a "legal secretary" when speaking about the Umayyad period.[47]

The "*baqṭ*" papyrus reveals a dichotomy between Upper Egypt, where justice was in the hands of *ʿummāl*, and Fustat where the qadi was probably dealing with daily legal affairs – and occasionally with more exceptional ones normally heard by the governor. As the same papyrus clearly shows, however, these different institutions were related to one another. Furthermore, a papyrus dating from the same period suggests that the office of the provincial *ʿāmil* and that of the qadi were closer than one might think. This trilingual Greek-Coptic-Arabic papyrus, which dates from the early Abbasid period,[48] mentions a sub-governor of Ikhmim and Tahta called Yazid b. ʿAbd Allah (unfortunately his official title has disappeared from both the Arabic and the Coptic versions of

45 Petra Sijpesteijn noticed that the title of *ʿāmil* could already designate a "pagarch" at the end of the Umayyad period. Sijpesteijn, *Shaping a Muslim State*, 117, 120.

46 al-Kindi, *The Governors and Judges of Egypt*, 356. Note that according to Ibn Hajar, he had been appointed by caliph al-Mansur (Ibn Hajar, *Rafʿ al-Isr ʿan Qudat Misr*, 300). But Ibn Hajar, who wrote much later than al-Kindi, is probably mistaken.

47 Joseph Schacht, *An Introduction to Islamic Law* (Oxford: Clarendon Press, 1982), 25.

48 According to Jelle Bruning, possible datings would be 132/late 749, 138/755 or 139/756 (Jelle Bruning, *The Rise of a Capital. On the development of al-Fustat's relationship with its hinterland, 18/639–132/750*, PhD thesis, Leiden University, 2014, 146–7).

the document).[49] Among his tasks, this Yazid b. ʿAbd Allah was apparently in charge of dispensing justice, and the papyrus states that he heard a complaint against a tax collector (*P.Cair.Arab.* III 167).[50] According to al-Kindi, Yazid b. ʿAbd Allah held the position of sub-governor (*wālī*) of Ikhmim in the 132/750s.[51] He subsequently became the scribe,[52] then the deputy (*khalīfa*) of qadi Ghawth b. Sulayman in 140/757. Ghawth b. Sulayman had to leave for a military campaign, and Yazid b. ʿAbd Allah took over his role as qadi of Fustat until his death four months after his appointment.[53] Owing to his judicial experience, a provincial *ʿāmil* could occasionally attain the position of the qadi of Fustat.

The Spread of Qadis' Courts in Upper Egypt

Documents Issued by Courts: an Islamic Jurisdiction in the Christian Landscape

The development of the legal administrative structure and the increasing use of written documents and archives had an important impact on the historical documentation from the beginning of the ninth century CE. onwards. After

---

49 If Grohmann's reading is correct, Yazid b. ʿAbd Allah is described as *ḥāfiẓ* [of the governor]. However, this noun is not attested elsewhere as an official title. It is likely that it characterizes the office otherwise known as that of pagarch or *ʿāmil*. Jelle Bruning, who considers the word *hāfiẓ* as an official title, hypothesizes that Yazid b. ʿAbd Allah could have been appointed twice in Ikhmim, first as *ḥāfiẓ*, and later as *wālī* or *qadi* (Bruning, *The Rise of a Capital*, 147–8). However, this interpretation may ascribe too much weight to an otherwise fluid terminology. I am grateful to Arietta Papaconstantinou, who helped me with the Coptic version of the document.

Ikhmim, about 300 km south of Fustat, was the administrative center of a pagarchy (*kūra*) in early Islam. See G. Wiet, « Akhmīm », *EI²*, I: 330. Tahta is about 35 km north of Ikhmim.

50 The Arabic version of this trilingual papyrus was first edited in Rhuvon Guest, "An Arabic Papyrus of the 8th Century," *Journal of the American Oriental Society* 43 (1923): 247–248.

51 Ibn Yunus, as quoted by Ibn Hajar in the fifteenth century, states that Yazid b. ʿAbd Allah was qadi of Ikhmim (Ibn Yunus, *Taʾrikh Ibn Yunus al-Misri*, ed. ʿAbd al-Fattah Fathi ʿAbd al-Fattah (Beirut: Dar al-kutub al-ʿilmiyya, 2000) 1:392; Ibn Ḥajar, *Rafʿ al-Isr ʿan Qudat Misr*, 467). This title, which would be the only attestation of a qadi in a small town of the Egyptian landscape at this period, is doubtful. Whatever his duties, it is likely that al-Kindi is closer to historical truth when he speaks of him as a *wālī*. About this issue, see Mathieu Tillier, "Introduction," in al-Kindi, *Histoire des cadis égyptiens*, 24.

52 Ibn Yunus, *Taʾrikh Ibn Yunus al-Misri*, 1: 392.

53 al-Kindi, *The Governors and Judges of Egypt*, 360.

that date, the number of preserved private legal documents (intended to support a claim) increases rapidly, which also testifies to a stronger presence of Muslims in the Egyptian countryside.[54] Likewise, documents clearly issued by Muslim courts begin to appear. A lacunar papyrus dated Shaʿbān 195/April-May 811 looks like the registration of a judgment concerning a succession. It is written at the order of a qadi named ʿAmr b. Abi Bakr and ends with a list of witnesses (*P.Cair.Arab.* I 51).[55] Another unedited fragmentary document from the ninth century may also have been issued by a Muslim court – perhaps a judgment or a court report (*maḥḍar*) – if we consider the few readable expressions such as *wa-shahida la-hu* ("he testified in his favor") or *wa-aqarra bi-hi* ("he confessed that") (*P.Khalili* II 149). Documents also begin to refer to judicial practices. In a letter from the ninth century, the author asks the addressee to inform a man called Abu l-Hasan that his name should not be cited in the *maḥḍar*, the report of an event that could result in a legal procedure, or the report of a qadi's hearing.[56]

The best documented judicial papyri are not fragments of qadi's archives, however, but rather summonses sent to litigants, most of whom were discovered in al-Ushmunayn in Upper Egypt (*Chrest.Khoury* I 79; *Chrest.Khoury* II 31= *P.Vindob.Arab.* III 77; *Chrest.Khoury* II 32= *P.Vindob.Arab.* III 76; *Chrest. Khoury* II 33= *P.Vindob.Arab.* III 75).[57] The earliest papyrus of the series dates from the third/ninth or fourth/tenth century according to Raif G. Khoury's estimation:

---

54 Sijpesteijn, *Shaping a Muslim State*, 111.

55 No Egyptian qadi is known to bear the name of ʿAmr b. Abi Bakr. It is noteworthy, however, that a qadi of Damascus bore this name at the time the document was written, between 183/799–800 and 194 or 195/809–811. See Ibn ʿAsakir, *Taʾrikh Madinat Dimashq*, ed. ʿUmar b. Jarama al-ʿAmrawi (Beirut: Dar al-Fikr, 1995), 43: 547–551; Ibn Tulun, *Qudat Dimashq. Al-Thaghr al-Bassam fi Dhikr man wulliya Qadaʾ al-Sham*, ed. Salah al-Din al-Munajjid (Damascus: al-Majmaʿ al-ʿilmi al-ʿarabi, 1956), 14. As a hypothesis, the document could be a letter written to another qadi by the judge of Damascus rather than a judgement issued by an Egyptian qadi. On this letter-based procedure, see Wael B. Hallaq, "*Qāḍīs* Communicating: Legal Change and the Law of Documentary Evidence," *al-Qantara* 20 (1999): 437–466; Mathieu Tillier, "Les réseaux judiciaires en Iraq à l'époque abbasside," in *Espaces et réseaux en Méditerranée, vol. II. La formation des réseaux*, ed. Damien Coulon, Christophe Picard, and Dominique Valérian (Paris: Bouchene, 2010), 91–107.

56 Petra M. Sijpesteijn, "The Archival Mind in Early Islamic Egypt," in *From al-Andalus to Khurasan. Documents from the Medieval Muslim World*, ed. Petra M. Sijpesteijn et al. (Leiden: Brill, 2007), 180.

57 For other summonses, see Tillier, "Deux papyrus," 419.

> In the name of God, the Merciful, the Compassionate. Praise be to the one God! Thiyudir b. Kayl and Fenūfe b. Abrāse, residing in Abū Qolte, shall come before the court (*majlis al-ḥukm*) of al-Ushmūnayn, in order to submit to justice's requirements, God willing. (*Chrest.Khoury* I 78)

This kind of summons has no apparent signature and does not mention any qadi, but the phrasing makes it clear that it was issued by a Muslim court. If we consider legal literature that theorized the functioning of the qadi's court during the same period, similar notes could be replaced by clay seals (*ṭīna*) authenticating the provenance of the summonses, at least in Iraq.[58] At any rate, this series of summonses attests to the presence of a Muslim court in al-Ushmunayn in the fourth/tenth century, and perhaps already in the third/ninth century.

The presence of a Muslim court did not mean that al-Ushmunayn now had a majority of Muslim inhabitants. In papyrus *Chrest.Khoury* I 78, translated above, litigants who are summoned bear Coptic names. If procedural rules developed by *fiqh* were active in Upper Egypt, non-Muslims had to answer to the Muslim court, especially when facing a Muslim adversary. This is what happens in a later papyrus (dated fourth/tenth century according to Khoury, but perhaps later – Fatimid? – judging by some of its expressions), in which Christian litigants (Qufra b. al-Qommos, Fawaris b. Fahr and Ibn Samawil) are summoned before the "sublime court" (*majlis al-ḥukm al-ʿazīz*) where they shall be brought face to face with the intendant (*khawlī*) Sulayman al-Qolobbi, most probably a Muslim. The litigation shall be decided according to "the noble Islamic law" (*al-sharʿ al-sharīf*) (*Chrest.Khoury* I 79). Although other documents from the fourth/tenth and fifth/eleventh centuries mention an increasing number of Muslim litigants, Christians do not disappear completely. In a fifth/eleventh century papyrus, a man called Daniyal is summoned before al-Ushmunayn's court to be brought face to face with his adversary, Balbeh (*Chrest.Khoury* II 33). Both of them appear to be Egyptian Christians.

It is thus possible to conclude that a Muslim court – most probably a qadi's court – was established in al-Ushmunayn in the third/ninth or the fourth/tenth century, when the town's population was still largely non-Muslim. At that time al-Ushmunayn had become one of the main Muslim garrisons of Upper Egypt. Al-Kindī mentions a *wālī l-ḥarb* (military governor) residing

58 al-Khassaf (with al-Jassas' commentary), *Kitab Adab al-Qadi*, ed. Farhat Ziyada (Cairo: The American University in Cairo Press, 1978), 238, 245. Cf. al-Simnani, *Rawdat al-Qudat wa-Tariq al-Najat*, ed. Salah al-Din al-Nahi (Beirut-Amman: Mu'assasat al-risala–Dar al-furqan, 1984), 1: 170, 173.

in this town when talking about events that occurred in 335/946, under the Ikhshidids.[59] Since al-Kindi manifests little interest in the Egyptian landscape outside Fustat, it is probable that the garrison existed before that date, and this permanent Muslim settlement may have justified the establishment of a qadi's court. Al-Kindi also mentions merchants (*tujjār*) who complained about the *wālī* of al-Ushmunayn.[60] We can speculate that the garrison attracted civil Muslim people, Arabs and converts,[61] and that it necessitated the installation of a legal system conforming to the now firmly established model of qadis' courts.[62] This Islamic institution could still attract Christian litigants too, even when they were not confronted by Muslim adversaries – as shown by *Chrest. Khoury* II 33.[63] Incidentally, the fact that summonses sent to Christian litigants were written in Arabic, perhaps as early as the third/ninth century, suggests that an important arabicization of al-Ushmunayn and its surrounding had already occurred.[64] When receiving such summons the addressee was supposedly able to read it or to find someone who was able to translate it. The judiciary system the Egyptian Christians had to submit to from time to time was not only Islamic but also Arabic.

Adab al-Qāḍī *in Practice*

The earliest court documents available from Upper Egypt are contemporary to the development of texts describing the rules regarding the organization and the procedures of the qadi's court – a part of *fiqh* called *adab al-qāḍī*. The first preserved books containing detailed prescriptions about procedures

59 al-Kindi, *The Governors and Judges of Egypt*, 295.

60 al-Kindi, *The Governors and Judges of Egypt*, 295.

61 Conversions to Islam in the Egyptian countryside are attested from the second/eighth century (see Sijpesteijn, "Landholding Patterns," 128). They certainly increased in the third/ninth century. Various hypotheses have been considered for the rapidity of Islamization in Egypt, most of whom regard the third/ninth century as crucial. Yaacov Lev, "Coptic Rebellions and the Islamization of Medieval Egypt (8th–10th Century): Medieval and Modern Perceptions," *Jerusalem Studies in Arabic and Islam* 39 (2012): 304–306.

62 It is noticeable that Ibn Hawqal describes several towns of the Delta having a Muslim judge in the fourth/tenth century. See Lev, "Coptic Rebellions," 333–334.

63 About the reasons why non-Muslims went to Muslim courts during the first centuries of Islam, see Uriel I.A. Simonsohn, *A Common Justice. The Legal Allegiances of Christians and Jews Under Early Islam* (Philadelphia: University of Pennsylvania Press, 2011), 178–191.

64 According to Sophia Björnesjö, a few eighth-century letters show that some Christians understood Arabic in Upper Egypt at that time. Sophia Björnesjö, "L'arabisation de l'Égypte: le témoignage papyrologique," *Égypte-Monde Arabe* 27–28 (1996): 93–106. Online: http://ema.revues.org/index1923.html (consulted on 05 December 2012).

are Ḥanafī works written by Iraqi scholars.[65] At the same period, prominent Egyptian scholars also composed chapters about procedural law, yet these were less detailed in respect to court organization than their Iraqi counterparts.[66] Practices reflected by judicial papyri cannot, therefore, be systematically compared to legal theory elaborated in the Egyptian province. However, judicial papyri echo some of the rules that we find in Iraqi legal literature. We have just seen that Egyptian summonses dating from the third/ninth or fourth/tenth century do not fundamentally differ from al-Khassaf's prescriptions. Other parallels between Egyptian practices and legal theory are noteworthy, some of them showing a high degree of standardization of Islamic procedures throughout the caliphate.

The series of summonses issued by al-Ushmunayn's tribunal provide indications concerning the extent of the courts' constituency. Several defendants' places of residence are mentioned in these papyri: Abu Qolte (*Chrest.Khoury* I 78), Itlidim (*Chrest.Khoury* II 31) and al-Rayramun (*Chrest.Khoury* I 79). As for one of the claimants, Sulayman al-Qolobbi, he was probably from a locality pertaining to Mellawi's district (*Chrest.Khoury* I 79). These villages were respectively at a distance of 10, 13, 5 and 8 km from al-Ushmunayn (see Figure 2.1 below). This indicates that the qadi of al-Ushmunayn's jurisdiction extended to the neighboring villages. In Iraq, the Hanafi jurist al-Khassaf considered that a qadi's district encompassed all the territories that were within walking distance of half a day, i.e. about a distance of 20 km.[67] The theory elaborated by Iraqi jurists appears to correspond to actual judicial practices in Upper Egypt.

Another document suggests that rules applied in Fustat regarding the reception of litigants in court also applied to those in Upper Egypt. In a petition of unknown origin, approximately dating from the second/eighth century or later according to Werner Diem, a claimant addresses an anonymous qadi to lodge a complaint against one of his sisters. After the death of their mother, he argues, his sister seized rental incomes that should have been divided between the legal heirs. It is possible that the claimant had already complained before the qadi and produced witnesses who had testified in his favor. For some unknown reason, the qadi has not yet rendered his judgment, and the petitioner urges him to give "everyone his due" ([…] *kull dhī ḥaqq ḥaqqa-hu*) (CPR XVI 3). In later literary sources, similar petitions are usually called *qiṣṣa*-s or *ruqʿa*-s.

65 Tillier, *Les cadis d'Iraq et l'État abbasside*, 48.

66 See for example al-Muzani (d. 264/878), *Mukhtasar al-Muzani fi Furuʿ al-Shafiʿiyya* (Beirut: Dar al-kutub al-ʿilmiyya, 1998), 393ff; al-Tahawi (d. 321/933), *Mukhtasar al-Tahawi*, ed. Abu l-Wafa' al-Afghani (Hyderabad: Lajnat ihya' al-maʿarif al-nuʿmaniyya, n.d.), 325ff.

67 Tillier, *Les cadis d'Iraq et l'État abbasside*, 297–298.

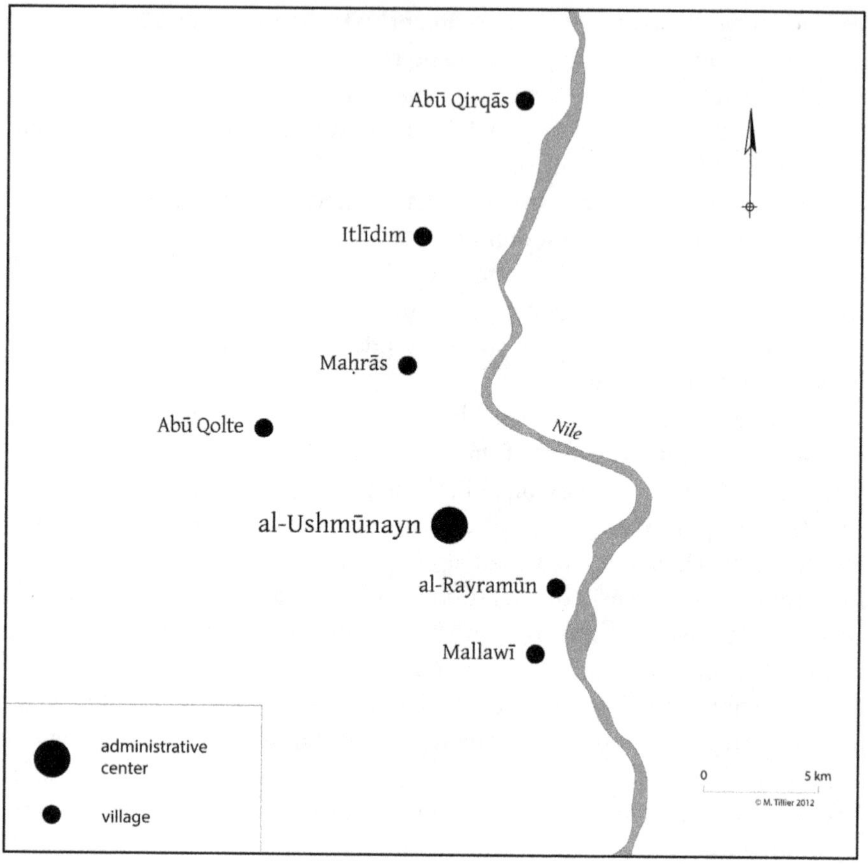

FIGURE 2.1 *Al-Ushmunayn and its area, ninth-tenth centuries* CE.

Waki' mentions the use of such petitions in Iraq (Basra) from the 140s/757s onwards.[68] In Egypt, the first mention of such petitions by al-Kindi relates to the 790s, under qadi al-Mufaddal b. Fadala[69] – the same qadi who is known for having developed the use of written documents in Fustat's court (see above).[70] According to al-Kindi, litigants brought their petitions to the court

68 Waki', *Akhbar al-Qudat*, 2:58, 70. As for Kufa, the same author relates that the much earlier qadi Shurayh (late seventh century) did not accept such written petitions. Waki', *Akhbar al-Qudat*, 2:307.

69 al-Kindi, *The Governors and Judges of Egypt*, 379.

70 Later, Ibn Ḥajar mentions a *ruq'a* under qadi Khayr b. Nu'aym (in office 133–135/751–753). However this is not the same kind of petition. In the anecdote reported by Ibn Hajar, a defendant is unable to counter his adversary's claim and appeals to the qadi's pity on a note that he gives him during the hearing (Ibn Hajar, *Raf' al-Isr 'an Qudat Misr*, 155).

and submitted them to the qadi.[71] Later legal theory recommends that such petitions be collected by the qadi's scribe at the beginning of every hearing.[72] Another fourth/tenth-century paper could well be a petition. The anonymous author appeals to a qadi, apparently requesting an interview in order to "inform him about his need." The note is partially damaged, however. Rather than representing a claim against an adversary, this petition could concern another of the qadi's duties, like management of properties (*Chrest.Khoury* I 81).

Other documents testify that qadis' courts in Upper Egypt became the center of notarial practices. From the fourth/tenth century onwards, some private legal documents bear certification marks, like *ṣaḥḥa* or *ṣaḥḥa dhālika* ("it is authentic"), written by a qadi or his scribe. Such marks certified the authenticity of the document and its legal value, enabling their production as evidence in later litigations (*CPR* XXVI 10, 40).[73] From then on, it seems that not only Muslims but also Christians came to the qadi's court to have their documents authenticated and have Muslim witnesses (perhaps attached to the tribunal) testify to the content of their deeds (*CPR* XXVI 10). Unlike other practices mentioned previously, such certification marks are not discussed in Iraqi Hanafi law. On the contrary, a tenth-century jurist like al-Jassas (d. 370/980) expresses some reluctance to the view that qadis could act as notaries and register evidence in anticipation of further litigations. For example, a qadi should refuse to write in advance a letter in which he would register testimonies about an agreement in case litigations occurred in the future.[74] Whether this refusal applies also to certification marks is unclear, but neither he nor al-Khassaf ever mentions such a practice. We can therefore wonder whether registration of legal documents did not begin as a specifically Egyptian practice.[75]

The development of the classical judicial system in Upper Egypt appears finally through documents that reflect the way courts were now part of a wider legal system led by the 'ulama'. A fourth/tenth-century paper of unknown

---

71 al-Kindi, *The Governors and Judges of Egypt*, 379.

72 al-Khassaf, *Kitab Adab al-Qadi*, 53, 123.

73 On this practice, see Adolf Grohmann, *Einführung und Chrestomathie zur arabischen Papyruskunde* (Prag: Státní Pedagogické Nakladatelství, 1954), 122–123; Adolf Grohmann, *Allgemeine Einführung in die arabischen Papyri* (Vienna: Burgverlag Ferdinand Zöllner, 1924), (Corpus Papyrorum Raineri III.I.1), 19.

74 al-Khassaf, *Kitab Adab al-Qadi*, 428.

75 The question of the origins of this practice is still unanswered. Apparently no Greek nor Coptic document is known for bearing such registration marks by a court, neither before nor after the Islamic conquest of Egypt. I am grateful to Alain Delattre, whose expertise I solicited on that matter.

origin appears as the draft of a demand for a fatwa regarding a judicial case.[76] The addressee (a "*shaykh*," probably a *faqīh*) is asked about a man who lodged a complaint against his aunt in court (*majlis al-ḥukm*), accusing her of selling wheat he had left in her care as deposit. The aunt confessed (*iʿtarafat*) and the judge (*ḥākim*) condemned her and wrote a judgment in favor of the claimant. However, the aunt died before she repaid her debt. In his demand, the author asks the mufti whether according to the law (literally "knowledge," *ʿilm*) the judge must demand her heir to reimburse the wheat in cash or in kind (*Chrest. Khoury* I 82–83). *Ḥākim* is regularly used in legal literature as a generic term for "judge." As the author of the demand asks both a general and theoretical question, it is likely that a qadi is meant here. It is possible that this demand for legal opinion was issued by the judiciary itself, and that its author was no other than a qadi (perhaps with the help of his scribes) concerned about dispensing the correct decision.

Conclusion

So far, no firm documentary evidence attests to the existence of qadis in Egypt during the Umayyad period. In this respect, papyri offer a picture of the early judiciary quite different from that given by literary sources for the main Egyptian cities. The absence of documents mentioning qadis in Fustat does not however imply that this institution did not exist there, and it is possible that future research on Fustat's papyri will change this picture. In the meantime, literary evidence suggests that under the Umayyads, the qadi's court in Fustat had a weak administrative structure which gradually developed its use of written documents and archival practices. Outside Fustat – and perhaps a major city like Alexandria – it is likely that the qadi's court did not yet exist in Egypt.

The situation changes with the early Abbasids. Arabic papyri mentioning qadis of Fustat appear in the 750s. The multiplication of references to qadis in subsequent documents, which we consider significant, probably reflects an increase in the production of documents by and for Fustat's court, and could also testify to a reinforcement of the qadi's position. Musa b. Kaʿb's letter, dating from 141/758, suggests that the qadi of Fustat was now regarded as an important judicial institution. It also shows, however, that the qadi was still an assistant of the provincial governor, and that justice was first and foremost a prerogative linked to political institutions.

---

76 The paper presents two versions of the same text on the recto and the verso, almost identical although written by two different hands. This suggests that the claimant prepared two versions of the text that he eventually sent to the mufti.

In Upper Egypt, the nature of legal administration also changed toward the end of the Umayyad or the early Abbasid period. Justice was no longer dispensed by pagarchs, but by Muslim administrators who replaced them. These administrators were now called ⲁⲙⲓⲣⲁ or *ʿāmil* – in Coptic and Arabic papyri; *wālī* according to literary sources – a title that reflects the complete integration of these administrators within a Muslim administrative structure. Since justice was rendered by these sub-governors – whose legal skills could eventually lead to an appointment as qadi in Fustat – judicial administration still appeared as an expression of political authorities, that of the governor and his delegates.

Qadis and their tribunals are only mentioned later in Upper Egypt, in the third/ninth century at the earliest. Henceforth, series of documents issued by local courts testify to the establishment of qadis who operated according to rules similar to those simultaneously written down by *fuqahāʾ*. Whether these courts were completely autonomous from political institutions is difficult to tell. What is obvious, however, is that they followed legal models shaped by private Muslim scholars and were no longer subjugated to administrative roles of sub-governors. Three or four centuries after the conquest of Egypt, the model of Islamic judiciary promoted by narrative sources was now spreading into the Egyptian countryside.

Bibliography

Papyri

CPR XVI = Diem, Werner. *Arabische Briefe auf Papyrus und Papier aus der Heidelberger Papyrus-Sammlung*. Wiesbaden: Otto Harrassowitz, 1991.

CPR XXVI = Thung, Michael E. *Arabische juristische Urkunden aus der Papyrussammlung der österreichischen Nationalbibliothek*. Leipzig: K.G. Saur München, 2006.

Chrest.Khoury I = Khoury, Raif G. *Chrestomathie de papyrologie arabe. Documents relatifs à la vie privée, sociale et administrative dans les premiers siècles islamiques*. Leiden: Brill, 1993.

Chrest.Khoury II = Khoury, Raif G. *Papyrologische Studien zum privaten und gesellschaftlischen Leben in den ersten islamischen Jahrhunderten*. Wiesbaden: Harrassowitz Verlag, 1995.

Guest, Rhuvon. "An Arabic Papyrus of the 8th Century." *Journal of the American Oriental Society* 43 (1923): 247–48.

Hinds, Martin, and Hamdi Sakkout. "A Letter from the Governor of Egypt to the King of Nubia and Muqurra Concerning Egyptian-Nubian Relations in 141/758." In *Studia Arabica et Islamica. Festschrift for Iḥsān ʿAbbās on his Sixtieth Birthday*, edited by Wadād al-Qāḍī, 209–229. Beirut: American University of Beirut, 1981.

MacCoull, Leslie S.B. (trans.). *Coptic Legal Documents. Law as Vernacular Text and Experience in Late Antique Egypt*. Tempe: Arizona Center for Medieval and Renaissance Studies, 2009.

P.Cair.Arab. III = Grohmann, Adolf. *Arabic Papyri in the Egyptian Library, vol. III, Administrative Texts*. Cairo: Egyptian Library Press, 1938.

P.MuslimState = Sijpesteijn, Petra M. *Shaping a Muslim State. The World of a Mid-Eighth-Century Egyptian Official*. Oxford: Oxford University Press, 2013.

P.Khalili II = Khan, Geoffrey. *Bills, Letters and Deeds. Arabic Papyri of the 7th to 11th Centuries*. London: The Nour Foundation, 1993.

P.Lond. IV = Bell, Harold Idris. *Greek Papyri in the British Museum*, IV. *The Aphrodito Papyri*. London: British Museum, 1910. English translation in Bell, Harold Idriss. 1911–1928. "Translations of the Greek Aphrodito Papyri in the British Museum," Parts I–VI. In *Der Islam*, 2: 269–283, 372–384; 3: 132–140, 369–373; 4: 87–93; 17: 4–8.

P.Mird = Grohmann, Adolf. *Arabic Papyri from Ḫirbet el-Mird*. Louvain: Bibliothèque du Muséon, 1963.

Plumley, J. Martin. "An Eighth Century Arabic Letter to the King of Nubia." *The Journal of Egyptian Archaeology* 61 (1975): 241–245.

Schiller, A. Arthur. "A Family Archive from Jeme." In *Studi in honore di Vincenzo Arangio-Ruiz*, 327–375. Napoli: Jovene, 1953.

Tillier, Mathieu. "Deux papyrus judiciaires de Fusṭāṭ (IIe/VIIIe siècle)." *Chronique d'Égypte* 89 (2014): 412–445.

Other Sources

Ibn ʿAsakir. *Taʾrikh Madinat Dimashq*. Edited by ʿUmar b. Jarama al-ʿAmrawi. Beirut: Dar al-Fikr, 1995.

Ibn Hajar al-ʿAsqalani. *Rafʿ al-Isr ʿan Qudat Misr*. Edited by ʿAli Muhammad ʿUmar. Cairo: Maktabat al-Khanji, 1998.

Ibn Tulun. *Qudat Dimashq. Al-Thaghr al-Bassam fi Dhikr man Wulliya Qadaʾ al-Sham*. Edited by Salah al-Din al-Munajjid. Damascus: al-Majmaʿ al-ʿilmi al-ʿarabi, 1956.

Ibn Yunus. *Taʾrikh Ibn Yunus al-Misri*. Edited by ʿAbd al-Fattah Fathi ʿAbd al-Fattah. Beirut: Dar al-kutub al-ʿilmiyya, 2000.

al-Khassaf (with al-Jassas' commentary). *Kitab Adab al-Qadi*. Edited by Farhat Ziyada. Cairo: The American University in Cairo Press, 1978.

al-Kindi. *The Governors and Judges of Egypt*. Edited by Rhuvon Guest. Leiden: E.J. Brill, 1912.

al-Muzani. *Mukhtasar al-Muzani fī Furuʿ al-Shafiʿiyya*. Beirut: Dar al-kutub al-ʿilmiyya, 1998.

al-Simnani. *Rawdat al-Qudat wa-Tariq al-Najat*. Edited by Salah al-Din al-Nahi. Beirut-Amman: Mu'assasat al-risala–Dar al-furqan, 1984.

al-Tahawi. *Mukhtasar al-Tahawi*. Edited by Abu l-Wafa' al-Afghani. Hyderabad: Lajnat ihya' al-maʿarif al-nuʿmaniyya, n.d.

Wakiʿ. *Akhbar al-Qudat*. Edited by ʿAbd al-ʿAziz Mustafa al-Maraghi. Cairo: Matbaʿat al-saʿada, 1947–1950.

Modern References

Abbott, Nabbia. *The Ḳurrah Papyri from Aphrodito in the Oriental Institute*. Chicago: The University of Chicago Press, 1938.

Abu Safiya, Jasir b. Khalid. *Bardiyyat Qurra b. Sharik al-ʿAbsi. Dirasa wa-Tahqiq*. Riyadh: Markaz al-Malik Faysal li-l-buhuth wa-l-dirasat al-islamiyya, 2004.

Bagnall, Roger S. *Reading Papyri, Writing Ancient History*. London: Routledge, 1995.

Björnesjö, Sophia. "L'arabisation de l'Égypte: le témoignage papyrologique." *Égypte-Monde Arabe* 27–28 (1996): 93–106. http://ema.revues.org/index1923.html (accessed 5 December 2012).

Bruning, Jelle. *The Rise of a Capital. On the Development of al-Fusṭāṭ's Relationship with its Hinterland, 18/639–132/750*. Ph.D diss., Leiden University, 2014.

Donner, Fred M. *Narratives of Islamic Origins. The Beginnings of Islamic Historical Writing*. Princeton: The Darwin Press, 1998.

Donner, Fred M. "Qur'anicization of Religio-Political Discourse in the Umayyad Period." *Revue des Mondes Musulmans et de la Méditerranée* 129 (2011): 79–92.

Grohmann, Adolf. *Allgemeine Einführung in die arabischen Papyri*, (Corpus Papyrorum Raineri III.I.1). Vienna: Burgverlag Ferdinand Zöllner, 1924.

Grohmann, Adolf. *Einführung und Chrestomathie zur arabischen Papyruskunde*. Prag: Státní Pedagogické Nakladatelství, 1954.

Hallaq, Wael B. "The *qāḍī*'s *dīwān* (*sijill*) before the Ottomans." *Bulletin of the School of Oriental and African Studies* 61, no. 3 (1998): 415–436.

Hallaq, Wael B. "*Qāḍīs* Communicating: Legal Change and the Law of Documentary Evidence." *al-Qantara* 20, no. 2 (1999): 437–466.

Hallaq, Wael B. *The Origins and Evolution of Islamic Law*. Cambridge: Cambridge University Press, 2005.

Lammens, Henri. "Un gouverneur omaiyade d'Égypte. Qorra ibn Šarîk d'après les papyrus arabes." *Bulletin de l'Institut d'Égypte*, 5e série, tome II (1908): 99–115.

Lev, Yaacov. "Coptic Rebellions and the Islamization of Medieval Egypt (8th–10th Century): Medieval and Modern Perceptions." *Jerusalem Studies in Arabic and Islam* 39 (2012): 303–344.

Morelli, Federico. "Consiglieri e comandanti: i titoli del governatore arabo d'Egitto *symboulos* e *amîr*." *Zeitschrift für Papyrologie und Epigraphik* 173 (2010): 158–166.

Nef, Annliese, and Mathieu Tillier. "Introduction: Les voies de l'innovation dans un empire polycentrique." *Annales Islamologiques* 45 (2011): 1–19.

Schacht, Joseph. *An Introduction to Islamic Law*. Oxford: Clarendon Press, 1982.

Sijpesteijn, Petra M. "The Archival Mind in Early Islamic Egypt." In *From al-Andalus to Khurasan. Documents from the Medieval Muslim World*, edited by Petra M. Sijpesteijn, Lennart Sundelin, Sofia T. Tovar, and Amalia Zomeno, 163–186. Leiden: Brill, 2007.

Sijpesteijn, Petra M. "Landholding Patterns in Early Islamic Egypt." *Journal of Agrarian Change* 9, no. 1 (2009): 120–133.

Sijpesteijn, Petra M. *Shaping a Muslim State. The World of a Mid-Eighth-Century Egyptian Official*. Oxford: Oxford University Press, 2013.

Simonsohn, Uriel I. *A Common Justice. The Legal Allegiances of Christians and Jews Under Early Islam*. Philadelphia: University of Pennsylvania Press, 2011.

Tillier, Mathieu. *Les cadis d'Iraq et l'État abbasside (132/750–334/945)*. Damascus: Presses de l'Ifpo, 2009.

Tillier, Mathieu. "Les réseaux judiciaires en Iraq à l'époque abbasside." In *Espaces et réseaux en Méditerranée, vol. II. La formation des réseaux*, edited by Damien Coulon, Christophe Picard, and Dominique Valérian, 91–107. Paris: Bouchène, 2010.

Tillier, Mathieu. "Scribes et enquêteurs. Note sur le personnel judiciaire en Égypte aux quatre premiers siècles de l'hégire." *Journal of the Economic and Social History of the Orient* 54, no. 3 (2011): 370–404.

Tillier, Mathieu. "Introduction." In al-Kindī, *Histoire des cadis égyptiens*, translated by Mathieu Tillier, 1–45. Cairo: Institut Français d'Archéologie Orientale, 2012.

Tillier, Mathieu. "Du pagarque au cadi: ruptures et continuités dans l'administration judiciaire de la Haute-Égypte (Ier–IIIe/VIIe–IXe siècle)." *Médiévales* 64, no. 1 (2013): 19–36.

Tillier, Mathieu. "Dispensing Justice in a Minority Context: The Judicial Administration of Upper Egypt under Muslim Rule (Early Eighth Century CE)." In *The Late Antique World of Early Islam: Muslims among Jews and Christians in the East Mediterranean*, edited by Robert Hoyland, 133–155. Princeton: The Darwin Press, 2015.

Tillier, Mathieu. *L'invention du cadi. La justice des musulmans, des juifs et des chrétiens aux premiers siècles de l'Islam*. Paris: Publications de la Sorbonne, 2017.

Tyan, Émile. *Histoire de l'organisation judiciaire en pays d'Islam*, 2nd edition. Leiden: E.J. Brill, 1960.

Wilfong, Terry G. *Women of Jeme. Lives in a Coptic Town in Late Antique Egypt*. Ann Arbor: University of Michigan Press, 2002.

CHAPTER 3

Delegation of Judicial Power in Abbasid Egypt

Petra M. Sijpesteijn

The papyrus edited in this article[1] and which forms the starting point of the discussion in it is typical in its sort: insignificant in appearance, but of hugely important historical meaning when placed in its proper context. Only partially preserved, so that its contents and even its genre remain unknown, and without an archeological context to place it firmly in a specific chronology and geography, the papyrus contains only a couple of lines. Typical too is that this apparently insignificant artifact preserved from a distant past offers on closer scrutiny important new information on the office of the qadi and his representatives in Abbasid Egypt, more specifically as a result of the administrative reforms introduced after the fourth *fitna* (811–819 CE).

Even the rich documentary record of Egypt attests only very few documents referring to qadis from the pre-Fatimid period so far. This dearth of information on the qadi is in stark contrast to the amount of legal documents – contracts of loan and sale, debt acknowledgements, marriage contracts and the like – that although small in the first Islamic century still greatly outnumbers that of documents referring to the judge's court.[2] This scarce presence of the qadi in the documentary record has been related to the slow development of the Islamic legal court system especially outside the garrison cities of Fustat and Alexandria.[3] Every new document that attests a qadi is thus a welcome addition to our understanding of the functioning of the judge's office. When, as in our case, the documents can be related to narrative sources, their

1 This publication is part of the project "The Formation of Islam: The View from Below" funded by the European Research Council (2009–2015). I would also like to thank the Andrew W. Mellon Foundation that funded my research stay at the Department of Papyri of the Austrian National Library (2013–2014) where I worked on this text. In preparation of this article I benefited from expertise of many colleagues. I would like to acknowledge especially Sobhi Bouderbala, Jelle Bruning, and Mathieu Tillier. Any remaining mistakes are, of course, my own.

2 To get an impression of the number of early Arabic legal documents, see the database of the project "Islamic Law Materialized" (http://cald.irht.cnrs.fr/php/ilm.php) under the direction of Christian Müller.

3 Mathieu Tillier, "Du pagarque au cadi: ruptures et continuités dans l'administration judiciaire de la Haute-Égypte (Ier–IIIe/VIe–IXe siècle)," *Médiévales* 64 (2013): 19–36.

 | DOI 10.1163/9789004343733_005

historiographical value even increases as they allow us to examine historical accounts in tandem with documentary sources. Connecting the papyrus to discussions in our literary sources from Egypt and elsewhere in the Muslim Empire, it even enlightens more general historical questions about the character and perception of judicial power in this period. Grateful for Ruud's sincere academic interest in legal documents for their own sake and as sources to illuminate historical and legal historical questions, this article is a tribute to his contagious enthusiasm for and academic achievements in the practical expressions of Islamic law.

Introduction

Sometime between 10 Rajab 212 AH (October 5 827 CE) and Ramaḍān 214 AH (2 November–1 December 829 CE) Hasan b. Yaʿqub produced an official document in which he identified himself as "representative (*khalīfa*) in the Fayyum of Yahya b. Saʿid who is the representative of the judge (qadi) ʿIsa b. al-Munkadir." ʿIsa b. al-Munkadir is the well-known chief judge of Fustat who held office in the first half of the ninth century.[4] Yahya b. Saʿid and Hasan b. Yaʿqub are not otherwise known from the sources. The practice of appointing lower judicial officers as deputies of the highest representative in the provincial capital is known from Egypt and other areas in the Muslim empire at this time as discussed in narrative sources.[5] How these lower officials expressed their association with higher forces, and thereby their relation with, degree of dependence on and measure of accountability towards the central authorities, however, is not. By examining the terminology used in this papyrus as well as anecdotal material from the narrative sources, this paper will discuss the nature of the delegation of judicial power from the top of the judicial hierarchy and the claim to authority that was exercised through it from the lower offices

4 See especially the exhaustive discussion of literary sources in the footnotes to Mathieu Tillier's translation of al-Kindi's biography of ʿIsa b. al-Munkadir (Mathieu Tillier, *Histoire des Cadis Égyptiens Aḫbār quḍāt Miṣr* [Cairo: Institut français d'archéologie orientale, 2012], 204–215). ʿIsa b. al-Munkadir appears in two other papyri from Egypt. A published debt acknowledgement (*P.Marchands* V/I 19.1) dated 214/829 mentions the qadi ʿIsa b. al-Munkadir (as identified in a corrected reading by Sobhi Bouderbala). An unpublished papyrus found at Istabl Antar in Fustat to be published by Sobhi Bouderbala equally mentions the judge in an official context. I would like to thank Sobhi Bouderbala for referring me to these two documents.

5 See below, the paragraph "Delegation and legitimization."

in the province. Attention will also be placed on the professionalization of the judiciary in Egypt at this time and the degree to which these offices and power structures formed a (legal) bureaucracy.

Before delving further into contextualizing the text of the papyrus, we should take a closer look at what it actually says.

Edition and Discussion of the Text

Currently preserved in the Papyrus Collection of the Austrian National Library under the inventory number AP 2090, the conditions of acquisition of this papyrus are not known beyond it having been purchased in Egypt. It has a light brown colour and the original cutting lines are preserved on the top and right sides. While the fibres on the left side are somewhat frayed, the remaining lines are complete on that side. There are some smaller holes in the papyrus due to worm holes and wear and tear. There is one diacritical dot written (l. 4 *bi*) and perhaps one other one (l. 1 *bi*). The text is written in a relatively practiced, fluid hand albeit not very carefully executed (see also the smudge that partially covers the *basmala* in line 1) in black ink with a thin pen parallel to the fibres. On the back the top of the letters of one word written in monumental script are preserved written in dark ink as well as traces of letters written in a smaller hand with black ink. The traces of the monumental writing on the back belong to a text that was written first on the papyrus, confirmed by the fact that that text is written perpendicular to the fibres.[6] The smaller writing on the back might be connected to the writing on the front. This might contain part of the address of the text on the front or some other text unrelated to the text on the front.

6 Continuing Byzantine practice, papyri in the Arab period were generally written *transversa charta*, with secondary texts being written parallel to the fibres. See my "Arabic Papyri and Islamic Egypt," in *The Oxford Handbook of Papyrology*, ed. R.S. Bagnall (Oxford: Oxford University Press, 2009), 452–472 for a discussion of the writing direction on papyri in the Arab period.

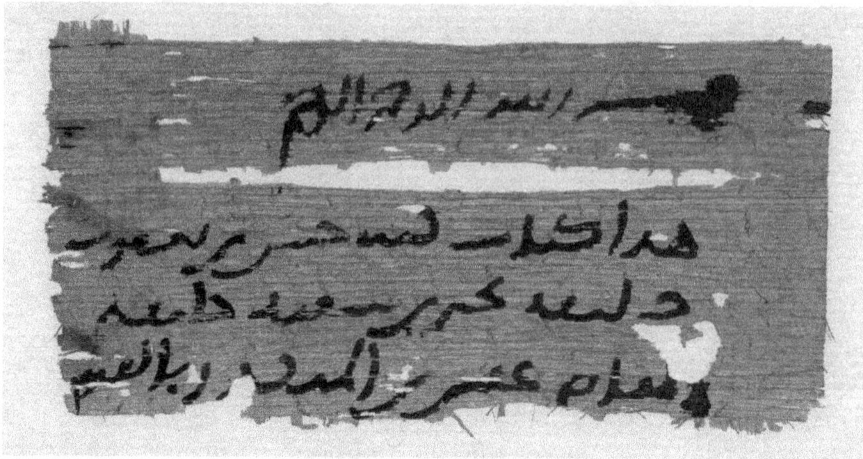

FIGURE 3.1A *P.Vindob. A.P. 2090 front.*
SOURCE: ÖSTERREICHISCHEN NATIONALBIBLIOTHEK, PAPYRUSSAMMLUNG UND PAPYRUSMUSEUM.

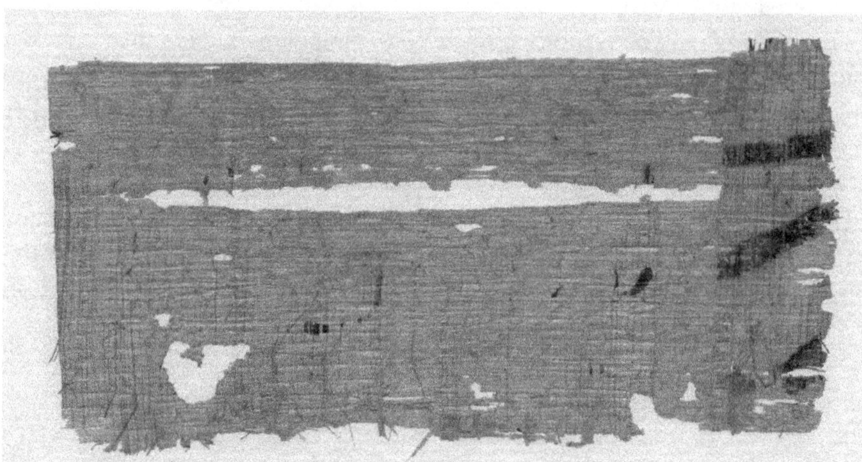

FIGURE 3.1B *P.Vindob. A.P. 2090 back.*
SOURCE: ÖSTERREICHISCHEN NATIONALBIBLIOTHEK, PAPYRUSSAMMLUNG UND PAPYRUSMUSEUM.

AP 2090[7]
5.5 × 11 cm
Text

1. بسم الله الرحمن الرحيم
2. هذا كتاب كتبه حسن بن يعقوب
3. خليفة يحيى بن سعيد خليفة
4. القاضي عيسى بن المنكدر بالفيوم

Diacritical dots:

1) بسم 2) بالفيوم

Translation

1. In the name of God, the Merciful, the Compassionate.
2. This is a document written by Hasan ibn Yaʿqub,
3. (who is a) representative of Yahya ibn Saʿid, (who is himself a) representative
4. of the judge ʿIsa ibn al-Munkadir, in the Fayyum

Commentary

1. A smudge has partially obscured the *basmala*. A dot under the line seems to belong to the *bāʾ* of *bi*.
2. Hasan ibn Yaʿqub is not known from the literary and documentary records.
3. Yahya ibn Saʿid is not attested in the documentary or literary sources. In the first word on the line, *khalīfa*, the *khāʾ* is separated from the *lām*.
4. ʿIsa ibn al-Munkadir is the well-known chief judge who was in office from 10 Rajab 212 AH (October 5 827 CE) to Ramaḍān 214 AH (2 November–1 December 829 CE) in Fustat.[8]

---

7 I would like to thank Bernhard Palme and Claudia Kreuzsaler of the Department of Papyri at the Austrian National Library for permission to publish this papyrus.

8 Tillier, *Histoire des Cadis Égyptiens*, 204–215.

Competition between the Centre and the Province

The papyrus under discussion dates from the mid-ninth century and reflects the new power relations and administrative structures in place in Egypt after the take-over by the Abbasid general ʿAbd Allah b. Tahir (d. 230/844). New arrangements between the earliest Arab settlers, Egyptians and new Arab, Turkish and Persian immigrants as well as the centralizing measures imposed on the administration by the Abbasid authorities from Baghdad as represented by their appointees in Egypt, are reflected in the affiliations with which the person who produced the papyrus identified himself.

The administrative organisation within Egypt as reflected in the text exhibits also larger empire-wide developments and concerns. The impact of the relation between the province and the caliphal court with Egypt's fiscal income and general wealth playing a crucially important role in the empire at large is expressed in the particular organizational structure that the papyrus' expressions belie. To understand the relationship between the judiciary office in Fustat and the caliph and his court, as well as with the other provincial high officials, especially the governor, and the judge's representatives throughout the province, a short overview of the developments that underpin the changed situation in the ninth century will be given first.

After the Arab conquest of Egypt in 642, governors were appointed over the province by the caliphs in Medina (632–661), then in Damascus (661–750) and after that in Baghdad (from 750). Governors were typically outsiders whose offices never lasted long enough to build up a local constituency. The *wujūh*, members of the Arab élite in Egypt who had settled there after the conquest, however, had their own agenda and lobbied to be ruled by a representative from their own ranks or at least someone sympathetic to their concerns.[9] The negotiation, sometimes expanding into outright clashes, between the interests of the caliphal center and that of the local élite members would be a continuum in the years to come.[10]

---

9 Even in the early ninth century the notables, when consulted concerning a suitable candidate to fill the post of chief judge, requested that he not be a "stranger" (*gharīb*). See al-Kindi (d. 350/961), *Kitab al-Wulat wa-Kitab al-Qudat* (*The Governors and Judges of Egypt*), in E.J.W. Gibb Memorial Series 19, ed. R. Guest, *The Governors and Judges of Egypt* (Leiden: Brill, 1912), 433.

10 Hugh Kennedy, "Egypt as a Province in the Islamic Caliphate, 641–868," in *The Cambridge History of Egypt. Volume 1: Islamic Egypt, 640–1517*, ed. Carl F. Petry (Cambridge: Cambridge University Press, 2008), 70.

The governors in their turn appointed members of the local Arab élite at the next level of offices: the head of police, *ṣāḥib al-shurṭa*, the financial officer, *ṣāḥib al-kharāj* and the chief judge, qadi, sometimes with the caliph getting involved as well. Especially the *ṣāḥib al-shurṭa* held a crucial position and belonged always to the *wujūh*, the local Arab notables. The governors were heavily dependent on, if not captives of these local Arab officers. Described as an oligarchy, their local knowledge and support amongst the *jund*, as well as their wealth and property made them indispensable for the governor's effectiveness in ruling the province.[11] Each of these positions relied of course on an extensive body of lower administrative officials, clerks, scribes, guards and other personnel, most of whom originated with the native Egyptian population.

A change in the power relations within the province occurred at the end of the seventh century. At ʿAbd Allah b. al-Zubayr's (d. 72/692) proclamation of caliph at the death of caliph Yazid I in 64/683, Arab-Egyptian kharijite supporters took control of the Egyptian capital and appointed a Zubayrid governor. Egypt's *wujūh*, however, overall continued in their support for the caliph in Damascus and cooperated with the reconquest of the province for the Umayyads by the caliph Marwan b. al-Hakam (d. 65/685) and his son ʿAbd al-ʿAziz (d. 86/705) in 64–65/684. While executing any élite members who did not retract their support of Ibn al-Zubayr, Marwan instructed his son, whom he appointed as governor in Egypt after recovering its control, to rule in full cooperation with the local Arab leaders.[12] From then on strong ties existed between the governor and the local élite, whose interdependency was from now on the basis of cooperation rather than competition, a policy continued under the Abbasids who maintained the locals' role in the administration.

Another phase in the relation between the capital of the caliphate and the province of Egypt began after the death of al-Harun in 193/809. The war between his sons and brothers al-Amin and al-Maʿmun (between 195/811 and 198/813) brought great disturbances to Egypt. Different Arab groups introduced in Egypt as soldiers, administrators or other kinds of settlers in attempts by the caliph to increase his control over the province, had begun to challenge the position of Egypt's earlier established Arab élite. With central control diminished, and new power constellations being formed, these groups openly started to fight for influence in the province.[13] Revolts, partially to protest fiscal burdens under the Arabs, partially in reaction to shifting alliances between Arab Egyptians, Christian Egyptians and incoming Arabs, which had

11 Kennedy, "Egypt as a Province in the Islamic Caliphate," 66.
12 Ibid., 71.
13 Ibid., 70–80.

been plaguing Egypt since the end of the seventh and early eighth century, added to the unrest and insecurity. From the last decade of the eighth century control of the province was effectively in the hands of ʿAbd al-ʿAziz al-Jarawi (d. 205/820) the appointed governor who controlled the Delta with the support of the Yamani tribes, and al-Sari b. al-Hakam (d. 205/820) who was in control of Fustat and the area to the south with the aid of the *abnāʾ*, the Khurasani troops which he had led to Egypt from Baghdad.[14] Andalusian refugees who arrived in 199/815 added to the disturbances, attacking and killing a number of *wujūh* in Alexandria in the following year.[15]

A return to safety in the province as well as the establishment of solid caliphal control, essential to secure the highly demanded fiscal revenues, clearly required a strong interference. This was realized in the person of ʿAbd Allah b. Tahir, son of al-Maʾmun's famous general whose taking control of Egypt resulted in increased centralization and influence from the East. Appointed in 206/821 as governor of the area between al-Raqqa on the Euphrates in the north and Egypt in the south and commander of the caliph's troops, ʿAbd Allah b. Tahir first established control in Syria and Palestine, moving his army into Egypt in 210 or 211/825–826.[16] With his large army, reinforced with naval ships from Syria, ʿAbd Allah was able to wrest the province from the hands of Ibn al-Sari (in office until 211/826) and Ibn al-Jarawi (d. 251/865), who had inherited their fathers' positions after 205/820, and defeat the Andalusians in Alexandria.[17] After more than 20 years, caliphal control was once again restored over the whole province.

ʿAbd Allah b. Tahir remained in Egypt until 212/827, but he ruled a very different province. The Egyptian *wujūh*'s power had been steadily declining at the expense of representatives of the ruling military élite from the caliphal capital in Iraq who had been settling in Egypt since the late eighth century. In the struggle between al-Jarawi and al-Sari and their sons, the old Arab élite of Egypt no longer played a decisive role. ʿAbd Allah b. Tahir's take-over and the measures he took decisively decimated the power of the old Arab leaders at the expense of new Arab and non-Arab population groups who obtained

---

14 Severus of El Ashmunein (d. 987), *History of the Patriarchs of the Coptic Church of Alexandria. Volume 4: Menas I to Joseph* (849), Arabic text edited, translated, and annotated by B. Evetts, *Patrologia Orientalis* 10 (1910): 428; al-Kindi, *Kitab al-Wulat*, 148, 151, 161–162.

15 Kennedy, "Egypt as a Province in the Islamic Caliphate," 81.

16 al-Tabari (d. 310/923), Muhammad ibn Jarir. *Tarikh al-Rusul wa-l-Muluk*, ed. Michael J. de Goeje (Leiden: Brill, 1879–1901), 3: 1087–1092.

17 al-Kindi, *Kitab al-Wulat*, 180.

influential positions in the administration and army, and thereby access to Egypt's resources.

ʿAbd Allah's army, which was now in control of the province, consisted of outsiders from the East, as did the army's commanders, mostly Persian-speaking Turks.[18] The tenth-century chronicler of Egypt's political and judicial structure, al-Kindi, writes how the governor ʿAbd Allah b. Tahir made use of eastern personnel. He replaced his earlier appointed head of police with a member of the *abnāʾ*.[19] Caliphal control over Egypt was put in effect by the governors appointed over the province. Representing the sovereigns who were assigned the western provinces by the caliph from 213/829 onwards, the governors belonged, like their masters, to the same class of eastern military commanders. Appointed for longer periods (3–4 years), the governors no longer relied on locals to fill the crucial positions of *ṣāḥib al-shurṭa, ṣāḥib al-kharāj* and qadi.[20] Instead, they appointed members from their own constituency, outsiders from the East like the governors. In other words, support and cooperation from the local *wujūh* was no longer essential to maintain control of the province, while a new class of administrators and bureaucrats working in a new system and with new practices was put in place.

The degree to which the caliph was involved in the affairs of the province beyond the organization of local administrative structures is exemplified by the caliph appointing his brother and future caliph al-Muʿtasim as sovereign in charge of the western provinces including Egypt in 213/829. Unlike most of the other sovereigns appointed over the western provinces who mainly stayed put at the caliphal court, al-Muʿtasim was in fact forced to come down in person to Egypt in 214/830 to put down a rebellion of Arabs in al-Hawf, the eastern part of the Delta. Soon, however, he left again, leaving his governor in place to rule for him. In 217/832 the caliph al-Maʾmun in his turn came to the province, in response to yet another uprising of Arab and Christian Egyptians. Significantly, the local rulers and their military forces were unable to deal with these uprisings, while each visit by an eastern army resulted in more newcomers staying on in the province. The final turn in the relation between Egypt's Arab population and the political center was reached in 218/833 when the newly appointed caliph al-Muʿtasim ordered his governor to abolish the *dīwān*, discontinuing the stipends (*ʿaṭāʾ*) for the Arabs in Egypt.[21] Relying on his own well-trained

18 See also the two "Persian" army generals from Khurasan whom ʿAbd Allah b. Tahir appointed at the head of the army he sent to Alexandria (al-Kindi, *Kitab al-Wulat*, 183–184).

19 Ibid., 183.

20 Occasionally outsider qadis had been appointed before, see Tillier, *Histoire des Cadis Égyptiens*, 36.

21 al-Kindi, *Kitab al-Wulat*, 193.

army of 'slave' soldiers, al-Mu'tasim's abolishment of the *dīwān* was one of his empire-wide measures to build a new constituency while breaking the influence of traditional power blocks. The virtual lack of protest against this measure indicates the changed power relations in the province where the loss of their privileged financial position was only the last formal stage witnessing the *wujūh*'s gradually diminishing place in the provincial hierarchy.

Also within the province itself the presence of Abbasid forces and administrators had resulted in centralizing measures, with stronger control being imposed from the capital Fustat in a new style and language showing eastern influences. Procedures were imposed to increase the taxes raised in the country, tightening the registration of property and with closer supervision of assessments, impositions and collections of taxes.[22] The documents reflect these changes in the administration where a new terminology and novel expressions are introduced representing new – 'Persian' – chancery traditions, while at the same time referring to the new organization based on a new hierarchical configuration put in place.[23] Especially well researched by Gladys Frantz-Murphy in the case of agricultural leases and receipts, the formulaic and semantic changes introduced in the documents suggest a professionalized bureaucracy relying on officials and subjects beholden to the state.[24] See for example the introduction of sultan, replacing "the Muslims" as a reference to the public authority of the province.[25] Those responsible for the tax-collection are referred to no longer in terms of personal relations between them and the governor, but as representatives of the authorities in general.[26] While these changes reflect the new administrative structure in place as part of the centralizing measures after the civil war, other evidence points to direct influence of eastern administrative traditions. The Persian word *jahbadh* replaces *qusṭāl* for

22 Resulting in new tax revolts in 212/828 (al-Kindi, *Kitab al-Wulat*, 185); Kosei Morimoto, *The Fiscal Administration of Egypt in the Early Islamic Period* (Kyoto: Dohosha, 1981), 228.

23 For the introduction of "Persian" administrative practices, see Gladys Frantz-Murphy, *Corpus Papyrorum Raineri XXI. Arabic Agricultural Leases and Tax Receipts from Egypt 148–427 AH/765–1035 AD* (Vienna: Brüder Hollinek, 2001); and Gladys Frantz-Murphy, "The Economics of State Formation in Early Islamic Egypt," in *From al-Andalus to Khurasan. Documents from the Medieval Muslim World*, ed. Petra M. Sijpesteijn et al. (Leiden: Brill, 2006), 101–114.

24 Frantz-Murphy, *Corpus Papyrorum Raineri XXI*, 40–44.

25 The first attestation of this term in an agricultural lease is dated 217/832, see Frantz-Murphy, *Corpus Papyrorum Raineri XXI*, 36–39.

26 Ibid., 122.

paymaster, while authenticating practices such as the use of seals and signatures also shows an influence from the eastern Islamic Empire.[27]

This then is the background against which our papyrus was written. Fundamental changes in the financial and administrative organization of the province and the empire at large had impacted the way the province of Egypt was run. Simultaneously, the penetrating presence of the Abbasid caliphate resulted in the more frequent attestation of members of the ruling family and their representatives in the form of eastern military élite members. Let us now turn to the effects of these changes on the organization of the judiciary connecting them to the situation represented in the papyrus.

Expanding Qadi Justice[28]

The qadi in the Abbasid period held indeed a very powerful position that only increased in importance with the rise of the prominence of religion-based law and its representatives or interpreters, the *fuqahāʾ*. In Egypt demographic changes added to the momentum of change. Through immigration and, to a lesser extent, through conversion of the local population, the Arab-Muslim population was growing significantly. From the eighth century onwards, migration outside the garrison cities added to the processes of conversion and acculturalisation of the Egyptian population. Developments internal to the Islamic judiciary coincided with these changes. As a consequence, significant modifications can be observed in the judicial organization in Egypt from the first half of the second/eighth century, characterized by an increased

27 For the introduction of *jahbadh*, see Frantz-Murphy, *Corpus Papyrorum Raineri XXI*, 122. For the authentication of documents, see Geoffrey Khan, "The Pre-Islamic Background of Muslim Legal Formularies," *ARAM* 6 (1994): 193–224; Geoffrey Khan, "Newly Discovered Arabic Documents from Early Abbasid Khurasan," in *From al-Andalus to Khurasan. Documents from the Medieval Muslim World*, ed. Petra M. Sijpesteijn et al. (Leiden: Brill, 2006), 199–216; Petra M. Sijpesteijn, "Seals and Papyri from Early Islamic Egypt," in *Seals and Sealing Practices in the Near East. Developments in Administration and Magic from Prehistory to the Islamic Period. Proceedings of an International Workshop at the Netherlands-Flemish Institute in Cairo on December 2–3, 2009*," ed. I. Regulski et al. (Louvain: Peeters, 2012).

28 The politics of the qadi's position in Egypt in this period is extensively described by Mathieu Tillier in his *Histoire des Cadis Égyptiens Aḫbār quḍāt Miṣr* (33), and in his "The Qāḍīs of Fustat-Miṣr under the Ṭūlūnids and the Ikhshīdids: The Judiciary and the Egyptian Autonomy," *Journal of the American Oriental Society* 131, no. 2 (2011): 207–222. I have relied heavily on his discussion for this overview.

professionalization on the one hand and an extended presence of the court on the other. A growing Arab-Muslim population in- and outside the garrison cities increasingly looked towards Arab-Islamic institutions to record their legal transactions and deal with their disputes. While Christian and Jewish authorities continued to play a role in legal matters, Muslim courts with their greater means of enforcement became an attractive alternative for Egypt's non-Muslim communities.[29] A developing Islamic judicial system on the other hand pushed for greater involvement,[30] while the long administrative and managerial arm from the capital Fustat also became more pronounced.[31] In short, the need for representatives of the qadi's court to operate outside Fustat increased and these representatives functioned in a more expert and disciplined fashion.[32]

These developments are exemplified by the emancipation of the qadi from other offices in the province. While early qadis regularly combined their office with that of the *ṣāḥib al-shurṭa*, the office of the judge was definitely separated from that of the head of police in the early eighth century, acknowledging the importance and volume of the law-giving and executive power.[33] At the same time, however, legal and administrative functions continued to be intertwined and exchangeable into the Abbasid period.[34] Similarly, while there are some attestations of qadis in the documentary record dating to this period, the documents offer no clear indication of the extent and character of their function, especially compared to other administrative offices.[35]

The ninth century saw the accumulative effects of these developments impacted by specific historical circumstances as reflected in the documentary

---

29 Maged S.A. Mikhail, *From Byzantine to Islamic Egypt: Religion, Identity and Politics after the Arab Conquest* (London/New York: I.B. Tauris, 2014), chapter 6; Petra M. Sijpesteijn, *Shaping a Muslim State: The World of a Mid-Eighth-Century Egyptian Official* (Oxford: Oxford University Press, 2013), 107–111.

30 Jelle Bruning, *The Rise of a Capital. On the Develoment of al-Fusṭāṭ's Relationship with its Hinterland, 18/639–132/750*. PhD dissertation (Leiden University, 2014), 151; Tillier, "The Qāḍīs of Fustat-Miṣr under the Ṭūlūnids and the Ikhshīdids."

31 Bruning, *The Rise of a Capital*, 148.

32 See also Mathieu Tillier's contribution to this volume.

33 Until 89/708 several qadis had also held the function of *ṣāḥib al-shurṭa*, see Tillier, *Histoire des Cadis Égyptiens Aḫbār quḍāt Miṣr*, 20.

34 See Tillier's discussion in this volume, extending Joseph Schacht's description of the Umayyad qadi as a legal secretary to the governor to the chief judge in early Abbasid Egypt.

35 See "Concerning the payment of a debt," text no. 26 in Sijpesteijn, *Shaping a Muslim State*, 398–403. See also the contribution of Tillier in this volume.

sources. A pronounced rise in the number of Arabic documents, including legal documents, shows that Egypt's population increasingly functioned in Arabic and did so also in Arabic-Muslim institutions.[36] Mathieu Tillier, in this volume, interprets this rise in extant legal documents as a sign of an increased professionalization of the judiciary relying on documentation and archival practices, and as a witness to a more active and involved court in Egypt's countryside.

A further development was the expansion of Egyptian legal practice to form part of an extensive legal system lead by legal scholars (*fuqahāʾ*).[37] The limited degree to which Egyptian scholars participated in empire-wide legal debates shows that this legal system was mostly locally defined, but there were some connections extending beyond the province.[38] Maturity of the Islamic legal system coincided with the new political and religious order with an increased role for religious scholars (ʿulamaʾ) as an independent voice of religious authority following the period of the *miḥna* introduced by caliph al-Maʾmun in 218/833 and continuing until 234/848 or 237/852.[39] While the document that is the subject of this article predates the *miḥna*, the development of religious scholarship leading to a discussion about who held the ultimate religious authority in the Muslim community was already a significant factor.

While Arabicisation and acculturalization as well as the growth of the Law definitely played a role in the increased presence of a professionalized Muslim

36 Sijpesteijn, *Shaping a Muslim State*, 111. See the Christians appearing in Arabic-Islamic contracts (Michael H. Thung, *Corpus Papyrorum Raineri XXVI. Arabische juristische Urkunden aus der Papyrussammlung der Österreichischen Nationalbibliothek* [Leipzig: De Gruyter, 2006]). See also the two tenth-century contracts written up in Arabic according to Islamic legal rules which had to be translated orally for the parties into Coptic (Gladys Frantz-Murphy, "A Comparison of the Arabic and Earlier Egyptian Contract Formularies. Part I: the Arab Contracts from Egypt [3rd/9th–5th/11th Centuries]." *Journal of Near Eastern Studies* 40, no. 1–2 [1981]: 203–225, 355–356.) and the Arabic marriage contracts drawn up for two Christian parties according to Islamic legal principles (Nabia Abbott, "Arabic Marriage Contracts among the Copts," *Zeitschrift der Deutschen morgenländischen Gesellschaft* 95 [1941]: 59–81.). All these documents originate in the Fayyum.

37 Discussed in this volume by Mathieu Tillier.

38 As discussed by Mathieu Tillier in his lecture "Local Tradition and Imperial Law in Umayyad Egypt," at the conference "Egypt Connected: Cultural, Economic, Political and Military Interactions (500–1000 CE)" which took place on June 18–20, 2015 at Leiden University.

39 Qadis cannot of course be equaled to *fuqahāʾ*. The qadis of Umayyad Egypt do not seem to have played an especially important role in religious scholarship of the time (G.H.A. Juynboll, *Muslim Tradition. Studies in Chronology, Provenance and Authorship of Early Hadith* [Cambridge: Cambridge University Press, 1983], 80); but see Mathieu Tillier, "Scribes et enquêteurs: note sur le personnel judiciaire en Égypte aux quatre premiers siècles de l'hégire," *Journal of the Social and Economic History of the Orient* 54 (2011): 370–404, n. 94.

court in Egypt's countryside, political-administrative measures were important too. The centralizing procedures undertaken by al-Ma'mun's regime after his victory in the civil war in the person of 'Abd Allah b. Tahir after his takeover of the province in 833 have already been described. Similarly, the impact of the arrival of Persian-Turkish administrators and militaries on the administrative infrastructure of the province have been discussed above. Both these developments greatly impacted the relation between the caliph and the qadi of Egypt as well as the position of the chief judge and his representatives in the province.

Contrary to governors who were always appointed directly by the caliph to the provinces, the qadi was a local appointee who was regularly installed by the governor, but was also often (re)confirmed by the caliph.[40] A clear pattern exists between centralizing efforts of the caliphal court and its involvement in the appointment of judges in Egypt, and the caliphs were always involved from al-Ma'mun's rule onwards.[41] Accountable to the official (governor or caliph) who invested him with his title and position, the qadi maintained direct contact with the ruler. This could restrict the judge's independence, but also transferred status onto him.[42] The caliph's ambitions of control over the provinces through the office of the qadi were, however, sometimes thwarted by weakness

---

40 See also the expression "qadi of the *amīr* (i.e. governor)" said of the qadi Ibrahim b. al-Jarrah (in office 205–211/820–826) (al-Kindi, *Qudat*, 431–432). Cf. Tillier, *Histoire des Cadis Égyptiens Aḫbār quḍāt Miṣr*, 31.

41 For an overview of who appointed the qadi in Fustat from the conquest until the Ṭūlūnid period, see the table in Tillier, *Histoire des Cadis Égyptiens Aḫbār quḍāt Miṣr*, 24–30; for the period 237–366/851–976, see Tillier, *Vies des cadis de Miṣr 237/851–366/976* (Cairo: Institut français d'archéologie orientale, 2002), 20–25. Even Ahmad b. Tulun (d. 270/884) as semi-independent viceroy of Egypt accepted the qadis appointed by the caliph (Tillier, *Vies des cadis de Miṣr 237/851–366/976*, 21–22). The governor 'Abd Allah b. Tahir appointed the qadi 'Isa b. al-Munkadir, the same of our papyrus, but he did so after long deliberation, and leaving the judgeship vacant for more than a year while legal cases were being dealt with in the maẓālim court whose heads were appointed by the governor too. Subsequent governors also sometimes appointed someone over the *maẓālim* court while the qadi was only appointed several years later by the caliph. See for example the appointment of Ishaq b. Isma'il (in office 215/830) by the governor 'Abdawayh b. Jabala (in office 215–216/830–831), Muhammad b. 'Abbad (in office 215–217/830–832) by the governor Kaydar Nasr b. 'Abd Allah (in office 217–219/832–834) and 'Isa b. Lahi'a (in office 235–237/850–851) by the governor Ishaq b. Yahya (in office 235–236/849–850).

42 For examples of direct involvement by the caliph al-Walid (r. 86–96/705–715) in Damascus in cases dealt with by the Egyptian qadi, see Yaacov Lev, "Coptic Rebellions and the Islamization of Medieval Egypt (8th–10th Century): Medieval and Modern Perceptions," *Jerusalem Studies in Arabic and Islam* 39 (2012): 303–344. 'Umar b. 'Abd

at the centre, for example at times of civil war, or by governors taking matters in their own hand.[43] Moreover, after the Abbasids' move of the capital to Baghdad, Egypt was sufficiently remote to make effective control difficult, especially when the local Arab élite or the governor opposed it.[44]

Even those qadis who were appointed by the caliph or their governors could form an opposing force. It is exactly when ʿAbd Allah b. Tahir was imposing direct and firm control on Egypt that he came into conflict with two consecutive judges. Ibrahim b. al-Jarrah (in office 206–211/821–826) was dismissed by the governor when the latter found out about Ibrahim's letter in support of the rebellious governor Ibn al-Sari. The post of qadi remained vacant for more than a year, with cases being dealt with in the *maẓālim* court. The *maẓalim* court of appeals fell directly under the governor.[45] It is interesting to note that in the process of choosing a new qadi ʿAbd Allah b. Tahir consulted the notables (*al-nās*) of Misr. Despite ʿAbd Allah b. Tahir's position as military conqueror and his exposing his absolute power by dismissing the qadi Ibrahim b. al-Jarrah and not installing a new qadi immediately, he obviously felt the need to involve the local notables and give them a voice and a feeling of empowerment in the process of the appointment of local officials. Finally, on 10 Rajab 212/ 5 October 827 ʿIsa b. al-Munkadir was appointed, seemingly as a compromise figure and after different candidates were put forward. The governor, of course, had the last say in the choice.[46] Besides having been dependent on the governor for his appointment, ʿIsa b. al-Munkadir had another reason to be grateful to the

al-ʿAziz (r. 98–101/7171–720) also communicated directly with the qadi of Egypt (Tillier, *Histoire des Cadis Égyptiens Aḫbār quḍāt Miṣr*, 31, n. 142).

43 In his *Histoire des Cadis Égyptiens Aḫbār quḍāt Miṣr* (32), Tillier describes several cases when Abbasid governors interfered in the appointment of the qadi.

44 Tillier writes that caliphal control over the office of the qadi seems to have been even harder to maintain in Egypt than in Iraq (*Histoire des Cadis Égyptiens Aḫbār quḍāt Miṣr*, 32).

45 Ibrahim b. al-Jarrah was removed from office in Rabīʿ I 211/June-July 826 (Ibn Hajar gives the alternative date Jumādā I 211/Augus 826. See Tillier, *Histoire des Cadis Égyptiens Aḫbār quḍāt Miṣr*, 204. n. 862), while ʿIsa b. al-Munkadir was not appointed until 10 Rajab 212/ 5 October 827. During this period the *maẓālim* court was headed by ʿAttaf b. Ghazwan (in office 211–212/826–827) (al-Kindi, *Kitab al-Wulat*, 432–433). Tillier showed how rulers resorted to installing (only) a *maẓālim* court while dismissing a troublesome qadi, see his "Qāḍī-s and the Political Use of the Maẓālim Jurisidiction under the ʿAbbāsids," in *Public Violence in Islamic Societies: Power, Discipline and the Construction of the Public Sphere, 7th–18th Centuries CE*, ed. C. Lange and M. Fierro (Edinburgh: Edinburgh University Press, 2009), 42–66.

46 al-Kindi, *Kitab al-Wulat*, 433–435 (tr. Tillier, *Histoire des Cadis Égyptiens Aḫbār quḍāt Miṣr*, 204–207).

governor, as the latter decided to provide him with a daily salary because he was "poor," besides a sign-up bonus of one thousand dinars.[47] The position of ʿIsa b. al-Munkadir, however, was compromised when he protested the appointment of the governor Abu Ishaq al-Muʿtasim over the western provinces in a letter to the caliph al-Maʾmun. In 214/829 Abu Ishaq al-Muʿtasim dismissed and imprisoned ʿIsa b. al-Munkadir. A year later Abu Ishaq al-Muʿtasim, who by now had left Egypt, ordered him to be exiled to Iraq where he died in prison in 220/835.[48]

Delegation and Legitimization

Unlike other provinces, where major towns often had two qadis, Fustat always only knew one chief judge who, together with his office, his scribes and other aids, was responsible for the maintenance of justice in the city and its dependent countryside.[49] Literary sources mention qadis in place in Alexandria from the end of the first/early eighth century, somewhat earlier than in other provinces of the Empire. The presence of qadis in Alexandria is presumably related to the city's dominant position in the province which remained at a par with the official capital Fustat.[50] At the same time the presence of a qadi in Alexandria at this early moment might explain why Fustat always only had one qadi whose work, with a partner in place in the other major Egyptian city, remained manageable.[51]

Qadis operating outside the capital, albeit without an indication of the extent of their mandate, start to be attested in the papyri from the mid-second/

47 Of seven dinars per day or four thousand dirhams per month. Al-Kindi writes this custom was standard from that moment onwards (al-Kindi, *Kitab al-Wulat*, 435). But see the receipt also recorded by al-Kindi (*Kitab al-Wulat*, 354) recording the payment of twenty dinars for two months of salary for the qadi ʿAbd al-Rahman b. Salim (in office Muḥarram 128/October 745-Ramaḍān 133/751). Cf. W. al-Qadi, "An Umayyad Papyrus in al-Kindī's Kitāb al-Quḍāt?," *Der Islam* 84 (2007): 200–245.

48 Tillier's translation of al-Kindi's biography of ʿIsa b. al-Munkadir contains exhaustive information from other Arabic sources on the judge's life. His death date is based on Ibn Yunus (d. 347/958), see Ibn Yunus, *Taʾrikh Ibn Yunus al-Sadafi*, ed. ʿA.F. ʿAbd al-Fattah (Beirut: Dar al-Kutub al-ʿIlmiyya, 2000), 215, n. 914.

49 Tillier, *Histoire des Cadis Égyptiens Aḫbār quḍāt Miṣr*, 23, n. 116.

50 Bruning, *The Rise of a Capital*, chapter 2. For the exceptional position of Fustat in having always only one qadi as opposed to Damascus and towns in Iraq, see Tillier, *Histoire des Cadis Égyptiens Aḫbār quḍāt Miṣr*, 23, n. 116; Tillier, "Qāḍī-s and the Political Use of the Maẓālim Jurisidiction under the ʿAbbāsids," 281–284.

51 Tillier, *Histoire des Cadis Égyptiens Aḫbār quḍāt Miṣr*, 23.

eighth century onwards. That is when in other provinces qadis are said to be appointed outside provincial capitals as well.[52] Besides Alexandria, the sources report that from the third/ninth century other towns such as Akhmim and Rashid (Rosetta) had qadis as well.[53] Although these officials were all equally called qadi, the judge in Fustat clearly topped the judicial hierarchy and important cases continued to be referred to the chief judge in the capital.[54]

Deputies of qadis are mentioned in the literary sources to have been in place from the end of the eighth/early ninth century onwards in the Fayyum and in Alexandria.[55] These sources use the same root *kh-l-f* to indicate the legal deputies.[56] The papyrus edited above not only mentions one representative, but a chain of representatives with the lowest office in the Fayyum oasis and

52 In his *The Rise of a Capital* (141–142), Bruning discusses examples from Egypt and Syria. Tillier lists examples from Iraq in his *Les cadis d'Iraq et l'État abbasside* (*132/750–334/945*) (Damascus: Presses de l'Institut français du Proche-Orient, 2009).

53 For Marthad b. ʿAbd Allah al-Yazani (d. 90/708–9) and other qadis in the first/seventh-second/eighth centuries, see Bruning, *The Rise of a Capital*, 141–148. For later examples, see Tillier, *Histoire des Cadis Égyptiens Aḫbār quḍāt Miṣr*, 23–24.

54 See also Bruning's reconstruction of the careers of Marthad b. ʿAbd Allah al-Yazani and Yazid b. ʿAbd Allah al-Hadrami, whose rise in the administrative hierarchy included a move from a provincial legal office to that of qadi in Fustat (*The Rise of a Capital*, 142–148). Mathieu Tillier warns against accepting the ascription of the title qadi by the narrative sources to judicial officials outside Fustat, suggesting that, especially for the earlier period, these should be interpreted rather as administrative officials wielding judicial power as part of their position (*Histoire des Cadis Égyptiens Aḫbār quḍāt Miṣr*, 24). The attestation of qadis in the papyri, however, suggests that such an office did exist (at times) beyond the capital, while the chief qadi located in Fustat might have been indicated with an adjusted title (See for example *qāḍī ahl miṣr* in the papyrus dating from 141/758–759 edited by Hinds and Sakkout, see Martin Hinds and Hamdi Sakkout, "A Letter from the Governor of Egypt to the King of Nubia and Muqurra Concerning Egyptian-Nubian Relations in 141/758," in *Studia Arabica et Islamica. Festschrift for Iḥsān ʿAbbās on his Sixtieth Birthday*, ed. Ihsan ʿAbbas et al. [Beirut: American University of Beirut, 1981], 202–229. The expression appears in line 46 of the document.). For an overview of the attestations of qadis in the papyri, see Sijpesteijn, *Shaping a Muslim State*, 85–86. For cases outside Fustat being referred to the main judge in Fustat, see for example the case of the killing of an Egyptian merchant in Nubia in a papyrus dating to the governorship of governor Musa b. Kaʿb (in office 141/758–759), see Hinds and Sakkout, "A Letter From the Governor of Egypt."

55 Tillier, *Histoire des Cadis Égyptiens Aḫbār quḍāt Miṣr*, 23.

56 *Wa-kataba ilayya an akhlafahu bi-l-fayyūm* (Qadi ʿIyad, *Tartib al-Madarik*, II, 463; *History of the Patriarchs*, vol. 4. All sources are cited in Tillier, *Histoire des Cadis Égyptiens Aḫbār quḍāt Miṣr*, 23, n. 117). See also the discussion in Hussein F.S. Kasassbeh, *The Office of Qāḍī in the Early ʿAbbāsid Caliphate* (*132–247/750–861*), PhD dissertation (London: SOAS,

another one in between that and the qadi's office in the capital Fustat. It shows not only the degree to which the judiciary and its institutions had expanded and proliferated, with offices multiplying and dependences of the provincial court in the countryside increasing, but also the level of centralization and hierarchy extending from the province's capital to its sub-regions. In those expanding and proliferating courts officials such as secretaries, scribes, examiners of witnesses and the like multiplied.[57]

ʿIsa b. al-Munkadir's office, the qadi under whose judgeship the papyrus was produced, shows these two processes in action. Appointed over the judiciary and the appeals courts (*maẓālim*) together, ʿIsa b. al-Munkadir was chosen to be the perfect representative of the caliph's interest after a period in which the ruler's representative in Egypt ʿAbd Allah b. Tahir had kept direct control over the law court through the office of the *maẓālim*. The centralizing ambitions of the regime in Egypt were expressed through the chain of representatives (*khalīfa*) that the sender of the papyrus Hasan b. Yaʿqub, who was located outside the capital in the oasis Fayyum, is identified with. At his appointment it is said that ʿIsa b. al-Munkadir appointed a new set of officials in his office: the main scribe and secretaries, a supervisor and the person in charge of examining upright witnesses are all replaced by him.[58] Not only does this action symbolize the arrival of a new powerbase put in place under the direct auspices of the caliphal court, it also refers to the bureaucracy on which the law court by now relied.

It is ironic that it is exactly ʿIsa b. al-Munkadir who defies the political hierarchy within the Empire by turning directly to the caliph al-Maʾmun to protest the appointment of the caliph's brother and heir apparent as sovereign over Egypt and the other western provinces. As described above the letter caused the judge's downfall and removal from office.

The new administrative and political order put in place by ʿAbd Allah b. Tahir enabled the rise of a service élite in Egypt. The status and authority of the new administrative notables were no longer based on their belonging to the earliest settled Arab families, but rather on their function within or relation with the state structure, which appears in the documents under the abstract term "sultan." Hence, association with representatives of that administration were more important when establishing one's position than personal relations.

1990), 289–292. I am grateful to Jelle Bruning for introducing me to this reference (see also Bruning *The Rise of a Capital*, 144, n. 75).

57 For the expansion of the lower officials working at the courts, see Tillier, "Scribes et enquêteurs," 370–404.

58 al-Kindi, *Kitab al-Wulat*, 435.

Social background remained of course important, with the Turkish-Persian military and bureaucratic culture now being dominant.

This emphasis on the administrative hierarchy is exemplified by the papyrus edited above. Hasan b. Yaʿqub, the sender of the document, identifies himself not only as being part of the judiciary headed by the qadi in Fustat in a general way, but connects himself through a chain of representatives, of whom he is the last and third one, directly with the qadi. While representing a government office in the Fayyum oasis, Hasan b. Yaʿqub also refers to the direct ties that link him in the countryside with the capital. It is an expression of extreme centralization when observed from the capital, with authority being referred onto the judge in the province through his link to the chief judge. Seen from Hasan b. Yaʿqub's point of view, however, the same chain empowers as it disseminates the court's power to lower layers in the judiciary. As identified in this papyrus, Hasan b. Yaʿqub is an official representative of the judiciary in the countryside and a member of Egypt's service elite. The same expression tying the official giving judgements in the Fayyum oasis to the court in Fustat operates both ways. It is a nice example of how centralised expressions of power implicated both sides of the chain in a reciprocal system of imposition and reception.

At the same time the first point of contact in the judicial hierarchy for Hasan b. Yaʿqub would have been Yahya ibn Saʿid, the official placed between himself and the qadi ʿIsa b. al-Munkadir. The papyrus also shows thus the different administrative layers that connected the district of the Fayyum oasis with the capital Fustat. The literary sources do not discuss such a tier in the judiciary, but one wonders whether it can be associated to a similar division in the fiscal administration. When the Arabs arrived in Egypt in 639, they initially maintained the division in five larger districts (eparchies) for administrative and fiscal purposes. From the end of the seventh century, however, documents and narrative sources describe the existence of a partition in two main subprovinces: the Saʿid (Upper Egypt) and Asfal al-Ard (the Delta).[59] While there were offices and officials working for the two districts in the capital Fustat, officials responsible for the Upper and Lower Egyptian areas were also located or at least operated in situ. This situation continued into the Abbasid period when the references in the documents to this division and the two offices in fact increase. Was the judiciary subjected to a similar division of the province in two with Yahya ibn Saʿid heading the Upper Egyptian one?

---

59 Sijpesteijn, *Shaping a Muslim State*, 107; 119, n. 14. For the changes in the administrative division of Egypt in the 8th century in general, see ibid., ch. 2.

Conclusion

With the edition of the papyrus in this article, ʿIsa b. al-Munkadir has become, with three papyrological attestations, the qadi most present in the documentary record.[60] The papyrus edited in this article places him, moreover, clearly at the top of a chain of offices extending from his position as qadi in Fustat via a delegate in the countryside to a judicial officer responsible for the Fayyum oasis. While delegated judicial officials operating in the Egyptian countryside occasionally occur in the papyrological record, the kind of hierarchical dependency as presented in this papyrus is not previously attested.[61] The qadi's presence in the form in which it occurs in this text confirms the changes in the administrative and political organization of the province imposed by ʿAbd Allah b. Tahir after his takeover of Egypt after the unrest surrounding the civil war between al-Amin and al-Ma'mun.

While clearly using the qadi in Fustat as the ultimate focus, the papyrus also points to the multitude of layers in the judiciary administrative hierarchy showing a complex system of control from the center over the smaller districts like the Fayyum. Offices in between the centrally located qadi and his local representatives diffused central rule and discipline, but also offered a reference point for local officials where cases could be dealt with before or without passing them on to the highest authority in the capital. It shows that within the tighter organized, centrally structured administration a multiple leveled hierarchy existed.

ʿAbd Allah b. Tahir took a while to appoint a new qadi after his arrival in Egypt, leaving the office vacant for two years, while all cases were dealt with in the *maẓālim* court which fell directly under his governorship. When he

60 For examples of other judges attested in the papyri, see for example: al-Mufaddal b. Fadala (d. ca. 181/797). Mathieu Tillier, "Deux papyrus judiciaires de Fusṭāṭ (IIe/VIIIe siècle)," *Chronique d'Egypte* 89 (2014): 412–445, text 2. Ghawth b. Sulayman (d. 168/784) appears in two papyri, see Tillier, "Deux papyrus judiciaires," text 1; Hinds and Sakkout, "A Letter from the Governor of Egypt," 209–229. See also the overview of attestations in the papyri in Mathieu Tillier's article in this volume.

61 While literary sources identify Yazid b. ʿAbd Allah al-Hadrami as representative of the qadi Ghawth b. Sulayman in Ikhmim and Tahta', in the single papyrus where he is attested he is referred to as *pagarch*, administrative governor of Ikhmim (Adolf Grohmann, *Arabic Papyri in the Egyptian Library III* (Cairo: Egyptian Library Press), 67–93; Bruning, *The Rise of a Capital*, 144–148; Mathieu Tillier, "Du pagarque au cadi: ruptures et continuités dans l'administration judiciaire de la Haute-Égypte [Ier–IIIe/VIIe–IXe siècle]," *Médiévales* 64 [2013]: 32).

appointed ʿIsa b. al-Munkadir he did so in consultation with the local notables.[62] Those notables no longer represented exclusively the interests of the first Arab settlers in Egypt, but consisted of the many new groups – Arab immigrants, Turkish-Persian administrators and militaries – that had obtained a position of power at the provincial court. While involving new groups in the administration of the province, the administration, including the judiciary, were profoundly reformed to allow for stronger central control from the caliphal capital through its representatives, the governors and chief judges in Egypt. Also within the province a centralization was imposed extending through the different branches of the administration.

Taking a local point of view, namely from the district of the Fayyum, our papyrus also shows the other side of this process. Namely that the ties that drew in the local legal representative, Hasan b. Yaʿqub, into the qadi's court and jurisdiction, the association with the chief judge also empowered this local official and legitimized his authority vis-à-vis his constituency. The emphasis on the judicial administrative pyramid, with its different layers, kept Hasan b. Yaʿqub attentative to his place in the pecking order, but also made him part of the larger structure, offering him a place in the judicial configuration with responsibilities, but also rights and entitlements.

By the mid-ninth century, Egyptians operated for a large part in Arabic in the written domain as the increase in public and private Arabic documents exchanged between Muslim and non-Muslim Egyptians shows. Many of these documents concern the legal domain, from administrative exchanges related to tax payments, to debt acknowledgements and property sales and even extending to marriage contracts. Non-Muslims, moreover, regularly sought recourse in Muslim law courts.[63] This development was as much a result of the Arabicisation and Islamicisation of the Egyptian population as of the expansion and professionalisation of the Muslim judiciary that replaced other forms of administrative legal practice and Christian and Jewish religious legal institutions.[64]

The papyrus edited in this paper shows how these two developments coincided – the advanced application and use by the population of the Muslim legal institutions and the imposition of more centralized administrative and judicial apparatus in the province presenting a new phase in Egypt's political structure. Presenting himself through a chain of representatives as the

---

62 al-Kindi, *Kitab al-Wulat*.

63 Uriel Simonsohn, *A Common Justice: The Legal Allegiances of Christians and Jews under Early Islam* (Philadelphia: University of Pennsylvania Press, 2011).

64 For such non-Islamic legal institutions, see Simonsohn, *A Common Justice*.

delegate in the Fayyūm oasis of the chief qadi in Fustat, the individual legal official who produced our papyrus reflects this new configuration. On the one hand his presence in the Fayyum oasis indicates to what extent the judiciary had expanded, while his association with the qadi in the provincial capital explicitly shows his ties with the central judiciary office.

The document thus offers in its minimalist and damaged form very important evidence of how these historical processes were expressed in practice. Or as this volume intends to show: how documents form important historical sources, correcting and adding to the information available from the literary texts.

Bibliography

Abbott, Nabia. "Arabic Marriage Contracts among the Copts." *Zeitschrift der Deutschen morgenländischen Gesellschaft* 95 (1941): 59–81.

Bligh-Abramski, Irit. "The Judiciary (*qāḍīs*) as a Governmental-Administrative Tool in Early Islam." *Journal of the Economic and Social History of the Orient* 35 (1992): 40–71.

Bruning, Jelle. *The Rise of a Capital. On the Develoment of al-Fusṭāṭ's Relationship with its Hinterland, 18/639–132/750*. PhD diss., Leiden University, 2014.

Michael H. Thung, *Corpus Papyrorum Raineri XXVI. Arabische juristische Urkunden aus der Papyrussammlung der Österreichischen Nationalbibliothek*. Leipzig: De Gruyter, 2006.

Frantz-Murphy, Gladys. "A Comparison of the Arabic and Earlier Egyptian Contract Formularies. Part 1: the Arab Contracts from Egypt (3rd/9th–5th/11th Centuries)." *Journal of Near Eastern Studies* 40, no. 1–2 (1981): 203–225, 355–356.

Frantz-Murphy, Gladys. *Corpus Papyrorum Raineri XXI. Arabic Agricultural Leases and Tax Receipts from Egypt 148–427 AH/765–1035 AD*. Vienna: Brüder Hollinek, 2001.

Frantz-Murphy, Gladys. "The Economics of State Formation in Early Islamic Egypt." In *From al-Andalus to Khurasan. Documents from the Medieval Muslim World*, edited by Petra M. Sijpesteijn, Lennart Sundelin, Sofia T. Tovar and Amalia Zomeño, 101–114. Leiden: Brill, 2006.

Hinds, Martin, and Hamdi Sakkout. "A Letter from the Governor of Egypt to the King of Nubia and Muqurra Concerning Egyptian-Nubian Relations in 141/758." In *Studia Arabica et Islamica. Festschrift for Ihsan 'Abbas on his Sixtieth Birthday*, edited by Ihsan Abbas, Wadad al-Qadi, Ramzi Baalbaki and Peter Bachmann, 202–229. Beirut: American University of Beirut, 1981.

Ibn Yunus (d. 347/958). *Ta'rikh Ibn Yunus al-Sadafi*. Edited by 'A.F. 'Abd al-Fattah. Beirut: Dar al-Kutub al-'Ilmiyya, 2000.

Juynboll, Gautier H.A. *Muslim Tradition. Studies in Chronology, Provenance and Authorship of Early Hadith.* Cambridge: Cambridge University Press, 1983.

Kasassbeh, Hussein F.S. *The Office of Qāḍī in the Early ʿAbbāsid Caliphate (132–247/750–861).* PhD diss., School of Oriental and African Studies, 1990.

Kennedy, Hugh. "Central Government and Provincial Élites in the Early ʿAbbāsid Caliphate." *Bulletin of the School of Oriental and African Studies* 44 (1981): 26–38.

Kennedy, Hugh. "Egypt as a Province in the Islamic Caliphate, 641–868." In *The Cambridge History of Egypt. Volume 1: Islamic Egypt, 640–1517*, edited by Carl F. Petry, 62–85. Cambridge: Cambridge University Press, 2008.

Khan, Geoffrey. "The Pre-Islamic Background of Muslim Legal Formularies." *ARAM* 6 (1994): 193–224.

Khan, Geoffrey. "Newly Discovered Arabic Documents from Early Abbasid Khurasan." In *From al-Andalus to Khurasan. Documents from the Medieval Muslim World*, edited by Petra M. Sijpesteijn, Lennart Sundelin, Sofia T. Tovar, and Amalia Zomeño, 199–216. Leiden: Brill, 2006.

al-Kindi (d. 350/961). *Kitab al-Wulat wa-Kitab al-Qudat.* E.J.W. Gibb Memorial Series 19, edited by R. Guest, *The Governors and Judges of Egypt.* Leiden: Brill, 1912.

Lev, Yaacov. "Coptic Rebellions and the Islamization of Medieval Egypt (8th–10th Century): Medieval and Modern Perceptions." *Jerusalem Studies in Arabic and Islam* 39 (2012): 303–344.

Mikhail, Maged S.A. *From Byzantine to Islamic Egypt: Religion, Identity and Politics after the Arab Conquest.* London/New York: I.B. Tauris, 2014.

Morimoto, Kosei. *The Fiscal Administration of Egypt in the Early Islamic Period.* Kyoto: Dohosha, 1981.

Adolf Grohmann. *Arabic Papyri in the Egyptian Library III.* Cairo: Egyptian Library Press, 1938.

Severus of El Ashmunein (Hermopolis). *History of the Patriarchs of the Coptic Church of Alexandria. Volume 4: Menas I to Joseph (849)*, Arabic text edited, translated, and annotated by B. Evetts. *Patrologia Orientalis* 10 (1910): 359–551.

Sijpesteijn, Petra M. "Arabic Papyri and Islamic Egypt." In *The Oxford Handbook of Papyrology*, edited by R.S. Bagnall, 452–472. Oxford: Oxford University Press, 2009.

Sijpesteijn, Petra M. "Seals and Papyri from Early Islamic Egypt." In *Seals and Sealing Practices in the Near East. Developments in Administration and Magic from Prehistory to the Islamic Period. Proceedings of an International Workshop at the Netherlands-Flemish Institute in Cairo on December 2–3, 2009.*" Edited by I. Regulski, K. Duistermaat and P. Verkinderen. Louvain: Peeters, 2012.

Sijpesteijn, Petra M. *Shaping a Muslim State: The World of a Mid-Eighth-Century Egyptian Official.* Oxford: Oxford University Press, 2013.

Simonsohn, Uriel. *A Common Justice: The Legal Allegiances of Christians and Jews under Early Islam.* Philadelphia: University of Pennsylvania Press, 2011.

al-Tabari (d. 310/923), Muhammad ibn Jarir. *Tarikh al-Rusul wa-l-Muluk*. Edited by Michael J. de Goeje et al. 3 vols. Leiden: Brill, 1879–1901.

Tillier, Mathieu. *Vies des cadis de Miṣr 237/851–366/976*. Cairo: Institut français d'archéologie orientale, 2002.

Tillier, Mathieu. "*Qāḍī*-s and the Political Use of the Maẓālim Jurisidiction under the ʿAbbāsids." In *Public Violence in Islamic Societies: Power, Discipline and the Construction of the Public Sphere, 7th–18th Centuries CE*, edited by C. Lange and M. Fierro, 42–66. Edinburgh: Edinburgh University Press, 2009.

Tillier, Mathieu. *Les cadis d'Iraq et l'État abbasside (132/750–334/945)*. Damascus: Presses de l'Institut français du Proche-Orient, 2009.

Tillier, Mathieu. "Les "premiers" cadis de Fustat et les dynamiques régionales de l'innovation judiciaire (750–833)." *Annales Islamologiques* 45 (2011): 213–242.

Tillier, Mathieu. "Scribes et enquêteurs : note sur le personnel judiciaire en Égypte aux quatre premiers siècles de l'hégire." *Journal of the Social and Economic History of the Orient* 54, no. 3 (2011): 370–404.

Tillier, Mathieu. "The Qāḍīs of Fustat-Miṣr under the Ṭūlūnids and the Ikhshīdids: The Judiciary and the Egyptian Autonomy." *Journal of the American Oriental Society* 131, no. 2 (2011): 207–222.

Tillier, Mathieu. *Histoire des Cadis Égyptiens Aḫbār quḍāt Miṣr*. Cairo: Institut français d'archéologie orientale, 2012.

Tillier, Mathieu. "Du pagarque au cadi : ruptures et continuités dans l'administration judiciaire de la Haute-Égypte (Ier–IIIe/VIe–IXe siècle)." *Médiévales* 64 (2013): 19–36.

Tillier, Mathieu. "Deux papyrus judiciaires de Fusṭāṭ (IIe/VIIIe siècle)." *Chronique d'Egypte* 89 (2014): 412–445.

CHAPTER 4

The Mahdi's Legal Opinion as an Instrument of Reform

Issues in Divorce, Inheritance, False Accusation of Unlawful Intercourse and Homicide

Aharon Layish

Introduction[1]

Muhammad Ahmad b. ʿAbdallah (1844–85) headed, as a self-proclaimed Mahdi, a millenarian, revival and reformist movement in Islam in the late nineteenth century, strongly inspired by Salafi ideas and Sufi traditions that formed the social and intellectual background of his formative period.[2] The Mahdi's vision was to restore the theocracy of the Prophet Muhammad and the "Righteous Caliphs" in Sudan. He claimed legitimacy on the grounds of being a successor to Muhammad, his ability to communicate with him, and his infallibility and moral authority. The Mahdi nominated successors to the orthodox caliphs, governors, military commanders and judges (qadis). Adherents to the Mahdiyya had to take a pledge of allegiance (*bayʿa*) entailing a commitment to

1 This paper is part of a comprehensive study entitled "Revival of Islamic Law in the Late 19th-Century Sudan: The Mahdi's Legal Methodology and Its Application" (in progress) based on the Mahdi's documents. I am most grateful to the late Prof. P.M. Holt who graciously placed his personal collection of the Mahdi's documents at my disposal during my sabbatical stay in Oxford in 1993. I am indebted to Ruud Peters of the University of Amsterdam for allowing me to consult in manuscript form chapters on Islamic family law (see bibl.). Gaby Warburg has initiated me into Sudanese studies and was very helpful in various ways for which he deserves my sincere thanks. Eliyahu Stern and David Powers read the annotated translations of the Mahdi's documents and made generous comments and suggestions for which I am most grateful. I am also indebted to Maaike van Berkel, Léon Buskens, Petra Sijpesteijn and Annemarie van Sandwijk for their substantive comments and editorial assistance. The research is supported by a grant from the Israel Science Foundation.

2 Aharon Layish, "The Sudanese Mahdi's Legal Methodology and Its Sufi Inspiration," *Jerusalem Studies in Arabic and Islam*, Special Issue in Honor of Yohanan Friedmann 33 (2007): 279–308.

 | DOI 10.1163/9789004343733_006

refrain from polytheism, offenses of the Qur'an and evading jihad, along with devotion to asceticism.[3]

The idea of Mahdism had manifested itself in Sudan as early as the seventeenth century. The Mahdist movement was motivated by eschatological expectations whose source of inspiration can be traced to Egypt in the 18th and 19th centuries.[4] In its initial stages the Mahdiyya had many of the characteristics of a social and political protest movement. Its main causes were the conquest of Sudan by Egypt under Muhammad 'Ali and the annexation of the former sultanate of Darfur by Egypt in 1874; the replacement, by the Turco-Egyptian régime, of the indigenous religious functionaries with orthodox 'ulama' imported from Egypt; and the attempts to put an end to the slave trade, contrary to Sudanese vested interests. Muhammad Ahmad's manifestation as the "Expected (*muntaẓar*) Mahdi" took place in the Egyptian Sudan in 1881. He overthrew the Turco-Egyptian régime and established instead a territorial state.[5]

The Mahdi did not leave behind any legal treatise in which he presents his reformist legal methodology. In this paper an attempt will be made to reconstruct this methodology on the basis of his legal documents issued for practical purposes in the course of his struggle to consolidate his new state. He left more than a thousand documents: legal opinions (fatwa, *jawāb*), decisions or rulings (*ḥukm*) and proclamations (*manshūr*) on an extremely broad range of administrative, political, religious, social and legal matters. In addition, "sayings" (*qawl*) – that is, traditions, and statements made in instructional sessions (*majlis*) – were attributed to him after his death. The documents were originally written in lithographic print. Over the years several editions of the documents were published, the last edition, *al-Athar al-Kamila li-l-Imam al-Mahdi*, consisting of seven volumes, appeared between 1990 and 1994.[6]

---

3 Muhammad Ibrahim Abu Salim, ed., *Al-Athar al-Kamila li-l-Imam al-Mahdi* (Khartoum: Dar Jami'at al-Khartum li-l-Nashr, 1992), 5: 13, 108. Cf. Peter M. Holt, *The Mahdist State in the Sudan, 1881–1898* (Oxford: Clarendon Press, 1970), 115, 117.

4 On the Mahdist idea and its connection to the Shi'a, see Holt, *The Mahdist State*, 22ff. Cf. Ahmad Ibrahim Abu Shuk, "Minhajiyyat al-Tashri' al-Mahdawi fi 'l-Sudan (1881–1885)," *Kitabat Sudaniyya* 9, Markaz al-Dirasat al-Sudaniyya, March 1999, 19, col. i.

5 Holt, *The Mahdist State*, 19ff.; P.M. Holt, "al-Mahdiyya," in *Encyclopaedia of Islam*, 2nd ed. (Leiden: Brill, 1986), 1247ff.; P.M. Holt & M.W. Daly, *The History of the Sudan from the Coming of Islam to the Present Day*. 3rd ed. (Boulder, Colorado: Westview Press, 1979), 87f.; Kim Searcy, *The Formation of the Sudanese Mahdist State, Ceremony and Symbols of Authority: 1882–1898*. (Leiden: Brill, 2010), 21–24.

6 For further detail, see R.S. O'Fahey (with the assistance of Muhammad Ibrahim Abu Salim, Albrecht Hofheinz, Yahya Muhammad Ibrahim, Bernd Radtke and Knut S. Vikør), *Arabic*

Some important contributions have been written on various aspects of the Mahdi's legal methodology; but no comprehensive, systematic research on this methodology and its application has so far been carried out on the basis of the entire corpus of the Mahdi's documents. Muhammad Ibrahim Abu Salim, the leading authority on the Mahdi's documents, who edited some of these editions, wrote instructive and useful introductions and annotations to the volumes with special reference to matters of law. Ahmad Ibrahim Abu Shuk wrote an important essay (see bibl.) in which he concentrates on the Mahdi's legal methodology and illustrates its application on the basis of some of his documents. P.M. Holt, the leading authority on the Mahdiyya, conducted extensive research on the political, religious and social history of the Mahdist state on the basis of these documents (see bibl.). Holt was concerned with the role of the Mahdi as a reformist legislator aiming to accommodate the shari'a to the changing political and social circumstances, and in this context he drew attention to the Mahdi's legal methodology. Haim Shaked's work on the biography of the Mahdi (see bibl.) concentrates mainly on the Mahdi as the initiator of a fundamentalist movement. Within this context such issues as the Mahdi's infallibility and observation of the Qur'an and the sunna come up for discussion. Al-Hasan b. Sa'd b. Muhammad al-'Abbadi (see bibl.) provides important information, in a rather polemical manner, on the Madhi's qualifications for *ijtihād*, his status as infallible (*maʿṣūm min al-khaṭa'*) legislator and his direct inspiration (*ilhām*) from the Prophet Muhammad.

The Judiciary and 'Ulama' in the Mahdist State

The Turco-Egyptian administration introduced the *sharʿī* legal system in Sudan. Although the Maliki school was the dominant school in the country,[7] the shari'a courts applied the Hanafi school. Egyptian 'ulama' were brought from Egypt and Sudanese students were trained in al-Azhar. The emergence of a class of trained 'ulama' threatened in the long run the prestige of the older *fakī*[8] class.[9] Most of the Egyptian-oriented 'ulama' did not cooperate with Muhammad Ahmad. They strongly criticized him for pretending to be the Expected Mahdi,

---

Literature of Africa, Vol. 1: The Writings of Eastern Sudanic Africa to c. 1900 (Leiden: E.J. Brill, 1994), 268ff.

7 Muhammad Ibrahim Abu Salim, *Buhuth fi Ta'rikh al-Sudan* (Beirut: Dar al-Jil, 1412/1992), 29.

8 *Fakī* is a dialect-form of *faqīh*, a religious teacher who propagates Islam in Sudan. See Holt, *The Mahdist State*, 18.

9 Ibid., 22.

a pretension that challenged the legitimacy of the Ottoman Sultan and his representative, the Egyptian Khedive.[10] Moreover, they could not tolerate the Mahdi's deviation from conventional Islamic legal methodology and *fiqh*, his denial of the schools of law[11] and the 'ulama''s historic role as the authoritative interpreters of the will of God. Further, they disqualified him as an *'ālim* capable of exercising *ijtihād*. The Mahdi reacted by excluding these 'ulama' from the elect community of his followers by stigmatizing them as unbelievers and by proclaiming them to be venal 'ulama' (*'ulamā' al-sū'*).[12]

The Mahdi delegated power to the caliphs, provincial governors, military commanders and commissioners; all were authorized to act as judges.[13] A so-called Qadi al-Islam, an office introduced by the Mahdi, headed the judiciary. He appointed *nuwwāb* (substitute qadis) subject to the Mahdi's approval. Judicial boards composed of three or four qadis functioned all over the Mahdist state.[14]

The Mahdi's Legal Methodology

The Mahdi promoted a unique legal methodology[15] providing him with unlimited authority to enact positive rules without any institutional restrictions on the part of the orthodox 'ulama'. He ignored all schools of law (*madhāhib*)

10 Ibid., 107ff. (the manifestos of Shakir al-Ghazzi and Ahmad al-Azhari b. Isma'il); Rudolph Peters, "Islam and the Legitimation of Power: The Mahdi-Revolt in the Sudan," in *Deutscher Orientalistentag* 21 (Berlin, März 1980): Ausgewählte Vorträge. Hrsg. von F. Steppat. (Wiesbaden, 1983) (ZDMG, Suppl., V), 412ff., 417ff., 419; 'Abdallah 'Ali Ibrahim, *Al-Sira' Bayna al-Mahdi wa'l-'Ulama'*. 2nd ed. (Cairo: Dar Nubar li'l-Tiba'a, 1994), 58 (referring to the anti-Mahdist mani *The Formation of the Sudanese Mahdist State* festo of Ahmad al-Azhari, the Mufti and Chief Judge of western Egyptian Sudan); Searcy, *The Sudanese Mahdist State*, 78–79.

11 Muhammad Ibrahim Abu Salim, *Al-Haraka al-Fikriyya fi al-Mahdiyya*, 3rd ed. (Khartoum: Matba'at Jami'at al-Khartum, 1989), 77; Ibrahim, *Al-Sira'*, 44. Cf. Holt, *The Mahdist State*, 210, fn. 2.

12 Abu Salim, ed., *Al-Athar al-Kamila*, 6: 183–84. Cf. Holt, *The Mahdist State*, 116; Abu Salim, *Al-Haraka al-Fikriyya*, 50, 168.

13 Holt, *The Mahdist State*, 132.

14 Husayn Sayyid Ahmad al-Mufti, *Tatawwur Nizam al-Qada' fi al-Sudan*, Part 1 (Khartoum: Matba'at Misr, 1378/1959), 130–33; Holt, *The Mahdist State*, 22, 131–32.

15 For a general review of the Mahdi's legal methodology, see Aharon Layish, "The Legal Methodology of the Mahdi in the Sudan, 1881–1885: Issues in Marriage and Divorce," *Sudanic Africa* 8 (1997): 37–66; Layish, "The Sudanese Mahdi's Legal Methodology and Its Sufi Inspiration," 279–308.

thus releasing himself from the burden of *taqlīd*, i.e., the positive law as consolidated by these schools. He acknowledged three sources of law: the Qur'an, prophetic sunna, and the inspiration (*ilhām*) communicated to him by the Prophet Muhammad. In terms of order of priority, the prophetic sunna may precede the Qur'an to the extent that the former can abrogate (*naskh*) the latter.[16] In the Mahdi's legal methodology, inspiration communicated by the Prophet replaces both the *qiyās*, systematic analogy from the textual sources, and the *ijmā'*, consensus of the *fuqahā'*. There is ample evidence in the Mahdi's documents to suggest that the Sufi orders (*tarīqas*) made a profound impact on him. The documents contain references to Sufi traditions to which the Mahdi had been exposed during various stages of his life and to mediators that may have served as links between the Mahdi and the doctrines of the founders of the *tarīqas*. Sufi concepts and ideas had a tremendous influence on the formulation of the Mahdi's legal methodology. Sufi figures, such as 'Abd al-Qadir al-Jilani (d. 561/1166) and Ibn al-'Arabi (d. 638/1240) participated in prophetic colloquies.[17]

There is isolated evidence in the Mahdi's documents of an unsophisticated concept of *maṣlaḥa*, public interest, as an auxiliary source for deriving law. Thus he proclaims: "We shall compile for you [instructions pertaining to state affairs] in accordance with what is required by the welfare of religion" (*nuḥarrir bi-mā taqtaḍīhi maṣlaḥat al-dīn*).[18] Moreover, the Mahdi argues that the procedure of abrogation of contradictory textual sources should be guided in light of *maṣlaḥa*:

> [Qur'anic] verses were abrogated (*tunsakhu*) during the time of the Prophet ... on account of the people's welfare (*'alā ḥasab maṣāliḥ al-khalq*). Likewise, hadiths [may] abrogate each other [today] on account of public welfare.[19]

The concept of *maṣlaḥa* in the Mahdi's documents is not connected in any way to the mechanism of deriving law by means of analogical reasoning that

---

16 See, e.g., Muhammad Ibrahim Abu Salim, ed., *Manshurat al-Imam al-Mahdi*. Vol. 3. *Al-Ahkam wa-l-Adab* (Khartoum: Idarat al-Mahfuzat al-Markaziyya, Wizarat al-Dakhiliyya, 1964), 101; Muhammad Ibrahim Abu Salim, ed., *Manshurat al-Mahdiyya* (Khartoum: Matba'at Jami'at al-Khartum, 1969), 227; Abu Salim, ed., *Al-Athar al-Kamila*, 5: 96.

17 For a detailed account of the impact of Sufism on the Mahdi's legal methodology, see Aharon Layish, *Revival of Islamic Law in the Late 19th-Century Sudan*, ch. 11.6.

18 Abu Salim, ed., *Al-Athar al-Kamila*, 5: 36, 42.

19 Ibid., 4: 417.

is totally ignored by the Mahdi. No reference is made to the role of *maṣlaḥa* in determining the suitability (*munāsaba*), a method required for establishing and verifying the reasoning of deriving law (*ʿilla, ratio legis*).[20]

Necessity (*ḍarūra*), which is a nuance of *maṣlaha*, renders permissible something which under normal circumstances is prohibited under the shariʿa with a view to avoiding harm (*ḍarar*), which is in itself another manifestation of *maṣlaḥa*. In an interpretation of Q. 5:3, as attributed to the Mahdi, he maintains:

> The exceptional eight sorts of food mentioned previously in the verse are lawfully permitted on the grounds of necessity (*taḥillu li-l-ḍarūra*) and he [the believer] may provide himself with these [prohibited sorts of food] until he manages to dispense with them.[21]

Finally, the term *yusr*, "ease" or "easiness," another variant of *maṣlaḥa*, is applied as a guiding principle in the Mahdi's legal methodology in the spirit of a hadith: "Make it easy and do not make it difficult" (*yassirū wa-lā tuʿassirū*).[22]

The Mahdi sought to deprive the ʿulama' of their historic role as the exclusive interpreters of the will of God. He did not exercise *ijtihād* in the conventional sense of the term. In the event of a lacuna in the textual sources, he would resort, after having exhausted the avenues of interpretation of the sources and the technique of abrogation, to a colloquy (*ḥaḍra*) with Muhammad for deriving the rule necessary for solving specific legal problems. The Mahdi, however, strongly denied the ʿulama''s allegations that he was a *mujtahid*.[23]

The following case illustrates the process of deriving a new law. The Mahdi was asked to issue a legal opinion as to whether a *khulʿ* divorce should be counted as one of the three repudiations after which an intermediate marriage is required in order for the man to legally remarry his ex-wife. The Mahdi concluded his fatwa by saying:

---

20 Cf. Wael B. Hallaq, *Islamic Legal Theories* (Cambridge: Cambridge University Press, 1997), 112.

21 Abu Salim, ed., *Al-Athar al-Kamila*, 7: 24. Cf. Wael B. Hallaq, *Shariʿa: Theory, Practice, Transformations* (Cambridge: Cambridge University Press, 2009), 427, 447; *The Qur'an*. Hebrew translation from the Arabic, annotations, appendices and index by Uri Rubin (Tel Aviv: Tel Aviv University Press and MAPA Publishers, 2005), 90 fn. 3; al-Hasan b. Saʿd b. Muhammad al-ʿAbbadi, *Al-Anwar al-Saniyya al-Mahiya li-Zalam al-Munkirin ʿalā al-Ḥadra al-Mahdiyya* (Omdurman: 1305/1887), 233 (necessity, *ḍarūra*, as an auxiliary source for *ijtihād*).

22 Abu Salim, ed., *Al-Athar al-Kamila*, 4: 462.

23 Ibid., 2: 183.

> I render my decision according to neither my personal legal reasoning [*ra'y*] nor my *ijtihād*; [rather, I decide] on the basis of what I find in the sunna and the book [Qur'an; and – in the event of a lacuna in the textual sources – I decide] in accordance with the inspiration (*ilhām*) that the Messenger of Allah, God bless him and grant him salvation, enlightens [me].[24]

A good notion of the Mahdi's qualifications as a *mujtahid* on the other hand may be derived from a treatise written by al-Hasan b. Saʿd al-ʿAbbadi (d. 1907), one of the Mahdi's closest companions whom he commissioned with administrative and religious tasks throughout the country.[25] Al-ʿAbbadi's treatise is a reply on behalf of the Mahdi against the ʿulama' who refuted his legal methodology and disqualified him for *ijtihād* and mahdiship.[26] Al-ʿAbbadi claims that the Mahdi ranks higher than a conventional *mujtahid* because he derives rules, in cases of doubt in the textual sources, by means of prophetic inspiration; hence the Mahdi is infallible (*maʿṣūm min al-khaṭa'*). Inspiration communicated by the Prophet makes personal reasoning (*ra'y*) or analogy (*qiyās*) redundant. Moreover, the Mahdi is exempt from the requirement to avail himself of the ordinary qualifications for *ijtihād* except for sanity (*ʿaql*), legal majority (*bulūgh*) and apprehension of the inner meanings (*fahm al-maʿānī*) communicated to him by Muhammad. Though the Mahdi may lack linguistic qualifications, he enjoys piety (*taqwā*) which is no less important than acquisition of the *sharʿī* sciences. The direct inspiration from Muhammad, as well as the Mahdi's status as Muhammad's successor (*khalīfa*) and his manifestation (*ẓuhūr*) as the "Expected Mahdi," legitimize his pretension to exercise *ijtihād*.[27]

The Mahdi's legal methodology provided him with almost unlimited authority to introduce far-reaching reforms in the shariʿa, outside the control of the ʿulama', which allowed him to achieve his political, social and economic goals. In what follows, a small sample of the Mahdi's legal opinions and rulings may provide some notion of the application of his legal methodology and innovative reforms in various domains of law.

---

24 Ibid., 3: 119; for an analysis of this fatwa, see below.

25 Abu Salim, *al-Haraka al-Fikriyya*, 65; Abu Salim, ed., *Al-Athar al-Kamila*, 5: 267–268.

26 Muhammad Ibrahim Abū Salim. *Al-ʿAlim al-Mujahid al-Hasan Saʿd al-ʿAbbadi. Safha min Khilaf al-ʿUlama' hawla al-Mahdiyya wa-Imara fi 'l-ʿAtabay* [unpublished MS], 66.

27 Ibid., 233, 235, 236, 239.

Khulʿ Does Not Count in the Quota for Intermediate Marriage

Khulʿ is a mode of dissolution of the marriage by mutual consent of the spouses for compensation (such as the nuptial gift) given to the husband. It is based on Q. 2:229 which allows the wife to redeem herself by compensating the husband as well as on a hadith based on the authority of Ibn ʿAbbas (d. 68/686–8). *Khulʿ* entails an irrevocable repudiation (*ṭalāq bāʾin*).[28] Under traditional shariʿa, after the third repudiation – whether revocable (*rajʿī*), which enables the husband to reinstate his wife during the waiting period without concluding a new marriage contract or irrevocable, which becomes operative immediately with all attendant legal effects – a divorced woman cannot be legally restored to her former husband unless she has married another man, that marriage has been dissolved and the waiting period (*ʿidda*) has been observed.[29] Ibn Taymiyya (d. 728/1328) maintains, on the strength of the authority of Ibn ʿAbbas, that *khulʿ* constitutes a *dissolution* (*faskh*) rather than irrevocable *repudiation*,[30] implying thereby that a woman divorced by *khulʿ* can be restored to her former husband without resorting to intermediate marriage.

In the case under review, the Mahdi is asked for a legal opinion as to whether a *khulʿ* constitutes a repudiation that should be taken into account within the quota of three divorces after which an intermediate marriage is required. The man asking the legal opinion (*mustaftī*) presumes that if *khulʿ* is not taken into account as a regular repudiation, then the divorced woman can be restored to her divorcing husband by a new marriage contract without having recourse

28 Rudolph Peters, "Islamic Family Law," University of Amsterdam, Department of Arabic Studies. Amsterdam, 1995 (unpublished), § 0.1.5.1.6.2, 0.1.5.2; ʿAbd al-Karim Zaydan, *Al-Mufassal fi Ahkam al-Marʾa wa-l-Bayt al-Muslim fi al-Shariʿa al-Islamiyya* (Beirut: Muʾassasat al-Risala, 1413/1993), 8: § 7824ff., 7830 (references to the hadith based on Ibn ʿAbbas), 8090ff. and the references there to the legal treatises; Muhammad Mustafa Shalabi, *Ahkam al-Usra fi al-Islam. Dirasa Muqarana bayn Fiqh al-Madhahib al-Sunniyya wa-l-Madhhab al-Jaʿfari wa-l-Qanun* (Beirut: Dar al-Nahda al-ʿArabiyya, 1393/1973), 530ff., 552f.; Hallaq, *Shariʿa*, 283–86.

29 Peters, "Islamic Family Law," § 0.1.5.1.3, 0.1.5.1.6; Hallaq, *Shariʿa*, 280ff.; Shalabi, *Ahkam al-Usra*, 489–91, 498ff. On intermediate marriage by means of *al-muḥallil min al-ṭalāq*, see Shalabi, *Ahkam al-Usra*, 511ff.; Zaydan, *Al-Mufassal*, 6: § 5648ff. Cf. Aharon Layish, *Women and Islamic Law in a Non-Muslim State. A Study Based on the Decisions of the Shariʿa Courts in Israel* (New York: John Wiley and Jerusalem: Israel Universities Press, 1975), 132, 173–75.

30 See Zaydan, *Al-Mufassal*, 8: § 8107–8. Cf. Hallaq, *Shariʿa*, 284; D.S. Powers, *Law, Society, and Culture in the Maghrib, 1300–1500* (Cambridge: Cambridge University Press, 2002), 70–71; Chafik Chehata, "Faskh," in *Encyclopaedia of Islam*, 2nd ed. (Leiden: Brill, 1965), 836.

to intermediate marriage. He derives support from Ibn ʿAbbas on this issue. In his legal opinion, the Mahdi rules as follows:

> I am referring to your question regarding someone who divorced his wife by *khulʿ* after having divorced her [previously] twice by [ordinary utterance of] repudiation (*ṭallaqahā marratayn*). [The question at stake is:] Does *khulʿ* constitute [in terms of legal consequences] a repudiation (*ṭalqa*) or rather [divorce that counts as] non-existence [i.e., the *khulʿ* does not count as repudiation] in which [the latter] case he [i.e., the divorcing husband] may restore her [his divorced wife] without resorting to another husband [i.e., intermediate marriage] (*hal yuʿaddu ka-l-ʿadam wa-yurājiʿuhā bi-dūn zawj*) on the strength of a view related on the authority of (*ruwiya ʿan*) Ibn ʿAbbas, or [alternatively, if *khulʿ* is counted as repudiation, then the husband] may not [restore his wife without intermediate marriage]?
>
> My opinion is in the affirmative (*aqūl naʿam*) [that is, that *khulʿ* does not constitute repudiation] if he [the husband] did not utter [while pronouncing *khulʿ*] the expression *ṭalāq*; if he did utter the expression *ṭalāq* along with the expression *khulʿ*, then [the wife] is not legally permissible to him unless an intermediate marriage has taken place (*lā taḥill lahu illā baʿda zawj*).[31]

The Mahdi seems to have been inspired by Ibn ʿAbbas probably because he belonged to the generation of Muhammad and due to his reputation as "the father of the Qur'anic exegesis."[32] The Mahdi may have also been motivated by the desire to diminish the harsh consequences of three divorces thus exempting both the wife and the husband, in the event of a hasty *khulʿ* agreement, from the distress of intermediate marriage.

Widow of a Martyr Takes the Entire Estate as Charity

Broadly speaking, the Sunni law of inheritance consists of two distinct categories of legal heirs: The Qur'anic heirs who take their prescribed portions (*ahl al-farāʾiḍ*) and the male agnates (*ʿaṣaba*), in a specific order of ascendants

---

31 Abu Salim, ed., *Al-Athar al-Kamila*, 3: 119. For a lithographic version of the document, see Abu Salim, ed., *Manshurat al-Imam al-Mahdi*. Vol. 3. *Al-Aḥkam wa-l-Adab*, 69–70.

32 L. Veccia Vaglieri, "ʿAbd Allāh b. al-ʿAbbās," in *Encyclopaedia of Islam*, 2nd ed. (Leiden: Brill, 1960), 40.

and descendants, who take the rest of the estate (the residuary heirs). Only in the absence of blood relatives of these two categories does the inheritance belong to the "outer family" or "cognates" (*dhawū al-arḥām*), relatives that are neither Qur'anic heirs nor male agnates. The category of the outer family is not recognized by the Maliki school. Hence, in the absence of legal heirs of the first two categories the Public Treasury (*bayt al-māl*) takes the entire estate as a residuary heir.[33]

Under traditional shariʿa, in the presence of a "descendant" (*walad*), i.e., a child or agnatic grandchild in the descending line, a wife (one of twelve Qur'anic heirs) takes one-eighth of the estate whereas in the absence of a "descendant," she takes one-quarter.[34] The Maliki school does not recognize the doctrine of *radd*, i.e., the right of the Qur'anic heirs to benefit from the residue of the estate after they have taken their prescribed portions and there are no male agnatic heirs. Under all three of the other Sunni schools only the wife and the husband, unlike other Qur'anic heirs, are barred from *radd*.[35]

The Qur'anic inheritance verses Q. 4:11–12 deal with the prescribed portions of the Qur'anic heirs, such as a husband and a wife, daughters, parents and brothers in the presence or absence of male agnatic heirs. Thus in the absence of a son, two daughters and more take two-thirds of the estate and one daughter takes one-half. A son converts a daughter into *ʿaṣaba* or residuary heir by virtue of the principle of *taʿṣīb* and takes twice as much as a daughter. These verses were revealed to Muhammad after the widow of the martyr Saʿd b. al-Rabiʿ (d. 625 AD) complained to him that her daughters' paternal uncle had taken possession of her husband's entire estate. She further complained that her daughters could not marry unless they had property. According to a hadith, Muhammad called Saʿd b. al-Rabiʿ's brother, i.e., the paternal uncle of the daughters, and said to him: "Give Saʿd's two daughters two-thirds of his property, give his wife one-eighth, and you take whatever remains." The case is discussed in *asbāb al-nuzūl*, lit. "the occasions or circumstances of the revelation," a genre of literature, which deals with the occasions or circumstances of the revelation of Qur'anic verses.[36]

33 For a detailed, systematic description of the inheritance law, see N.J. Coulson, *Succession in the Muslim Family* (Cambridge: Cambridge University Press, 1971). For a concise description, see Hallaq, *Shariʿa*, 289–95.

34 Zaydan, *Al-Mufassal*, 11: § 12185ff.; Coulson, *Succession*, 41, 49–51.

35 Coulson, *Succession*, 49–51.

36 For further discussion, see Coulson, *Succession*, 29–30; D.S. Powers, *Studies in Qur'an and Hadith* (Berkeley and Los Angeles: University of California Press, 1986), 189–190, 195.

In the case under review, Zaynab bint Ahmad Muhammad Sharaf, a widow of ʿAbdallah Sharaf, a martyr (*shahīd*) who died in a battle against the "infidel" Turks, complained to the Mahdi that she had been given in marriage against her will. She was probably taken as a captive by one of the *Ikhwān* or the *Anṣār*, the Mahdi's followers.[37] The Mahdi dissolved the marriage, probably on behalf of the husband (*taṭlīq*) and on that occasion referred to the widow's rights in her late husband's estate:

> I warn you [i.e., the man who contracted the second marriage] not to interfere with any of [the widow's] rights, especially those pertaining to the estate of her [late] husband ʿAbdallah Sharaf who was killed as a martyr; we left to her [the entire estate] as charity from us (*taraknāhā lahā iḥsānan minnā ilayhā*).[38]

The Mahdi's document does not indicate whether the martyr left any legal heirs other than his widow. Had he left any male agnatic heir [such as children], he would have – after the widow had taken her prescribed Qurʾanic portion – exhausted the residue of the estate. Had the widow been the only legal heir, the Public Treasury as a residuary heir would have taken the remainder of the estate. Neither is there any reference in the document to the doctrine of *radd* in the event that the widow was the only legal heir or when there were other Qurʾanic heirs besides her, but no male agnatic heirs; in neither case would the widow have benefited from the *radd*. As mentioned above, according to all schools of law with the exception of the Maliki school, Qurʾanic heirs other than the widow would have benefited from the *radd*.

As a gesture of gratitude for the martyr's contribution to the cause of the Mahdiyya the Mahdi offered the widow the *entire* estate although as a matter of law she was only entitled to her Qurʾanic portion. Had the widow been the only legal heir this gesture would have been at the expense of the Public Treasury as a residuary heir. Had there been other heirs besides the widow this gesture would have been at their expense. In any case, the gesture toward

---

37 See Abu Salim, ed., *Al-Athar al-Kamila*, 4: 286–87 where the Mahdi warns the Anṣār not to marry free women, whether married or unmarried, who were residing in military camps in Turco-Egyptian territory. He refers to cases of abduction.

38 Abu Salim, ed., *Al-Athar al-Kamila*, 4: 473. Cf. Ibid., 2: 94. For a lithographic version of the document, see Durham University library, SAD 97/5/17, col. i; *Manshurat al-Imam al-Mahdi fi al-Ḥudud wa-Ghayriha min al-Ahkam* (London: The School of Oriental and African Studies, accession no. 101493 [File DG.L.VII.416.2]), 45, 57–58.

the martyr's widow served the Mahdi's political and social agenda: promoting jihad and improving women's status.

The circumstance or *sabab* of the revelation of the Qur'anic verses, that is, the personal appeal to Muhammad by the widow of Sa'd b. al-Rabi' and the latter's decision to divide the estate in a manner that was compatible with the special conditions of the case, could have inspired the Mahdi in the case under review. However, whereas Muhammad's gesture to the widow was transformed into law within the framework of the Qur'anic inheritance verses, there is no evidence in the Mahdi's documents to the effect that the Mahdi's gesture of generosity became a binding precedent. Although there is no explicit reference to the case of the widow of Sa'd b. al-Rabi' in the Mahdi's decision, there is good reason to believe that the Mahdi was fully aware of the *sabab* of the revelation of the Qur'anic verses. Hence, the possibility that the Mahdi attempted to create the impression that he was acting under circumstances similar to those of Muhammad in order to justify his deviation from the Qur'anic verses cannot be ruled out.

A Widow's Waiting-Period Maintenance Out of the Estate

A widow's right to maintenance out of the estate during her waiting period is disputed among the schools. According to the Hanafis, she is entitled to neither maintenance (*nafaqa*) nor a dwelling (*suknā*) out of her deceased husband's estate, regardless of whether she is barren (*ḥā'il*)[39] or pregnant (*ḥāmil*), because the estate belongs to the legal heirs from the moment of its owner's death.

According to the Malikis, the widow is entitled to maintenance (but not to a dwelling) out of the estate, provided she was capable of having sexual relations and the marriage was consummated; if she is not capable of having sexual relations she is not entitled, unless her husband had provided her with a dwelling prior to his death.

According to the dominant view in the Shafi'i school, the widow is entitled to a dwelling (but not to food or clothing) out of the estate, on the strength of a prophetic hadith.

According to the Hanbalis, if the widow is barren she is entitled to neither a dwelling nor maintenance because the marriage ceases to exist at the moment of the husband's death. If the widow is pregnant, there are two views:

39 J.G. Hava, *Al-Fara'id al-Durriyya fi al-Lughatayn al-'Arabiyya wa-l-Inkliziyya* (Beirut: Catholic Press, 1951), 151, col. i.

1) The widow is entitled to both maintenance and a dwelling out of the estate, as if her husband had divorced her while she was pregnant.
2) The widow is entitled to neither maintenance nor a dwelling out of the estate, because the estate belongs to the legal heirs, and they are not required to provide the widow with maintenance or a dwelling during her pregnancy; each heir is expected to cover his/her expenses from his/her share (*naṣīb*) of the estate. This suggests that expenses for maintenance and dwelling should be collected from the share of the widow in the estate or that of the product of her pregnancy.[40]

According to Ibn Hazm al-Zahiri (d. 456/1064), the widow is entitled to neither a dwelling nor maintenance out of the estate, or from any legal heir, under any circumstances, during her waiting period.[41]

In the case under review, Khalifa ʿAli al-Hilu[42] asks the Mahdi for a legal opinion regarding the division of Tatay's estate among his heirs, some of whom reside outside Mahdist territory. Tatay's sons died in battle against the "infidel" Turks. Before they died, they appointed the aforementioned Khalifa as a testamentary executor (*waṣī*) of the property of all their children, including minor children (i.e., Tatay's grandchildren), that is, of their shares in the estate as well as rights (*ḥuqūq*) in other, movable [?] property and in "members of their households" (such as slaves or domestics) (*ahālī buyūtihim*). Since it is not clear whether legal heirs who reside in Turco-Egyptian territory are to be treated as booty (*ghanīma*), the Khalifa asks the Mahdi to clarify the following issues:

1) Regarding the descendants and widows of the martyrs, are both those residing in Mahdist territory and those residing in Turco-Egyptian territory entitled to their shares in the estate?
2) May the waiting-period maintenance of the martyrs' widows be collected out of the estate, that is, before the division of the estate among the heirs?
3) In the event that the widows of the martyrs do not marry after the termination of their waiting period, will they be entitled to maintenance out of the estate?[43]

---

40 A child in embryo who is born alive is deemed a legal heir from the time of its conception. For further details, see Coulson, *Succession*, 204ff.

41 Zaydan, *Al-Mufassal*, 9: § 9559ff.

42 The Mahdi nominated ʿAli b. Muhammad Hilu (ʿAli wad Hilu) as Khalifat al-Faruk (ʿUmar); see Holt, *The Mahdist State*, 116.

43 Abu Salim, ed., *Al-Athar al-Kamila*, 2: 283.

The Mahdi's Legal Opinion

Since the aforementioned *Ikhwān* [those who died in the jihad] were faithful [to the cause of the Mahdiyya], their descendants (*wuld*) present here [in Mahdist territory in control of] their property, and their wives [i.e., widows] are entitled to whatever is found of their property; they may apportion [Tatay's] estate among themselves according to the rules of inheritance prescribed in the Qur'an.

As to the absent [heirs] and the property [in their control outside Mahdist territory], they are treated as absentees (*al-ghā'ib … ka-l-ghā'ib*) until God brings all of them together [in Mahdist territory], whereupon [their property will be handled] in accordance with what is written in the Qur'an and the sunna (*'alā ḥasab al-wārid min allāh wa-rasūlihi*).

The [widows' waiting-period] maintenance is provided out of the aforementioned property [i.e., Tatay's estate] (*wa-nafaqatuhum* [*sic*] *min dhālika al-māl al-madhkūr*). [However,] after the end of their waiting period, they are entitled only to their [portions of the] estate, regardless of whether or not they re-marry.[44]

The Mahdi makes a clear distinction between legal heirs residing in Mahdist territory and those residing in Turco-Egyptian territory. Only the former are entitled to their shares of the estate as prescribed in the Qur'anic inheritance verses. As for those residing in non-Mahdist territory (the absentees), they are temporarily denied their inheritance rights. The term "absentee" (*ghā'ib*) implies a temporary status (rather than legally non-existent heirs, that is, those not counted for the purpose of division of the estate) pending repentance and forgiveness by the Mahdi, that is, until they join the Mahdiyya.[45] Taking into account the martyrs' contribution to the cause of the Mahdiyya, the Mahdi demonstrates willingness to forgive the absentees; once they join the Mahdiyya they will be entitled to their *shar'ī* rights in the estate.[46] However, if they fail to repent they will be excluded from inheritance on the grounds of difference

---

44 Ibid., 2: 284. For a lithographic version of the fatwa, see Abu Salim, ed., *Manshurat al-Imam al-Mahdi.* Vol. 3. *Al-Aḥkam wa-l-Adab*, 35–36.

45 Abu Salim, ed., *Al-Athar al-Kamila*, 5: 35 where the people of the province of Kassala apply for submission to the Mahdiyya after having approached God repentantly asking for a pledge of security for themselves, their children and their property. Cf. Holt, *The Mahdist State*, 59.

46 Cf. Abu Salim, ed., *Al-Athar al-Kamila*, 4: 245 (a man was killed in a Turkish fortified camp in the cause of the Mahdiyya and his property there was confiscated by the Turco-Egyptian commander. The martyr's legal heirs immigrated to Mahdist territory. The Mahdi instructs Khalifa 'Abdallahi to return the martyr's movable property to his heirs

of religion (*ikhtilāf al-dīn*) or apostasy. This implies practically that the legal heirs residing in Mahdist territory will receive their respective shares in Tatay's estate whereas the shares of the absentee heirs will be kept until some future date by the Treasury on their behalf: If they join the Mahdiyya the Treasury will release their respective shares to them; if, however, they fail to join the Mahdiyya their shares will be confiscated forever to the Treasury.

The Mahdi rules that during their waiting period the widows of martyrs are entitled to maintenance, *nafaqa* (without specifying the components of the technical term) *out of the estate, before its apportionment among the legal heirs.* In other words, the Mahdi conceives of the waiting-period maintenance as a debt on the estate that legally must be settled like any other debt, prior to the division of the estate among the legal heirs.[47] He does not suggest, however, any specific interim arrangements until division of the estate takes place. He further contends – unlike some of the Sunni schools – that a widow's right in this regard is not subject to such preconditions as consummation of the marriage or pregnancy. The Mahdi's reform is extremely generous; it contrasts with the view that once the owner of an estate dies his or her property belongs to the legal heirs and each of them takes care of his/her own expenses from his/her own share of the estate. According to the Mahdi, only upon termination of the waiting period is the estate divided among the legal heirs, at which time each widow receives her share of the estate regardless of whether or not she remarries. Again, the Mahdi is eager to secure the widow's economic status, even at the risk that she might marry outside the family and transfer her share in Tatay's estate to her new family.[48]

A Husband Sentenced Successively to *Ḥadd* Punishment for *Qadhf* and to Compulsory Execution for Killing his Wife's Alleged Sexual Harasser

Q. 24:4–5 provides that if a person accuses a woman of unlawful intercourse without supporting his accusation by four eyewitnesses, he is liable to the punishment of *qadhf*, which is 80 lashes and deprivation of the right to testify.

---

without delay; the martyr's immovable estate in the camp will be returned to the heirs once the camp is captured by the Mahdi's forces).

47 Zaydan, *Al-Mufassal*, 11: § 12007 (the settlement of a debt is first in priority).

48 Cf. Layish, *Women*, 104, 213, 281f., 317; Aharon Layish, *Shari'a and Custom in Libyan Tribal Society. An Annotated Translation of Decisions from the Shari'a Courts of Ajdabiya and Kufra* (Leiden: Brill, 2005), doc. 53.

According to most schools, for the penalty to be applied, the woman whose chastity is the object of the defamation must be, in addition to fulfilling the usual conditions of "immunity" (*iḥṣān*)[49] applicable to the parties of illicit sex, a person who has never been convicted of unlawful sexual intercourse or been subjected to the *liʿān* procedure.[50] The punishment of *qadhf* belongs to both private and public law. The Hanafi doctrine gives more weight to the public aspect of the offense. Hence it maintains that the injured party cannot withdraw his claim for punishment. The Maliki doctrine, on the other hand, allows the injured party to withdraw his claim provided he is motivated by the protection of his own reputation; hence after his death his heirs may demand punishment if the allegation of unlawful sexual intercourse (*zinā*) also affects their honor.[51]

The husband may kill with impunity a person in the very act of committing a sexual crime against his wife (*flagrante delicto*) provided the killing is the only way to stop the continuation of the crime.[52] The schools differ regarding the evidence that the defendant must produce in order for this defense to be accepted. The Hanafis and the Shafiʿis require that the act of the unlawful sexual intercourse be proven by four male eyewitnesses (*bayyina*), whereas the other schools accept the testimony of two witnesses on the assumption that the witnesses are required as a defense against a charge of homicide.[53] The subject is discussed intensively in the hadith.[54] The majority of jurists maintain that four witnesses or, in their absence, the acknowledgment of the harasser's heirs are indispensable conditions for the husband to be exempt from retribution (*qiṣāṣ*). The dominant view among the jurists is that the husband may kill the harasser (as well as his own wife if she collaborated with the harasser). If there are witnesses to the adultery or, in their absence, if the harasser's blood avenger (*walī* [*al-dam*]),[55] acknowledges the adultery, the husband is liable to

49 "Immune" (*muḥṣan*) is a Muslim, free adult who has previously consummated a valid marriage. See Rudolph Peters, *Crime and Punishment in Islamic Law. Theory and Practice from the Sixteenth to the Twenty-first Century* (Cambridge: Cambridge University Press, 2005), 61.

50 *Liʿān* is a procedure, by means of which a husband can deny the paternity of a child born in wedlock. See Shalabi, *Ahkam al-Usra*, 597ff.; Zaydan, *Al-Mufassal*, 8: § 8396ff.

51 Peters, *Crime*, 63–64; Zaydan, *Al-Mufassal*, 5: § 4329, 4334f.

52 One may kill a man in the very act of committing a crime on two grounds: defense of one's honor and the necessity of halting a crime in progress. See Peters, *Crime*, 26.

53 Peters, *Crime*, 26–27.

54 E.g., Zaydan, *Al-Mufassal*, 5: § 4207, 4209.

55 All the schools except the Malikis hold that the blood avengers are the victim's heirs regardless of their sex. Some of the schools exclude the spouse relict. According to the Maliki school, which adopted the pre-Islamic tribal blood-money group, the avengers are

neither retribution nor payment of blood money (*diya*); if the avenger does not acknowledge but there is circumstantial evidence (*qarā'in*) as to the adultery, such as the husband finding the harasser in his own house with his kin "on one mattress (*firāsh*)" or in a "situation arousing suspicion" (*waḍ' murīb*), the husband is exempt from retribution but he must pay blood money because of the doubt (*shubha*) as to the option of retribution.[56]

In the case under review, a man complained to a commander of an encampment (*ṣāḥib al-ḥilla, al-ḥākim*) that someone was "treating friendly" (*mukhālil*), i.e., wooing, the man's wife. The commander warned the wife's "deceiver" (*mukhāwin*), i.e., the alleged harasser, that he would take legal action against him if he continued to enter the complainant's matrimonial home. The alleged harasser seems to have ignored the warning. Subsequently the husband came across the alleged harasser in his home in what he claimed to be a state of privacy (*khalā'*) with his wife. No witnesses were present at the scene. According to the husband's version, he was furious because of the repeated intrusions, and when the harasser began insulting him he could not bear the provocation any longer and killed him. The Mahdi, who was asked for a legal opinion on the case, ruled as follows:

> Since [the husband] did not prove [that an act of unlawful sexual intercourse (*zinā*) had taken place] by means of eyewitnesses, [his accusation against the victim] is nothing but (*mujarrad*) an unfounded accusation of unlawful intercourse (*qadhf*) with respect to the aforementioned man [the victim that allegedly] had insulted him (*sabbahu*). Hence it is imperative [that the husband] be punished [successively] by the sanction prescribed for unproven accusation of *zinā* and be executed [by way of retribution] for killing a person (*fa-yalzam ḥadd al-qadhf wa'l-qatl 'an al-raqaba allatī qatalahā*) in accordance with what God, be He Exalted, says [in Q. 24:4]: "And those who accuse honorable women but bring not four witnesses," etc.[57]

---

the victim's closest male agnates in the order of inheritance: the descendants, the ascendants, the brothers and their descendants, the paternal uncles and their descendants, the paternal great-uncles and their descendants (agnates of a higher class exclude those of a lower class). See Peters, *Crime*, 44ff.; Frank H. Stewart, "Tha'r," in *Encyclopaedia of Islam*, 2nd ed. (Leiden: Brill, 1998), 442–443.

56 Zaydan, *Al-Mufassal*, 5: § 4210–4211, 4220. The entire procedure takes place in court and the *qadi*'s discretion plays a vital role.

57 Abu Salim, ed., *Al-Athar al-Kamila*, 3: 110, 112. For a lithographic version of the document, see Abu Salim, ed., *Manshurat al-Imam al-Mahdi*. Vol. 3. *Al-Aḥkam wa-l-Adab*, 10.

The Mahdi's legal opinion deals with two different issues, the first belonging to public law and the second to private law. The punishment on *qadhf* is a matter of public law. The husband could not provide eyewitnesses to the act of adultery. The Mahdi declined to regard the mere entrance of the alleged harasser into the husband's home as tantamount to a state of privacy (*khalāʾ*) with the wife. Nor did he regard the commander's warning to take legal action against the alleged intruder if the latter continued to enter into the complainant's matrimonial home as a circumstantial evidence to the charge that an illegal intercourse or privacy between the victim and the wife had taken place. Hence the Mahdi convicted the husband to the *ḥadd al-qadhf*, which is 80 lashes.[58] The Mahdi's conviction and punishment on the charge of *qadhf* is compatible with the literal reading of Q. 24:4–5.

Homicide is a matter of private law. The Mahdi might have been impressed by the husband's acknowledgment to have killed the intruder as a result of the latter's provocation, but in the absence of a proven charge of illegal intercourse between the victim and the wife the option that the husband was entitled to benefit from the good defense of having killed with impunity the alleged harasser in the very act of committing the crime was irrelevant. Inexplicably, the Mahdi decided that the killing husband *must* be executed by way of retribution (*qiṣāṣ*) without leaving the victim's blood avenger the option of blood money (*diya*). The compulsory retribution is in line with another case where the Mahdi ruled that intentional homicide entails compulsory retribution with no option of forgiveness.[59] The denial of the option of monetary compensation while establishing retribution as the only option in cases of intentional homicide, is not compatible with the spirit of Q. 5:45 which commends forgiveness. The compulsory retribution bears the nature of punishment, which is alien to private law.[60] The expansion of the public domain at the expense of private domain seems to have been in line with the Mahdi's political and social

58 On an earlier occasion, in an attempt to elevate the moralistic behavior of his followers, the Mahdi added 20 lashes to the punishment of *qadhf*, thus fixing the punishment at 100 lashes. After the Mahdiyya "consolidated" (*istaqarrat*) itself, the Mahdi restored Muhammad's original legal norm (*ḥukm*), which is 80 lashes. See Abu Salim, ed., *Al-Athar al-Kamila*, 2: 93–94.

59 Abu Salim, ed., *Al-Athar al-Kamila*, 1: 306–7 (the Mahdi: "Since the conquest [of El Obeid] the law applying to intentional homicide (*al-qatl ʿamdan*) [has been changed to the effect] that the only option available is retribution (*yataʿayyan fīhi al-qiṣāṣ faqaṭ*), nothing else").

60 See Peters, *Crime*, 39ff.

agenda, that is, to secure law and order in the country; more precisely, to deter against intentional killing.[61]

Conclusion

The Mahdi's legal opinions and proclamations are based on the Qur'an, the prophetic sunna and the inspiration (*ilhām*) communicated to him by the Prophet Muhammad as well as on the Mahdi's personal legal discretion. The Mahdi does not resort to such traditional legal sources as systematic analogy (*qiyās*) or jurists' consensus (*ijmāʿ*); nor does he resort to the legal literature as elaborated by any of the schools of law, the only exception being *fuqahā'* belonging to the generation of Muhammad. A case in point is the Mahdi's reliance on Ibn ʿAbbas with respect to the legal consequences of *khulʿ*.[62] It seems safe to conclude that the Mahdi enlists his legal methodology combined with an extensive legal discretion as an instrument for promoting his political and social agenda. Thus he rules that *khulʿ* divorce does not count in the quota for intermediate marriage, that a martyr's widow is entitled to the entire estate rather than her prescribed portion as a Qurʿanic heir, that a widow has a right to waiting-period maintenance out of the estate before its division among the legal heirs, and that killing entails a punishment of compulsory execution thus extending the domain of public law at the expense of private law.

The Mahdi's legal experiment is unique in the sense that it was strongly influenced by Sufism, the most important manifestation of which is the elevation of inspiration (*ilhām*) communicated by the Prophet to a central source of law in his legal methodology. It is also unique due to the fact that it was elaborated outside the ʿulama''s control. It is doubtful, however, whether the Mahdi's legal methodology and its application have left any substantial imprint on contemporary Islamic legal theory or positive law. Moreover, it has left almost no impact on Islamic law in modern Sudan.[63]

---

61 For a discussion on the transition of Islamic law from tortious to penal law within the context of *ʿāqila* (solidarity group liable collectively for payment of blood money), see Layish, *Revival of Islamic Law in the Late 19th-Century Sudan*, doc. 51 and a reference there to Nurit Tsafrir's work.

62 There is ample evidence in the Mahdi's documents of his reliance on such jurists as ʿIkrima (d. 105/723–4), al-Dahhak (d. c.105–6/723–24), Ubayy b. Kaʿb (d. c.29–34/649–54) and Mujahid (d. c. 100–04/718–22). See Layish, *Revival of Islamic Law in the Late 19th-Century Sudan*, e.g., doc. 20.

63 Thus the legal methodology of Hasan al-Turabi who played a decisive role in Jaʿfar al-Numayri's legal experiment of reinstating the shariʿa was inspired by a combination of

Bibliography

Primary Sources

Abu Salim, Muhammad Ibrahim. *Manshurat al-Imam al-Mahdi.* Vol. 3. *Al-Aḥkam wa-l-Adab*. Khartoum: Idarat al-Mahfuzat al-Markaziyya, Wizarat al-Dakhiliyya, 1964.

Abu Salim, Muhammad Ibrahim. *Manshurat al-Mahdiyya*. Khartoum: Matbaʿat Jamiʿat al-Khartum, 1969.

Abu Salim, Muhammad Ibrahim, ed. *Al-Athar al-Kamila li-l-Imam al-Mahdi*, 7 vols. Khartoum: Dar Jamiʿat al-Khartum li-l-Nashr, 1990–94.

Durham University Library: Files, SAD 97/5/1–6, 97/5/10–17(v); 97/5/84–85, 97/5/86–91.

Manshurat al-Imam al-Mahdi fi al-Hudud wa-Ghayriha min al-Ahkam. Photographic reproduction from the original Arabic manuscript, dated 1881–1885. The School of Oriental and African Studies, London, accession no. 101493 [File SG.L.VII.416.2] [lithograph].

Secondary Sources

Al-ʿAbbadi, al-Hasan b. Saʿd b. Muhammad. *Al-Anwar al-Saniyya al-Mahiya li-Zalam al-Munkirin ʿala al-Ḥadra al-Mahdiyya*. Omdurman: 1305/1887 [lithograph].

Abu Salim, Muhammad Ibrahim. *Al-Haraka al-Fikriyya fi al-Mahdiyya*, 3rd ed. Khartoum: Matbaʿat Jamiʿat al-Khartum, 1989.

Abu Salim, Muhammad Ibrahim. *Buhuth fi Taʾrikh al-Sudan*. Beirut: Dar al-Jil, 1412/1992.

Abu Salim, Muhammad Ibrahim. *Al-ʿAlim al-Mujahid al-Hasan Saʿd al-ʿAbbadi. Safha min Khilaf al-ʿUlamaʾ hawla al-Mahdiyya wa-Imara fi ʾl-ʿAtabay* [Unpublished MS].

Abu Shuk, Ahmad Ibrahim. "Minhajiyyat al-Tashriʿ al-Mahdawi fi ʾl-Sudan (1881–1885)." *Kitabat Sudaniyya* 9. Markaz al-Dirasat al-Sudaniyya, March 1999, 10–30.

Chehata, Chafik. "Faskh." In *Encyclopaedia of Islam*, 2nd ed. Leiden: Brill, 1965.

Coulson, N.J. *Succession in the Muslim Family*. Cambridge: Cambridge University Press, 1971.

Hallaq, Wael B. *Islamic Legal Theories*. Cambridge: Cambridge University Press, 1997.

Hallaq, Wael B. *Sharīʿa: Theory, Practice, Transformations*. Cambridge: Cambridge University Press, 2009.

Hava, J.G. *Al-Faraʾid al-Durriyya fi al-Lughatayn al-ʿArabiyya wa-l-Inkliziyya*. Beirut: Catholic Press, 1951.

---

the traditional Islamic legal theory and Western legal doctrines, a combination that can by no means be reconciled with the Mahdi's legal methodology. See Aharon Layish and G.R. Warburg, *The Reinstatement of Islamic Law in Sudan under Numayri: An Evaluation of a Legal Experiment in the Light of Its Historical Context, Methodology, and Repercussions* (Leiden: Brill, 2002), 89–90, 286; Aharon Layish, "Hasan al-Turabi (1932–)," in *Islamic Legal Thought: A Compendium of Muslim Jurists*, ed. Oussama Arabi, D.S., Powers, and Susan Spectorsky (Leiden: Brill, 2013), 513–532.

Holt, Peter M. *The Mahdist State in the Sudan, 1881–1898*. Oxford: Clarendon Press, 1970.
Holt, Peter M. "Al-Mahdiyya." In *Encyclopaedia of Islam*, 2nd ed. Leiden: Brill, 1986.
Holt, Peter M. and M.W. Daly. *The History of the Sudan from the Coming of Islam to the Present Day*, 3rd ed. Boulder, Colorado: Westview Press, 1979.
Ibrahim, ʿAbdallah ʿAli. *Al-Siraʿ bayna al-Mahdi wa'l-ʿUlama'*, 2nd ed. Cairo: Dar Nubar li'l-Tibaʿa, 1994.
Layish, Aharon. *Women and Islamic Law in a Non-Muslim State. A Study Based on the Decisions of the Shariʿa Courts in Israel.* New York: John Wiley and Jerusalem: Israel Universities Press, 1975.
Layish, Aharon. "The Legal Methodology of the Mahdi in the Sudan, 1881–1885: Issues in Marriage and Divorce." *Sudanic Africa* 8 (1997): 37–66.
Layish, Aharon. *Sharīʿa and Custom in Libyan Tribal Society. An Annotated Translation of Decisions from the Sharīʿa Courts of Ajdābiya and Kufra.* Leiden: Brill, 2005.
Layish, Aharon. "The Sudanese Mahdi's Legal Methodology and Its Sufi Inspiration." *Jerusalem Studies in Arabic and Islam* (Special Issue in Honor of Yohanan Friedmann) 33 (2007): 279–308.
Layish, Aharon. "Hasan al-Turabi (1932–)." In *Islamic Legal Thought: A Compendium of Muslim Jurists*, edited by Oussama Arabi, D.S Powers, and Susan Spectorsky, 513–532. Leiden: Brill, 2013.
Layish, Aharon. *Revival of Islamic Law in the Late 19th-Century Sudan: The Mahdi's Legal Methodology and Its Application* (in progress).
Layish, Aharon and G.R. Warburg. *The Reinstatement of Islamic Law in Sudan under Numayrī: An Evaluation of a Legal Experiment in the Light of Its Historical Context, Methodology, and Repercussions*. Leiden: Brill, 2002.
Al-Mufti, Husayn Sayyid Ahmad. *Tatawwur Nizam al-Qaḍa' fi al-Sudan*, Part 1. Khartoum: Matbaʿat Misr, 1378/1959.
O'Fahey, R.S. (with the assistance of Muhammad Ibrahim Abu Salim, Albrecht Hofheinz, Yahya Muhammad Ibrahim, Bernd Radtke and Knut S. Vikør). *Arabic Literature of Africa, Vol. 1: The Writings of Eastern Sudanic Africa to c. 1900*. Leiden: E.J. Brill, 1994.
Peters, Rudolph. "Islam and the Legitimation of Power: The Mahdi-Revolt in the Sudan." In *Deutscher Orientalistentag* 21 (Berlin, März 1980): Ausgewählte Vorträge. Hrsg. von F. Steppat. Wiesbaden, 1983 (ZDMG, Suppl., V), 409–420.
Peters, Rudolph. *Crime and Punishment in Islamic Law. Theory and Practice from the Sixteenth to the Twenty-first Century*. Cambridge: Cambridge University Press, 2005.
Peters, Rudolph. "Islamic Family Law." University of Amsterdam, Department of Arabic Studies. Amsterdam, 1995 (unpublished).
Powers, David S. *Studies in Qur'ān and Ḥadīth*. Berkeley and Los Angeles: University of California Press, 1986.
Powers, David S. *Law, Society, and Culture in the Maghrib, 1300–1500*. Cambridge: Cambridge University Press, 2002.

The Qur'an. Hebrew translation from the Arabic, annotations, appendices and index by Uri Rubin. Tel Aviv: Tel Aviv University Press and MAPA Publishers, 2005.

Searcy, Kim. *The Sudanese Mahdist State. Ceremony and Symbols of Authority: 1882–1898.* Leiden: Brill, 2010.

Shalabi, Muhammad Mustafa. *Ahkam al-Usra fi al-Islam. Dirasa Muqarana bayn Fiqh al-Madhahib al-Sunniyya wa-l-Madhhab al-Jaʿfari wa-l-Qanun*. Beirut: Dar al-Nahda al-ʿArabiyya, 1393/1973.

Stewart, Frank H. "Tha'r." In *Encyclopaedia of Islam*, 2nd ed. Leiden: Brill, 1998.

Veccia Vaglieri, L. "ʿAbd Allāh b. al-ʿAbbās." In *Encyclopaedia of Islam*, 2nd ed. Leiden: Brill, 1960.

Zaydan, ʿAbd al-Karim. *Al-Mufaṣṣal fi Ahkam al-Mar'a wa-l-Bayt al-Muslim fi al-Shariʿa al-Islamiyya*, 11 vols. Beirut: Mu'assasat al-Risala, 1413/1993.

PART 2

Practices of Recording and Verifying

CHAPTER 5

Identifying the *ʿudūl* in Fifteenth-Century Granada

Sergio Carro Martín and Amalia Zomeño

Introduction and Purpose[1]

The archives and libraries of Granada preserve several collections of Arabic legal documents dated mostly in the second half of the fifteenth century.[2] They were written down and signed by notaries, who were in charge of drafting the legal transactions demanded by the inhabitants of Granada and guaranteeing their validity and effectiveness in court. According to Emile Tyan: "dans beaucoup d'actes notariés, la formule religieuse est précédée d'une formule qui porte tout à la fois certification du contenue du document et indication du nom du notaire-rédacteur."[3] This formula is not present in Granadan documents. There is no certification of the contents nor a mention of the notaries' names before the *basmallāh*. In addition, the signatures in the documents are

1 This paper is the result of several of our previous studies, but also based on endless discussions on the formalities of the Granadan documents. We would like to thank the useful comments given to a preliminary version of this paper on 11 May 2011 in Amsterdam and later on by Christian Müller and Tamer el-Leithy on different occasions. The paper was possible thanks to the amazing database Comparing Arabic Legal Documents, elaborated by Christian Müller in the IRHT (Paris), with its results available online in the *Corpus of Arabic Legal Documents* (http://cald.irht.cnrs.fr/php/ilm.php). We would also like to express our gratitude to Teresa Espejo and her team in Granada, for generously giving us their magnificent photographs of the documents. We would also like to thank the Biblioteca del Hospital Real for granting us permission for the reproduction of these photographs. The present contribution was elaborated within the framework of the research projects FFI2012–39567 and FFI2012–37775, financed by the Spanish Ministry of Economy.

2 On these different collections, see Carmen Barceló and Ana Labarta, "Los documentos árabes del Reino de Granada. Bibliografía y perspectivas," *Cuadernos de la Alhambra* 26 (1990): 113–119; Camilo Álvarez de Morales, "La geografía documental arábigogranadina," in *Documentos y manuscritos árabes del Occidente musulmán medieval*, ed. Nuria Martínez de Castilla (Madrid: CSIC, 2010), 205–223; Francisco Vidal, "Un tipo de manuscritos "documentales": Las escrituras árabes notariales en al-Andalus naṣrí (s. XIII–XVI)," in *Manuscritos: papel, técnicas y dimensión cultural. IV Primavera del Manuscrito Andalusí*, ed. Mostafa Ammadi (Casablanca-Rabat: Universidad Hassan II-Bouregreg, 2012), 23–57.

3 Emile Tyan, "Le notariat et le régime de la preuve par écrit dans la pratique du droit musulman," *Annales de l'École Française de Droit de Beyrouth* 2 (1945): 52.

 | DOI 10.1163/9789004343733_007

not at all readable: as is common nowadays as well, instead of clearly spelling out their names, the notaries used to design an elaborated signature. However, we know that in Granada, the signatures were identifiable and the documents were ascribed to their writer-notaries. An example of this is a document written in Baza in 889/1484, validating a previous one dated fifty years before by identifying the handwriting of the notaries:

> The witnesses who sign this document have examined the testimony (*shahāda*) of the two honourable jurists (*al-faqīhayn al-ʿadālayn*) Abū Jaʿfar Aḥmad b. Muḥammad son of Abū Bakr al-Jayyānī and Abū ʿAbd Allāh Muḥammad b. ʿAlī al-Qaysī, and have carefully deciphered the forms of their letters (*ishkāl ḥurūfihimā*), and it seems clear to them that such testimony was written by their hand (*bi-khaṭṭ yadayhimā*) and that they were two of the *ʿudūl* of Baza –May God protect this city-. They also know that they gave their testimonies and continued their function as notaries (*ʿadālatuhumā*) until the moment of their death.[4]

Our purpose is to do something similar in this study as these medieval witnesses did in Baza: to identify and single out the notaries through the examination of the documents they wrote. We will try to decipher the "forms of their characters," both in their style of writing and in their signatures. We will also describe some of the writing conventions used by all of them, the *mise en page* of the Granadan documents, which will help to discern the specificities or divergences from these general writing conventions by individual notaries. We will especially focus on some of those conventions and rules related with the legal validation of the documents. At the end of this paper, we will provide a characterisation of one of these notaries and describe some traces of his relationship with his "clients," the inhabitants of Granada at the end of the fifteenth century.

The Collection

The most important collection of legal documents in Granada is preserved in the Biblioteca del Hospital Real (University of Granada); it will be the main

4 Luis Seco de Lucena, *Documentos arábigo-granadinos* (Madrid: Instituto Egipcio de Estudios Islámicos, 1961), 6 (no. 2b).

source for this work.[5] It contains 167 handwriting pieces,[6] although we have to exclude 16 items from our study because some are not Granadan legal documents and some others cannot be read because of their bad condition.[7] Therefore, this study comprises 151 Arabic legal documents.[8]

The documents range from the end of the fourteenth century to the end of the fifteenth century: the earliest in 15 Rabīʿ II 792/2 April 1390, and the later in 24 Ṣafar 905/30 September 1499 and therefore eight years after the conquest of

5 On this collection, see Amalia Zomeño, "Repertorio documental arábigo-granadino: Los documentos árabes de la Biblioteca Universitaria de Granada," *Qurtuba. Estudios Andalusíes* 6 (2002): 275–296.

6 These Arabic texts are distributed in two boxes (*caja* in Spanish), although this arrangement seems to be the result of the modern history of the Library. In box 27 (containing 110 items), the documents are numbered from 32950 to 33041 (a little file encloses the number 33040, including 17 items) and 33096–33097. Box 69 (containing 57 items) is also numbered from 5-01 to 5-48 and from 5-53 to 5-57 (this last number contains three items). In subsequent pages we will refer to the documents as Biblioteca del Hospital Real (=BHR), the number of the box, and the number of the document in it.

7 These are six parchments almost completely erased (BHR C-27 33009, BHR C-69 5–51, 5–53, 5–54, 5–55, 5–56), three Moroccan documents (BHR C-69 5–01, 5–03, 5–12), four separated folia of different manuscripts (BHR C-69 5–02, 5–57, 5–57, 5–57), a letter (BHR C-69 5–11), an amulet (BHR C-69 5–50) and a modern transcription of an unknown document (BHR C-27 33041).

8 We are currently working on the complete edition of this collection, but some have already been published in Seco de Lucena, *Documentos arábigo-granadinos*, with the numbers 1, 3, 8, 9, 12, 16–24, 27, 29, 31, 33, 36, 38–41, 43–44, 47, 54, 59, 61–64, 87, 90, 92–93; Francisco Vidal, "Water and Farm Estates in the Arabic Documents of the Nasrid Kingdom of Granada," in *From al-Andalus to Khurasan. Documents from the Medieval Muslim World*, ed. Petra M. Sijpesteijn et al. (Leiden: Brill, 2006), 39–58; Amalia Zomeño, "Notaries and Their Formulas: The Legacies from the University Library of Granada," in *From al-Andalus to Khurasan. Documents from the Medieval Muslim World*, ed. Petra M. Sijpesteijn et al. (Leiden: Brill, 2006), 59–77; María Dolores Rodríguez, "Les *maṣārī* de Grenade d'après quelques documents arabes (1442–1490)," *Bibliotheca Orientalis* 65 no. 5/6 (2008): 555–594; María Dolores Rodríguez and Salud María Domínguez, "La compraventa de fincas urbanas en la Granada del siglo XV a través de dos documentos notariales árabes," *Anaquel de Estudios Árabes* 19 (2008): 175–199; María Dolores Rodríguez, Emilio Molina, and Carmen Jiménez Mata, "La emisión monetaria de Muley Hacén. Cuestiones políticas y socioeconómicas que suscita," in *VII Estudios de Frontera: Islam y cristiandad (siglos XI–XVI). Los Banū Saʿīd*, ed. Francisco Toro and José Rodríguez (Jaén: Diputación de Jaén, 2010), 773–783; María Dolores Rodríguez and Francisco Vidal, "Fāṭima bint Muḥammad vende una finca de regadío. Sobre mujeres nazaríes y propiedades en la Granada del siglo XV," in *VIII Estudios de Frontera: Mujeres y fronteras*, ed. Francisco Toro and José Rodríguez (Jaén: Diputación Provincial de Jaén, 2011), 415–430.

the Nasrid Emirate by the Catholic Monarchs in 1492.[9] However, the bulk of the writings belongs to the 80s of the fifteenth century.

The Writing of a Legal Document (*Kitāba*) in Granada

The most common type of legal document in this collection is a text written on a piece of paper with a narration of a legal fact in the past tense. Preceded by a *basmallāh*, always followed by a *taṣliya*, most of the documents end, immediately after the date, with two signatures. Sometimes, the completion of the legal facts needed another visit, or visits, to the notaries, and therefore, another writing was added, on the same piece of paper, following on the recto or using the verso, now starting with a *ḥamdallāh* and finishing again with the signatures of two witnesses. A common version of this kind of document are sales contracts with the addition of a deferred payment or payments.[10] Also very frequent was the copy of an appraisal of certain properties by experts (*ahl al-baṣr wa-l-maʿrifa*) followed by the distribution of those properties among the heirs in a *qisma* document (division of inheritance).

There is a consistent layout in the documents. Almost all the notaries used the same kind of paper with a similar size and very rarely utilized parchment.[11] They also elaborated or purchased a similar ink and a similar kind of pen.[12] They prepared their pieces of paper maintaining regular margins and distances to the edges of the writing surface, writing until the left border and starting two to two and a half centimetres from the right margin. The main text of the documents is always located on the top left part of the piece.

---

9 The documents were used after the conquest and well into the 16th century, as many of them bear annotations in the margins mentioning the contents of the transaction. These annotations are in vernacular Arabic by a non-expert hand or in Romance maybe by a clerk of the Castilian administration.

10 In the collection, 105 documents contain only one writing, 24 documents contain 2 writings, 11 contain 3, and 9 documents contain 4 writings. Exceptional are those containing 5, 6 and 7 writings.

11 Only seven – out of 151 – documents were written on parchment (although we have to add here the six excluded because of their bad condition); five sale contracts and two marriage contracts.

12 A first analysis of Granadan documents' ink were published in Teresa Espejo et al., "Caracterización material y proceso de conservación de la colección de documentos árabes manuscritos del Archivo Histórico Provincial de Granada," *Al-Qantara* 32 (2011): 519–532.

Signing the Documents

As a general rule, the documents in this Granadan collection are signed by two witnesses,[13] but, how did the notaries proceed in the signing of the texts? Who signed what?

As we said before, the notaries do not write their names but insert a design with a signature, and even if they are diverse, we could make the following classification: First, we find simple signatures, made by a single design with the notary's name indicated with words disposed in several lines. Second, and more frequently, we find that a notary makes a compound signature, drawing his name by designing two segments only linked by an enlargement of the last character and thus uniting both segments horizontally (see figure 5.1).

Simple signatures		Compound signatures	
BHR C-69 5-47		BHR C-27 32958	
BHR C-27 32985		BHR C-27 32960	
BHR C-27 32987		BHR C-27 32969	
		BHR C-27 32981	

FIGURE 5.1 *Simple and compound signatures.*
SOURCE: BIBLIOTECA DEL HOSPITAL REAL, UNIVERSITY OF GRANADA.

13 It is well known that two witnesses are required for the validity of legal documents, see Tyan, *Le notariat*, 55.

At first look, a compound signature might be mistaken as two signatures of different notaries, but every design is usually followed and wrapped up by a stroke similar to the *hā*,[14] and are separated by a *wāw* between them.

Although we tried to read the names hidden in the designs, we did not succeed in understanding any of them. Besides some potential "Muhammads," "Ahmads" or "'Isas" no surely identifiable segment of a proper name could be read. The designs are repeated in several of the documents, as we will describe later, and therefore we can see the development of the design of a notary through a period of time.

However, some of the writings in the documents of the collection diverge from the general rule since they do not have the two signatures. In fact, ten have only one, that of the writer-notary who might not have needed to take the effort to search for the assistance of another witness to complete the two necessary testimonies,[15] turning these texts into mere records of legal acts not constituting evidence to be presented in court.[16] In five other documents, the writer-notary did not even sign the legal writing himself, so they do not have even one single signature. What is surprising in these documents is the fact that they are complete in the sense that they all have a complete *basmallāh* and *taṣliya*, contain all the legal requirements for the transactions to be valid, and are fully dated.[17] Even if they are exceptional and scarce, these insufficiently validated writings might show the practice of drafting legal documents without immediately making them public through the adding of the signatures.

Kitāba and *Shahāda*

For our identification of the notaries, the position of the signatures is relevant. They placed their signatures at the end of the document, inserted most of the times immediately after the body of the text. Therefore, if there is enough space, the first signature would be added after the end of the last line. The second signature would start on a new line, on the right. If there is not enough

14 This sign resembles the one described by Nico van den Boogert in a Maghribi manuscript meaning *intahā* (finished), and it might have the same meaning in these notarial documents. See Nico van den Boogert, "Some Notes on Maghribī Script," *Manuscripts of the Middle East* 4 (1989): 34.

15 Tyan, *Le notariat*, 55–6.

16 They are BHR C-27 32967, 32969, 32991, 33003, 33023, BHR C-69 5–04, 5–10, 5–15, 5–30 and 5–33.

17 They are BHR C-27 32959, 33031, 33034, BHR C-69 5–31 and 5–34.

space to add the first signature, the writer adds some formula after the date in order to finish the line.[18]

The positioning of the signatures in the document might not be random, but rather intentional. Following Tyan,[19] our hypothesis is that also in Granada the first signer-notary, the one who draws his signature immediately after the text, is the one who writes the whole text, while the second one only testifies. In other words, the first signature informs us of which notary has exercised the two functions, *kitāba* (writing) and *shahāda* (testimony), while the second signer-notary only exercises his function as witness.

This hypothesis, even if it sounds only logical, needs further confirmation and proof. We have provided that by examining whether the documents that were signed by the same first witness are written in the same hand. In the following table (figure 5.2) we show three documents signed by the same two notaries. The palaeographic samples given (*al-raḥīm* and *Muhammad*) make it clear that the palaeography of the body of the text always corresponds with the signature placed in the first position. When the first signer-notary of documents BHR C-27 32951 and BHR C-69 5–45 signs on the second position, as in document BHR C-27 32955, the palaeography is clearly not the same. In document BHR C-27 32951, the first signature is placed in the margin on the left, leaving no space after the body of the text. The same signature appears in document BHR C-69 5–45 at the right, now beginning a new line since there was no space on the previous line. As he signs in the first position in both cases, he was the writer of both documents, which is corroborated by the same hand being used to write the documents as seen in the examples. However, in document BHR C-27 32955, the notary who signed in the second position in the other documents, now signs in the first position, and the palaeography, therefore, changes. Figure 5.3 offers other examples.

In addition, an analysis of the inks used in the Arabic legal documents of Granada demonstrates that the composition of the ink used in almost all of them is usually the same, but the proportions between the different components varies a lot. These analyses show that the proportions found in the body of the texts are the same as the ones used in the first signatures, while the second signature differs from it.[20]

18 In Granadan documents, they write *ʿarafa Allāh khayr dhālika*, but not *ṣaḥḥ*, as in Tyan, *Le notariat*, 58 (note 2).

19 Tyan, *Le notariat*, 55.

20 The publication of the results of this ink analysis is still forthcoming. See Teresa Espejo, "La colección de manuscritos árabes del Archivo Histórico Provincial de Granada: caracterización y conservación," forthcoming.

Document	Signatures	Example 1	Example 2
BHR C-27 32951		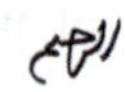	
BHR C-69 5–45	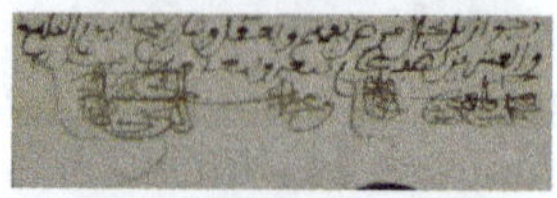		
BHR C-27 32955			

FIGURE 5.2 *Combination of two signers-notaries.*
SOURCE: BIBLIOTECA DEL HOSPITAL REAL, UNIVERSITY OF GRANADA.

Document	Signatures	Example 1	Example 2
BHR C-27 32966		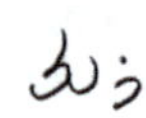	
BHR C-27 32968	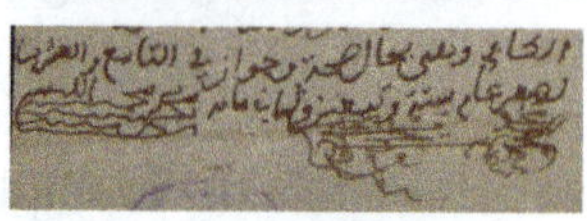		
BHR C-27 32963			

FIGURE 5.3 *Combination of two signers-notaries.*
SOURCE: BIBLIOTECA DEL HOSPITAL REAL, UNIVERSITY OF GRANADA.

This concordance between signature, palaeography and ink holds true for many other documents, and therefore we could conclude that there is a conventional order and a system established among Granadan notaries for the writing of a document and on how it should be subsequently signed.

Some Notes on Palaeography

It might come as no surprise if we say that the Granadan legal documents were written in a Maghribi script, as it is the Arabic script traditionally assigned to the area of our study.[21] Beyond this general label, it would be interesting to see whether there was a standardized palaeography used in the administration of justice in Granada and, on the other hand, whether significant variations of its forms are discernible. In fact, our documents provide a new and fruitful sample that allows us to understand better this script as used in daily practice.

Nico van den Boogert already presented the main features of the Maghribi script,[22] and, in general, our Arabic documents fit these features. It will be complicated to give a simple list of the palaeographical features found in the documents, since the different notaries developed a personal style. However, it should be mentioned from the start that the script is quick, very cursive and deprived of any intention of ornament, beauty or even care.[23] In any case, the documents present a clear horizontal disposition on the flat baseline which guides the words. The letters' sizes are usually the same in all lines and almost identical spaces exist between words. There are no paragraphs so the texts are presented always as a single block without spaces, nor punctuations. They wrote the words in slopes and enlarged the ending strokes of letters, inclining them over the small spaces between lines and most of the times extending over other lines.

In summary, among the characteristics of the documents of Granada we find the following:

- *basmallāh* and *taṣliya* always written together on the same line, never on two lines
- horizontal lines of writing
- standard size of right and upper margins
- diacritical punctuation of the letters *fāʾ* and *qāf* is unconventional
- frequent absence of diacriticals and vowels, as well as other signs of writing
- systematic absence of diacritics in final characters, especially in *tāʾ marbūṭa*

21 See Octave Houdas, "Essai sur l'écriture maghrebine," in *Nouveaux mélanges orientaux* 19 (1886): 83–117; van den Boogert, "Some Notes on the Maghribi Script"; François Déroche, "O. Houdas et les écritures maghrébines," in *Le manuscrit arabe et la codicologie*, ed. Ahmed-Chouqui Binebine (Rabat: Université Mohammed v, Colloques et séminaires, no. 33, 1994), 75–81.

22 These are: final *alif* drawn from top to bottom; stems of *alif, lām, lām-alif,* and *ṭāʾ/ẓāʾ* have club like extensions to the left of their top point; loop of *ṣād/ḍād* is identical with that of *ṭāʾ/ẓāʾ*; stem of *ṭāʾ/ẓāʾ* is drawn diagonally; *qāf* and *fāʾ* have unconventional diacritical points; final and separate *dāl/dhāl* are very similar to initial and medial *kāf, see* Van den Boogert, "Some Notes on Maghribi Script," 30–43.

23 As it is the convention, see Tyan, *Le notariat*, 50.

- frequent absence of vocalization, only present in some geographical and proper names
- letters with open strokes extend their length when there are no ligatures
- vertical strokes descend below the writing line and frequently adopt a slight diagonal tilt in the same writing direction
- letters *dāl* and *dhāl*, in initial position, acquire the form of a 45° triangle. When ligatured to the precedent letter they adopt the shape of a *rāʾ*
- presence of a large number of unconventional ligatures.

Although these general characteristics in the documents of Granada are common in all of them, we cannot maintain the idea that all notaries of Granada wrote their documents alike. In fact, we should keep in mind that the differences between them, as happened with their signatures, were taken into account by the judges themselves, in order to verify their legal validity.

Validating the Documents

We said that the general convention was that every legal document should start with a *basmallāh*, followed by a *taṣliya* and, if subsequent writings needed to be added, they should start only with a *ḥamdallāh*, indicating that the second writing depended on the previous one on the document. This general rule applies to 142 out of the 151 documents studied here, but we also find some exceptions. First, six documents with different writings use the *basmallāh-taṣliya* in all the different transactions of the document, rather than using the *ḥamdallāh* in the subsequent transactions.[24] Maybe in this way the notaries preferred to give to the second legal writing a superior status not dependent on the first one.

Secondly, some documents only have a *ḥamdallāh* on an independent piece of paper, apparently with no connection to, or need of, other transactions.[25] It is true that all the documents with this feature are dated after the conquest of Granada, so this exception to the rule might be explained by the fact that the notaries remaining in Granada lost touch with earlier conventions. However, it might also mean that the previous writing not included in the piece, as we will see later, existed as a separate document that did not survive. In any case, we found no connection between the *basmallāh-taṣliya* and the validating process, which seems to be always represented at the end of the writing.

24 These are BHR C-27 32952, 32965, 32981, 33001, 33040-xii and BHR C-69 5–10.

25 These are BHR C-27 32967, 33012, 33040-vii and BHR C-69 5–06, 5–18 and 5–37.

Another group of 21 documents show the lack of signatures of the witnesses but they are validated by the judge. All these start in the present tense – instead of the past as in the others – and provide the testimony of qualified witnesses. All of them are documents of the same nature: they are either experts' testimonies or eye-witnesses, but never what Claude Cahen calls "témoins instrumentaires."[26] Ten of them start – after the *basmallāh* and *taṣliya* –, with the sentence "the witnesses of this document, those from the people of science and knowledge, testify …" (*waqafa shuhūduhu min ahl al-baṣr wa-l-maʿrifa bi-mā yushahidūn bi-hi fī-hi …*). Five others start by "the witnesses of this document know … and inform that …" (*yuʿrafu shuhūduhu … wa-yaʿlamūna anna …*) and two others "the witnesses know the ownership of … and inform that …" (*yaḥūzu shuhūduhu … wa-yaʿlamūna*).[27] These show that the practice in Granada was that the experts did not sign the documents, but that their names were annotated in a clear and readable manner, aligned after the text. Most of these documents bring the testimony of at least two experts, but it is possible to find writings with three or even more; two of them give the names of eleven qualified witnesses.

These legal writings have another peculiarity not found in most of the documents signed by "professionals": over their names someone wrote the word *shahida* (he testified), with a different ink and between the lines. In addition, outside the bloc of the text, all of them include a formula with the validation by the judge; this formula is "sufficient" (*iktafā*) (figure 5.4).

This layout shows a procedure. Our hypothesis is that their testimony had to be validated by the judge and so, after the recording of their testimony, they went to court and repeated their testimony orally in front of the judge. Once they did so, the judge himself, or the court secretary (*kātib*), confirmed their individual testimony by writing *shahida* over their names and, in the end, adding the validation, thus meaning "sufficient" to establish a legal proof.[28]

---

26 See Claude Cahen, "A pròpos des *shuhūd*," *Studia Islamica* 31 (1970): 71.

27 Of a similar nature, but using different wording, are those starting with "the witnesses who placed their names after the date, testify about their knowledge of …" or "those who write their names after the date, testify about their knowledge of …"

28 Although we might need a further study on these kinds of documents, the procedure seems to be the same as the one described by Christian Müller, "Écrire pour établir la prevue oral en Islam. La pratique d'un tribunal à Jérusalem au XIV^{è} siècle," in *Les outils de la pensée. Études historique et comparatives des "textes,"* ed. Akira Saito and Yusuke Nakamure (Paris: Les editions de la Maison des sciences de l'homme, 2010), 63–97, esp. 72 and 85.

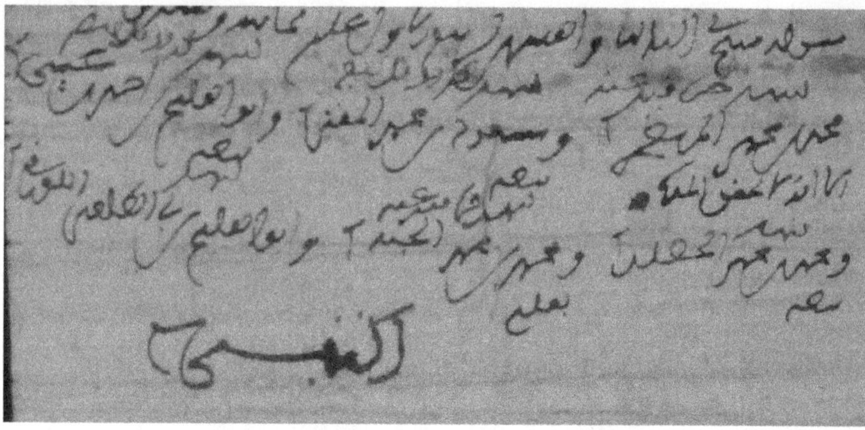

FIGURE 5.4 *Non-professional witnesses' names. Document number* BHR C-27 32982.
SOURCE: BIBLIOTECA DEL HOSPITAL REAL, UNIVERSITY OF GRANADA.

Three other documents do not only show the *iktafā*, but include a mention that the judge deemed the legal facts or rights mentioned in the documents to be valid: "[the judge] informs of the sufficiency of the document, may God give him success" (*aʿlama bi-ktifāʾihi* [unreadable signature] *wafaqahu Allāh*). This signed information might have been needed when the document was not used in this judge court, but maybe when the information should be sent to another judge in another court or city.

Therefore, most of the documents in the collection under study bear two signatures of professional witnesses and, when the witnesses are not directly those in charge of the redaction-testimony, but experts or eye-witnesses, the document should be presented in court and the judge intervenes in order to validate the proof.

Finally, only six documents signed by professional witnesses are also validated by the judge. Now, the formula changes and we do not find the word *iktafā* but *thabata* (stands firm) or *thubita* (it was made firm). Again, in these six documents, "he testified" is written over the signatures and, when necessary, "he informs of its confirmation (*aʿlama bi-thubūtihi*).

All in all, only 27 of the documents preserved in the Biblioteca del Hospital Real – the total was 151 – were presented in court. In our opinion, this is very relevant when we try to study the relationship between the notaries and their "clients," the subjects of the application of Justice in fifteenth-century Granada. Does this mean that the population of Granada did not need fully validated documents? Rather, we would like to suggest that the documents, while not constituting full evidence according to Islamic law, certainly had – because they bear these signatures – a potential legal effectiveness, exactly in case they might need to be used at court. In the meantime, the documents will have had only a "latent" validity in the hands of the parties.[29]

To sum up: even if each of the notaries of Granada was free to write the text of a legal document in his own way, we have shown that they were following certain conventions that were necessary to provide the validity and effectiveness of the documents. The existence of these conventions also shows that the notaries belonged to a specialized group of professionals that received a similar formation on Islamic legal procedures, as well as a similar education on chancery, within the legal system of Granada.[30]

The Notary and His Clients

The design of the signatures in the documents, as well as the palaeography and *mise en page*, helped us to identify the witnesses in the documents. Now, in addition, we would like to know what their relationship was with their clients, the inhabitants of Granada. In order to understand this relationship, we will follow the activity of one of these identified notaries, whose name we only guess, but whose documents we will be able to analyse.

He signed nine documents of the collection (see figure 5.5) and is, without doubt, the most illustrative case since eight of them refer to transactions made by the same person, Umm al-Fath bint Muhammad al-Shalyani.[31] From this we might conclude that to Umm al-Fath he is not just another clerk of the administration of justice who stays as the other notaries do in their offices around the city mosque,[32] but someone she especially trusts for guaranteeing the validity of her documents and her rights.

29 For a comparison with other collections, see Müller, "Écrire pour établir la prevue oral en Islam," 85.

30 Sergio Carro, "*Kātib* or *Muwaththiq*?: Toward a Paleography of Private Arabic Documents" (forthcoming).

31 There are a total of 20 documents related to this Umm al-Fath and her husband Muhammad in the collection. On both of them, see Amalia Zomeño, "Documentos árabes y biografías mudéjares: Umm al-Fatḥ al-Šalyānī y Muḥammad Baḥṭān (1448–1496)," in *Biografías mudéjares o la experiencia de ser minoría: Biografías islámicas en la España cristiana*, ed. Ana Echevarría (Madrid: CSIC, 2008), 291–325.

32 On the notaries of Granada, in general terms, see Maribel Calero Secall, "La justicia, cadíes y otros magistrados," in *El Reino Nazarí de Granada (1232–1492). Política. Instituciones. Espacio y economía*, ed. María Jesús Viguera (Madrid: Espasa Calpe, 2000), 401–403.

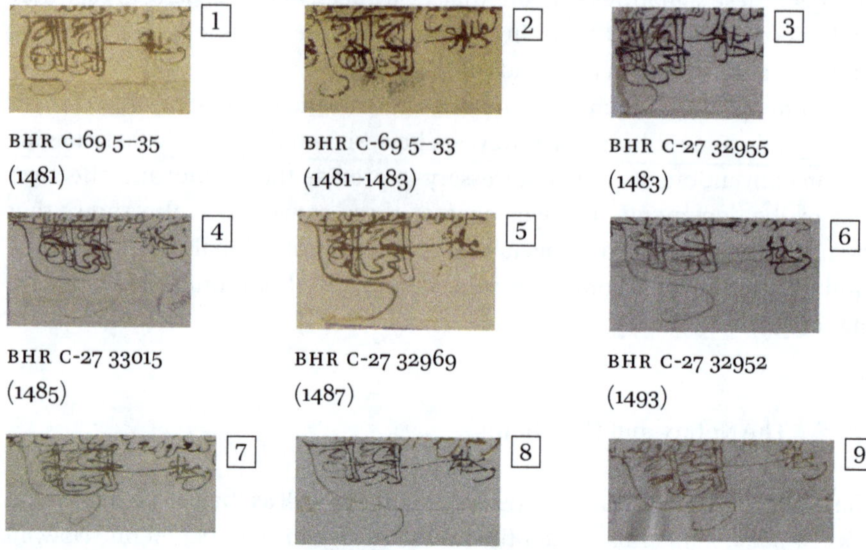

BHR C-69 5–35 (1481) | BHR C-69 5–33 (1481–1483) | BHR C-27 32955 (1483)

BHR C-27 33015 (1485) | BHR C-27 32969 (1487) | BHR C-27 32952 (1493)

BHR C-69 5–45 (1493) | BHR C-69 5–46 (1494) | BHR C-27 32951 (1496)

FIGURE 5.5 *Signatures of the same notary from 1481 to 1496.*
SOURCE: BIBLIOTECA DEL HOSPITAL REAL, UNIVERSITY OF GRANADA.

His signature is a compound one that ends with a stroke closing the second segment of his design. Although he signs the nine documents, he is the writer of only two of them, showing a characteristic hand that extends the strokes above and below the lines and typically includes unconventional ligatures all over the text, with an absolute absence of diacritics, vowels and *hamza*.

He stayed in Granada after the conquest in his function as notary-witness, in fact, from 1481 to 1496. After the conquest he always signed with the same partner-notary and he appears only in his role of witness, never more as notary-writer.

The relationship between him and Umm al-Fath could be traced then through eight episodes:

First: on 885/1481, together with her father-in-law, Abu al-Hasan ʿAli b. al-Ahsan al-Husayni, she asked for his testimony (*ashhada*) in order to make public the duty of Abu al-Hasan to pay the maintenance (*nafaqa*) of his daughter ʿA'isha, while Umm al-Fath will be in charge of her full custody (*ḥaḍānatuhā*

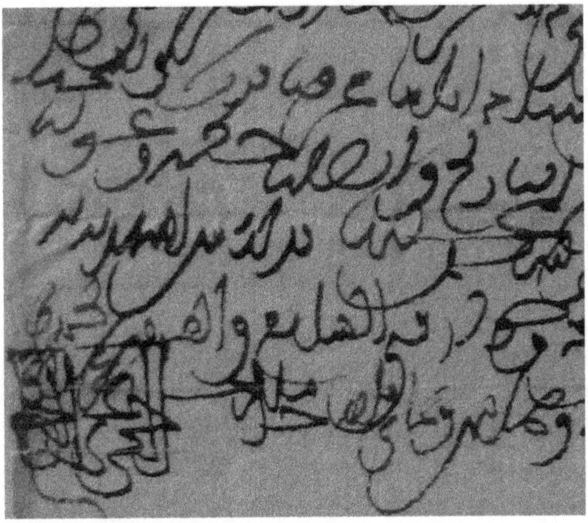

FIGURE 5.6
Sample of writing.
SOURCE: BIBLIOTECA DEL HOSPITAL REAL, UNIVERSITY OF GRANADA.

wa-kafālatuhā).[33] From previous documents we know that after the death of her husband, Umm al-Fath's mother remarried and had another daughter, ʿA'isha.[34]

Second: on 885/1481 Umm al-Fath buys some properties from her father-in-law, Abu al-Hasan, in order to establish a shop in the centre of Granada.[35]

Third, on 888/1483 Umm al-Fath, perhaps with the advice of our notary, dictated a first will and now he writes the text himself.[36] The legacy resembles those written in Granada by other notaries:[37] the testator gives some money to the poor of the city and the rest of the one third that she is allowed to dispense of freely according to Islamic law she donates the largest part to her father-in-law, Abu al-Hasan. She might thereby have thought to benefit indirectly her

33 BHR C-69 5–35, see Seco de Lucena, *Documentos arábigo-granadinos*, no. 41. On *nafaqa*, see Ibn Juzayy, *al-Qawanin al-Fiqhiyya* (Libia: al-Dar al-Arabiyya li-l-Kitab, 1982), 226–229; J. Lapanne-Joinville, "L'Obligation d'entretien (*nafaqa*) en droit malekite," *Revue Marocaine de Droit* (1949): 166–182.

34 See note 34.

35 BHR C-69 5–33, see Seco de Lucena, *Documentos arábigo-granadinos*, no. 39.

36 BHR C-27 32955.

37 On charitable legacies, see Amalia Zomeño, "When Death Will Fall Upon Him": Charitable Legacies in 15th Century Granada," in *Charity and Giving in Monotheistic Religions*, ed. Miriam Frenkel and Yaacov Lev (Berlin – New York: De Gruyter, 2009), 217–233.

own sister who is now under her custody but who is dependent of his economic means. In fact, according to the law, she cannot give it to her sister directly.[38]

Fourth, two years later, Umm al-Fath's husband, Muhammad Bahtan, makes his own legacy, witnessed by our notary 1.[39] Her husband also gave the freely disposable third of his properties entirely to charity.

On 893/1487, our notary signs another document, although this one is not related to Umm al-Fath. Now he testified that a certain Fatima bt. Muhammad al-Munturi was the owner of a half of a house in the al-Bayazin quarter in the city of Granada.[40]

After the conquest of Granada in 1492, when the *Capitulaciones* were still observed and the properties and documents written by the Muslim community respected,[41] the relationship between our notary and Umm al-Fath clearly strengthened, now including her husband and, therefore, the interests of both of them. The notary helps them both when they develop a strategy for the transmission of their patrimony.

Five and six, on 19 Ṣafar 899/29 November 1493, Muhammad Bahtan, Umm al-Fath's husband, asked for two notaries to write up and witness two documents. The first is his will and the second a document by which he acknowledges that he has no rights against his wife – a document unique in the Granadan collections.[42] In the legacy, Muhammad changes his first will, and now, instead of giving the complete third to charity, he reduces the charitable part to 30 silver dirhams and gives most of it to his pupils (*rabīb/rabība*) 'A'isha and 'Isa, the offspring of the late Muhammad b. Muhammad Mahdi and his widow Umm al-Fath bt. Yusuf b. Abi Hadid (related to Bahtan by his mother).

Therefore, this is a significant change in his will, since instead of the charity given to the poor (*masākīn*) in Nasrid Granada and in times of war, he now prefers to benefit the members of his family in need and under Christian rule. This change might have been the result of the recommendation of the notaries in the now Mudejar community of Granada.

38 On the restrictions on legacies in Islamic Law, see Rudolf Peeters, "Waṣiyya," *EI²*, 171–2. See also David S. Powers, "The Islamic Inheritance System: A Socio-Historical Approach," in *Islamic Family Law*, ed. Chibli Mallat and Jane Connors (London-Dordrecht-Boston: 1990), 11–29.

39 BHR C-27 33015.

40 BHR C-27 32969.

41 See Manuel Garrido Atienza, *Las capitulaciones para la entrega de Granada* (Granada: Universidad, 1992); José Enrique López de Coca Castañer, "Las capitulaciones y la Granada mudéjar," in *La incorporación de Granada a la Corona de Castilla*, ed. Miguel Ángel Ladero Quesada (Granada: Diputación, 1993), 263–305.

42 Both are BHR C-69 5–45 and BHR C-27 32952. This second document does only start with the *ḥamdallah*, thus indicating its relation with the first, written the very same day.

Seven, a year later, in 899/1494, both husband and wife are again asking for the testimony of the same two witnesses when they declare that they will economically maintain both ʿA'isha and ʿIsa – the two beneficiaries in Muhammad's will.[43]

Finally, in 902/1496, Umm al-Fath also makes a second will, with the same two notaries, now giving the third of her properties to their pupils, instead of the charitable legacies.

From this narration of several legal events in the lives of Umm al-Fath and her husband, what is most surprising is the continuous presence of the same notary through 15 years. He might be familiar with the social and economic situation of the married couple – I did not find a mention of them having children – and, therefore, of their legal needs and possibilities within the framework of Islamic law. In fact, they both changed their legacies when the political situation changed. Although, it is true that we will never know whether they changed them because of a recommendation of the notaries, because of the events of 1492 or just because they knew their rights and options, we certainly know that their relationship was close and continuous throughout time.

This example also shows how the notaries might have been working with a preferred partner in the two roles as writers of legal documents and witnesses of the facts contained in them. However, this is only represented here after the conquest of Granada.

Conclusions

The end of the fifteenth century in Granada provides a very exceptional case in Islamic medieval history since for a quite limited period of time – the last quarter of the century – it provides an important *corpus* of Arabic legal documents. These texts shed light on the legal procedures in pre-modern Islamic courts, especially on the use of writing in the practice of the law.

The documents were drafted by a group of professionals who shared formal conventions in order to know how to write the legal documents. In fact, some of them seem to master a very specialized knowledge on chancery and apply this knowledge to write legal documents.

The majority of the documents in the University Library collection in Granada were never used in court. Even if the notaries gave them a public nature and they might be used to establish the veracity of facts and the rights of the individuals involved in each transaction, their effective validity in case

43 BHR C-69 5–46, see Seco de Lucena, *Documentos arábigo-granadinos*, no. 90. This document was wrongly understood as an adoption by Seco de Lucena.

of litigation would directly depend on the procedure of *adāʾ al-shahāda* (the deposition of the witnesses orally in front of the judge).[44] Only a very small number of documents show traces of this procedure.

The notaries of Granada did not write their names in the documents; rather they signed them in a complicated manner. Therefore, we cannot see their names and we will not be able to follow them in the biographical dictionaries. However, their signatures can be identified and subsequently their documents could be analysed through time, so that we can see how they did not specialize in specific subjects of the law. On the other hand, the notary we studied here preferred his function as witness, second witness in a document, while he was pairing his job with a colleague who proceeded as a scribe, but relied on him for the testimony.

Writing a potentially valid document, public by the presence of the two witnesses, was frequent and maybe necessary in fifteenth century Granada. Family duties and rights, economic transactions, and all kinds of legal obligations were written down. The inhabitants of Granada kept these writings for some time[45] and they certainly were in use for social and economic purpose, although they were only prepared in case litigations occurred, or maybe to prevent them.

Umm al-Fath al-Shalyani is one of the most mentioned people in the University Library of Granada. But what is also striking is that she almost always visited the same notary, the same as her husband Muhammad Bahtan. We might think of many reasons why she chose him to supervise her wills, or to advice her on how to distribute her legacy. Especially after the Conquest of Granada by the Catholic Monarchs in 1492, the Mudejar community was in need of brokers and intermediaries, not only to negotiate with the new political power, but also to maintain the application of Islamic law as before. The notaries fulfilled this duty and role, as they did before the conquest.

Bibliography

Atienza, Manuel G. *Las capitulaciones para la entrega de Granada*. Granada: Universidad, 1992.

---

44 Müller, "Écrire pour établir la prevue orale en Islam," 85.

45 For a case of a family archive, see Amalia Zomeño, "Un archive, una familia y una pequeña historia de Baza a finales del siglo XV," *Revista del Centro de Estudios Históricos de Granada y su Reino* 27 (2015), 63–77.

Boogert, Nico van den. "Some Notes on Maghribī Script." *Manuscripts of the Middle East* 4(1989): 30–43.

Cahen, Claude. "A pròpos des *shuhūd*." *Studia Islamica* 31 (1970): 71–79.

Castañer, José Enrique López de Coca. "Las capitulaciones y la Granada mudéjar." In *La incorporación de Granada a la Corona de Castilla*, edited by Miguel Á.L. Quesada, 263–305. Granada: Diputación, 1993.

Déroche, François. "O. Houdas et les écritures maghrébines." In *Le manuscrit arabe et la codicologie*, edited by Ahmed-Chouqui Binebine, 75–81. Rabat: Université Mohammed V, 1994.

Espejo, Teresa, Irenia L. Stoytcheva, Domingo Campillo, Ana Durán, and María del Carmen Jiménez de Haro. "Caracterización material y proceso de conservación de la colección de documentos árabes manuscritos del Archivo Histórico Provincial de Granada." *Al-Qantara* 32 (2011): 519–532.

Houdas, Octave. "Essai sur l'écriture maghrebine." In *Nouveaux mélanges orientaux* 19 (1886): 83–117.

Ibn Juzayy. *al-Qawanin al-Fiqhiyya*. Libia: al-Dar al-Arabiyya li-l-Kitab, 1982.

Lapanne-Joinville, J. "L'Obligation d'entretien (*nafaqa*) en droit malekite." *Revue Marocaine de Droit* (1949): 166–182.

Lucena, Luis Seco de. *Documentos arábigo-granadinos*. Madrid: Instituto Egipcio de Estudios Islámicos, 1961.

Müller, Christian. "Écrire pour établir la prevue oral en Islam. La pratique d'un tribunal à Jérusalem au XIVè siècle." In *Les outils de la pensée. Études historique et comparatives des "textes,"* edited by Yusuke Nakamure and Akira Saito, 63–97. Paris: Les editions de la Maison des sciences de l'homme, 2010.

Powers, David S. "The Islamic Inheritance System: A Socio-Historical Approach." In *Islamic Family Law*, edited by Chibli Mallat and Jane Connors, 11–29. London, Dordrecht and Boston: Graham & Trotman, 1990.

Rodríguez, María D. "Les *maṣārī* de Grenade d'après quelques documents arabes (1442–1490)." *Bibliotheca Orientalis* 65, no. 5/6 (2008): 555–594.

Rodríguez, María D., and Salud M. Domínguez. "La compraventa de fincas urbanas en la Granada del siglo XV a través de dos documentos notariales árabes." *Anaquel de Estudios Árabes* 19 (2008): 175–199.

Rodríguez, María D., Emilio Molina, and Carmen Jiménez Mata. "La emisión monetaria de Muley Hacén. Cuestiones políticas y socioeconómicas que suscita." In *VII Estudios de Frontera: Islam y cristiandad (siglos XI–XVI). Los Banū Saʿīd*, edited by Francisco Toro and José Rodríguez, 773–783. Jaén: Diputación de Jaén, 2010.

Rodríguez, María D., and Francisco Vidal. "Fāṭima bint Muḥammad vende una finca de regadío. Sobre mujeres nazaríes y propiedades en la Granada del siglo XV." In *VIII Estudios de Frontera: Mujeres y fronteras*, edited by Francisco Toro and José Rodríguez, 415–430. Jaén: Diputación Provincial de Jaén, 2011.

Secall, Maribel C. "La justicia, cadíes y otros magistrados." In *El Reino Nazarí de Granada (1232–1492). Política. Instituciones. Espacio y economía*, edited by María J. Viguera, 365–427. Madrid: Espasa Calpe, 2000.

Tyan, Emile. "Le notariat et le régime de la preuve par écrit dans la pratique du droit musulman." *Annales de l'École Française de Droit de Beyrouth* 2 (1945): 1–99.

Vidal, Francisco. "Water and Farm Estates in the Arabic Documents of the Nasrid Kingdom of Granada." In *From al-Andalus to Khurasan. Documents from the Medieval Muslim World*, edited by Petra M. Sijpesteijn, Lennart Sundelin, Sofia T. Tovar, and Amalia Zomeño, 39–58. Leiden: Brill, 2006.

Zomeño, Amalia. "Notaries and Their Formulas: The Legacies from the University Library of Granada." In *From al-Andalus to Khurasan. Documents from the Medieval Muslim World*, edited by Petra M. Sijpesteijn, Lennart Sundelin, Sofia T. Tovar, and Amalia Zomeño, 59–77. Leiden: Brill, 2006.

Zomeño, Amalia. "Documentos árabes y biografías mudéjares: Umm al-Fatḥ al-Šalyānī y Muḥammad Baḥṭān (1448–1496)." In *Biografías mudéjares o la experiencia de ser minoría: Biografías islámicas en la España cristiana*, edited by Ana Echevarría, 291–325. Madrid: CSIC, 2008.

Zomeño, Amalia. "'When Death Will Fall Upon Him': Charitable Legacies in 15th Century Granada." In *Charity and Giving in Monotheistic Religions*, edited by Miriam Frenkel and Yaacov Lev, 217–233. Berlin and New York: De Gruyter, 2009.

Zomeño, Amalia. "Un archive, una familia y una pequeña historia de Baza a finales del siglo XV." *Revista del Centro de Estudios Históricos de Granada y su Reino* 27 (2015): 63–77.

CHAPTER 6

Crimes without Criminals?

Legal Documents on Fourteenth-Century Injury and Homicide Cases from the Haram Collection in Jerusalem

Christian Müller

Punishment and crime in the Mamluk period are attracting increasing scholarly interest.[1] These studies draw on rich material from chronicles,[2] in which, it seems, the qadi plays only a minor role as a judge in criminal matters. The documents presented here go beyond historiographical information for two reasons: first, as originals, they reflect judicial and administrative procedures in vigor, not historiographical narration; and second, they concern a type of non-spectacular homicide and injury cases that chronicles hardly ever mention. Therefore, the following analysis provides new insights into the functioning of Mamluk institutions in the field of bodily offenses.

The six documents of this study are conserved in the Haram al-Sharif Collection in Jerusalem.[3] They cover different aspects of how the qadi and Mamluk officials dealt with homicide and injury cases, as they notarize ongoing affairs, not always court sentences. Although varying in form and content, all documents were notarized by professional witnesses in the service of the qadi court: Document #30 reports on two armed attacks on villagers outside Jerusalem, the implication of Mamluk authorities in investigating the affairs, and the victims' claims. Report #642 describes the circumstances of a sword

1 This study was prepared as part of the ERC FP7 project ILM "Islamic Law Materialised." I would like to thank Lahcen Daaif for valuable advice. A version of this article with fully transliterated Arabic terms will be published in HAL: https://hal.archives-ouvertes.fr.

2 Bernadette Martel-Thoumian, *Délinquance et ordre social. L'État mamlouk syro-égyptien face au crime à la fin du IXe–XVe siècle* (Pessac/Paris: Ausonius, 2012); Carl F. Petry, "Al-Maqrīzī's Discussion of Imprisonment and Description of Jails in the Khiṭaṭ," *Mamlūk Studies Review* 7, no. 2 (2003): 137–143. On civilian crime in Cairo see C. Petry, "Disruptive 'Others' as Depicted in Chronicles of the Late Mamlūk Period," In *The Historiography of Islamic Egypt (c. 950–1800)*, ed. H. Kennedy (Leiden: Brill, 2001), 180ff.; M. Espéronnier, "La mort violente à l'époque mamlouke: Le crime et le châtiment: Les témoignages de Maqrīzī et d'Ibn Iyās," *Der Islam* 74, no. 1 (1997): 137–155.

3 Christian Müller, *Der Kadi und seine Zeugen. Studie der mamlukischen Ḥaram-Dokumente in Jerusalem* (Wiesbaden: Harrassowitz, 2013); Donald Little, *A Catalogue of the Islamic Documents from al-Ḥaram aš-Šarīf in Jerusalem* (Beirut: Orient-Institut der Deutschen Morgenländischen Gesellschaft, 1984).

 | DOI 10.1163/9789004343733_008

attack against a peasant by two pairs of brothers from his own village. Four other documents circumscribe legally relevant facts, not the course of events: injuries resulting from violent attacks (#292, #373, #628) and the victims' deaths (#373, #75), and finally notarized subjective rights, such as the acceptance of a financial compensation (#75) or the waiving of any claim (*barāʾa*) due to the described injury (#628).

In modern terms the events described constitute "criminal cases" since they include murder and armed attacks against human beings. Our sources, however, never refer to these facts in the generic term of crime (*jarīma*) or punishment (*ʿuqūba*), but mention the specific offense and its consequences for the victim, bodily harm or death. A "crime" to be punished according to the rules of Islamic law concerns primarily *ḥadd* delicts.[4] Islamic law's finality in offenses was "compensation for life, limb and property."[5] Most of the documents presented here notarize the subjective rights of victims and perpetrators. The rights of victims are described by the type of injury or death caused by the offense. The rights of perpetrators are involved when the victim, or next-of-kin prosecutors, refrain from retaliation (*qiṣāṣ*) as a form of compensation, or when any further claim against the perpetrator becomes excluded. As will be shown, these documents reflect the application of *fiqh* norms by the Mamluk qadi.

As the documents frequently mention Mamluk officials who investigated crime and then contacted the qadi court of law, this illustrates the twofold aspect of their activities: maintaining public order and repressing crime on the one hand and a role as executive agents for enforcing Islamic law on the other. If we consider "criminality" as a notion that legitimizes the modern state to exercise, in the form of penal law, the exclusive right of punishment,[6] then our documents add interesting insights into the legal reality of "fighting crime" in the Mamluk state.[7] Public crime repression, as inefficient as some of the

---

4 Cf. On the classical doctrine see Rudolph Peters, *Crime and Punishment in Islamic Law: Theory and Practice from the Sixteenth to the Twenty-first Century* (Cambridge: Cambridge University Press, 2005), 6–68.

5 Wael Hallaq, *Sharīʿa. Theory, Practice, Transformations* (Cambridge: Cambridge University Press, 2009), 309.

6 Cf. Hallaq, *Sharīʿa*, 308f.

7 Cf. C. Petry, "The Politics of Insult: The Mamluk Sultanate's Response to Criminal Affronts," *Mamluk Studies Review* 15 (2011): 87–115; Petry, "'Quis Custodiet Custodes?' Revisited: The Prosecution of Crime in the Late Mamluk Sultanate," *Mamluk Studies Review* 3 (1999): 13–30; Bernadette Martel-Thoumian, "Pouvoir et justice sous les derniers sultans circassiens (872–922/1468–1516)," in *Continuity and Change in the Realms of Islam: Studies in Honour of Professor Urbain Vermeulen*, ed. K. D'Hulster and J. van Steenbergen (Leuven: Peeters, 2008), 451–467.

documents may depict it as being, was never detached from the claim for private legal rights. Mamluk authorities and qadi courts of law represented different institutions that interacted in the field of bodily harm and homicide cases.

Notarizing the Rights of Victims and Perpetrators

Three documents center around a description of inflicted wounds and, eventually, the victims' deaths:

1) In document 373, dated 8 Rajab 796/9 May 1394, witnesses inspected two dead men who were struck by sword blows and later carried to the Bab Hitta in Jerusalem. The first victim, a villager from al-Zira'a, bore injuries to his head. Sword blows had cut off fingers of his left hand and broken his hand at an angle; his right leg was cut above the knee (#373 l. 5–7). The second victim, Muhammad, from Bayt al-Rama, had the flesh of his right leg cut to the bone (#373 l. 8–9). The witnesses mention the victims' clothes, as they do in other estate inventories. They confirm that nobody among those present explained the circumstances of the attack, or designated the attackers (#373 l. 11–12). This document, written on the back of a reused lease-contract paper, was neither completed nor signed, contrary to the hundreds of estate inventories that exist for this period.[8] Its connection with the case described in #30 (see below) may explain this particularity.[9]

2) In document 292 from 18 Shaʿbān 784/ 27 October 1382, the *mutawallī* of al-Salt presented himself to the qadi court and summoned witnesses to attest that a certain Ibrahim b. ʿAbd Allah b. Qubsa was hit by a stone that cut his brows next to his eyes, and that no perpetrator (*gharīm*) was designated.[10]

3) Document 642, 1 Shaʿbān 796/ 1 June 1394, frames the description of injuries with a report on who mandated the witnesses and wound expert to inspect the victim. The victim, a peasant from Taquʿ, had been attacked by four Christians of his own village while heading to his onion field. When he

8 On the 429 estate inventories in the Haram Corpus see Müller, *Der Kadi*, 390–400, on different legal formulations ibid., 62 (note 102), 86f. and 89–94; with Little, *Catalogue*, 63–186 on *wuqūf*-inventories and *passim* on other forms.

9 All the four witnesses of document 30 include in their attestation – in one way or another – that they had seen the two dead bodies brought to Jerusalem, whose inspection was the subject of the unsigned document #373.

10 First edited by al-ʿAsali (Kamil Jamil al-ʿAsali, *Watha'iq Maqdisiyya Ta'rikhiyya* (Amman: 1983/1985), 2:76) with a different interpretation, see below. On the implicit presence at the qadi court, i.e. "*bayna yaday,*" line 2, already proposed in al-ʿAsali, *Watha'iq*, 2:76, note 1.

was brought to Jerusalem, the wound expert noted many sword strokes on his body; one of them had cut off his left hand and another had hit his forehead and cut through skin, muscles and veins to the bone. The victim identified the perpetrator who had cut his hand. (#642, l. 10–14).

Two other documents exceed the description of the victim's injuries and determine the legal rights and obligations that follow from the offense:

4) In document 628, dated 2 Shawwāl 795/11 August 1393, the victim renounces any rights stemming from the wounds inflicted by his aggressor: an intentional (*ʿamd*) sword blow that cut the right-hand second and middle fingers off where they joined the palm (#628, l. 4–5). This implies in legal terms that blood money had been paid, and the document excludes further claims for this same offense.

5) The last victim was killed. No description of the wounds is given (#75). This court attestation (*maḥḍar*), issued by the qadi court of Hebron on 22 Jumādā I 706/29 November 1306, reports the claim of three brothers from Dura against two brothers, the barbers of the neighboring village of Idna,[11] who had killed their brother with intention (*qatl ʿamd*).[12] In court, they desisted from a retaliation punishment and opted for the payment of the blood money. The judge "gave them credence" and summoned the defendants, who accepted and thus avoided execution.[13]

Case Contexts Provided by the Documents

The legal contexts of the six notarizations vary, and this offers to today's reader a certain level of detail regarding the circumstances of the case: in document #373, witnesses inspect (*waqafa ʿalā*) two dead villagers brought to Bab Hitta in Jerusalem though no reason is given for their inspection. This document resembles the more than 400 estate inventories of dead or dying persons from the Haram corpus,[14] without however indicating the victims' heirs, or their personal belongings other than their clothes. Several aspects, the date of the inventory, 8 Rajab 796, the origin of the two victims from the villages al-Ziraʿa and Bayt al-Rama, as well as the place of the inspection, Bab Hitta, make it

11 On both villages, Dura and Idna see Wolf-Dieter Hütteroth and Kamal Abdulfattah, *Historical Geography of Palestine, Transjordan and Southern Syria in the late 16th Century* (Erlangen: Palm und Enke, 1977), 124, cf. Little, *Catalogue*, 263.

12 In fact by means of an "object", not necessarily by intention.

13 Cf. Little, *Catalogue*, 263, who does not mention the stake of the blood money.

14 See note 8, above.

possible to identify them as the two victims of the attack at Bi'r al-ʿAdd the day before, mentioned in document #30, l. 12. Document #373 is silent on this attack and only mentions the injuries caused by sword blows. This inventory was then certainly used later to write the report on several violent conflicts among villagers, dated to the end of Rajab 796/end of May 1394, that mentions the witnesses' inspection without going into the medical details (l. 17–18).[15]

Document #292 contains the description of wounds inflicted by throwing stones and names two persons: the "great emir al-Nasiri *mutawallī* of al-Salt" (l. 3) and a certain Ibrahim b. ʿAbd Allah b. Qubsa (l. 4–5). Its exact meaning is difficult to assess, since the text grammatically allows for various readings that designate different persons as victim or perpetrator. Beyond doubt, the text begins with somebody presenting himself to the witnesses (l. 2).

One grammatically correct reading possibility considers "*bayna yaday*" ("before a person," l. 2) as the first part of a syntactical construction with *mutawallī* as its second component: an unnamed "person presented himself to the witnesses in presence of the *mutawallī* and had attested that Ibrahim hit him (*ḍarabahu*, line 5) with a stone, without involving another adversary." With such a reading, the document designates the aggressor, not the victim, and then describes the injuries inflicted by him. It would also mean that the person who "called upon witnesses to attest to a fact" (*ashhada ʿalayhi*) was not named, a unique case among all other documents of this kind.[16] For these reasons, "*bayna yaday*" should mean, as it does in many other documents, "before the judge" – with the exception that here, in document 292, the judge is not named.

If we accept the omission of the qadi's name, the person presenting himself to the witnesses in presence of the unnamed judge was the *mutawallī*. He summoned the witnesses on his behalf concerning the fact that followed. This understanding of the text corresponds to a common document style that opens two further interpretations:

1) Grammatically correct, the text reads that the *mutawallī* had summoned the witnesses to attest that "Ibrahim hit him [that is the *mutawallī*] with a stone inflicting the described injuries and that he was the only attacker."[17] If this were indeed the meaning, why did the *mutawallī*, a high Mamluk official, not obtain from his attacker a confession or an acknowledgement since he was

15 #30, edition by al-ʿAsali, *Wathaʾiq*, 2:132–134.

16 Cf. Müller, *Der Kadi*, 56–64 partially revising Little, *Catalogue*, 224–244.

17 This reading corresponds roughly to the summary given by al-ʿAsali, which he considers as strange, all the more since the witnesses confirm "having seen the blow," *op. cit.*

known to the authorities? An *ishhād* document primarily engages the person summoning the witnesses (here the *mutawallī*), whereas an acknowledgment (*iqrār*) would be valid even if the potential aggressor (Ibrahim) later retracted it. That Mamluk judges and officials often used the *ishhād* form to have facts and events under their authority certified is an additional reason to suppose that the *mutawallī* acted here as a police officer, not as a victim.

2) In a third reading corresponding to administrative practice, it was the *mutawallī* who summoned the witnesses to the judge's presence to testify that "Ibrahim was hit by a stone inflicting the described injuries and that there is no other adversary." The text does not name any aggressor or person who struck the victim. This may explain the syntactical problem in the sentence, which probably followed a well known semantic structure: naming the victim (bearer of the right to blood money), then the aggressor and finally the inflicted wounds. In the present document however, the *mutawallī* did not know of another participant (*lam yukawwan lahu gharīmun ghayrahu*), either because he was in fact unidentified or since the victim had not given his name to the police. As a legal document, the text affirms that the *mutawallī*s investigated the case, and it might serve exactly for this purpose of identifying the incident and protecting the *mutawallī* against any suspicion of non-activity. Since the stone-hit was not qualified as "*ʿamḍan*," the inflicted injuries were not subject to claims for financial compensation. The filing note on the *verso* indirectly confirms this interpretation. Usually referring to the content, with names and places mentioned in the document, it reads: "*ḥujja* of ʿAbd Allah b. Jundub." If we exclude the first, highly improbable reading in which the victim does not figure at all in the text, this name must refer to the *mutawallī* since the only named person was called Ibrahim b. ʿAbd Allah b. Qusba.[18] To sum up, document 292 was the police report of a stone-hit causing injury without a designated aggressor, which was filed under the name of the Mamluk official, the *mutawallī* of al-Salt, *al-amīr al-kabīr* Nasir al-Din ʿAbd Allah b. Jundub. Since we do not dispose of other similar documents that defy standard grammar and establish a specific administrative usage, my reading remains an interpretation. In any case, however, this document illustrates that the *mutawallī* dealt with injury cases and summoned the witnesses to the qadi court of law for a legally valid account of injury cases.

Record 642 includes the description of the victim, a peasant from Taquʿ, in a report on various preceding administrative actions. The *mutawallī al-layl* delivered a letter (*risāla*) through the major-domo of the Mamluk viceroy of

---

18 The name element in line 2, his *laqab* Nasir al-Din, is complementary to his *ism* ʿAbd Allah and that of his father Jundub.

Jerusalem to the Shafiʿi judge. This letter demanded that the judge send court witnesses attesting to the state of health of an injured person from the Taquʿ village, near Jerusalem, who was brought to the Viceroy's residence that day. Upon the judge's written order (l. 7), the undersigning witnesses attended the examination by the "wound expert" (*jarāʾiḥī*) al-Hajj Musa b. Muhammad and saw that the victim's left hand had been cut off. The wound expert pointed to a sword blow that had hit the victim's forehead and cut into muscles, talons and bones. In the presence of these witnesses, the victim mentioned how he headed for his onion field this morning when four Christians of his own village, two pairs of brothers, assaulted and beat him. He then identified one of his assailants as the person who cut off his hand.[19]

The judicial attestation (*maḥḍar*) of the qadi court settlement on blood money for the murder of a peasant from Dura in Hebron (doc. 75) indicates that the prosecutors (*wulāt al-dam*) were sent by Bulghaq, Overseer of the Haram Foundations in Syria[20] to which their village, Dura, belonged (#75, lines 3–4). Once the judge was convinced that they refrained from retaliation and accepted the blood money, he summoned the perpetrators – possibly from prison – and the case could be settled with them. Five witnesses, present at the court session, attested to the mutual acknowledgement. Two of them wrote that they did "know the totality" of the case,[21] which implies that the others did not know the identity of the persons present at court. The judge authenticated this document with his *ʿalāma* (in a different script): according to legal standards, this implied his presence during the session, for otherwise the law would require an affirmation by court-witness attestations.[22]

The exclusion of further claims against the perpetrator of his injuries, drawn up as a "private witness document" without any reference to judicial authorities in the text (doc. 628), bears a notation in the right margin that the document was issued according to the written order (*marsūm*) of the Mamluk Viceroy. The Shafiʿi judge of Jerusalem, Sharaf al-Din ʿIsa, authenticated this court attestation with his *ʿalāma* notification. In this document, the former slave Mubarak summoned witnesses at the Shafiʿi court of law in Jerusalem to attest that he acquitted Ahmad from any obligations due to cutting off two of his, Mubarak's, right-hand fingers, and that he desisted from any future claim

19 #642, see edition al-ʿAsali, *Wathaʾiq*, 1:224–226.

20 This Mamluk officer, #075, l. 3–4, is also mentioned in Haram documents numbers 320, 332 and 763.

21 See both signatures in bottom line.

22 On this Müller, *Der Kadi*, 354–357.

in this case.[23] The injury was probably not accidental since the injuries were caused by a sword. It is not mentioned whether the victim had received the blood money or had inflicted retaliation on the perpetrator: legally both possibilities conform to his rights. The expression "that he acquitted the obligation (*dhimma*) of Ahmad (*annahu tabarra'a dhimmat Ahmad*)"[24] points rather to the acquittal of a monetary obligation, not retaliation. The final formulation excluding further claims and procedures is common usage. The Viceroy's order in this document illustrates the implication of Mamluk authorities in cases of bodily harm.

The Implication of Mamluk Officials in Offense Cases and Connected Private Claims

Haram document number 30 provides important information on the role of Mamluk officials in homicide cases: after the deadly attack on 19. Dhū l-Ḥijja 795, killing one and wounding several persons, the inhabitants of the village of al-Qusur presented their case several times to the viceroy of Jerusalem. The later claimed (v. excused himself) that he could solve the case only with a Sultan's order (*marsūm sharīf*). The victims' families then addressed a petition to the Noble Gate and obtained the sultan's decree (#30, l. 6–7). It is unclear from the text how long this took. The Monastery of St. Catherine conserves several petitions and decrees ordering Mamluk officials to protect and to act on behalf of the petitioners.[25] When this document was written at the end of Rajab 796, seven months after the attack, the case was still pending (#30, l. 8). What was certainly an authority's failure to act may relate to administrative events: during this seven-month period, the Viceroy in Jerusalem changed three times. The Viceroy on the day of the first crime, Buluwwa, who had been in office since Shawwāl 795, roughly three months, was replaced on 12th Jumādā I 796by the Emir Qardam al-Hasani. This official was replaced only weeks later on 25th Jumādā II by the Emir Ahmad al-Yaghmuri, who stayed in office at least until Muḥarram 797.[26] His son (l. 9–10), the "*janāb ʿālī*," ordered

23 #628, cf. Little, *Catalogue*, 267.

24 #628, line 4.

25 For the Mamluk period see Hans Ernst, *Die mamlukischen Sultansurkunden des Sinai-Klosters* (Wiesbaden: Harrassowitz, 1960); D.S. Richards, *Mamluk Administrative Documents from St Catherine's Monastery* (Leuven: Peeters, 2011).

26 These dates are partially based on estate inventories that mention their companions; cf. Müller, *Der Kadi*, 415f. The first mention of al-Sayfī Buluwwa occurs on #628, cf. also

the report to be written at the end of Rajab 796 (l. 22), which was notarized and signed by court witnesses, then confirmed by the judge with the notation "that he had heard what the witnesses had said in this case" (above the text).

The same document explains that for the second attack, on 7th Rajab 796, the *mutawallī al-layl* ʿAli b. ʿUmar came to the *janāb ʿālī* Shaʿban, son of the Mamluk viceroy of Jerusalem, accompanied by two villagers near Jericho who carried two dead bodies and reported on eight more dead victims at a place called Biʾr al-ʿAdd. The two bodies carried to Jerusalem originated from al-Ziraʿa and Bayt al-Rama, villages near Nablus, the eight other victims from al-ʿAwjaʾ. During the morning of the same day, the viceroy's son went to the qadi court and demanded two witnesses (*shāhidayn*) to inspect the two dead bodies (l. 9–12). The judge mandated the witnesses (l. 14) and two of them accompanied the *mutawallī* of Jerusalem Nasir b. Muhammad b. Fursan and his Mamluk staff to inspect the bodies at the mentioned Biʾr al-ʿAdd.[27] They found two dead young men, hit by several sword blows, but nobody who could inform them about the victims (l. 15–17). The document does not insist on the difference between eight bodies initially indicated and two found at the scene of crime: relatives might already have carried away the six missing bodies for a speedy burial.

This document also summarizes the inspection of the bodies brought to Jerusalem on the 7th of Rajab. It mentions that the two villagers who had carried them could not be heard by the witnesses and nobody knew their whereabouts (l. 17–19). The above-mentioned document of this inspection, dated 8th Rajab, number #373, gives the wound expert's description of the inflicted wounds. Since the victims were brought to Jerusalem on the morning of 7th Rajab and the inspection took place on 8th Rajab, the two villagers might well not have stayed over night and returned home. Other members of the victims' group stayed, since the witnesses learned from one of them that the group was warned against a potential attack by the habitants of al-Qusur when passing ʿAziriya, a village east of Jerusalem. When they had reached Biʾr al-ʿAdd, their

Mujir al-Din al-ʿUlaymi, *al-Uns al-Jalil bi-Taʾrikh al-Quds wa-l-Khalil* (Najaf: 1968), 2: 273. On Qardam see Shihab al-Din Abu l-ʿAbbas Ahmad al-Saʿdi al-Husbani Ibn Hijji (751–816), *Taʾrikh Ibn Hijji*, ed. Abu Yahya ʿAbd Allah al-Kundari (Beirut: Dar Ibn Hazm, 1424/2003), vol. 1: 92; Taqi al-Din ibn Qadi Shuhba, *Taʾrikh Ibn Qadi Shuhba*, ed. ʿAdnan Darwish (Damascus: al-Maʿhad al-ʿIlmi al-Faransi li-l-Dirasat al-ʿArabiyya, 1977–1997), 3: 511, lines 18f, and 3: 566 lines 3f. On al-Yaghmuri cf. al-ʿUlaymi, *al-Uns*, 2: 94, 2: 273.

27 On witness attestations see below (the first witness confirms that he saw the deaths "in all places," numbers two and four only mention the two victims in Jerusalem at Bab Hitta, the third witness affirms "that he saw the victims" in the plural. #30, right margin from top to bottom.

group was attacked and two of his companions killed. The eyewitness confirmed that he did not know whether the attackers came from al-Qusur or not (#30, l. 19–22). All these events are reported at the end of Rajab on behalf of the *janāb ʿālī* Shaʿban, the Viceroy's son: he ordered the writing of this act (*rassama bi-kitābat hādhihi al-ṣūra*, ibid). This document summarizes the facts of several murder cases investigated (sometimes not sufficiently) by Mamluk officials. For this it takes the form of an attested legal document that might serve as the basis for a qadi sentence on blood money or *talio* in the future.

Mamluk officials investigating bodily offenses who ask the judge to mandate witnesses for an inspection of victims do not only figure in the above-mentioned document (#30, l. 9–12). In another case, the majordomo of the Viceroy wrote a letter (*risāla*) to the judge saying that he should send his witnesses to see the wounded peasant from Taquʿ at the Viceroy's seat in Jerusalem (#642, lines 2, 6–7). In such a context, it is highly probable that the *mutawallī* of al-Salt summoned witnesses to attest to the injuries of a person in document 292, and not the victim himself (see above). According to this document, the victim was presented to the witnesses, who confirmed that they had seen the injury. And it was the Mamluk official who had the competence *ex officio* to notarize facts concerning corporal offenses. Given the fact that the victim did not designate his aggressor, may we suppose that the official acted here against the victim's will?

The direct implication of Mamluk officials in the notarization of legal documents becomes evident in most of the documents under study here. Next to those already mentioned, it was the Nāẓir al-Ḥaramayn Bulghaq who sent the private prosecutors in the Hebron murder case to the qadi court (#75, l. 3–4). When they refrained from retaliation and both sides accepted the financial compensation, the judge concluded and ratified the witness document for the case.

Although the witness documents #373 and #628 do not mention Mamluk authorities in the text, both specimens are linked to the actions of Mamluk executory agents: inventory #373 concerned victims of the second murder case reported in #30. And document #628, a waiver of claims for injuries, bears a marginal note that mentions the Viceroy's order to write the document. Did Mamluk authorities exercise pressure on the victims to resolve corporal offenses in such a way? Or had the judge hesitated to notarize the waiver of claims without such an order? From the Islamic law perspective that determined the written form, the victim had privately summoned the witnesses "by free will etc." (l. 3) to certify that he desisted from further claims against his aggressor. Legally, the Mamluk official did not interfere in the claims between victim and perpetrator.

Mamluk Titles and Offices

The present documents designate Mamluk officers with four different hierarchical ranks. These ranks tell us at what level Mamluk officials dealt with the investigation of crime in a provincial administration like that of Jerusalem:

1) The *mutawallī l-layl* (night commissary) was called *al-amīr al-ajall*,[28] according to Qalqashandi the 10th and least important rank that corresponded to the soldiers of an emir.[29] The same title was used for the *mutawallī* al-Salt, some 90 years earlier (#292). When two dead bodies were carried to Jerusalem at sunrise, the *mutawallī l-layl* brought them to the major-domo of the Viceroy (#30, l. 9). Was he responsible for public security during the night? At any rate, he was certainly not only a civilian watchman (*ḥāris*).[30]

2) The *mutawallī* al-Quds, investigating the crime scene at Bi'r ʿAdd (#30, l. 15), was designated in other documents as *al-majlis al-sāmī*.[31] This corresponded to the second rank of the Mamluk *ḥalqa*, which was two ranks higher than the *mutawallī l-layl*.[32]

3) The major-domo (*ustādār*) of the Viceroy in Jerusalem was addressed as *al-janāb al-ʿālī*, an emir of twenty, corresponding to the fifth military rank by Qalqashandi.[33] The Viceroy's son held the same rank of a *al-janāb al-ʿālī*. In both cases studied here, the orders given to the qadi emanated from this level of the Mamluk hierarchy, not from lower ranks. The "Overseer of the two Sanctuaries" Bulghaq (#75) was also addressed as *al-janāb al-ʿālī*.[34] As a

28 #642, l.

29 Ahmad al-Qalqashandi, *Subh al-Aʿsha fi Sinaʿat al-Insha'* (Cairo: 1913–1919), 12: 287. The term *al-amīr al-ajall* is frequently used in the Haram documents, specifically in documents 193, 331, 360, 483, 593, 642. Its attribution to specific offices merits further study.

30 Cf. Huda Lutfi, *Al Quds al-Mamlûkiyya. A History of Mamlûk Jerusalem Based on the Ḥaram Documents* (Berlin: Klaus Schwarz Verlag, 1985), 306, referring to document #513.

31 Document #772a. al-Qalqashandi mentions "*al-majlis al-sāmiyya*" as seventh rank and "*al-majlis al-sāmī*" as eighth rank, al-Qalqashandi, *Subh al-Aʿsha*, 12:286f. The cursive writing of the Haram documents does not allow for a distinction, so I opted for the lesser rank.

32 The Jerusalem estate inventories mention the implication of the *mutawallī* l-Quds (#300), never the *mutawallī l-layl*.

33 al-Qalqashandi, *Subh al-Aʿsha*, 12:286. According to Shams al-Din Muhammad al-Manhaji al-Asyuti, *Jawahir al-ʿUqud wa-Muʿin al-Qudah wa'l-Muwaqqiʿin wa-l-Shuhud*, ed. Musʿad ʿAbd al-Hamid al-Saʿdani (Beirut: 1996), 2: 590, this was the lowest rank above the emirs of the *ḥalqa*.

34 Documents #596 and #763, as well in #75, l. 3 as "*al-janāb al-karīm al-ʿālī*."

civil servant, the "representative of the Public Treasury" (*wakīl bayt al-māl*) in Jerusalem held the same rank.[35]

4) The viceroy (*nāʾib al-salṭana*) was the highest representative of the Mamluk state in Jerusalem. He was designated as *al-maqarr al-karīm*.[36] According to Qalqashandi, this referred to the second rank of an emir of one thousand.[37] This Mamluk representative was not directly involved with investigating the murder cases. But he issued the order (*marsūm*) to notarize document #628. The victims of the attack near Jericho on 19 Ḏū l-Ḥijja 795 appealed to him for a solution, and he directed the claimants to obtain a Sultan's decree for this (#30, l. 5–7). In Jerusalem, the office of a viceroy was created as late as 777/1375,[38] some 20 years before these two documents were produced. As we have seen in the sources, he nominated a majordomo who dealt with current affairs. Speculations that the district of Jerusalem was too unimportant and did not reflect Mamluk authority levels must therefore be rejected.[39]

Narrative sources and Qalqashandī, to the best of my knowledge, only mention the Viceroy of Jerusalem in a quite secondary position.[40] They never refer to the lower Mamluk officers, the *mutawallī* of Quds or its "night commissary" (*mutawallī l-layl*). Both titles designate different offices held by different persons: in the year 796 AH, the *mutawallī l-layl* was ʿAlaʾ al-Din ʿAli b. ʿUmar al-Kurdi,[41] and the *mutawallī l-Quds* was Nasir b. M. b. Faris. Further references for the years 795 and 797 AH[42] mention the *mutawallī* [*l-Quds*] Sharaf al-Din Musa (al-Marjani) and the *mutawallī bil-Quds* Sayf al-Din Abu Bakr.[43] Neither of the lower-ranking officers had the competence to ask the judge to send court witnesses to crime scenes. This was the prerogative of an emir of twenty

35 Participating in estate inventories: documents 093, 148, 153, 257, 258, 299, 337, 338, 419, 427, 461, 466, 483, 496, 521, 545, 561, 572, 594, 663, 689, 705, 728, 738, 742, responsible for selling inheritances: documents 530, 580, 586, 589, 591, 767t; cf. al-Qalqashandi, *Subh al-Aʿsha*, 12:289, as the fourth rank in the civil administration.

36 #642, l. 2–3.

37 al-Qalqashandi, *Subh al-Aʿsha*, 12:285.

38 Cf. Lutfi, *al-Quds al-Mamlûkiyya.*, 154f.; cf. al-Qalqashandī, *Subh Aʿsha*, 4:199.

39 *Pace* Lutfi, *al-Quds al-Mamlûkiyya*, 176, and more generally *ibid.*, 154ff.

40 The same is true for *al-Quds*, and for the model given for the province of Alep, cf. Lutfi, *al-Quds al-Mamlûkiyya*, 158f; cf. al-Qalqashandī, *Subh al-Aʿsha*, 8:219, with the *nāʾib* of al-Quds among the 8th rank.

41 See #30. In estate inventory #457, a person died in the house of the *mutawallī al-layl* ʿAlaʾ (?) al-Din ʿAli – who might be the same person, but the name is too frequent to exclude a homonym.

42 See Lutfi, *al-Quds al-Mamlûkiyya*, 174f., with references to #767 (in 795) and #772a (in 797).

43 #300.

janāb ʿālī, and in the cases examined here either the majordomo or the son of the viceroy.

Legal Significance of the Documents

A final aspect concerns the legal consequences of these documents, which, as was stated above, cover different stages of a case, not always its final outcome. All documents presented here bear witness signatures, but no authentication marks by the Mamluk state administration. As such, they may be considered as "legal documents", in the sense that contents and authentication by a qadi determine their legal significance, according to the norms of Islamic law. Islamic law does not consider writing (*kitāb*) as legal proof. Any qadi judgment is based on facts that were established either by the judge's knowledge of them and by the testimony of "honorable" witnesses, often professional notaries who were accredited with the qadi.[44] This is why the present documents were signed by witnesses who, in the end, could testify orally to their contents in court and "legally establish" the facts (*thubūt*). In juridical terms, signing a document as a witness, introduced by a phrase such as "I attest to this" (*shahidtu bi-dhālika*), corresponded to accepting the individual duty of attesting to this fact (*taḥammul al-shahāda*). The witness complied with this duty when the judge called for the oral performance of testimony (*adāʾ al-shahāda*).[45] This juridical distinction explains why a signed witness document does not constitute legal "proof" – unless it passes through attestation in the presence of a qadi. Consequently, and according to authentication criteria, documents may

---

44 See my analysis of more than 400 documents with over one thousand signatures from Jerusalem, in Müller, *Der Kadi*, 280–318. Three of the documents presented here were signed in Jerusalem, by the following witnesses, document #30: ʿAli b. ʿAbd al-Qadir al-[…] {P 8} with 36 signatures from 774–796 AH, Ahmad b. Thabit al-Ansari {P 37} with 35 signatures from 784–798 AH, Ahmad b. Sulayman {P 53} with 94 signatures 790–797 AH, Ahmad b. Ibrahim {P 67} with 37 signatures 771–797 AH; document #628: Yusuf b. Yaʿqub al-Hanafi {P 298} with 55 signatures 787–796 AH, Ahmad b. Ahmad ibn al-Jalal {P 68} with 39 signatures 795–797 AH, Khalil b. Yusuf {P 287} with 34 signatures 790–796 AH; document #642: Muhammad b. Aʿala al-Hanafi {P 612}with 4 signatures 792–796 AH, ʿAbd al-Munʿim b. Muhammad al-Ansari {P 100} with 77 signatures 793–797 AH, and ʿAbd Allah b. Muhammad al-Misri {P 560} with 38 signatures 793–797 AH. The number in {P …} refers to the identification in Müller, *Der Kadi*, 531ff., where all signed documents are listed.

45 On judicial procedures that accompany oral attestation in the qadi court see Müller, *Der Kadi*, 349–351.

contain the certification of a legal right by the qadi, or simply notarize legal facts that were of importance to a case.

Several authentication levels existed in Mamluk judicial practice:

1) the witness attestations, usually written separately below the text;
2) qadi notations on whether he was present or confirmed the notarized facts etc., usually written by himself above the text;
3) the qadi's ratification of a legal right that was established according to the terms of the law. In Mamluk documents this was indicated by the judge's motto (*ʿalāma*) written by him at the top, next to the *basmala*. The *ʿalāma* implied that the judge had accepted the oral attestation as legal proof (*bayyina*).[46]

1) Witness attestations as a basic level of authentication: all documents were signed by witnesses with the exception of #373, since this inspection of two killed persons complemented report document #30, where the signatures of its witnesses are conserved. In such a context, #373 may have been preserved as an unsigned memory aid. Among the other documents, only number 292 bears no authentication marks other than witness' signatures. With the presence of the – unnamed – qadi mentioned at the beginning, this attestation concerning a police officer's role in an injury case already constituted a "legal proof document," as it was filed as "*ḥujja*." The lack of further authentication marks may be explained by the fact that neither the officer nor the victim could claim a financial compensation on the basis of this document, which did not specify the aggressor.

2) Qadi notations: all three judicial notations in our sources were applied by the qadi ʿIsa b. Ghanim al-Shafiʿi who officiated in Jerusalem between 793/1391 and 797/1395.[47] He noted on document #628, containing the victim's disavowal of any further right or claim against the perpetrator of his injuries, that "this happened in this way." By this, the judge signaled his presence during the attestation and he therefore "knew the facts." With this document in hand, the perpetrator could counter future claims since a judge had confirmed the facts.[48]

---

46 Müller, *Der Kadi*, 353–358.

47 With full name Sharaf al-Din Abu l-Ruh ʿIsa b. Ghanim b. ʿIsa b. Ghanim al-Ansari al-Khazraji, cf. #610/2; on him see Müller, *Der Kadi*, 250–253 and *passim*; cf. also Little, *Catalogue*.

48 Unless if the judge's conduct was at stake: this particular judge, ʿIsa b. Ghanim, was accused of corruption and a case was opened against him after his death, see Müller, *Der Kadi*, 509ff.

Since the notarized facts are negative statements – the exclusion of further action – the law prohibits its confirmation by a court sentence (*ḥukm*). The same judge applied the notation that he "mandated the witnesses" to the report on an attack against a peasant, #642. The police officer had demanded their presence at the inspection of injuries. At that stage no *ḥukm* was required. The financial compensation for the cut fingers, the legal right of the victim, would be determined later on the basis of these attestations. The report on two deadly incidents, #30, bore the judge's confirmation, that he "heard what the witnesses said." Although he does not confirm the totality of the described events, he could use the present document as the basis of future decisions, possibly concerning the blood money for the victims.

3) Ratified documents: document #75 notarizes the legal rights of the persecutors (*wulāt al-dam*) to obtain the blood money for their murdered brother and the rights of the murderers not to be killed for this. By applying his *ʿalāma* "Praise to God, Master of the World," the judge certifies the legal rights in this case. In terms of the distinction between legal facts and legal rights, only this last document establishes legal rights while the others refer to legal facts.

From a legal point of view, none of these documents mention a punishment by state authorities or by the qadi in the form of *taʿzīr*, nor the "expiation of a sin" (*kaffāra*) for certain offenses and crimes according to Islamic law.[49] Significantly enough, no case was qualified as a *ḥadd* offense, not even the robbing of villagers on their way to the market of Hisban in Document 30, lines 2–8. This event obviously was considered a normal homicide (*jināya*), not banditry (*muḥāraba* or *qaṭʿ al-ṭarīq*), since relatives claimed their right with the authorities. This document also states the inaction of the Mamluk authorities to inquire into this crime. The perpetrators were designated as "*gharīm*," opponent or attacker (#292, #373 and #642), never as criminal (*mujrim*) or as suspect in a crime case (*tuhma*). Since the term *gharīm* also applied to litigations on economic matters,[50] its use did not presuppose *per se* a criminal action. Assuming that Islamic law ignores the concept of a criminal, however, would mean to throw out the baby with the bath. It simply means that these documents deal with a specific aspect of what we would call "criminal cases" today.

No document mentions a sentence (*ḥukm*). This does not, however, signify that Mamluk qadis could not pass a sentence in offense cases. The analyzed documents represent earlier stages of legal procedures that would finally pass through the "establishment of facts" (*thubūt*) in a court-session, and, upon the claimants request, lead to the sentence. In order to be valid, the *ḥukm*

49 On the notion of *kaffāra* for unintentional homicide, cf. al-Asyuti, *Jawahir*, 2: 215.

50 Cf. i.e. al-Asyuti, *Jawahir*, 1: 124, 1: 130.

document was certified by the qadi's *ʿalāma* and his "call for attestation" (*ishhād*) to the legality of the procedure by court witnesses. All *ḥukm* documents from the Haram corpus follow this procedure,[51] and Asyuti's manual provides corresponding model documents for qadi trials in cases of homicide.[52] In the Hebron murder case, the prosecutors' pardon (*ʿafw*) and acceptance of financial compensation obviously did not require a *ḥukm* since the judge had not yet fixed the amount of the compensation.

Islamic law in Mamluk times established the compensation (*diya*) for the loss of life and limb. If the loss was only partial, or if it concerned smaller injuries, the manual refers to a proportional compensation fixed according to the qadi's discretion, called "*ḥukūma*."[53] These rules were more than legal theory, as is illustrated by #628, where the victim, who had lost two fingers by a sword blow, excluded for the future, among other aspects and claims, "any *diya* and any *ḥukūma*" (#628, l. 7). Other than a claim for retaliation, a claim for financial compensation did not require the identification of the perpetrator by "proof": Islamic law considers the payment of the *diya* by the liability group (*ʿāqila*). It is difficult to accept that this institution fell into disuse at an early date,[54] since Asyuti's manual reports later legal positions on how the payment was to be effected in the case of unintended homicide,[55] as he does in other fields of law. According to these rules, the victims of the murderous attacks near Jericho and at Biʾr ʿAdd would receive compensation within three years of the judgment, paid by the village near to where the victims were found, even if the culprits were not identified. This judicial claim was the stake behind documents #30 and #373.[56]

Conclusion

Each document was dressed to serve a specific need within the practice of law in Mamluk society. At their time, they constituted different "cards" to be played in the game called "law and society." These records and attestations

51 Cf. Müller, *Der Kadi*, 329–383.

52 al-Asyuti, *Jawahir*, 2: 229ff.

53 See the definition for *ḥukūma* in al-Asyuti, *Jawahir*, 2:211, with references in the section on various limbs, ibid., 2:209–211. Here *ḥukūma* stands next to the fixed *diya*.

54 *Pace* Joseph Schacht, *An Introduction to Islamic Law* (London: The Clarendon Press, 1982), 186.

55 al-Asyuti, *Jawahir*, 2:214f.

56 Cf. the model for such a claim in al-Asyuti, *Jawahir*, 2: 245.

illustrate the close interaction between Mamluk authorities and the qadi court in the field of offenses and homicide.

Documents give insights into the importance of Islamic law as normative reference for obtaining compensation in offenses against life or limbs of a person: None of the cited documents match with a police-report of the exact details and circumstances, nor with a medical expertise. The reported facts concern the kind of injury (i.e. loss of limb)[57] or the kind of murder (i.e. *qatl ʿamd*).[58] These aspects were precisely necessary to determine the compensation for injury and homicide cases. Situated between a medical expertise and a police record, the attested descriptions made of injuries correspond exactly to the exigencies of *fiqh*[59] and prepare the ground for court action.

Our sources reflect on the role of the qadi and his court to certify a legally relevant situation that is conditioned by the interaction with Mamluk authorities: The first step is that authorities demanded witnesses to effect attestations at scenes of crime or to inspect victims (#30, #642). At certain stages of their investigation of offenses, Mamluk officials presented cases (in form of their protagonists, one may say) to the qadi, who then treated them as private claims or affairs.[60] This collaboration counters an old argument against an effective qadi jurisdiction in criminal cases, who was limited to cases presented to him (*accusatio*-competence) and not entitled to investigate upon suspicion.[61] For this see the Overseer of the Sanctuaries, who sends the protagonists of a homicide to the qadi of Hebron #75; and the Viceroy who is at the origin of a waiver of claims in an injury case #628. The interaction went into both directions: The police addressed the qadi court to notarize and render legally acceptable/receivable certain facts during the investigation of cases. A police officer went to court for attesting the state of a not yet resolved enquiry #292, and the report on deadly attacks on villagers was dressed by the Viceroy's son #30.

The interaction of the Mamluk qadi and executive officials in cases of bodily offenses goes parallel with the evolution of legal doctrine in so called "trials of suspicion" (*daʿāwī al-tuham*) that Mamluk authorities may organize.[62]

57 Cf. #642.

58 Cf. #075.

59 Cf. the chapter on injuries (*al-jirāḥ*) in al-Asyuti, *Jawahir*, 2: 200–215, and on claims for blood-money, *ibid.*, 2: 216–251.

60 The documents do not describe how the process at the qadi court was conducted. On a summary for the Ottoman practice and enforcement agencies see Peters, *Crime and Punishment in Islamic Law*, 75ff.

61 Cf. E. Tyan, *Histoire de l'organisation judiciaire en pays d'Islam*, 2nd ed. (Leiden: Brill, 1960).

62 Cf. B. Johansen, "Signs as Evidence: The Doctrine of Ibn Taymiyya (1263–1328) and Ibn Qayyim al-Jawziyya (d. 1351) on Proof," *ILS* 9 (2002), 168–193, esp. 190f. For the Ottoman

Circumstances of a case constitute signs that may create a suspicion and allow for torturing the suspect to obtain information and acknowledgements. According to the classical doctrine, an acknowledgment is only valid when given out of free will without constraint (*ikrāh*). The present documents do not cover certain aspects of police investigation, arrest and custody: we do not know the conditions in which the perpetrators where identified and acknowledged the facts when they were presented to the qadi. But if police interrogation bordered torture, the acknowledgement would be receivable according to the new legal doctrine. The qadi court as institution was fully integrated into the Mamluk system of governance. The enforcement of subjective rights according to Islamic law passed by Mamluk executive agents who collaborate with the qadi court in its task to certify these rights.[63] The analysis of law through one of its primary products, legal documents, offers important insights into spheres of its application that chronicles, the major source for criminal cases in Mamluk times, hardly ever provide. Law seen from the bottom-up perspective of legal documents allows glimpses into a historical reality that contrasts with and complements the fascinating stories told by literary sources. The underlying administrative and juridical realities of Mamluk society beyond juridical and historiographical narratives are just beginning to emerge.

Editions

Document Number 30 (*Figures 6.1a and b*)

Little, *Catalogue*, p. 271

26,5 × 35,5 cms.

Date: 27th [?] Rajab 796[64] / 28th [?] May 1394

Edition ʿAsali, *op. cit.* 2: 132–4, no. 47.

---

period cf. Peters, *Crime and Punishment in Islamic Law*, 83, on the minority ḥanafite position that executive officials were under certain circumstances allowed to use torture in order to find the truth.

63 *Pace* Kristen Stilt, *Islamic Law in Action. Authority, Discretion and Everyday Experience in Mamluk Egypt* (Oxford: Oxford University Press, 2011), 89ff., who mentions no injury and homicide cases among crimes and offenses.

64 Little's date 7 Rajab 796 /8 May refers to the second incident, line 8, not to the redaction of the document, line 23, where the scribe adds to the 7 something that remains under consideration.

[1] بسم الله الرحمن الرحيم

[2] لما كان بتاريخ تاسع عشر الحجة سنة خمس وتسعين وسبعمائة توجه جماعة من أهل قرية القصور الجارية في أوقاف النبي صلى الله عليه وسلم إلى

[3] حسبان ومعهم مالهم إلى الجهة المذكورة ليبتاعوا به زبيبا وحب رمان وغير ذلك فمروا بالدرب عن قرية أريحا الغور في الليل

[4] فطلع عليهم جماعة من أهل قرية أريحا المذكورة بعددهم وأسلحتهم وقتلوا شيخهم الشيخ علي بن علوان وجرحوا جماعة من أهل

[5] قرية القصور المذكورة وحمل القتيل المذكور والجرحى إلى القدس الشريف وتكرر طلبهم لأخذ حقهم من المذكورين أهل

[6] قرية أريحا ورفعوا أمرهم غير مرة لنائب السلطنة الشريفة بالقدس الشريف إذ ذاك واعتذر بأنه لا يمكن الحل في ذلك

[7] إلا بمرسوم شريف فتوجه أقارب القتيل والجرحى إلى الباب الشريف وشكوا حالتهم فبرز المرسوم الشريف بخلاص حقهم

[8] فتمادى الأمر في ذلك إلى أن كان ليلة يسفر صباحها عن سابع شهر رجب الفرد سنة ست وتسعين وسبعمائة حضر

[9] علاء الدين علي بن عمر متولي الليل بالقدس الشريف ومعه اثنين من فلاحي الغور إلى بين يدي الجناب العالي الأميري الزيني شعبان

[10] ابن المقر الكريم العالي الشهابي اليغموري الظاهري نائب السلطنة الشريفة بالقدس الشريف وبلد سيدنا الخليل عليه السلام وناظر الحرمين

[11] الشريفين أدام الله نعمه وصحبتهما رجلان مقتولان ذكر الجناب المشار إليه أن أحد القتلى من قرية بيت الرامة والآخر من قرية الزراعة

[12] من الغور وذكر الفلاحان للجناب المشار إليه أن ثمن قتلى من قرية العوجا ببئر العد ظاهر القدس الشريف و إنه لما كان صبيحة الليلة المذكورة أعلاه

[13] حضر الجناب العالي الزيني المشار إليه مجلس الحكم العزيز الشافعي بالقدس الشريف أجله الله تعالى وطلب شاهدين للوقوف على القتلى المذكورين

[14] فندب الحاكم المشار إليه أعلاه أيده الله تعالى الواضع خطه أعلاه شهودا للوقوف على القتلى المذكورين أعلاه فتوجه من يعين رسم شهادته آخره

[15] نفران منهم للوقوف على القتلى الذين ببئر العد المذكور ومعهم متولي القدس الشريف ناصر بن محمد بن فرسان ومن عين معه من دار النيابة المعظمة

[16] بالقدس الشريف فوجدوا جميعا قتيلين رجلين شايين وهما ميتان لا روح فيهما وبهما ضربات سيوف في أماكن متفرقة ولم يوجد عندهم

[17] أحد يعلم بخبرهم ووقف الشهود المندوبين من مجلس الحكم العزيز بأجمعهم على القتيلين المحضرين صحبة الفلاحين المذكورين الحاضرين بهما

[18] إلى القدس الشريف وهما ميتان لا روح فيهما وبهما ضربات سيوف بشعة في أماكن متفرقة ولم يوجد الفلاحين الذين أحضراهما ولم

[19] يسمع الشهود كلا مهما ولا حضر من أعلم بحالهما فتولى شخص ذكر أن اسمه عبد بن محيسن من قرية خربتي من عمل القدس الشريف الموكل بقرية العوجا المذكورة

[20] بذكره وأنه كان رفيقا للمقتولين المذكورين وأنهم مروا من قرية العازرية ظاهر القدس الشريف عند الغروب لحضر معهم جماعة من أهل القرية المذكورة وذكروا

[21] لهم أن جماعة من أهل قرية القصور المذكورة أعلاه تقدموكم بالدرب وذلك أنه لما وصلوا إلى بئر العد قام عليهم جماعة قتلوا المذكورين ولم يعلم هل القاتلين

[22] من أهل قرية القصور أو من غيرها فلما تكامل ذلك رسم الجناب العالي المشار إليه أعلاه بكتابة هذه الصورة فكتب بتاريخه حسب ما رسم به والحمد لله وحده

[23] في سابع |وعشرين [؟]| شهر رجب سنة ستة وتسعين وسبعمائة

[بالهاشي اليميني من الفوق إلى التحت]

[1] وقفت على القتلى المذكورين أمامه جميعهم في الأماكن المذكورة وعاينت القتلى على الحالة المذكورة كتبه علي بن عبد القادر ال...

[2] وقفت على القتيلين المحضرين للشهابي بالقدس الشريف وعاينت الجراحات بهما وهما ميتان لا روح فيهما في تاريخه المعين أعلاه كتبه أحمد بن سليمان

[3] وقفت على القتلى المذكورين أعلاه في تاريخه كتبه أحمد بن إبراهيم

[4] وقفت على القتيلين المحضرين إلى باب حطة بالقدس الشريف وعاينت الجراحات وهما ميتان لا روح فيهما كتبه أحمد بن ثابت الأنصاري

[أعلى الوثيقة يسار البسملة]

سمعت كلام شهوده بذلك | كتبه عيسى بن غانم الشافعي | لطف الله تعالى به

Translation of Document 30

1 In the name of God the Compassionate, the Merciful

2 On the date of 19. Dhū l-Ḥijja 795 a group of persons from the village al-Qusur that belongs to the Foundations of the Prophet [Khalil] reached for

3 Hisban. They carried money to buy dried grapes, grains of pomegranate and other items. When they passed the way (*darb*) along the village Jericho al-Ghawr during the night

4 they were attacked by a group of habitants of that village with their equipment and weapons. The [assailants] killed their Sheik, al-Shaykh ʿAli b. ʿUlwan and injured several inhabitants of the

5 mentioned village al-Qusur. The mentioned dead body and injured persons were carried to Jerusalem the Noble. The [villagers] repeatedly demanded their right from the mentioned inhabitants

6 of Jericho and brought their case several times to the viceroy of Jerusalem the Noble at that time. The latter excused himself that he could solve the case

7 only with a Sultan's order (*marsūm sharīf*). Relatives of the dead and the wounded addressed the Noble Gate [the Sultan] complaining about their situation. As consequence, a sultan's decree ordering to solve their rights came up.

8 The affair dragged on like this [without result] when in the early morning of the 7th Rajab of the year 796

9 the *mutawallī al-layl* of Jerusalem, ʿAlaʾ al-Din ʿAli b. ʿUmar presented himself and two peasants of the Ghawr-plain at [the viceroy's son at Jerusalem], *al-janāb al-ʿālī* Zayn al-Din Shaʿban,

10 son of *al-maqarr al-karīm al-ʿālī* Shihab al-Din al-Yaghmuri al-Zahiri, Viceroy of Jerusalem the Noble and Hebron, Overseer of the two Sacred

11 Shrines, may God protect his benefaction; the two [villagers] were in presence of two dead men. The mentioned *janāb* [i.e. the Viceroy's son] stated that one of the dead came from the village Bayt al-Rama and the second from the village al-Ziraʿa

12 in the Ghawr. The peasants told the mentioned *janāb* that eight dead bodies from the village al-ʿAwga' lay at a place called Bi'r al-ʿAdd outside Jerusalem. In the morning of the above-mentioned day (w. night),

13 the mentioned *janāb ʿālī* Zayn al-Din went to the Shafiʿi qadi court of law in Jerusalem, may God dignify him, and demanded (*ṭalaba*) that two witnesses were sent for inspecting the two dead bodies.

14 The above-mentioned judge, may God help him, who put his writing on top of [the document], mandated witnesses to inspecting the two above-mentioned dead persons. Thereupon the two witness, who are assigned with their witness-notification below, headed to

15 inspect the dead bodies at the mentioned Bi'r al-ʿAdd. Together with them went the Mutawallī of Jerusalem, Nasir b. Muhammad b. Fursan and those he had assigned [belonging to] the Viceroy-Ship

16 in Jerusalem, the Noble. Altogether they found two young men dead, without a sign of life, bearing sword blows at various places [of the body]. Nobody was there

17 to inform them on these [persons]. All witnesses mandated by the qadi court inspected the two dead who had been accompanied by the mentioned peasants

18 to Jerusalem the Noble. The two [victims] were dead, without a sign of live, and they bore heavy sword-blows at various parts [of their body]. The [witnesses] did not meet the two peasants that had brought the bodies [to Jerusalem]. They did not

19 listen their deposition (*kalām*), and nobody present knew their whereabouts (*ḥāl*). A person who called himself ʿAbd b. Muhaysan (?) from the village al-Khurbati (?) in the District of Jerusalem, and, according to his own saying, was mandated (*muwakkal*) by the mentioned village al-ʿAwja', took in hand [the affair] (*tawallā*):

20 He was a companion of the mentioned dead, and when they passed the village al-ʿAziriyya, outside Jerusalem at sunset, several inhabitants of this village came to them and told

21 them: "several inhabitants of the above-mentioned village al-Qusur precede you at the pass-way." And when they reached Bi'r al-ʿAdd, a group attacked them and killed those mentioned. He did not know whether the murders

22 belonged to al-Qusur or to another village. When this was done, the abovementioned *janāb ʿālī* had the writing completed in this shape (*ṣūra*). And this was written on the date, according to what was recorded, and Praise alone to God,

23 on the 27th [?] Rajab in the year 796.

[four attestations at the right margin, from top to bottom:]

1 I inspected all the victims mentioned ahead [this sheet] at the mentioned places and and saw the dead in the state as mentioned. Written by ʿAli b. ʿAbd al-Qadir al- …
2 I inspected the two victims that were brought to Shihab al-Din in Jerusalem and saw their injuries and they were dead without a sign of life at the date indicated above, written by Ahmad b. Sulayman
3 I inspected the above-mentioned victims at the above-indicated date, written by Ahmad b. Ibrahim.
4 I inspected the two victims that were brought to Bab Hitta at Jerusalem and saw their injuries and they were dead without a sign of life, written my Ahmad b. Thabit al-Ansari.

[*ʿalāma*-notification on top of the writing:]
I listened to the witnesses saying this, written by ʿIsa b. Ghanim al-Shafiʿi, may God be graceful with him.

***Document Number 075* (*Figures 6.2a and b*)**
Little, *Catalogue*, p. 263
26 × 38 cms.
Date: 22 Jumādā I 706/ 29 November 1306

الحمد لله رب العالمين

[1] بسم الله الرحمن الرحيم وصلى الله على سيدنا محمد وآله وصحبه وسلم

[2] حضر إلى مجلس الحكم العزيز بمدينة الخليل عليه وعلى نبينا أفضل الصلاة والسلام والرحمة

[3] من ذكر أنه حضر من مجلس الجناب الكريم العالي [؟] المولوي الأميري الكبيري الاسفهسلاري الكفيلي الزعيمي العوني الغياثي

[4] السيفي بلغاق الملكي الناصري المنصوري ناظر أوقاف الحرمين الشريفين بالشام المحروس من أسبغ الله ظله ورفع محله

[5] كل واحد من ملك بن راجح بن وال وأخويه وشقيقيه راشد وغازي الرئيسين [!] قرية دورى الوقف على حرم الخليل

[6] عليه السلام وادعوا أن كل واحد من عبد الله بن محمد بن نادر و نجم بن شليطا بن خميط الخلاقين [؟]

[7] من قرية إدنا قتل أخاهم شقيقهم مبارك بن راجح وذلك قتلا عمدا عدوانا وأنهم استحقوا

[8] ديته عليهما وقد عفوا عنهما من القصاص بالدية ابتغا لوجه الله تعالى وطلبا لمرضاته صدقه عليهما ذلك

[9] وحضر بحضورهم المدعى عليهما عبد الله ونجم رضياهم على ذلك وقبلا منهم البراءة قبولا شرعيا وبه شهد

[10] عليهم بتاريخ الثاني والعشرين من جمادى الأول سنة ست وسبعمائة

[11|15 شهادة يمنى] حضرت المجلس المذكور وشهدت على إقرار المذكورين بما فيه وكتب عبد الله بن مالك

[11|15 شهادة وسطى] حضرت المجلس المذكور وشهدت على إقرار المذكورين بما فيه كتب عبد الله بن أبي بكر عمران في تاريخه

[11|15 شهادة يسرى] حضرت المجلس المذكور وشهدت على إقرار المذكورين بذلك كتبه محمد بن يوسف [؟] بن سليمان المقدسي المالكي

[16|19 شهادة وسطى] حضرت المجلس المذكور وشهدت على إقرار المذكورين بذلك وأنا بالجميع عارف كتبه خليل بن فرح بن محمد الحنفي

[19|16] شهادة يسرى] حضرت المجلس المذكور وشهدت على إقرار المذكورين بذلك وأنا بالجميع عارف كتبه عثمان بن عمر بن علي المقرئ بالمقام الشريف

[verso]

محضر اخوان [؟] ودورى وإقرارهم لبعضهما بعضا السند [؟] في شهور سنة ست وسبعمائة

Translation of Document 075

1 In the name of God the Compassionate, the Merciful. God bless our prophet Muhammad, his family and companions and grant salvation.

2 There came to the qadi court in Hebron (Khalil), be on him and on our prophet the best prayers, peace and blessing,

3 some persons who stated that they came from the siege of *al-janāb al-karīm* [...] al-Isfahsalari [...]

4 Sayf al-Din Bulghaq al-Malaki al-Nasiri al-Mansuri, overseer of the two Sanctuaries in Syria the Protected, may God provide his shadow and elevate his position.

5 They were Malik b. Rajih b. Walin and his two brothers Rashid and Ghazi, the two headmen of the village Dura [which] belonged to the foundation of Khalil,

6 Peace upon him, and they claimed that ʿAbd Allah b. Muhammad b. Nadir, Najm b. Shallita b. Khumayt, two barbers

7 from the village Idna[65] had killed their full-brother Mubarak b. Rajih with intention (*qatl ʿamd*)[66] in a hostile action. They required

8 blood-money for him from them, desisting from killing them in retaliation, in the desire to face God and to seek his gratification. [The judge] deemed this credible

9 and summoned in their presence the defendants ʿAbd Allah and Najm, who agreed with them and accepted the acquittal [from retaliation or the payment] in the legal form. This was attested

10 on their behalf on the 22nd Jumādā I in the year 706.[67]

---

65 On both villages, Dura and Idna s. above, note 11.

66 Actually by means of an "object", not necessarily by intention.

67 The *waw* is attached to the six. This reading is confirmed by the filing notation on verso.

lines 11–15)

[right attestation:]
I assisted at the indicated court session and attested to the acknowledgments as they are [described] in the [document], written by ʿAbd Allah b. Malik

[middle attestation:]
I assisted at the indicated court session and attested to the acknowledgments as they are [described] in the [document], written by ʿAbd Allah b. Abi Bakr ʿUmran on that date

[left attestation:]
I assisted at the indicated court session and attested to the acknowledgments by this, written by Muhammad b. Yusuf (?) b. Sulayman al-Maqdisi al-Maliki

lines 16–19)

[middle attestation:]
I assisted at the indicated court session and attested to the acknowledgments by this and I know all this, written by Khalil b. Faraj b. Muhammad al-Hanafi

[left attestation:]
I assisted at the indicated court session and attested to the acknowledgments by this and I know all this, written by ʿUthman b. ʿUmar b. ʿAli, recitor at the Noble Sacred Place.

[A *ʿalāma* next of a long *basmala*]
Praise to God, Master of the World.

[verso:]
a *maḥḍar*: the brothers from Dura and their mutual acknowledgments, the legal instrument (?) during the months of the year 706.

***Document Number 292* (*Figures 6.3a and b*)**

Little, *Catalogue*, p. 243
12 × 30 cms.
date: 18 Shaʿbān 784/ 27 October 1382
ed. ʿAsali, *Watha'iq Maqdisiyya Ta'rikhiyya*, 2: 76, Notice num. 23

[1] بسم الله الرحمن الرحيم

[2] حضر إلى شهوده يوم تاريخه بين يدي

[3] الأميري الكبيري الناصري متولي الصلت المحروس أعزه الله تعالى

[4] وأشهد على نفسه من غير إكراه ولا إلزام أن إبراهيم

[5] بن عبد الله بن قبصة ضربه بحجر ففجه في جبنه[68] عند

[6] عينه وأن الشهود الواضعين خطوطهم فيه عاينوا

[7] الضربة وأنه لم يكون له غريم[69] غيره[70] وبذلك

[8] أشهد عليه في ثماني[71] عشر شعبان المبارك

[9] سنة أربعة وثمانين وسبعمائة

[10] أشهد عليه بذلك   أشهد عليه بذلك

[11] كتبه محمد بن عمر ال.عر[؟] الشافعي   وكتبه عمر بن يحيى بن عثمان

verso:[72]

حجة عبد الله بن جندب

verso at bottom, other writing direction:

على يد الحاج إبراهم |درهم وثمن صابون |على يد الجارية نصف [؟] وثمن زيت

68 التحرير: جبينه.

69 التحرير: غرم.

70 التحرير: عنده.

71 التحرير: ثاني.

72 Not edited by al-ʿAsali.

Translation of Document 292

1 In the name of God the Compassionate, the Merciful
2 There came to the witnesses on the date of its writing in [the judge's] presence
3 the Great Emir Nasir al-Din, Mutawallī of al-Salt the Protected, may God give him strength,
4 who summoned upon himself as witness, without constraint nor coercion, that Ibrāhīm
5 Ibn ʿAbd Allah b. Qubsa was hit by a stone that cleaved his brows (pl. *jubun*) next to
6 his eye; that the witnesses who put their writing on the [document] had seen
7 the blow [i.e. the injury]; and that no other perpetrator (*gharīm*)[73] was designated to him.[74] This
8 he had testified upon himself on the 18th Shaʿbān
9 of the year 784.
10 he called upon my testimony on this, / he called upon my testimony on this
11 written by Muhammad b. Umar al-? al-Shafiʿi / written by ʿUmar b. Yahya b. ʿUthman

verso: *ḥujja* of ʿAbd Allah b. Jundub

verso at bottom upside down: a notation on obligations with no obvious link to the case on *recto*.

Document Number 373 (verso) (*Figure 6.4b*)

Little, *Catalogue*, p. 174
9 × 15 cms.
Date: 8 Rajab 796/ 9 May 1394

[1] الحمد لله

[2] بتاريخ ثماني رجب المعظم سنة ست وتسعين وسبعمائة وقف من يضع خطه

[3] على رجلين ميتين لا روح فيهما أحضرا من باب حطة ذكر

73 The editor's choice "*ghurm*" (damage) does not correspond to the handwriting.

74 I prefer reading *lam yukawwan lahu gharīm* over "*lam yakūn*", which deviates from the standard grammar.

[4] أن اسم أحدهما معتوق من الزراعة

[5] به جراحات بيده اليسرى ضربه سيف قاطع لأصابعه

[6] وقصه يده من الكوع وضربه سيف قاطع لرجله

[7] اليمنى من فوق الركبة وبرأسه جراحات

[8] والثاني يدعى محمد من بيت الرامة برجله

[9] اليمنى ضربة قاطعة ألحم والعصب وهما ميتان

[10] على محمد قميص أبيض وجبة طرح وفروة وعلى

[11] المـ......قميص وعباءة فروة عتيقة [؟] ولم يحضر أحد

[12] عند شهوده يذكر أمرهم ولا من هو غريمهم ولا

[13] [ولا] تهم

Translation of Document 373 (*verso*)

1 Praise to God
2 On the date of eighth[75] Rajab of the year 796, those who put their signature [on it] inspected
3 two dead men, without any life, they were present at (?) Bab Hitta. It was said
4 that the name of one of them was Freedman,[76] a freedman from al-Zira'a.[77]
5 He bore injuries at his left hand, hit by a sword that cut the fingers
6 and cut him of his hand from the bend (elbow; angle) on. He was hit by a sword cutting his
7 right leg above the knee (*rukba*) and he bore injuries at his head.
8 The second person was called Muhammad, from Bayt al-Rama. On his
9 right leg a blow cut meat parts and the bone. Both were dead.

---

75 The comparison with document 30, dated on the seventh, excludes the reading "two," cf. Little, *Catalogue*, 174, with 2 Rajab 796/3 May 1394.

76 cf. Little, *Catalogue*, 174, has Maʿtuq, does not mention the village al-Ziraʿa. The last letter of the person resembles more a letter *nūn* than a *qāf*.

77 The same village is mentioned in #30.

10 Muhammad wore a white shirt, a *ṭarḥ*-overcoat, and a fur; the
11 [? first indicated person wore] a shirt and an old [?] cloak-like fur wrap. Nobody was present
12 with the witnesses to explain their case, who were their perpetrators and who were
13 their [prosecutors]

[no witness signatures]

***Document Number 628* (*Figures 6.5a and b*)**
Little, *Catalogue*, p. 267,
28,5 × 38 cms.
date 2 Shawwāl 795/11 August 1393

جرى الأمر كذلك

كتبه عيسى بن غانم الشافعي لطف الله تعالى به

[1] بسم الله الرحمن الرحيم

[2] حضر إلى مجلس الحكم العزيز الشافعي بالقدس الشريف أجله الله تعالى
وأدام أيام متوليه مبارك بن عبد الله عتاقه

[3] الحاج محمد العريشي فقيه جالود وقف سيدنا خليل عليه الصلاة والسلام
وأشهد عليه طائعا مختارا في صحة منه وسلامة وجواز أمر

[4] أنه تبرأ ذمة أحمد بن إبرهيم بن حمزة عرف بابن البقرة الخليلي مما
جناه عليه بأن جرم بسيف عمدا فانقطعت اصبعيه الثاني

[5] والوسطى من يد اليمنى من الفصل المتصل بالكف ومن الدية على ذلك
وأقر مبارك المذكور أعلاه أنه لا يستحق

[6] ولا يستوجب في ذمة أحمد المذكور أعلاه ولا عنده ولا تحت يده حقا
ولا بقية من حق ولا جناية ولا أمر [؟] من جناية ولا قضاء ولا

[7] عملا ولا دية ولا حكومة ولا عوضا عن ذلك ولا دعوى ولا مطالبة ولا
شيئا قل ولا جل بوجه من الوجوه ولا سبب

[8] من الأسباب ومتى ادعى بدعوى يخالف هذا الإقرار أو ادعى احد
بسببه كانت دعواه ودعوى من يدعى سببه زورا

[9] وبهتانا وإثما وعدوانا باطلة لا حقيقة لها عرف الحق في ذلك فأقر به
والصدق فاتبع لا تبعة في ذلك إنكاره ولا جحوده

[10] ووكل في ثبوته وبه شهد في ثاني شهر شوال المبارك من شهور سنة خمسة
تسعين وسبعماية - والحمد لله وحده

[شهادة يمنى] شهدت على إقراره يوسف بن يعقوب الحنفي

[شهادة وسطى] شهدت على إقراره بذلك أحمد بن محمد بن الجلال الش

[شهادة يسرى] أشهد على إقراره خليل بن يوسف الحنفي

right margin:

وسطر ذلك حسب المرسوم الكريم العالي السيفية نائب السلطنة وناظر
الحرمين الشريفين أعز الله أنصاره........أحمد المقر المشار إليه أعلاه
في تاريخه أعلاه

Translation of Document 628

The matter happened in that way,
written by ʿIsa b. Ghanim al-Shafiʿi, may God be graceful to him

1 In the name of God the Compassionate, the Merciful

2 There came to the Honored Shafiʿi Court in Jerusalem the Noble, may God the Exalted dignify it and prolong the days of its magistrate, Mubarak

3 Ibn ʿAbd Allah, the freed-man by al-Hajj Muhammad al-ʿArishi, jurist in Jalud, which is part of the Foundation of Our Master Khalil, Prayers and Peace upon him, and called upon himself to attest voluntarily and by own choice, while he was in a sound state and legally capable to conduct his affairs,

4 that he acquitted the person of Ahmad b. Ibrahim b. Hamza, known als Ibn al-Baqara (Cow-Son) al-Khalili, from all obligation resulting from injuries that he inflicted on him intentionally (*ʿamdan*) by sword, that is cutting the second

5 and the middle right-hand fingers off the palm, and from the payment of the blood-money. The above-mentioned Mubarak acknowledged that he does not claim a right,

6 does not request from the personality-right of the above-mentioned Ahmad, nor with him, nor in his possession any right, nor the rest of a right, nor an injury or any matter linked to an injury, no court-sentence, no

7 action, no blood-money, no partial settling of a blood-money, no substitute to that, no court-claim, nor demand, no thing small or big in any aspect, from any reason.

8 Should he, or anybody else raise a claim on behalf of these reasons in contradiction to this acknowledgement, it is a lie,

9 a slander, a sin and an invalid hostile action without veracity: the rightful (*ḥaqq*) in this matter is known. To this he acknowledges in trueness. His denying or refusing this has no (legal) consequences.

10 He authorized this to be established as fact (*thubūt*). This was testified on the second Shawwāl of the year 795. Praise be to God alone.[78]

Attestation right:	I bore witness to this acknowledgment, Yusuf b. Yaʿqub al-Hanafī
Attestation middle:	I bore witness to this acknowledgment by this, Ahmad b. Muhammad b. al-Jalal
Attestation left:	I attest to this acknowledgement Khalil b. Yusuf al-Hanafi

marginal note: written according the distinguished and high ordinance (*marsūm*) of Sayf al-Din (w. al-sayfī), Viceroy and Overseer of the two Noble Sanctuaries, may God enforce his partisans, … Ahmad, the mentioned beneficiary on the date [mentioned] above.

***Document Number 642* (*Figures 6.6a and b*)**

Little, *Catalogue*, p. 272,
28 × 38 cms
Date: 1 Shaʿbān 796/ 1 June 1394
Edition: ʿAsali, *Wathaʾiq Maqdisiyya taʾrikhiyya*, 1: 224, Notice num. 27

78 Written by a different hand.

ندبت شهوده لذلك

كتبه عيسى بن غانم الشافعي

لطف الله تعالى به

[1] بسم الله الرحمن الرحيم

[2] بتاريخ مستهل شهر شعبان المكرم سنة ست وتسعين وسبعمائة حضرت رسالة من الجناب العالي الشهابي أستادار المقر الكريم العالي المولوي الأميري الشهابي

[3] أحمد اليغموري الظاهري نائب السلطنة المعظمة بالقدس الشريف وبلد سيدنا الخليل عليه السلام وناظر الحرمين الشريفين أعز الله أنصاره على يد الأمير

[4] الأجل علائي علي الكردي متولي الليل بالقدس الشريف إلى بين يدي سيدنا ومولانا العبد الفقير إلى الله تعالى القضائي الشرفي الأنصاري

[5] الخزرجي الشافعي الحاكم بالقدس الشريف وأعمالها وناظر أوقافها المبرورة ومضافاتها وشيخ الشيوخ أدام الله تعالى نعمه عليه وأحسن في الدنيا والآخرة

[6] إليه أن يندب شهودا للوقوف على رجل مجروح من أهل قرية تقوع من عمل القدس الشريف أحضر يوم تاريخه إلى القدس الشريف إلى

[7] دار النيابة الكريمة فعند ذلك رسم سيدنا ومولانا الحاكم المشار اليه أعلاه أيده الله تعالى للواضعين خطوطهم آخره أن

[8] يتوجهوا للوقوف على المذكور وصحبتهم جرائحي من أرباب الخبرة فتوجه من يضع خطه من شهود المندوبين من مجلس الحكم

[9] العزيز الشافعي المشار إليه أدام الله تعالى أيام متوليه وصحبتهم الحاج موسى بن محمد الجرائحي بالقدس الشريف فوجدوا رجلا جريحا يدعى نصير

[10] بن نصر الله بن محمد من أهل قرية تقوع وصحبته والده نصر الله وغيره من القرية المذكورة من الرجال والنساء وبه ضربات عديدة مقطوع

[11] اليد اليسرى عاينها شهوده وذكر الجرائحي المذكور أن به ضربة سيف في مقدمة دماغه قاطعة الكيمخت ثم العظم

[12] ثم العصب ثم العظم وذكر أنه لم يكز به خلاف ذلك وذكر نصير الجريح المذكور أنه كان ليلة يسفر صباحها عن يوم

[13] تاريخه بمزرعة له بها بصل بالقرية المذكور ة ظاهر النوادر فحضر إليه إلى المزرعة المذكور ة كل واحد من

[14] إبراهيم بن جرجس وشقيقه يعقوب و صلاح بن صالح وشقيقه مفرح الجميع النصارى من القرية المذكورة وتحاملو [!] عليه وضربوه

[15] وأن الذي تولا قطع يده إبراهيم المبدأ بذكره أعلاه وليس له غريم في ذلك سوى من عين فيه فلما تكامل ذلك رسم كتابة هذه الصورة

[16] فكتب في تاريخه المعين أعلاه ـ الحمد لله وحسبنا الله ونعم الوكيل

witness-attestations lines 17–20

[شهادة يمنى] وقفت على المذكور وعاينت يده المفصولة منه وشهدت عليه بذلك وعلى الجرائحي بما نسب اليهما فيه محمد بن اعلى الحنفي؟

[شهادة وسطى] وقفت على المذكور وعاينت يده المفصولة منه وشهدت عليه بذلك وعلى الجرائحي بما نسب اليهما فيه كتبه عبد المنعم بن محمد الأنصاري

[شهادة يسرى] وقفت على المذكور وعاينت يده المفصولة منه وشهدت عليه بذلك وعلى الجرائحي بما نسب اليهما فيه كتبه عبد الله بن أحمد المصري

Translation of Document 642

1 In the name of God the Compassionate, the Merciful

2 On the date of first Sha'bān in the year 796, a letter by *al-Janab al-'Ali* Shihab al-Din, Major-domo of *al-Maqarr al-Karim* [...] Shihab al-Din

3 Ahmad, Viceroy of Jerusalem and Hebron [...] and Overseer of the two Sanctuaries, may God strengthen his partisans, through the hand of the

4 Great Emir 'Ala' al-Din 'Ali al-Kurdi, *mutawallī al-layl* in Jerusalem the Noble, [was delivered] to our Lord and Master, the Needy of God the Exalted, the qadi Sharaf al-Din al-Ansari

5 al-Khazraji al-Shafi'i, judge of Jerusalem the Noble and its district, Overseer of its blessed foundations and its annexes, Sheik of the Sheiks, may God prolong his benefaction on him and do him good in this world and the thereafter

6 that he should mandate his witnesses to inspect a wounded person from Taqu',[79] a village of the District of Jerusalem, who was brought today to Jerusalem to the

7 seat of the Noble Viceroy-ship. Upon this, our Lord and Master, the above-mentioned judge, may God the Exalted help him, wrote to the undersigning persons that they

8 head to inspect the mentioned person in the company of the wound-expert. And the undersigning witnesses, who are assigned

9 by the above-mentioned qadi court, may God prolong the days of its keeper, in the company of al-Hajj Musa b. Muhammad, the wound-expert in Jerusalem the Noble then found a wounded man called Nuṣayr

---

79 Hütteroth, *Historical Geography*, 114.

10 b. Nasr Allah b. Muhammad from the inhabitants of the village Taquʿ, accompanied by his father Nasr Allah and other man and women of the same village. He bore many strokes that cut

11 his left hand. The witnesses of this [document] saw the [blows] and the mentioned wound-expert explained that a sword blow to the front head (w. of his brain) cut his skin (*kaymakht*), then the muscles (*ʿaḍal* for *ʿathal*),

12 then the veins (*ʿaṣab*, also nerves), then the bone (*ʿaẓm*), and that he did not heavily bleed besides this. The wounded Nuṣayr said that he left in the morning of this day

13 for his field of onions in the mentioned village outside the stacks,[80] when in his mentioned field

14 Ibrahim b. Jurjus and his brother Yaʿqub [together with] Salaḥ b. Salih and his brother Mafrah showed up. They are all Christians from the mentioned village. They attacked and struck him. The one whom he holds responsible (*tawallā*) for cutting his hand is the initially mentioned Ibrahim, no other perpetrator (*gharīm*) except

15 the one designated in this [document]. When this was accomplished, he dressed the writing in this form

16 and it was written on the above-mentioned date. Praise to God. God is our sufficiency. How excellent a Keeper is He!

17–20) attestation at the right:
I inspected the mentioned person and saw his cut-off hand; and I attested on this and on the wound-expert and what is attributed to both of them.
written by Muhammad b. Aʿla (?) al-Hanafi

17–20) attestation in the middle:
I inspected the mentioned person and saw his cut-off hand; and I attested on this and on the wound-expert and what is attributed to both of them.
written by ʿAbd al-Munʿim b. Muhammad al-Ansari

17–20) attestation at the left:
I inspected the mentioned person and saw his cut-off hand; and I attested on this and on the wound-expert and what is attributed to both of them.
written by ʿAbd Allah b. Ahmad al-Misri

80 Dozy, Supplément aux dictionnaires arabes (Leiden: E.J. Brill, 1881), has "meule" for *andar*, pl. *nawādir*, which may signify haystack or charcoal stack.

On top at left:
I mandated the witnesses to this, written by ʿIsa b. Ghanim al-Shafiʿi, may God be graceful to him

Bibliography

al-ʿAsali, Kamil Jamil. *Watha'iq Maqdisiyya Ta'rikhiyya*, 2 vols. Amman: Matbaʿat al-tawfiq, 1983 and 1985.

al-Asyuti, Shams al-Din Muhammad al-Manhaji. *Jawahir al-ʿUqud wa-Muʿin al-Qudah wa'l-Muwaqqiʿin wa-l-Shuhud*. Edited by Musʿad ʿAbd al-Hamid al-Saʿdani. Beirut: Dar al-kutub al-ʿilmiyya, 1996.

Dozy, R. Supplément aux dictionnaires arabes, 2 vols. Leiden: E.J. Brill, 1881.

Espéronnier, M. "La mort violente à l'époque mamlouke: Le crime et le châtiment: Les temoignages de Maqrīzī et d'Ibn Iyās." *Der Islam* 74, no. 1 (1997): 137–155.

Ernst, Hans. *Die mamlukischen Sultansurkunden des Sinai-Klosters*. Wiesbaden: Harrassowitz, 1960.

Hallaq, Wael B. *Sharīʿa: Theory, Practice, Transformations*. Cambridge: Cambridge University Press, 2009.

Hütteroth, Wolf-Dieter and Kamal Abdulfattah. *Historical Geography of Palestine, Transjordan and Southern Syria in the late 16th Century*. Erlangen: Palm und Enke, 1977.

Ibn Hijji, Shihab al-Din Abu l-ʿAbbas Ahmad al-Saʿdi al-Husbani (751–816). *Ta'rikh Ibn Hijji*. Edited by Abu Yahya ʿAbd Allah al-Kundari, 2 vols. Beirut: Dar Ibn Hazm, 1424/2003.

Ibn Qadi Shuhba, Taqi al-Din. *Ta'rikh Ibn Qadi Shuhba*. Edited by ʿAdnan Darwish, 4 vols. Damascus: al-Maʿhad al-ʿIlmi al-Faransi li-l-Dirasat al-ʿArabiyya, 1977–1997.

Little, Donald. *A Catalogue of the Islamic Documents from al-Ḥaram ash-Sharīf in Jerusalem*. Beirut: Orient-Institut der Deutschen Morgenländischen Gesellschaft, 1984.

Lutfi, Huda. *Al Quds al-Mamlûkiyya. A History of Mamlûk Jerusalem Based on the Ḥaram Documents*. Berlin: Klaus Schwarz Verlag, 1985.

Martel-Thoumian, Bernadette. "Pouvoir et justice sous les derniers sultans circassiens (872–922/1468–1516)." In *Continuity and Change in the Realms of Islam: Studies in Honour of Professor Urbain Vermeulen*. Edited by K. D'Hulster and J. Van Steenbergen, 451–467. Leuven: Peeters, 2008.

Martel-Thoumian, Bernadette. *Délinquance et ordre social. L'État mamlouk syro-égyptien face au crime à la fin du IXe–XVe siècle*. Pessac/Paris: Ausonius, 2012.

Müller, Christian. "Écrire pour établir la preuve orale en Islam: la pratique d'un tribunal à Jérusalem au XIVe siècle." In *Les outils de la pensée. Étude historique et comparative des "textes,"* edited by Akira Saito and Yusuke Nakamura, 63–97. Paris: Maison des sciences de l'homme, 2010.

Müller, Christian. *Der Kadi und seine Zeugen. Studie der mamlukischen Ḥaram-Dokumente in Jerusalem*. Wiesbaden: Harrassowitz, 2013.

Mujir al-Din, al-ʿUlaymi. *Al-Uns al-Jalil bi-Taʾrikh al-Quds wa-l-Khalil*. 2 vols. Najaf: 1968.

Peters, Rudolph. *Crime and Punishment in Islamic Law: Theory and Practice from the Sixteenth to the Twenty-first Century*. Cambridge: Cambridge University Press, 2005.

Petry, Carl. "'Quis Custodiet Custodes?' Revisited: The Prosecution of Crime in the Late Mamluk Sultanate." *Mamluk Studies Review* 3 (1999): 13–30.

Petry, Carl. "Disruptive 'Others' as Depicted in Chronicles of the Late Mamlūk Period." In *The Historiography of Islamic Egypt (c. 950–1800)*, edited by Hugh Kennedy, 167–194. Leiden: Brill, 2001.

Petry, Carl. "Al-Maqrīzī's Discussion of Imprisonment and Description of Jails in the Khiṭaṭ." *Mamluk Studies Review* 7, no. 2 (2003): 137–143.

Petry, Carl. "The Politics of Insult: The Mamluk Sultanate's Response to Criminal Affronts." *Mamluk Studies Review* 15 (2011): 87–115.

al-Qalqashandi, Ahmad. *Subh al-Aʿsha fī Sinaʿat al-Inshaʾ*. 14 vols. Cairo: 1913–1919.

Richards, Donald S. *Mamluk Administrative Documents from St Catherine's Monastery*. Leuven: Peeters, 2011.

Schacht, Joseph. *An Introduction to Islamic Law*. London: The Clarendon Press, 1982.

Stilt, Kristen. *Islamic Law in Action. Authority, Discretion and Everyday Experience in Mamluk Egypt*. Oxford: Oxford University Press, 2011.

Tyan, Émile. *Histoire de l'organisation judiciaire en pays d'Islam*. 2nd ed. Leiden: Brill, 1960.

Plates

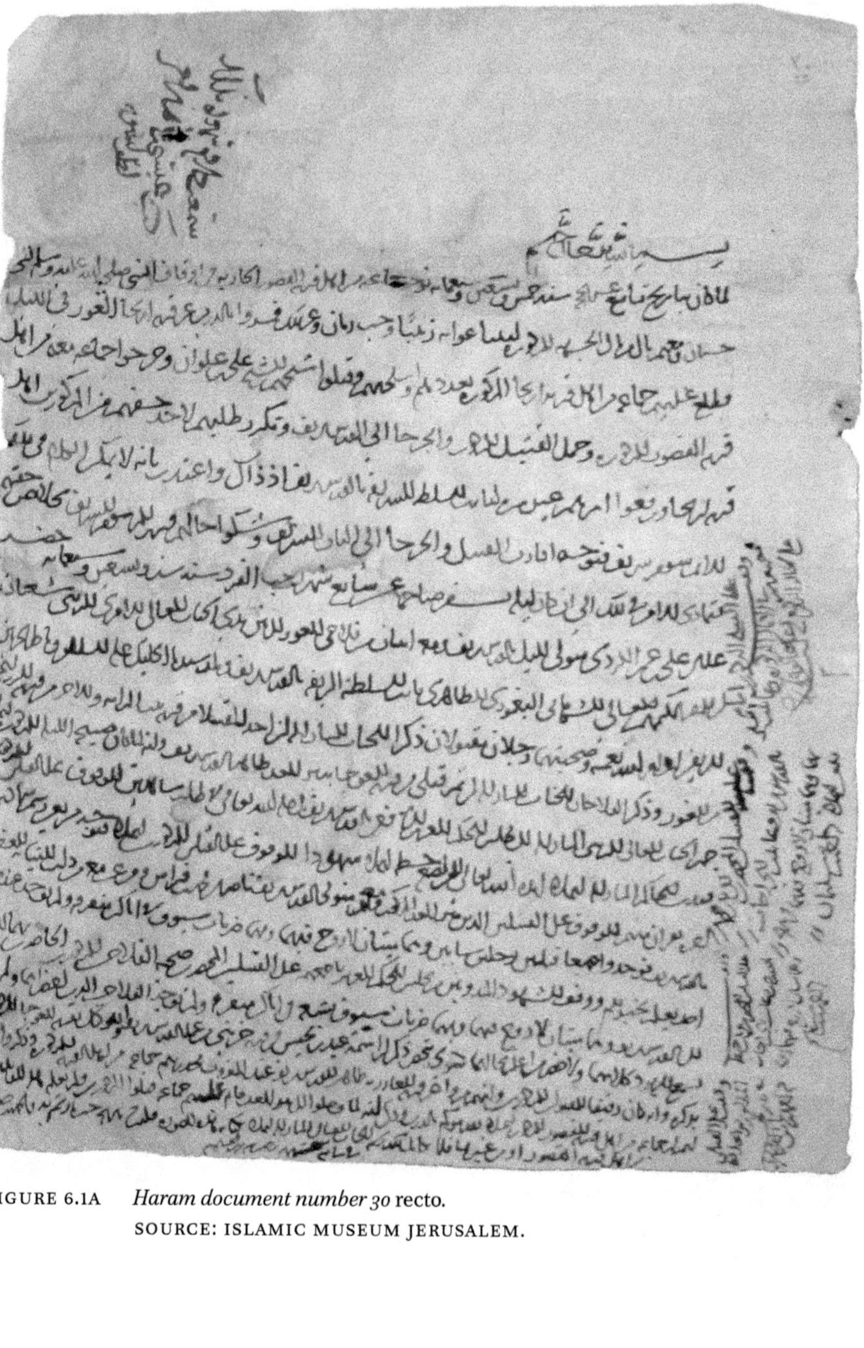

FIGURE 6.1A *Haram document number 30* recto.
SOURCE: ISLAMIC MUSEUM JERUSALEM.

FIGURE 6.1B *Haram document number 30* verso.
SOURCE: ISLAMIC MUSEUM JERUSALEM.

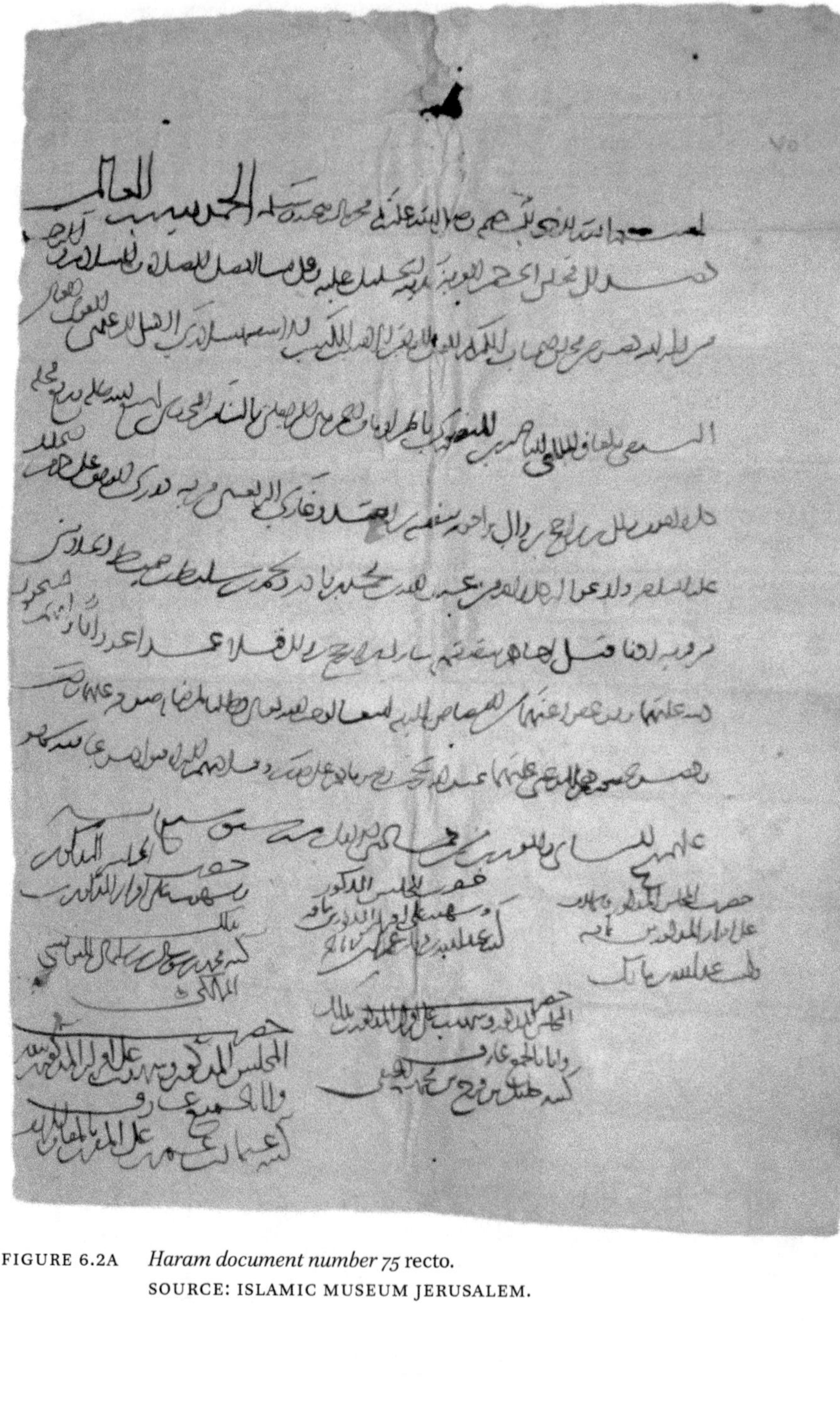

FIGURE 6.2A *Haram document number 75* recto.
SOURCE: ISLAMIC MUSEUM JERUSALEM.

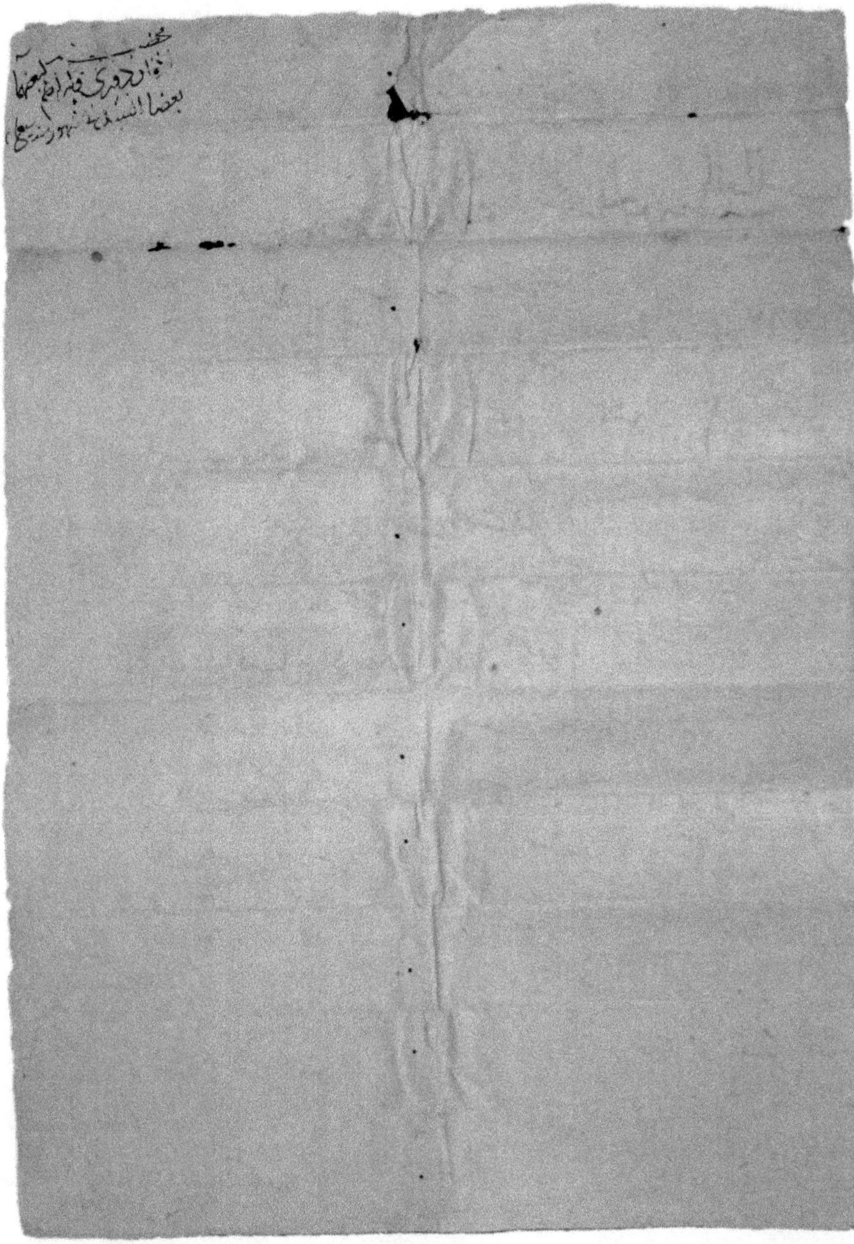

FIGURE 6.2B *Haram document number 75* verso.
SOURCE: ISLAMIC MUSEUM JERUSALEM.

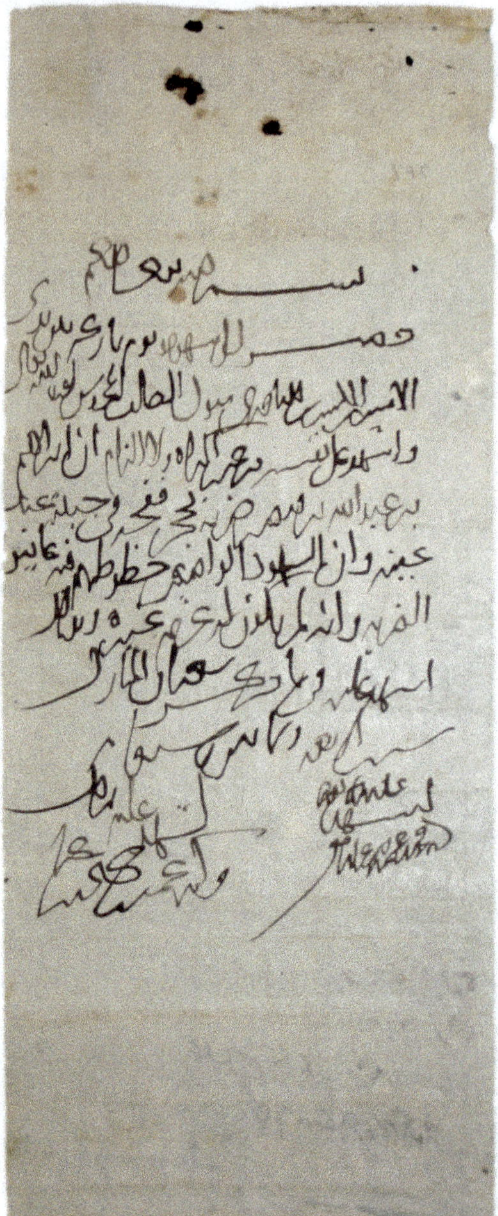

FIGURE 6.3A *Haram document number 292* recto.
SOURCE: ISLAMIC MUSEUM JERUSALEM.

FIGURE 6.3B *Haram document number 292* verso.
SOURCE: ISLAMIC MUSEUM JERUSALEM.

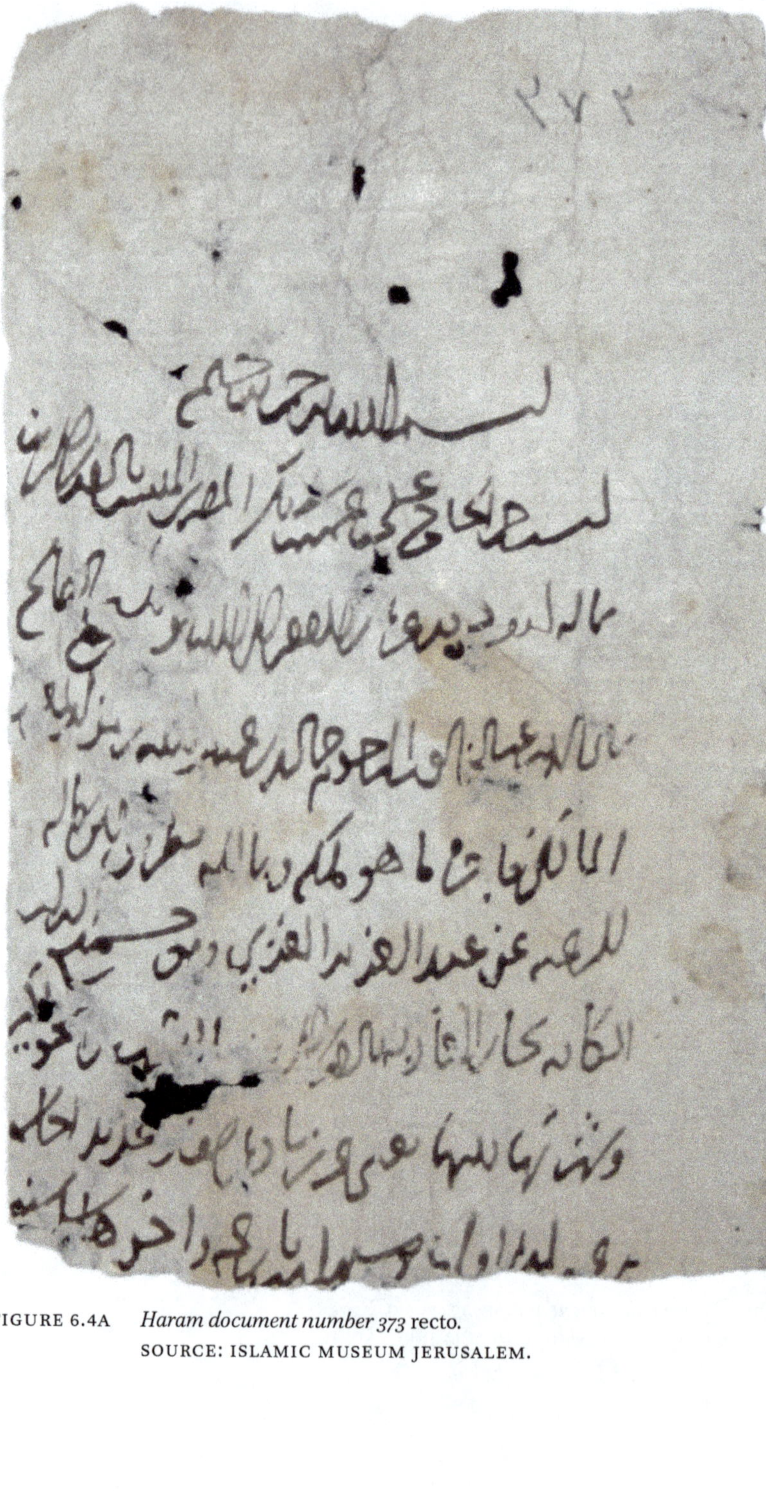

FIGURE 6.4A *Haram document number 373* recto.
SOURCE: ISLAMIC MUSEUM JERUSALEM.

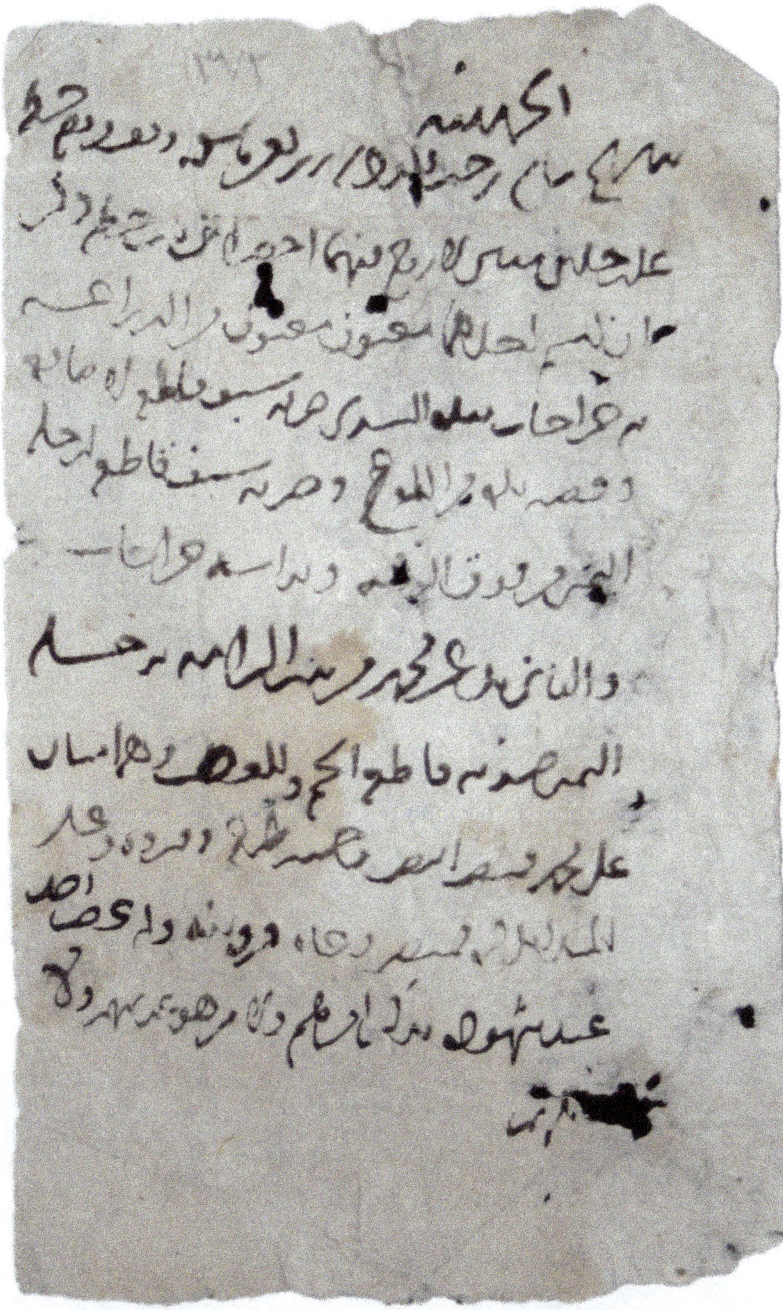

FIGURE 6.4B *Haram document number 373* verso.
SOURCE: ISLAMIC MUSEUM JERUSALEM.

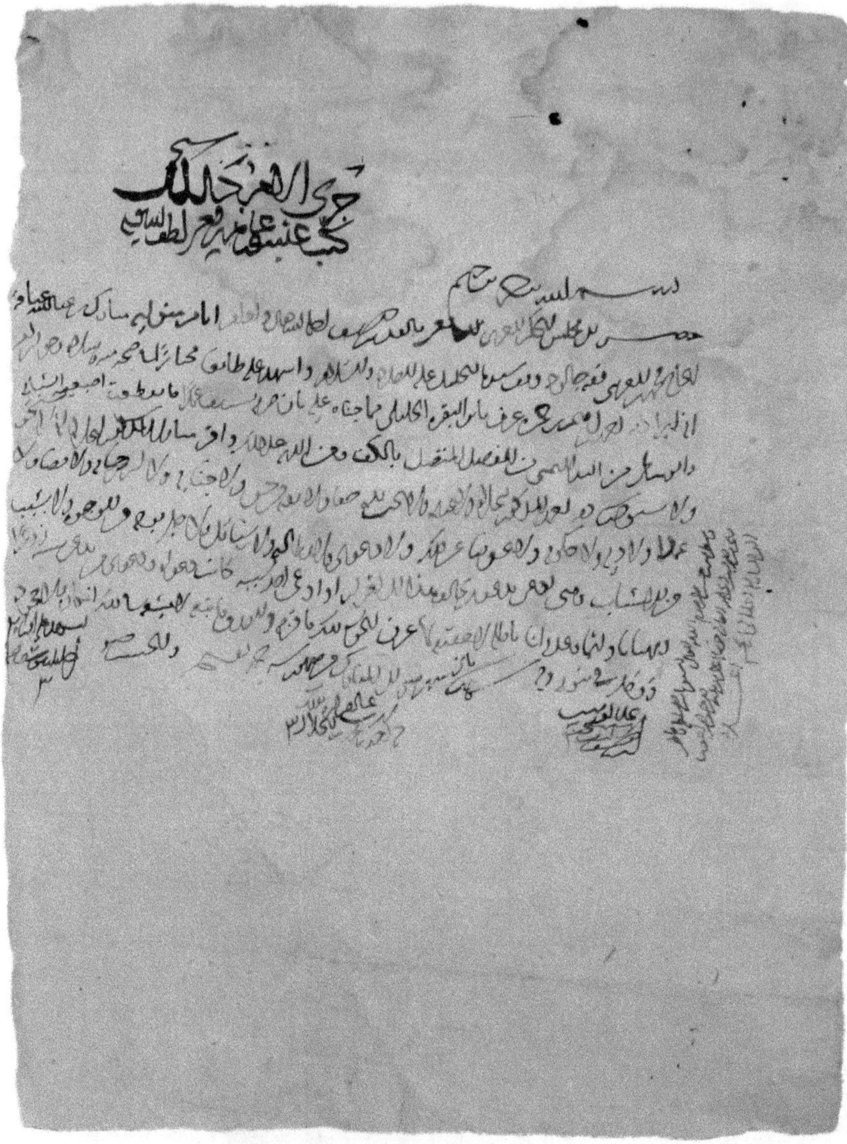

FIGURE 6.5A *Haram document number 628* recto.
SOURCE: ISLAMIC MUSEUM JERUSALEM.

FIGURE 6.5B *Haram document number 628* verso.
SOURCE: ISLAMIC MUSEUM JERUSALEM.

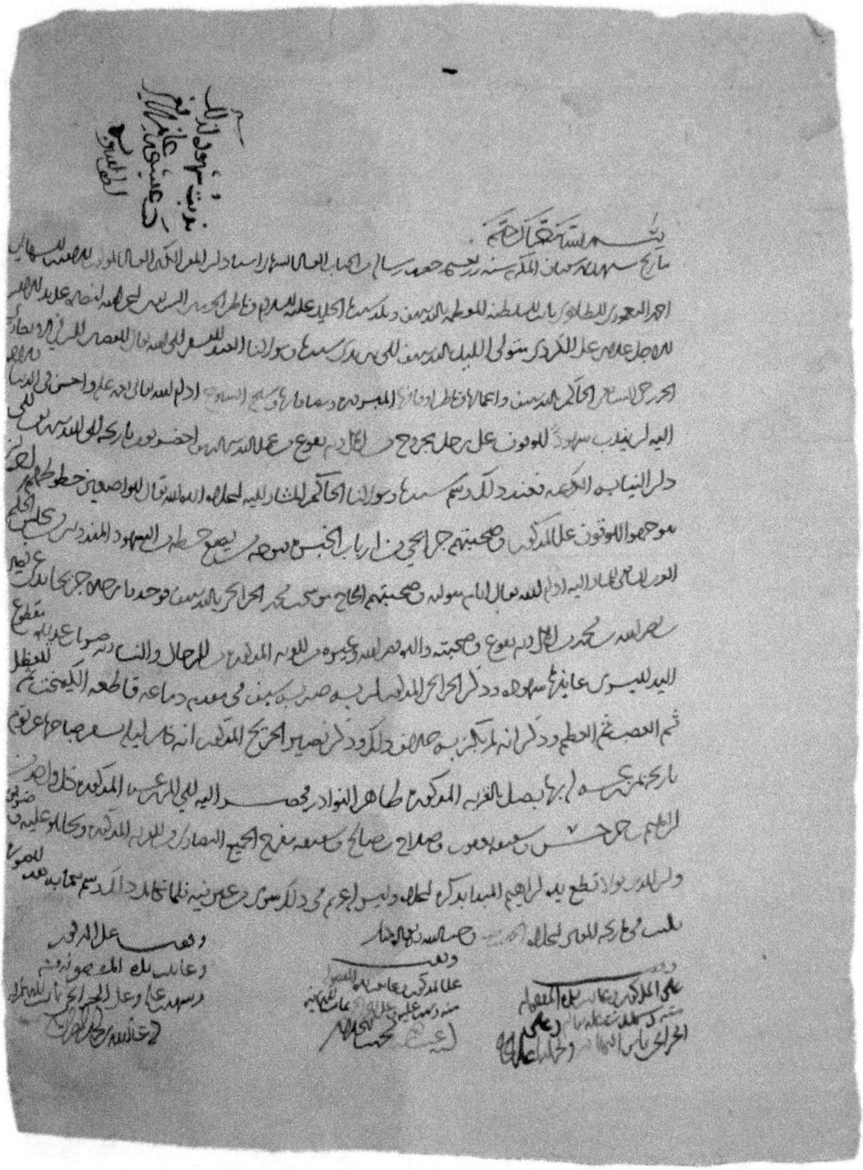

FIGURE 6.6A *Haram document number 642* recto.
SOURCE: ISLAMIC MUSEUM JERUSALEM.

FIGURE 6.6B *Haram document number 642* verso.
SOURCE: ISLAMIC MUSEUM JERUSALEM.

CHAPTER 7

From Trash to Treasure

Ethnographic Notes on Collecting Legal Documents in Morocco

Léon Buskens

Introduction[1]

Rudolph Peters recently published a hefty volume with editions of legal documents from the oasis of Dakhla in Egypt.[2] This book is the latest in a series of studies on legal practice in modern Egypt before the twentieth century. His historical work has profoundly contributed to changing our understanding of the relations between theory and practice, the central issue in the Western academic study of Islamic law since Snouck Hurgronje and Schacht. Peters argues that the gap between the law books and actual legal practice that Schacht postulated does not show in the primary sources, mainly court records, that he studied in Cairene archives. Actual legal documents bring us even closer to practice. In fact, as Christian Müller shows in his seminal work on the medieval legal tradition, they are as close as we can get.

Western legal scholars realised the relevance of documents for the study of Islamic legal practice quite soon. Joseph Schacht was one of the pioneers in this field by editing model books for legal witnesses. Janet Wakin followed her teacher by editing another formulary with an important introduction.[3] In the French tradition Jacques Berque showed interest in legal documents and

---

1 I would like to thank Patricia Spyer and Baudouin Dupret for the questions and suggestions which they generously offered as a reaction to my presentation of part of the material during the NISIS spring school in Rabat in March 2015. I also thank Mercedes Volait, François Pouillon, Jean-Philippe Bras, Nathalie Bernard-Maugiron and Christian Müller for their comments during various presentations while being their guest in Paris in spring 2015 at the invitation of the Institut d'études de l'Islam et des Sociétés du Monde Musulman (IISMM). I am very grateful to Annemarie van Sandwijk for her patience and good care in the editing of my contribution.

2 Rudolph Peters, *Watha'iq Madinat al-Qasr fi al-Wahat al-Dakhila Masdaran li-Tarikh Misr fi al-ʿAsr al-ʿUthmani* (The documents of the town of al-Qasr in the Dakhla Oasis as a source for the history of Egypt in the Ottoman periode). Silsilat Dirasat Watha'iqiyya, 1. Cairo: Dar al-Watha'iq al-Qawmiyya (National Archive), 2011.

3 Jeanette A. Wakin, ed., *The Function of Documents in Islamic Law. The Chapters on Sales from Ṭaḥāwī's* Kitāb al-shurūṭ al-kabīr (Albany: State University of New York Press, 1972).

 | DOI 10.1163/9789004343733_009

judicial practice.[4] Until recently legal documents from al-Andalus were among the best exploited sources, thanks to the work of Luis Seco de Lucena and Wilhelm Hoenerbach, to which tradition Amalia Zomeño also contributes in this book. The social history of the Ottoman period was revolutionised by the study of court records, initiated by the Syrian historian Abdul-Karim Rafeq. Maaike van Berkel studied the activities of the scribe, *kātib*, one of the main actors in the production of written records, and one of the most famous manuals guiding his work.[5] Papyrology contributes to our study of early legal practice by the careful edition of the documents that gradually surface from the garbage dumps of early medieval Egypt, as Petra Sijpesteijn shows.[6]

Most of the studies use the records as sources, instead of questioning them as social and historical phenomena in themselves. In anthropology and social history Brinkley Messick and Ghislaine Lydon have done seminal work for the understanding of the culture of writing and reading in Yemen and the Sahara region. Messick holds a huge archive of photographed documents from the town of Ibb in his office at Columbia University in New York, which he has steadily been mining during the past decades. He recently wrote a methodological reflection on the anthropologist as a reader of such documents.[7] These anthropologists extensively use documents both as objects of and sources for research. Another important study of legal documents was made by Aharon Layish on the basis of documents gathered by the British anthropologist John Davis during his fieldwork in Libya. Layish focuses in his work on documents as sources rather than as objects of study in themselves, nor does he question the coming into being of the corpora of materials that he handles.

Some of the scholars mentioned, such as Messick, actively sought for documents in the framework of their fieldwork. But many accidentally "found" their materials, as in the case of Rudolph Peters who came across them as left behind in deserted houses, or "discovered" them by chance in archives.

---

4 Jacques Berque, "Petits documents d'histoire sociale marocaine: les archives d'un cadi rural," *Revue africaine* 94, no.1–2/422–423 (1950): 113–124; reprinted in: Jacques Berque, *Opera minora II. Histoire et anthropologie du Maghreb* (Paris: Editions Bouchène, 2001).

5 Maaike van Berkel, *Accountants and Men of Letters. Status and Position of Civil Servants in Early Tenth Century Baghdad* (Amsterdam: PhD thesis University of Amsterdam, 2003); Maaike van Berkel, "Reconstructing Archival Practices in Abbasid Baghdad," *Journal of Abbasid Studies* 1, no. 1 (2014): 7–22.

6 Petra M. Sijpesteijn, *Shaping a Muslim State. The World of a Mid-Eighth-Century Egyptian Official* (Oxford: Oxford University Press, 2013).

7 Brinkley Messick, "Islamic Texts: The Anthropologist as Reader," in *Islamic Studies in the Twenty-first Century: Transformations and Continuities*, eds. Léon Buskens and Annemarie van Sandwijk (Amsterdam: Amsterdam University Press, 2016), 29–46.

The editors of the documents rarely give us insight in how these documents "survived" before they fell into their hands, nor do they question their existence or survival. In the existing literature it is much more common to lament the absence of archives[8] than to ask why people would keep their papers instead of throwing them away. Often archival practices existing in modern Western societies, with considerable historical roots, are taken for granted instead of studied as specific cultural phenomena. The documents studied seem not to have had any history or owners prior to falling into the hands of their editors. They ironically appear almost as *res nullius*, similar to the overseas territories to be colonised in former times.

Among the few exceptions to the scholarly neglect of the history and social conditions of the transmission of documents and of their "materiality" is a special issue of the Spanish journal *Al-Qantara*.[9] Tamer el-Leithy opens the issue with a stimulating plea for a historical archaeology of medieval archives, which is very similar to my concerns here. Unfortunately, he limits himself to references to historical studies, whereas he could have strengthened his case for a microhistorical approach by also taking anthropological work into consideration. Christian Müller reconstructs the reasons behind the survival of a specific set of documents from the Haram al-Sharif papers in Jerusalem as related to a judicial inquiry into abuse that was accidentally never closed. His article is a valuable sequel and correction to Wael Hallaq's seminal study in which he argues that judicial archives existed before the Ottoman period.[10] Amalia Zomeño also investigates the survival of Nasrid legal documents in Christian archives in Granada, asking the fundamental question why documents have been kept instead of thrown away.[11] The two other contributions to the special issue deal with more specific questions of translation and the material aspects of documents kept in Granada. In the introduction to the recent edition of eight documents on vellum kept in the Toyo Bunko library in Tokyo, Toru Miura carefully reconstructs the arrival of the documents in Japan and manages to trace back the trajectory of these precious materials to the market

8 Cf. Jacques Berque and Dominique Chevallier, eds., *Les Arabes par leurs archives: XVIe–XXe siècles* (Paris: Editions du CNRS, 1976).

9 *Al-Qantara* 32, no. 2 (2011).

10 Wael B. Hallaq, "The *qāḍī*'s *dīwān* (*sijill*) before the Ottomans," *Bulletin of the School of Oriental and African Studies* 61, no. 3 (1998): 415–436.

11 Amalia Zomeño, "From Private Collections to Archives: How Christians Kept Arabic Legal Documents in Granada," *Al-Qantara* 32, no. 2 (2011): 461–479.

for manuscripts in Fez.[12] One of the most famous cases of paper trash turned into scholarly treasure is the "discovery" of the Cairo Geniza, the huge medieval garbage heap of the Jewish community, whose story has recently been told by Adina Hoffman and Peter Cole.[13]

The present ethnographic case study is intended as a contribution to the study of the production of legal documents and the way people deal with papers in different settings. The keeping of archives is just one of these social practices that varies according to time and place. In an earlier essay I studied the production of a marriage deed in contemporary Morocco in detail.[14] Here I focus on the "finding" and "collecting" of legal documents for research as yet another stage in their social life. The conditions of acquiring the documents reveal important information about the changes in their meaning.

Collecting was for a long time a crucial research technique in many branches of scholarship. During the last decades it has fallen into disrepute, a tendency now strengthened by the idea of "virtual collections." Lately the study of its history has become quite fashionable in art history and anthropology, for example. My contribution is related to recent trends in the anthropological study of material culture. Since the famous collection of essays edited by Arjun Appadurai, *The Social Life of Things* (1986), anthropologists and historians have become increasingly interested in the ways in which people deal with objects as important aspects of their culture. This has resulted in the construction of "cultural biographies" of things, to borrow the expression of Igor Kopytoff's contribution to the volume.[15] Since then, a considerable body of studies has been written in which the materiality of objects has obtained growing

12 Toru Miura and Sato Kentaro, eds., *The Vellum Contract Documents in Morocco in the Sixteenth to Nineteenth Centuries. Part I* (Tokyo: The Toyo Bunko, 2015).

13 Adina Hoffman and Peter Cole, *Sacred Trash. The Lost and Found World of the Cairo Geniza* (New York, Schocken Books, 2011). A kindred story is the "saving" of a tenth century copy of the Hebrew Bible, the "Aleppo codex" as told by Matti Friedman, *The Aleppo Codex. A True Story of Obsession, Faith, and the Pursuit of an Ancient Bible* (Chapel Hill, North Carolina, Algonquin Books of Chapel Hill, 2012).

14 Léon Buskens, "Tales according to the Book. Professional Witnesses (*ʿUdul*) as Cultural Brokers in Morocco," in *Narratives of Truth in Islamic Law*, Baudouin Dupret, Barbara Drieskens and Annelies Moors eds., (London and New York: I.B. Tauris & Co., 2008), 143–160 and 340 (notes).

15 Igor Kopytoff, "The Cultural Biography of Things: Commoditization as Process," in Arjun Appadurai ed., *The Social Life of Things. Commodities in Cultural Perspective*, (Cambridge, Cambridge University Press, 1986), 64–91.

attention, resulting in the urge to take things seriously as "objects."[16] So far few researchers have applied this material perspective to legal documents as objects, in order to understand more about the ways in people used them in different social settings, forgot about them, discarded them, or sold them.

The present essay is meant as a contribution to the social history of legal documents in Morocco, on the basis of my own research in this field since 1988, initially undertaken with my dear friend, the late Mostapha Naji. As such it is part of a bigger project, with two main lines of inquiry: social practices of legal writing, reading, and storage;[17] and an ethnography of the manuscript trade.[18]

I will first present some ethnographic cases of collecting legal documents in Morocco during the last three decades. Then we will look at the physical aspects of the collected documents, studying them as material objects, and see what we can learn from their appearance about their social life and meaning. I will conclude by reconstructing their trajectories from legal documents to treasures in orientalist library collections.

Some Ethnographic Notes on Collecting Documents in Morocco

Due to the fact that legal documents are often related to aspects of life that people value and consider private, these papers can often not be collected

---

16 Christopher Tilley et al., eds., *Handbook of Material Culture* (London: SAGE Publications Ltd., 2006).

17 Cf. Léon Buskens, "Islamic Commentaries and French Codes: The Confrontation and Accommodation of Two Forms of Textualization of Family Law in Morocco," in *The Politics of Ethnographic Reading and Writing. Confrontations of Western and Indigenous Views*, ed. Henk Driessen (Saarbrücken and Fort Lauderdale: Verlag Breitenbach Publishers, 1993), 65–100; Léon Buskens, "Maliki Formularies and Legal Documents: Changes in the Manuscript Culture of the *'Udul* (Professional Witnesses) in Morocco," in *The Codicology of Islamic Manuscripts. Proceedings of the Second Conference of Al-Furqan Islamic Heritage Foundation, 4–5 December 1993*, ed. Yasin Dutton (London: Al-Furqan Islamic Heritage Foundation, 1995), 137–145; Léon Buskens, "Tales according to the Book."

18 Cf. Léon Buskens, "Conversations with Mostapha: Learning about Islamic Law in a Bookshop in Rabat," in *Cultural Styles in Knowledge Transmission. Essays in Honour of Ad Borsboom*, ed. Jean Kommers and Eric Venbrux (Amsterdam: Aksant Academic Publishers, 2008), 19–24; Léon Buskens, "Paper Worlds. A *Nesrani* Ethnographer Entering the Manuscript Trade in Morocco," in *Pratiquer les sciences sociales au Maghreb. Textes pour Driss Mansouri. Avec un choix de ses articles*, ed. François Pouillon and Mohammed Almoubaker (Casablanca: Fondation du Roi Abdul-Aziz Al Saoud pour les Etudes Islamiques et les Sciences Humaines, 2014), 239–265.

easily or by the exercise of sheer force or pressure. At some point in the lives of these documents the relationship that the owners have with them might have changed to the effect that they might be willing to part with them. Hence, my main questions are: *who* can collect *what* at *what time* and under *which conditions*? What is *not* collectable or obtainable? As a (historical) anthropologist I consider these questions as sociological problems. Collecting is a social activity, which depends on social relations that the people involved maintain. I try to understand these relations and exchanges in the context of a specific time and social constellations. The power balance between actors, which is related to larger structures such as colonialism and economics, is vital to situate these relations properly. In this section I offer a description of a series of cases that I have witnessed, or in which I was even an actor, during the more than thirty years that I have been involved in fieldwork in Morocco. I focus particularly on encounters during the twelve years between 1988 and 2000 that I had the privilege to be on the road with my dear friend Mostapha in a quest for manuscripts.

In 1985, during my fieldwork for my MA thesis in the port town of Larache on the Atlantic, I got into contact with the son of a once wealthy and influential family. They lived in a magnificent old house in the *mdina*, which was in a bad state. The decorations of *zellij*, mosaics, and stucco were crumbling, giving a faint impression of past grandeur. I was struck by the fact that his mother and sisters smoked cigarettes in my presence, hardly knowing what to make of this: utmost liberty or depravity. Apart from my interest in the old house, an important reason for my visit was to look at their collection of family documents. This turned out to be highly problematic. I was allowed to see the *dahir*, decree of the sultan, that the family kept to demonstrate its claim to social status, and after some begging even to make a photocopy of it. The son told me that I could not see the rest of the family archive because it was too sensitive. His parents did not know what was really amongst these papers, but feared that their unknown contents might spark off new inheritance disputes.

My first contact with legal documents in Morocco immediately showed me one of the dominant attitudes of people: documents are dangerous because they can kindle disputes about property and should therefore remain hidden. This attitude is quite widespread in many societies. Another gross instance I witnessed many years later was in 2012, when I had the privilege to see the remains of a family archive in the old town of Hila on the North coast of Ambon in the Moluccas. I was impressed to see that the family had managed to preserve old papers even going back to the times of the Dutch trading company in the eighteenth century and urged them to take good care of them. The present keeper reacted by telling me that they had owned even more papers, but had decided to burn them, as they might only create trouble about inheritance rights.[19]

During the same fieldwork stint in 1985, I also went to see a *fqih*, a teacher of the Qur'an for children and writer of amulets "for women" in the shanty town of Kelito at the outskirts of Larache. The old man lived in very poor conditions in a barrack made of salvaged materials. Maybe he felt somehow flattered by my respect for his learning. He told me that he could not afford to buy books, but had enough time to copy them by hand. He tried to sell me a manuscript copy of a manual on how to write *wathāʾiq*, which he had in his possession. Having hardly an idea what the book was about I kindly declined his offer, something that I have regretted ever since.

After a few months of almost daily visits to, and acquisitions in, his bookshop Dar al-Turāth in Rabat, Mostapha Naji invited me to accompany him on a book hunting trip to Meknes and Fez in June 1988.[20] In Meknes we went to see the heirs of a scholar from whom Mostapha had already bought many books, among which was a collection of lithographed editions that I in my turn had acquired for the library of Leiden University. In a somewhat dilapidated house full of stray papers we encountered the remains of what had been once the library of a scholar versed in the Islamic sciences, serving the community as a preacher, imam, and judge. I was free to choose whatever was of my liking. For the grandchildren, the legal documents, notes for sermons, and amulets were hardly more than waste paper. They were happy to meet a strange young man who was apparently interested to the extent that he wanted to offer some money. However, there was one object that turned out to be out of bounds. On the wall hung a wooden slate inscribed with verses from the Qur'an, a *lawḥ*. Despite my vivid interest the heirs refused to sell it, explaining that they wanted to keep their grandfather's diploma certifying his memorization of the Qur'an by heart. Of course, I immediately respected this filial piety.

Later that day I would meet with the grandson of an *ʿadl*, a professional witness, who offered a few bundles of legal documents from the papers of his grandfather for sale. Mostapha was not interested in buying these legal documents, since he would not have customers for this rather common material. However, he was quite happy that I wanted to acquire them for my research, since this would help to maintain his relation with this local middleman.

19 For a study of these papers and further references: Franz and Keebet von Benda-Beckmann, "Texts in Context: Historical Documents as Political Commodity on Islamic Ambon," in *Social Security between Past and Future. Ambonese Networks of Care and Support*, ed. by Franz and Keebet von Benda-Beckmann (Berlin, Lit Verlag, 2007), 137–158.

20 Cf. Buskens, "Conversations with Mostapha"; Buskens, "Paper Worlds."

In hindsight, these two experiences as a collector already showed me a basic pattern in the lives of legal documents. Legal documents that were no longer meaningful to the present owner entered a kind of limbo state: they were in the attic, but one stage away from becoming waste to be thrown away. At this point a dealer or collector might enter the scene, which will lead to an interaction that turns the waste paper into a commodity, a collectible, and eventually a source for scholarly research.

The next stop on our first bookhunting trip was Fez. With beginners' luck I would find here one of the finest pieces for my future collection of legal documents. In a souvenirshop close to the famous fountain at the Place en-Nejjarin in the heart of the *mdina*, a showcase displayed a legal document on vellum nearly four centuries old.[21] Although we both considered the asking price of a thousand dirhams quite high, Mostapha encouraged me to buy this rare and important piece, which would be like a *clou* in my collection. At several occasions Mostapha would explain to me that every good collection would need one or more exceptional pieces to make it really good, and hence also desirable for other collectors.

In the spring of 1988 my dear friend and colleague Marjo Buitelaar, who was doing anthropological fieldwork in Marrakech, offered me two small wooden tablets or sticks on which were written legal texts in ink. She did not know what they were but had found them in the curio shops in the *mdina*, catering to tourists' desire for souvenirs. In due time I would find out more about these *alwāḥ* (sing. *lawḥ*; pl. in tashelhit *tilluaht*), which used to be common forms of legal documents in Southern Morocco. While visiting the house of a French arabist in Rabat in spring 1990 I saw some of them on display as decorations. Gradually I would see more and more of them for sale on the market. Mostapha also offered me several lots of dozens of pieces. Moroccan scholars would also start to study these, first with an article in the national encyclopaedia, and later with a monograph published by the ministry of religious affairs, and with reproductions of individual documents in regional histories.[22]

21 On legal documents on vellum from Morocco see Miura and Kentaro, eds., *The Vellum Contract Documents*.

22 The entry "al-ʾAlwāh" by ʿUmar Afa in *Maʿalimat al-Maghrib*, vol. 2 (1984), 656–657. A monograph on the wooden boards is Mhammad al-ʿUthmani, *Alwah Jazula wa-l-Tashriʿ al-Islami. Dirasa li-Aʿraf Qabaʾil Sus fi dawʾ al-Tashriʿ al-Islami* (al-Ribat, Manshurat Wizarat al-Awqaf wa-l-Shuʾun al-Islamiyya, 2004). For a regional history with some reproductions of these documents: Muhammad Amshra, *Dhakira Ayt ʿAbd Allah. Dirasa fi taqalid wa-ʿadat al-mujtamaʿ bi-janub al-Maghrib* (s.l. [Rabat]: s.e. [Rabat Net Maroc], 2014). Recently Boguslaw R. Zagorski published an essay on these wooden documents, "Malo znany typ rekopisu arabskiego: marokanskie umowy na drewienkach," in *Badania nad swiatem*

The documents would be promoted to ethnographic museum pieces in an exhibition on Moroccan folk culture in Brussels organised by the well-known Belgian ethnographer, collector and dealer Ivo Grammet from Essaouira, who reproduced in the catalogue a staged photograph of local men taking these property deeds from their clay vessel in the setting of an *agadir* (collective storage) in the Western Anti-Atlas.[23] Some of the documents carry indications of a former life, stamps in red ink mentioning "Service des affaires indigènes – Contrôle des actes," indicating French colonial supervision in the use of these sticks as legal instruments.

I encountered a further form of their commodification in the shop of the National Museum of Ethnology in Leiden during the exhibition on the *Hajj* in September 2013, where a few tablets were offered for sale as specimens of "Islamic art and culture." When I returned to the museum store shortly afterwards with my camera to document this new stage in their life I was disappointed find them gone. The staff explained to me that they had been acquired by the manager during a trip to Marrakech to buy materials to sell in the shop, which was considered to be an important fundraising venue in the new strategy of the museum. Almost immediately after the opening of the exhibition a fellow Arabist from Leiden had bought all of them for his collection. A Moroccan historian laments the rape of this "heritage" from Southern Moroccan in a recent article in the popular historical monthly *Zamane* and calls for its protection against plunder.[24]

Acquiring legal documents was not always as easy as entering the market for commodities of the curio business. During my quest for materials for my collections, I encountered several occasions where documents turned out to be inalienable possessions, because of the special meanings people attached to them. Early on in my research on family law, I sensed how sensitive people were about speaking about the legal, or personal, aspects of their own family life. Asking to see the marriage deed, and thereby getting to know all the financial and legal details of the marriage, did not seem to be polite. A unique opportunity to witness the process of the creation of a marriage document presented itself when in autumn 1989 Latif, the assistant in Mostapha's bookstore, asked me for a loan in order to pay for the *ʿudūl*, professional witnesses, who would come to his mother's house in order to write down his marriage

islamu. Dzieje, dzien dzisiejszy, perspektywy, eds. Marty Wozniak and Doroty Scislewskiej (Lodz: Uniwersytet Lodzki, Katedra Bliskiego Wschodu i Polnocnej Afryki, 2015), 89–98.

23 Ivo Grammet and Min De Meersman, eds., *Splendeurs du Maroc* (Tervuren: Musée royal de l'Agrique centrale, 1998), 62.

24 Hamid Triki, "Un patrimoine violé," *Zamane* (February 2015): 62–63.

contract. Mostapha immediately understood how important it would be for my research to be present at this occasion, and asked Latif politely whether he would invite me. Later on Latif allowed me to copy the marriage deed. I transformed my presence into an ethnographic report in my thesis, and later into a separate article on the reactions between the models available to the witnesses and their actual practices.[25] Unfortunately, Latif's choice turned out to be an unhappy one; his spouse did not get along with his mother, hence he divorced her before even consumating the marriage. When he married again in 1991, he allowed me to photocopy this deed as well, and I of course offered him a present to celebrate this happy news.

My landlord Paul lived together with a Moroccan family, whom he had adopted as his kin. His "son" Driss had a cousin who married into an old family from the town of Salé that was proud of their urban roots. This cousin was a school teacher who met occasionally with Paul to discuss current social developments, but also to ask for financial assistance. When he heard about my research he offered to show me the marriage deed of his wife's grandparents from 1915. This turned out to be a calligraphic document on paper sumptuously decorated with geometric ornaments in coloured and silver ink. My acquisitiveness was easily raised, but he explained to me that his parents-in-law were very attached to this heirloom and that they preferred to keep it. However, I was allowed to take pictures of it, which I later reproduced as a frontispiece for my book on Islamic law and family relations in Morocco.[26]

In the life of these family heirlooms, we may again observe certain changes. A few years later Mostapha announced that he had managed to obtain a real *clou* for my collection, a "Mona Lisa," on a visit to the son of the famous historian Ibn Suda. Among the papers and manuscripts that he was selling, Mostapha had found a beautifully written and gold illuminated marriage document on parchment, which would be the pride of my collection. Apparently for this descendant this sumptuous document was no longer a heirloom, nor a source for historical research, but a commodity.

On the other extreme of this gliding scale from inalienable to alienable papers is the category of waste and trash. In the 1990s, Mostapha and I went on one of our many trips to Southern Morocco to hunt for manuscripts. As always our first stop was Marrakech. We met some of his usual contacts, mostly young men acting as *des tuyaux*, runners scouring the flea markets and auction, *dallāla*, for interesting materials and information. Then he took me to

25 Cf. Buskens, "Tales according to the Book."

26 Léon Buskens, *Islamitisch recht en familiebetrekkingen in Marokko* (Amsterdam: Bulaaq, 1999).

a house in the middle of the *mdina* full of a bizarre assemblage of objects: stuffed animals, antlers, fake African sculptures, cracked pottery, old furniture, and much more to behold. I felt as if I were entering Ali Bab's cave and wanted to see it all. Mostapha looked at me in an amused way, but was focused on his business. The owners of the house took out several big boxes full of papers: legal documents in Hebrew written by *sofrim*, Jewish professional witnesses, signed with their typical signatures which reminded me of the scribal culture of their Muslim counterparts, and big stacks of letters and copies of letters written in French, but also in English, exchanged between different members of the Corcos family, residing in Marrakech, Essaouira, and Manchester. Our hosts explained that they had found these papers one day in the street, as trash to be thrown away. Since it was their profession to search the dustbins for anything sellable, they had recognised these papers as objects for which they might find a client, which in fact had arrived that very moment. Frugality made me only buy the materials in Hebrew for the Leiden University library, considering these documents to be a useful complement to my collection of Islamic legal materials in Arabic.

The hero of this story of adventure and discovery is of course my dear friend Mostapha Naji. Much more than a businessman he was a reader, an erudite and a booklover. He put his creative talents in collecting interesting materials and in sharing these with other scholars who might make good use of them. Early on in our friendship he showed me a formulary for professional witnesses and offered it for sale. At that time I still managed to resist, claiming that I would not become a collector of manuscripts. The manual went to the library of the Fondation du roi Abdulaziz Al Saoud in Casablanca. But because of reading Clifford Geertz' essay "Local Knowledge", I had already taken a strong interest in studying the *'udūl*, although my supervisor at that time would not allow me to make it the main subject of my thesis, and Moroccan colleagues also did not find any interest in it.[27] While the friendship between Mostapha and me developped, our shared interest in professional witnesses and their material traces also grew. Mostapha published three editions of formularies, partly edited by himself as well, on the basis of manuscripts that he had discovered, and either bought or photocopied.[28] He hoped to make some money with these small booklets published by his "Markaz Ihya' al-Turath

27 Clifford Geertz, "Local Knowledge: Fact and Law in Comparative Perspective," in Clifford Geertz, *Local Knowledge. Further Essays in Interpretive Anthropology* (New York: Basic Books, 1983), 167–234.

28 For example M. Naji, ed., *Al-Watha'iq al-Mukhtasara li-l-Qadi 'Abi 'Ishaq al-Gharnati (t.: 579 h.)* (al-Ribat: Markaz 'ihya' al-Turath al-Maghribi, 1988) and M. Naji, ed.,

al-Maghribi," "The Centre for the revivification of the Moroccan heritage." That hope was not realised; twenty-five years later many copies are still in stock for those who know where to find them. But he enjoyed himself while working on these materials and rendered a lasting service to scholarship.

The basis of this scholarship was his talent for finding and collecting, rooted in his curiosity and appetite for knowledge and adventure. Mostapha liked to tell me stories about his years as a hippy, on the road in Europe in his early twenties. These travels already showed his openness to people and new experiences, and his sense of adventure and enjoying life. He became a bookdealer because he liked to read, and this trade would provide him with a continuous influx of new books. Soon after, he married the daughter of a small streetvendor of second hand books in Fez. Gradually, Mostapha developed an interest in the classical writings of scholars who are considered to form the Islamic heritage, *turāth*, especially in mysticism, *tasawwuf*, and jurisprudence, *fiqh*. I was lucky that we became friends and that I found a mentor in my study of classical Islamic law in Morocco.[29] Mostapha was in continuous exchange, both intellectually and materially, with scholars from Morocco and from abroad. For example, Si Boukhobza, a former librarian in Tetouan, came to his bookstore regularly and received Mostapha at his house. He copied books by hand for him and for his customers, but also offered materials for sale that he did not want to keep himself. Thus I could acquire a collection of legal documents that he seemed to have carefully studied before selling them. Pin-holes indicated that he had removed receipts and separated documents that were attached to each other, reordering the materials in his own way.

In the course of twelve years I would acquire numerous collections of legal documents from Mostapha, from various sources. Some would come from scholars, others from the waste paper market or from intermediaries. Mostapha tried to offer me a range of material manifestations of the writing culture of the *ʿudūl* as wide as possible, with documents on paper, parchment and wood, plied, or kept rolled in metal boxes or reed tubes. He was also continuously on the lookout for formularies, collections of *fatāwā*, treatises on *fiqh*, and other scholarly literature that would provide a learned context for the documents. As such, he played a decisive role in the formation of my collection.

When Mostapha decided to buy a bigger house in the *mdina* of Rabat he offered me his own collection of materials on legal documents for sale, which

Al-Watha'iq al-Sijilmasiyya li-'Abi 'Abd Allah Muhammad al-Masmudi (al-qarn 11 h.) (al-Ribat: 'ihya' al-Turath al-Maghribi, 1988).

29 Buskens, "Conversations with Mostapha."

he had carefully assembled during years of searching and studying. Unlike me, Mostapha had not kept many documents, but had focused on the learned treatises. He had a considerable collection of both original manuscripts and photocopies of formularies, collections of *fatāwā* and other related materials. His collection contained many rare lithograph and printed editions. He also offered me his almost complete collection of printed books of Octave Pesle, a French scholar who had devoted his life to the study of Maliki *fiqh* in the Maghrib. Because Pesle's books had been published during the French protectorate in Morocco they were quite difficult to find. When he moved into the new house he found a heap of dusty and damaged papers under the stairs. His neighbours explained that the former owners had burned many papers before leaving, but that they had apparently forgotten about these. Mostapha sent them to Leiden as a gift for all my help, once again transforming trash into treasure.

His collection went far beyond what he might need to edit texts which he would publish in order to make a profit. Mostapha was first of all a collector with the interests of an erudite. But he was not so possessive that he could not let go his gleanings. We shared this interest in professional witnesses, their manuals and their documents. By selling his collection to me, Mostapha knew that he would always keep full access to his discoveries. At the end of the 1990s Mostapha decided to close his bookstore to concentrate completely on his search for manuscripts. He started to carefully study the biographical dictionaries of al-Andalus to compile a list of authors of formularies, which he intended to publish together with me as part of our joint research project.

Of course, Mostapha Naji was not only an erudite, a collector, and a friend, but also a businessman, who had to make a profit in order to make a living for his family. We can see his agency working at several levels: in selecting what to buy as a profitable asset, and what to leave to his travelling companion, who would contribute to the maintenance of the network by his own acquisitions, what to keep for his own reading and collections, and what to sell, and to whom. As I explained in a previous article, the market for manuscripts and rare books in Morocco, as elsewhere, has its own peculiarities, in which social relations and notions of reciprocity, "placing" certain important pieces, and "granting" patrons specific pieces which "belong" to them, all play an important role, which might be more important than the short term aim of maximising profit.[30] For this paper the most important aspect is the fact that Mostapha played a decisive role in recognising and selecting materials which

30 Buskens, "Paper Worlds."

for the sellers were often found objects which other people had thrown away or left behind and which they tried to turn into commodities. With his knowledge and discerning eye, and through his studies of the classical literature and the writings of "Orientalist" scholars, Mostapha added value to these "findings" by transforming them into sources for historical research.

For me the personal dimension of collecting was apparently also so important that I stopped buying after Mostapha's untimely death in September 2000. But when in the spring of 2015 NISIS, together with colleagues from Paris and Morocco, organised its spring school in Rabat on "Images, Objects, Collections," I indulged in an experiment in order to demonstrate to our students the workings of the old paper trade. On the Sunday afternoon preceding the beginning of our school I went to the *Jutia*, the flea market in the *mdina*, to dealers in found objects and second hand books which keep small shops there, together with my friends François Pouillon and Mercedes Volait. When I asked for documents, one dealer, who seemed to sell whatever came into his hands, from fake modern art to spare parts of household appliances, rummaged a bit and came up with two *wathāʾiq*. His neighbours who specialised in second hand books, and occasionally sold manuscripts and lithographs, showed me two plastic bags full of loose sheets of papers. One contained mainly amulets, but the other had sewn together quires with small religious texts and a number of legal documents. A few of these had holes at the places where the *ʿudūl* had written down their signatures. Upon closer inspection these holes proved to be no accident, but intentional: a previous owner had invalidated the documents by taking out the *ashkāl*, a common practice. Acquiring these documents in order to show them during my lecture later that week proved to be quite a hassle. I considered the asking price to be quite unfair. The seller claimed that he had bought them from a *fqih*, who had asked them almost the same amount as he was charging me. From this I learned that the previous owner had been at least a man of some education, who considered these old papers to be possible commodities, and who had apparently made a selection before selling them.

An intriguing example of an "indigenous collection" of materials relating to *ʿudūl* is embodied by a scrapbook that the earlier mentioned historian Ibn Suda put together. A colleague from Leiden University acquired it from his son in order to resell it, despite protests from Mostapha that it would be an important source for our research. It consisted of an old French style account book, which opened on the inside of its front cover with a handcopied fatwa about the use of documents as legal proof. The rest of the ledger was filled with *ashkāl* of professional witnesses cut out of original legal documents. Apparently this book contained a collection of sources for Ibn Suda's studies in the intellectual

FIGURE 7.1 *A small store selling second-hand books and documents. Flea market* mdina *Rabat, March 2015.*
PHOTOGRAPH BY LÉON BUSKENS.

history of Fez, which resulted in a posthumous publication of his history of the judges of Fez.[31]

Mostapha told me about at least one other example of these local forms of collecting. He offered me a photocopy of a sheet of paper containing the signatures of the professional witnesses of the town of Sefrou, as they had deposed them with the judge controlling their work, as part of the procedure accepting them as witnesses, *tazkiya*. Mostapha was quite interested to acquire this unique piece, but its owner only allowed him to take a photocopy.

One of the few institutional collections of legal documents that I came across during my research in Morocco were the extensive holdings of *wathāʾiq* in the Sbīhiyya library in Salé. This private library was founded by members of the prominent Sbīhī family who had played an important role in the city's history, as merchants, administrators and scholars. They had brought together their family's manuscripts and printed books in a new library building, just

31 ʿAbd al-Salam b. Suda, *Qudat Fas* (al-Ribat, Manshurat Mudiriyyat al-Watha'iq al-Malakiyya, 2009).

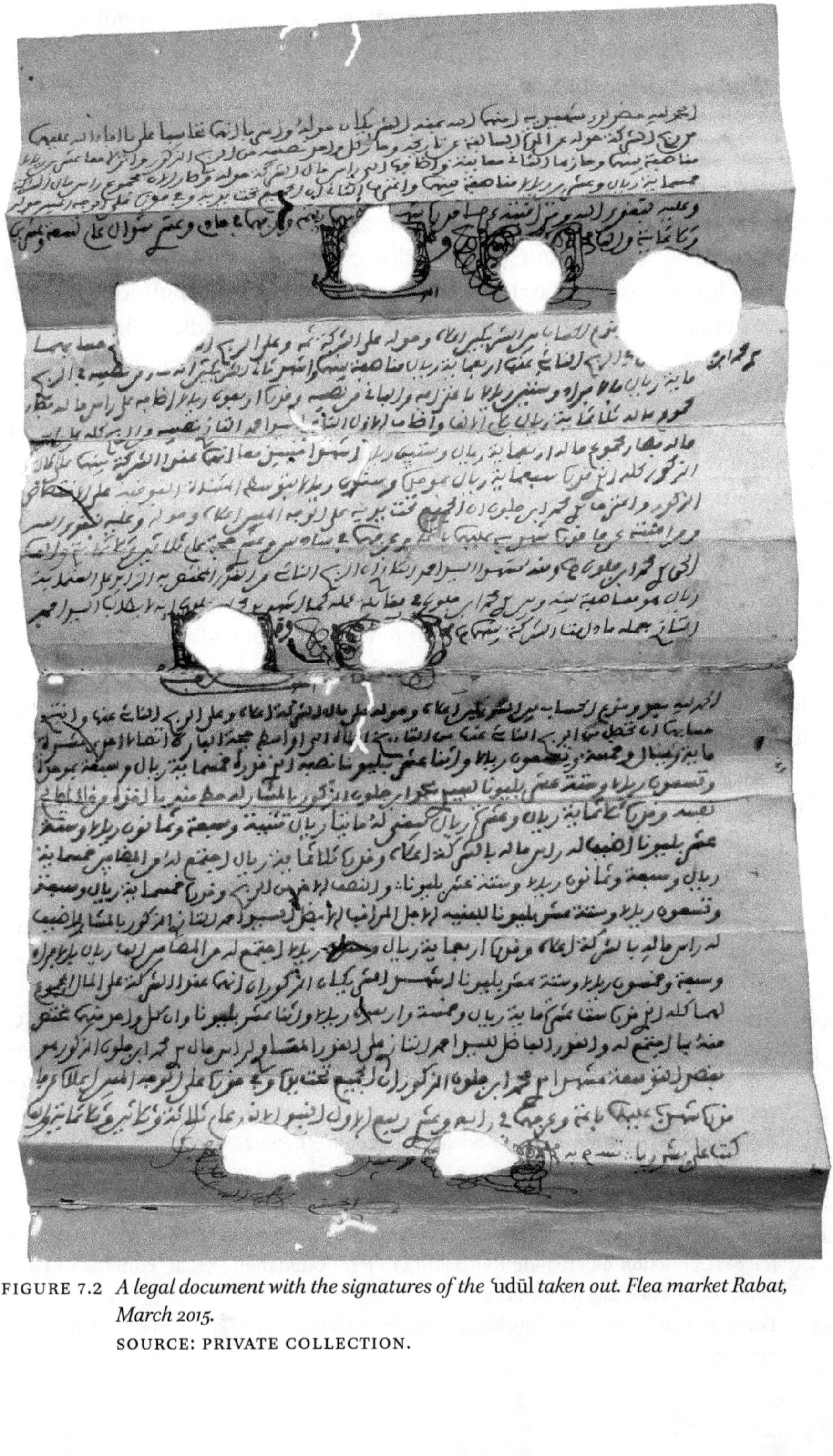

FIGURE 7.2 *A legal document with the signatures of the* ʿudūl *taken out. Flea market Rabat, March 2015.*
SOURCE: PRIVATE COLLECTION.

outside the old city's walls. The library offered space to high school and university students to quietly prepare their homework. It also housed important sources for the history of Salé, to which the owners tried to add new materials, and on which they published their own books, especially editions of texts.

Occasionally researchers would also come across locally held smaller collections of documents, often held by prominent families.[32] Sociologist Paul Pascon and his collaborators "found" on 2 February 1983 in the village Aït Yassine a collection of about 300 legal documents in reed tubes kept in a big oil drum during their research in the Ounein valley in the High Atlas.[33] Until now this collection has unfortunately not been further studied. Similar traces of local collections can be gleaned from publications on regional history, as already mentioned earlier.

European travellers and scholars have from early on demonstrated interest in the role of professional witnesses in Islamic legal practice in Morocco, as shows the famous book of Georg Høst, who was consul in Morocco in the second half of the eighteenth century.[34] With the competition for the colonisation of North Africa in the nineteenth century, the interest among European scholars in Islamic law and documents increased. French scholars published collections of facsimiles of legal documents with translations and wordlists based on materials gathered in Algeria. As Morocco was one of the few not yet colonised territories at the end of the nineteenth century, German scholars started to study these useful issues in Morocco as well.[35] Philipp Vassel published an overview of Moroccan legal practice, with an edition and translation of three specimens of court records, in which he also gives an introduction to

32 For an example of a Moroccan researcher presenting documents from his own family's archive: Hassan Jouad, "Les chroniques familiales du Haut-Atlas," *Etudes et Documents Berbères* 5 (1989): 22–31.

33 Personal communication by Paolo de Mas, 17 December 1990 and letter 12 January 1991. Cf. Paul Pascon, "Histoire du peuplement de l'Ounein," *30 Ans de sociologie du Maroc (Textes anciens et inédits). Bulletin économique et social du Maroc* 155–156 (1986): 87–96. In a study resulting from the same project we find references to the use of *rusum*, legal documents, for claiming irrigation rights: Abdellah Herzenni, "L'Ounein: Modes d'utilisation des eaux d'irrigation et rapports sociaux," *Bulletin économique et social du Maroc* 159–160–161 (1987): 85–111.

34 Georg Høst, *Relations sur les Royaumes de Marrakech et Fès recueillis dans ces pays de 1760 à 1768*, traduction de Frédéric Damgaard et Pierre Gailhanou (Rabat, Editions La Porte, 2002; orig. Copenhagen 1779), 189.

35 For further references see: Buskens, *Islamitisch recht en familiebetrekkingen in Marokko*, 217–219.

the work of the *ʿudūl*.[36] A famous publication on a collection of legal documents is the two volume book *Les Habous de Tanger. Registre officiel d'actes et de documents. Analyse et extraits* that Edmond Michaux-Bellaire published in 1914, two years after Morocco became a French and Spanish protectorate, in the series *Archives marocaines*. This is one of several such source publications of legal materials, others being for example Louis Milliot's four volume *Recueil de jurisprudence chérifienne* or his study on collective ownership of land, which were not only of scholarly interest, but also of prime importance for the legal administration of Morocco and access to its valuable land and other immovable property. With these colonial studies of local collections we move to another, earlier stage in the social life of Moroccan legal documents.

Taking Documents Seriously as Objects

The discarding and selling of legal documents as described in the previous section is just one stage in their life-cycle. The documents themselves offer many traces of earlier stages once we start to take them seriously as objects, without even necessarily immediately reducing them to texts by reading their contents.

The first striking physical characteristic is that a legal document is often not just a sheet of neatly written paper, but an intricately plied or rolled series of papers glued to each other, sometimes adding up to more than a metre, or even several metres of length, although its width normally does not exceed thirty centimetres. The classical manuals for scribes give all kinds of instructions for storing, sometimes suggesting to first roll a document and then flatten it. Modern Moroccan documents are often so neatly and intricately folded that they seem to have been plied from the beginning. In Southern Morocco they sometimes were rolled and then stored in hollow bamboo tubes, or in specially made tin tubes or boxes. The documents on parchment are often plied in a similar way as those on paper, which makes it quite difficult to unfolded them once the material has hardened.

On the final fold which serves as the outer cover we often find a small manuscript note indicating the subject of the document, such as "sale," "marriage" or "divorce." Once we start to unfold the carefully plied document we may find that it is composed of many sheets of paper, of different sizes and appearance, which are glued together at the lower and upper ends, following each other in chronological order. Such an accumulation of documents normally refers to

36 Philipp Vassel, "Über marokkanische Processpraxis," *Mitteilungen des Seminars für orientalische Sprachen* 5, Abt. 2 (1902): 170–232.

FIGURE 7.3A AND 7.3B *The outer fold of a document from the Meknes collection on the transfer of property, showing an indication of its subject matter, tax seals and stamps concerning its registration.*
SOURCE: PRIVATE COLLECTION.

the transfer of real estate, where each document proves the rights of the proprietor to transfer his property to the subsequent owner. These documents can be valuable sources for the history of houses.[37]

The lay-out of a document complies with certain conventions: the right-hand margin is normally left blank, while the text runs on the left hand side to the very end of the sheet, not allowing for the addition of any word. This convention is meant to prevent any tampering with the contents of a legal document. The right hand margin might be used for adding further legal deeds related to the original document, as can be seen in older specimens, resulting

37 See the studies by Ali Amahan of legal documents in J. Revault et al., *Palais et demeures de Fès*, 3 vols. (Paris: Editions du CNRS, 1985–1992).

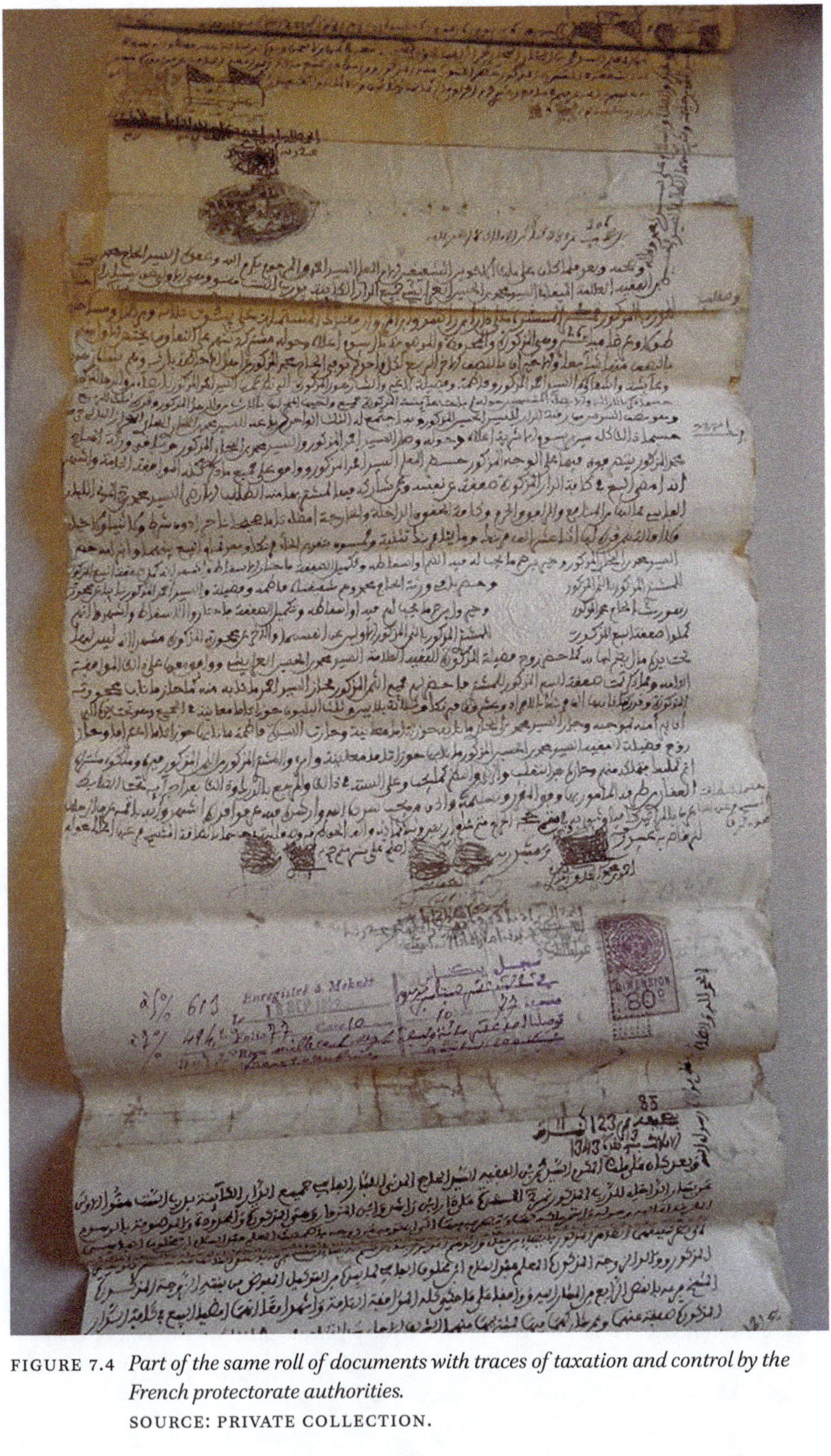

FIGURE 7.4 *Part of the same roll of documents with traces of taxation and control by the French protectorate authorities.*
SOURCE: PRIVATE COLLECTION.

in the sheet of paper to be covered by many texts on both sides, to read in different directions. In more recent documents the professional witnesses normally use the right-hand margin for all kinds of administrative purposes, such as a stamp with the name of the court, and blank spaces in which is filled in the subject, and a number under which they have copied the text of the deed in a specific register. This is also the space for affixing stamps for the payment of dues, or for the tax stamps which have already been embossed on the paper in the case of the so-called *papier timbré*. Further additions might be receipts for the registration of the transfer of property with specific tax institutions, such as the *percepteur*, which in former times were pinned on to the document, and further stamps indicating registration, often also on the backside of the sheet of paper.

Accumulations of documents stuck together in general nicely demonstrate the changes in the writing culture of the *ʿudūl* during the past century. Gradually we witness the coming into use of *papier timbré*, stamps, seals, written forms with pre-printed rubrics, and finally the use of computers and text processing. Changes in decoration of the marriage deeds are also apparent, apart from variations relating to the amount of money spent. During the 1990s, and maybe even earlier, printed forms with multi-colour decorations became available on the market.

Once we move beyond the direct materiality of the document as an object and we start to look at the document as a text, we may notice that in some cases several related documents have been written on the same sheet, for example deeds certifying marriage, repudiation, and revocation of the repudiation, or successive transfers of the same piece of land. It might also be the case that older documents have been recopied on a new sheet of paper or parchment, to which a more recent document has been added, followed by later transactions, in order to certify the status of a certain property, thus incorporating older deeds in newer documents.[38]

The texts of the deeds themselves, as well as the indications in the margins, refer to registers with copies of the documents kept in court archives, or to additional administrative certificates required for the establishment of the legal status of a person, such as national identity cards. These references indicate increasing forms of control and formalisation, especially through the use of registers and archives, and other new forms of legal technologies. A document may refer to an archive or not. Until the introduction by the French of

38 Cf. Sato Kentaro, "Form and Use of the Vellum Documents," in *The Vellum Contract Documents in Morocco in the Sixteenth to Nineteenth Centuries. Part I*, ed. Toru Miura and Sato Kentaro (Tokyo: The Toyo Bunko, 2015), 8–22.

new rules for control during their protectorate, many deeds existed only in the form of one "original." This original might be kept among private papers, which might take the form of a family archive. Other archives of a more or less institutional kind might exist as well, such as the papers of a judge or a *ʿadl*, or of the overseer of pious foundations, *ḥubūs*.

Changes in registration and in archival practices, as increasing formalisation and taxation of documents, are all related to increasing state control, in which the introduction of new legal technologies is related to the incorporation of the classical institution of the professional witnesses in positive state law modelled on a French example. The protectorate period, with its confrontation of Islamic and French understandings of normativity, proved to be a turning point.[39] The new rules, stipulated in legal texts such as laws, imposed a new framework for the production and life of the documents.[40] We could study these changes and turns in the close reading of a specific accumulation of legal documents, but that should be explored in another article. Such a case study would present the intersection of history and the biography of a specific document, to retake C. Wright Mills' characterisation of sociology.

Conclusions: From Legal Instrument to Collectable Commodity

The main focus in this essay has been on the collecting of legal documents in Morocco for scholarly purposes, which may be situated in the Orientalist tradition. This case study is meant to contribute to an understanding of what the acts of "finding" and "taking" materials for scholarly purposes mean. Scholars have at least since the 1970s lost their innocence which permitted them to accept these naïve terms at face value. However, the notion of "plunder," full of post-colonial anger, seems to be equally unproductive, but rather a condemnation which is itself part of a history of appropriations. The history of the collecting of books and documents is in some ways similar to those of ethnographic and archaeological specimens and might profit from the recent work done on these subjects. Scholarly collecting of legal documents is a social

39 Buskens, "Islamic Commentaries and French Codes"; Buskens, "Maliki Formularies"; Léon Buskens and Baudouin Dupret, "The Invention of Islamic Law: A History of Western Studies of Islamic Normativity and Their Spread in the Orient," in *After Orientalism. Critical Perspectives on Western Agency and Eastern Re-appropriations*, ed. François Pouillon and Jean-Claude Vatin (Leiden and Boston: Brill, 2014), 31–47.

40 J. Lapanne-Joinville, "Les actes adoulaires marocains sont-ils authentiques," *Revue marocaine de droit* 9 (1957): 337–384.

phenomenon, and might be understood as yet another stage in a history of paper keeping.

The conditions of obtaining should be themselves the object of research. Why have papers been kept, rather than thrown away? Archives are a historical phenomenon, related to specific social and political purposes. The same goes for the making of scholarly collections and archives. Gaining insight in the history of collections helps us to understand their possibilities and limitations for research. What may scholars obtain, and what do they have to leave untouched? What do they select? The sources for the biographies of these documents are both external, such as the stories that I have related here about my travels with Mostapha, and internal, which means taking documents seriously as objects and gleaning information from their materiality.

Documents often mark important moments in the lives of people, such as marriage, divorce, or the transfer of a house or a piece of land. They may serve as legal proof that the event has actually taken place and that a person is married, divorced, or the owner of a house. As such, people may attach great value to documents and keep them carefully in a kind of personal archive. In some families, often with significant means, people guard these papers over several generations and hence constitute a "family archive." At some point a family dies out or heirs lose interest, which leads to the old papers changing meaning and becoming "something" in the attic, or even trash. Similar biographies might be constructed for the papers of judges and *ʿudūl*. They might have kept at their houses old documents that they copied in newer versions, which later on lost meaning to their heirs as legal instruments and became trash or commodities.

The ways of collecting described in this essay present various possibilities: descendants of the original owners who did not see any other interest than monetary in these old papers, middlemen who found papers as trash, dealers who offered souvenirs or collectibles, collectors who parted with materials that they no longer had any use for, and a highly knowledgeable bookseller who understood very well what I was looking for and who actively formed my collection which would offer the sources for a joint research project.

Parallel to this history of collecting, I might present an alternative history of the formation of archives and collections of legal documents in Morocco. Some documents have become part of institutional archives, which belong either to the legal or the educational system in Morocco. Whether they serve as legal instruments or as scholarly sources, they have become inalienable possessions. The formation of these public collections is related to the coming into being of a modern state with positive law and a national system of education and research. Next to this Morocco has private scholarly collections of documents with a long history. For example the Sbīhiyya library in Salé is a continuation of a family library, which has started to collect documents as historical sources on a larger scale.

The collecting of legal documents is related to a process in which the documents seem to start "to speak in a different language": from legal instruments they become souvenirs, collectibles, primary sources for historical research, in short: commodities. The key to understanding collecting as a social process is to focus on the social relations between the actors. Three concepts are crucial in this analysis. First of all, the related notions of exchange and reciprocity. In the cases described here the documents are objects of business transactions in which they are a commodity with a certain value that is created in this exchange. The second notion is agency. Parties in these exchanges make choices and select materials which they are willing to exchange. Sellers might not always fully understand the interest of the collectors and the value they attach to the materials, but they consciously decide to part with the materials in their possession which for them are first of all commodities in a market in which buyers are not so easy to find. The third notion is that of the context of power relations. The stories of collection presented here took place in a post-colonial context, in which the economic power balance between a young Dutch collector and many Moroccan sellers was often quite favourable for the foreign collector, but where he lacked any coercive powers to obtain materials without a counter gift which the possessors might deem appropriate. They were meeting and exchanging in what was basically a market place, although in a world structured by economic inequalities.

In the reconstruction of the social lives of the legal documents we observe changes in their meaning. From instruments for legal proof in an archive they moved to the attic, or another space in between, to even the trash can, and hence they became commodities, curiosities, and souvenirs, and then again primary sources in a library or treasures in a collection. Again an alternative story might be constructed which stresses the unevenness of the exchanges, and which understands the documents as national heritage and looted cultural property, which has been lost for the nation. Heritage making and the creation of cultural property are relatively new forms of appropriation, related to the creation of the nation state and the independence of former colonies. In post-colonial debates, collecting and removing objects "from their context" have become important ethical issues. According to recent views scholars should no longer take sources from their country of origin, but leave them there, satisfying their curiosity by making copies and images. This view implies a radical rupture with classical Orientalist research techniques in which collecting played a crucial role.

This debates leads us to a final useful analytical notion, that of "transcultural objects." Orientalism flourished because of an interest in the "Other," going beyond the own culture of the researchers. By now we know that these studies were less disinterested than their practitioners liked to present them. But collecting by taking objects out of their "original context" and moving them into new contexts, such as libraries, archives, museums, universities and studies created new meanings and new perspectives. Rescuing objects from destruction, from the dustbin and the rubbish heaps used to be a justification for this collecting, turning them into treasures of universal scholarship. Nowadays, some scholars claim that we should rather leave them among the trash than meddle with other people's affairs.

Bibliography

Afa, ʿUmar. "al-ʾAlwāh." In *Maʿlamat al-Maghrib*, vol. 2, 656–657. Sala: Matabiʿ Sala, 1984.

Amshra, Muhammad. *Dhakira Ayt ʿAbd Allah. Dirasa fī Taqalid wa-ʿAdat al-Mujtamaʿ bi-Janub al-Maghrib*. s.l. [Rabat]: s.e. [Rabat Net Maroc], 2014.

Appadurai, Arjun, ed. *The Social Life of Things. Commodities in Cultural Perspective*. Cambridge: Cambridge University Press, 1986.

Von Benda-Beckmann, Franz and Keebet von Benda-Beckmann. *Social Security between Past and Future. Ambonese Networks of Care and Support*. Berlin: Lit Verlag, 2007.

Van Berkel, Maaike. *Accountants and Men of Letters. Status and Position of Civil Servants in Early Tenth Century Baghdad*. Amsterdam: PhD diss., University of Amsterdam, 2003.

Van Berkel, Maaike. "Reconstructing Archival Practices in Abbasid Baghdad." *Journal of Abbasid Studies* 1, no. 1 (2014): 7–22.

Berque, Jacques. "Petits documents d'histoire sociale marocaine: les archives d'un cadi rural." *Revue africaine* 94, no.1–2/422–423 (1950): 113–124. Reprinted in Jacques Berque, *Opera minora II. Histoire et anthropologie du Maghreb*. Paris: Editions Bouchène, 2001.

Berque, Jacques and Dominique Chevallier, eds. *Les Arabes par leurs archives: XVIe–XXe* siècles. Paris: Editions du CNRS, 1976.

Buskens, Léon. "Islamic Commentaries and French Codes: The Confrontation and Accommodation of Two Forms of Textualization of Family Law in Morocco." In *The Politics of Ethnographic Reading and Writing. Confrontations of Western and Indigenous Views*, edited by Henk Driessen, 65–100. Saarbrücken and Fort Lauderdale: Verlag Breitenbach Publishers, 1993.

Buskens, Léon. "Maliki Formularies and Legal Documents: Changes in the Manuscript Culture of the *'Udūl* (Professional Witnesses) in Morocco." In *The Codicology of Islamic Manuscripts. Proceedings of the Second Conference of Al-Furqan Islamic Heritage Foundation, 4–5 December 1993*, edited by Yasin Dutton, 137–145. London: Al-Furqan Islamic Heritage Foundation, 1995.

Buskens, Léon. *Islamitisch recht en familiebetrekkingen in Marokko*. Amsterdam: Bulaaq, 1999.

Buskens, Léon. "Conversations with Mostapha: Learning about Islamic Law in a Bookshop in Rabat." In *Cultural Styles in Knowledge Transmission. Essays in Honour of Ad Borsboom*, edited by Jean Kommers and Eric Venbrux, 19–24. Amsterdam: Aksant Academic Publishers, 2008.

Buskens, Léon. "Tales according to the Book. Professional Witnesses (*'Udul*) as Cultural Brokers in Morocco." In *Narratives of Truth in Islamic Law*, edited by Baudouin Dupret, Barbara Drieskens and Annelies Moors, 143–160 and p. 340 (notes). London and New York: I.B. Tauris & Co., 2008.

Buskens, Léon. "Paper Worlds. A *Nesrani* Ethnographer Entering the Manuscript Trade in Morocco." In *Pratiquer les sciences sociales au Maghreb. Textes pour Driss Mansouri. Avec un choix de ses articles*, edited by François Pouillon and Mohammed Almoubaker, 239–265. Casablanca: Fondation du Roi Abdul-Aziz Al Saoud pour les Etudes Islamiques et les Sciences Humaines, 2014.

Buskens, Léon and Baudouin Dupret. "The Invention of Islamic Law: A History of Western Studies of Islamic Normativity and Their Spread in the Orient." In *After Orientalism. Critical Perspectives on Western Agency and Eastern Re-appropriations*, edited by François Pouillon and Jean-Claude Vatin, 31–47. Leiden and Boston: Brill, 2014.

Friedman, Matti. *The Aleppo Codex. A True Story of Obsession, Faith, and the Pursuit of an Ancient Bible*. Chapel Hill, North Carolina, Algonquin Books of Chapel Hill, 2012.

Geertz, Clifford. *Local Knowledge. Further Essays in Interpretive Anthropology*. New York: Basic Books, 1983.

Grammet, Ivo and Min de Meersman, eds. *Splendeurs du Maroc*. Tervuren: Musée royal de l'Afrique centrale, 1998.

Hallaq, Wael B. "The *qāḍī*'s *dīwān* (*sijill*) before the Ottomans." *Bulletin of the School of Oriental and African Studies* 61, no. 3 (1998): 415–436.

Herzenni, Abdellah. "L'Ounein: Modes d'utilisation des eaux d'irrigation et rapports sociaux." *Bulletin économique et social du Maroc* 159–160–161 (1987): 85–111.

Hoffman, Adina and Peter Cole. *Sacred Trash. The Lost and Found World of the Cairo Geniza*. New York: Schocken Books, 2011.

Høst, Georg. *Relations sur les Royaumes de Marrakech et Fès recueillis dans ces pays de 1760 à 1768*. Traduction de Frédéric Damgaard et Pierre Gailhanou. Rabat: Editions La Porte, 2002 (orig. Copenhagen 1779).

Jouad, Hassan. "Les chroniques familiales du Haut-Atlas." *Etudes et Documents Berbères* 5 (1989): 22–31.

Kentaro, Sato. "Form and Use of the Vellum Documents." In *The Vellum Contract Documents in Morocco in the Sixteenth to Nineteenth Centuries. Part I*, edited by Toru Miura and Sato Kentaro, 8–22. Tokyo: The Toyo Bunko, 2015.

Kopytoff, Igor. "The Cultural Biography of Things: Commoditization as Process." In *The Social Life of Things. Commodities in Cultural Perspective*, edited by Arjun Appadurai, 64–91. Cambridge: Cambridge University Press, 1986.

Lapanne-Joinville, J. "Les actes adoulaires marocains sont-ils authentiques." *Revue marocaine de droit* 9 (1957): 337–384.

El-Leithy, Tamer. "Living Documents, Dying Archives: Towards a Historical Anthropology of Medieval Arabic Archives." *Al-Qantara* 32, no. 2 (2011): 389–434.

Messick, Brinkley. "Islamic Texts: The Anthropologist as Reader." In *Islamic Studies in the Twenty-first Century: Transformations and Continuities*, edited by Léon Buskens and Annemarie van Sandwijk, 29–46. Amsterdam: Amsterdam University Press, 2016.

Miura, Toru and Sato Kentaro, eds. *The Vellum Contract Documents in Morocco in the Sixteenth to Nineteenth Centuries. Part I.* Tokyo: The Toyo Bunko, 2015.

Müller, Christian. "The Ḥaram al-Šarīf Collection of Arabic Legal Documents in Jerusalem: A Mamlūk Court Archive?" *Al-Qantara* 32, no. 2 (2011): 435–459.

Naji, M., ed. *Al-Watha'iq al-Mukhtasara li-l-Qadi Abī Ishaq al-Gharnati (t.: 579 h.)*. Al-Ribat: Markaz 'Ihya' al-Turath al-Maghribi, 1988.

Naji, M., ed. *Al-Watha'iq al-Sijilmasiyya li-Abi 'Abd Allah Muhammad al-Masmudi (al-qarn 11 h.)*. Al-Ribat: Markaz 'Ihya' al-Turath al-Maghribi, 1988.

Pascon, Paul. "Histoire du peuplement de l'Ounein." *30 Ans de sociologie du Maroc (Textes anciens et inédits). Bulletin économique et social du Maroc* 155–156 (1986): 87–96.

Peters, Rudolph. *Watha'iq Madinat al-Qasr fi al-Wahat al-Dakhila Masdaran li-Tarikh Misr fi al-'Asr al-'Uthmani* (The documents of the town of al-Qasr in the Dakhla Oasis as a source for the history of Egypt in the Ottoman periode). Silsilat Dirasat Watha'iqiyya, 1. Cairo: Dar al-Watha'iq al-Qawmiyya (National Archive), 2011.

Revault, Jacques, Lucien Golvin and Ali Amahan. *Palais et demeures de Fès*, 3 vols. Paris: Editions du CNRS, 1985–1992.

Sijpesteijn, Petra M. *Shaping a Muslim State. The World of a Mid-Eighth-Century Egyptian Official.* Oxford: Oxford University Press, 2013.

'Abd al-Salam b. Suda. *Qudat Fas*. al-Ribat, Manshurat Mudiriyyat al-Watha'iq al-Malakiyya, 2009.

Tilley, Christopher, Webb Keane, Susanne Kuechler-Fogden, Mike Rowlands, and Patricia Spyer, eds. *Handbook of Material Culture*. London: SAGE Publications Ltd., 2006.

Triki, Hamid. "Un patrimoine violé." *Zamane* (February 2015): 62–63.

al-ʿUthmani, Muhammad. *Alwah Jazula wa-l-Tashriʿ al-Islami. Dirasa li-Aʿraf Qabaʾil Sus fi Dawʾ al-Tashriʿ al-Islami.* Al-Ribat (Rabat): Manshurat Wizarat al-Awqaf wa-l-Shuʾun al-Islamiyya, 2004.

Vassel, Philipp. "Über marokkanische Processpraxis." *Mitteilungen des Seminars für orientalische Sprachen* 5, Abt. 2 (1902): 170–232.

Wakin, Jeanette A. *The Function of Documents in Islamic Law. The Chapters on Sales from Tahawi's* Kitab al-Shurut al-Kabir. Albany: State University of New York Press, 1972.

Zagorski, Boguslaw R. "Malo znany typ rekopisu arabskiego: marokanskie umowy na drewienkach." In *Badania nad swiatem islamu. Dzieje, dzien dzisiejszy, perspektywy*, edited by Marty Wozniak and Doroty Scislewskiej, 89–98. Lodz: Uniwersytet Lodzki, Katedra Bliskiego Wschodu i Polnocnej Afryki, 2015.

Zomeño, Amalia. "From Private Collections to Archives: How Christians Kept Arabic Legal Documents in Granada." *Al-Qantara* 32, no. 2 (2011): 461–479.

CHAPTER 8

Notes for a Local History of Falsehood

Brinkley Messick

Legal studies figures among the many fields of substantive inquiry impacted by the work of Michel Foucault, in particular by his *Discipline and Punish*, a challenging, unconventional history of the transformation of western penal institutions.[1] In recent years, however, another Foucault, or at least another aspect of his oeuvre, has emerged with the publication, and ensuing English translation, of his lectures at the Collège de France.[2] Alongside his finished, historical-analytic works such as *Discipline and Punish* – in which he engages in critical readings of western professional literatures, such as that on penal institutions – his lectures (re)introduce us to Foucault the philologist. In his lectures he appears as a careful and insightful reader of, for example, early Greek texts, who provides transliterations of key terms much in the manner of an Islamicist working with Arabic texts.

A well-known frame for *Discipline and Punish* is as the study of a "system of truth" or, more famously, a "regime of truth."[3] It is interesting to note that, at least in this particular book, Foucault chose not to pursue this frame of analysis with respect to processes in courts of law, which represent another essential institution in a realm of truth. Likewise, in his separately published piece on "Truth and Juridical Form," he elected to concentrate on the "field of penal law."[4] Yet one of the topical interventions in his lectures at the Collège concerns the transition from the ancient ordeal, or test, to the judicial procedure of "inquiry," an institution for the production of truth. Throughout, his focus is on the West, on "the history of truth" in "our societies."[5] But he also notes that, in the modern era, this history assumed a global relevance. He writes that the

1 Michel Foucault, *Discipline and Punish: The Birth of the Prison*, trans. Alan Sheridan (New York: Vintage Books, 1979).

2 E.g., Michel Foucault, *The Courage of Truth*, trans. Graham Burchell (New York: Picador, 2011); Foucault, *Lectures on the Will to Know*, trans. Graham Burchell (New York: Picador, 2013).

3 Foucault, *Discipline and Punish*, 23; cf. Michel Foucault, "Political Function of the Intellectual," trans. Colin Gordon, *Radical Philosophy* 17, 1977: 12–14: "each society has its regime of truth," 13.

4 Michel Foucault, "Truth and Juridical Forms," in *Power*, ed. James S. Faubion (New York: New Press, 2000), 4, 15.

5 Foucault, "Truth and Juridical Forms," 4, 15.

 | DOI 10.1163/9789004343733_010

juridical "forms" he discusses were not only "absolutely essential for the history of Europe" – where they "still circulate" – but also "for the history of the whole world, inasmuch as Europe violently imposed its domination on the entire surface of the earth."[6]

In the following discussion, I approach what may be termed a non-western, specifically, an Islamic "regime of truth," but my approach is indirect. With reference to a historically specific institutional world, I seek, in more precise terms, to sketch elements of what might be thought of as the inverse or the foil of truth, namely, falsehood. Truth and falsehood, I suggest, represent reciprocal elements and co-determinants of a "regime of truth," although the features of the latter component are little examined.[7] Is it that falsehood is more elusive and therefore difficult to study? Is it that while the truth may appear finite or unitary, falsehood is neither? Finally, if "truth itself has a history," as Foucault states, may the same be said of falsehood?[8]

To pursue this discussion I will examine the particular institutionalization of truth and of falsehood in historical shariʿa courts, mainly through examples of witness testimony recorded in litigation transcripts. The courts in question are those of the highland Yemen town of Ibb in the first half of the twentieth century.[9] In this era, in the post-Ottoman and pre-nation state period of rule of the last two Zaydi imams, the highlands also stood apart from the dramatic legal changes associated with direct colonial rule, that is, the sorts of imposed westernizing changes referred to by Foucault. In this period in Yemen,

---

6 Ibid., 40.

7 Cf., his reference, in passing, to "the interdependent system of truth and falsity," Foucault, *Will to Know*, 4.

8 Foucault, "Truth and Juridical Forms," 2.

9 The three cases cited in the following are 1) a marriage contract case from 1378 (1958) decided by Judge Ismaʿil ʿAbd al-Rahman al-Mansur. See Brinkley Messick, "Interpreting Tears: A Marriage Case from Imamic Yemen," in *The Islamic Marriage Contract: Studies in Islamic Family Law*, ed. Asifa Quraishi and Frank E. Vogel (Cambridge: Harvard University Press, 2008), 156–179; 2) a rural murder case from 1380 (1961), decided by Judge Hasan Ahmad al-Iryani. See Brinkley Messick, "L'Écriture en procès: Les récits d'un meurtre devant un tribunal *sharʿī*," *Droit et Société* 39 (1998): 237–56; and 3) an endowment and inheritance case involving landed property in a powerful and wealthy town family decided in 1366 (1947) by Judge ʿAbd Allah b. ʿAli al-Yamani (al-Yadumi), a Taʿizz-based Judge of the Provincial Seat, who was assigned to the case by Imam Yahya. See Brinkley Messick, "Textual Properties: Writing and Wealth in a Case," *Anthropological Quarterly* 68, no. 3 (1995): 157–170. Since these original and final judgment documents issued by the courts to the litigant have the physical form of rolls, I cite them by line. (Copies of the same judgments were preserved in court registers). Rather than using pseudonyms for people and places, I employ a blank (–).

the shariʿa remained uncodified and there was no modern constitution for the imamic polity; judges were formed in classical-style madrasas, studying traditional *fiqh* works; a public prosecutorial institution did not exist, and there were no trained lawyers; and the courts heard the gamut of justiciable matters, including property and murder cases, rather than being confined to personal status matters, as in colonial settings and in the turn-of-the-century shariʿa jurisdictions of the Ottoman Empire. In addition, as opposed to the radically summarized records kept in many historical shariʿa jurisdictions, including those of the Ottoman centuries, Yemeni litigation transcripts of the period tended to be lengthy, and intermittently verbatim in character, and thus offer rich material on witness testimony. Oral testimony, of course, appears in written form in the court transcripts.

We may think of the ideal or "just witness" (*shāhid al-ʿadl*) as an individual in the witness role who engages in what Foucault refers to conceptually as "truth-telling."[10] Rather than focusing upon this truth-teller, I look briefly into what may be learned from these period courts about the the *shāhid al-zūr*, the witness who lies. While the general topic of the witness and testimony is treated in detail in the doctrinal law books,[11] the perspective I develop here mainly depends on what may be gleaned from litigation records about the related logic of court practice. This includes the strategies of litigants and the discourses of the witnesses who testify on their behalf. While texts similar in their theoretical or conceptual status to those read by Foucault concerning western institutions certainly existed for that of the witness and court testimony in Yemen (and in other Islamic times and regions), I consider a quite different, archival level of texts.

This is to point out the existence of a little known substratum of assumptions and strategies related in primary evidential texts, both spoken and written. Dipping into the heavily populated and turbulent worlds of the period case records, I give examples of how such assumptions were articulated and the strategies pursued by litigants through the medium of testimony. False testimony was a known threat to justice, as was false writing. From a doctrinal

10 Foucault, *The Courage of Truth*; Foucault, *Wrong-Doing and Truth-Telling: The Function of Avowal in Justice*, trans. Stephen W. Sawyer (Chicago: University of Chicago Press, 2014). While exploring its various "modalities," Foucault anchors his approach to "truth-telling" to related analyses of types of knowledge, structures of "governmentality" and the "care of the self."

11 Rudolph Peters, "Shāhid," *Encyclopaedia of Islam*, 2nd ed. (Leiden: Brill, 1997), vol. 9: 207–208. For the Zaydi doctrine, see Brinkley Messick, "Evidence: From Memory to Archive," *Islamic Law and Society* 9, no. 2 (2002): 231–270.

position quite close to court practice, Imam Yahya (ruled 1918–1948) issued a formal opinion (a "choice," *ikhtiyār*) on the acceptance of sound writings as evidence in court. Issued to guide the appointed judges of his judiciary, the specific purpose of this opinion was to counter the efforts of the "practitioners of forgery" (*arbāb al-tazwīr*) in his day. In court cases, of course, false testimony and forgery were not theoretical but actual, pressing, and, at times, unresolved problems.

The powerful did not necessarily prevail in these lawsuits. Although he was the ruling head of the polity in this era in the highlands, Imam Yahya famously lost a suit in which he figured (with representation) as a litigant party. Court transcripts of the era also do not shy away from recounting forms of oppression and they also document fights for justice. They detail the acts of the wrong doers and the tribulations of the wronged. They quote angry words and pleas for judgments. Yet theirs is a textual terrain of both truths and falsehoods.

These were not sanitized records. An example of the unexpurgated character of recorded witness testimony will suffice. In a marriage case, the fact that a man tried to coerce his niece to grant him an agency is reported in the case record in the following entry based on the testimony of a witness:

> He [the witness] said that he went out [of the room where the men were sitting] to go to her, and she was in a room next to the kitchen. He asked her about the agency by her, and she pleaded with him, by God and by the shariʿa, to leave her alone and [she said] that she was not granting agency to anyone and that she was a minor. He returned to the room and informed them of this. And [the uncle] went out and in his hand there was a ... stick and he beat her with this stick three [times], with the witness behind him watching. Then – [the uncle] jumped on the aforementioned, stepping on her stomach with his foot, he [the witness] said, "until we saw her urine on her clothes and on the floor covering." Then the witness went with – [the uncle] into the room where – [the eventual notarial writer] and his son were. They said, "What did she say?" And the witness told them that she did not consent.[12]

The reporting of facts in this segment of testimony does not avoid an account of shameful and violent behavior, whether by omission, indirection or euphemism. The record of what may be described as "truth-telling," in short, seems quite full. At the same time, however, it usually is difficult to verify that a particular testimony was truthful, since judges tend not to respond in detail to

12 Marriage case, lines 320–323.

specific testimonies. Truthfulness on the part of witnesses ordinarily must be understood from the general terms and findings of a judge's final judgment. In some judgments, however, judges state that they consider, or suspect, that particular witnesses were untruthful. At the conclusion of the marriage case, for example, the judge's ruling states that the notarial writer of the marriage contract contractor "is just and trustworthy (*ʿādil thiqa*)." But he goes on to say that, "He [the notary] stated that she [the niece] did not appear before him but that her consent and her permission to her paternal uncle for the contract and [the fact of] her legal majority were sworn to by … [three named men] and they are known to me for their non-justness."[13]

Jarḥ and *Taʿdīl*

This pair of terms defines the dual mechanism for, respectively, the "attack" upon and the "verification" of justness (*ʿadāla*) on the part of a particular witness. The two terms are much better known from their application to the evaluation of hadith transmitters, but they figure as well in the realm of evidential testimony, in the negative and positive evaluation of witness credibility, typically on moral-religious grounds. They are presented as such in the Zaydi school doctrine on "testimony," where some technical aspects are discussed, such as whether the individuals who appear in the roles of *jarḥ* or *taʿdīl* are themselves witnesses, who convey "knowledge," or simply bearers of "information."[14] I leave these interesting doctrinal details aside here to concentrate on how these mechanisms, *jarḥ* in particular, figured in actual litigation. The point I nevertheless want to emphasize at the outset is that this pair of concepts served as organizational tools in the shariʿa "regime of truth," a system of ideas and practices that explicitly encompassed the phenomenon of falsehood. As elaborated and implemented in this historically specific "regime of truth," these reciprocal mechanisms contributed to either refuting or establishing the potential of a given witness for "truth-telling." Falsehood, or the moral propensity to "false-telling," thus receives conceptual recognition.

To repeat, the level of analysis in the following discussion is not that of the pertinent doctrine. My examples instead tap the untutored discourse of the archive. As I will demonstrate in the remainder of this discussion, in these court records one finds not only straightforward instances of truthfulness and lying, but also regular patterns, together with the occasional meta-statement.

13 Marriage case, 364–365, 366.

14 Messick, "Evidence," 254–261.

Attending to such regularities in and reflexive comments about the relevant testimonies makes it possible to begin to sketch a practical logic of falsehood. Concerning the records to be cited, I should point out that, as opposed to the doctrinally normative mode of litigation in which only the plaintiff presents evidence, these cases exemplify the practical norm according to which both sides presented evidence.[15]

In a rural murder case from the mid-twentieth century, witnesses for the private claimants, the father and mother of the deceased, testified to the facts of the killing, by a stab of a dagger.[16] While the defendant, the accused murderer, was a locally powerful shaykh, the murdered individual was a humble tenant cultivator. One of the witnesses for the claimants was the Headman of a neighboring village who happened to be present in connection with matters of crop evaluation (for zakat-tax purposes). This individual's testimony early in the trial is reported as follows:

> He testified that he arrived in the adjacent village of – on the day of the occurrence of the killing of – and encountered – [the defendant, the accused], who was present at the event. He asked him, "Why did you do that deed," that is, kill –, and he replied, "I did it, I am the killer of him and the shraʿ [shariʿa] will deal with me." This was at the time of noon on the day of the occurrence, Monday, six o'clock, and this was in the cemetery. And the witness stated that he had arrived from his place to [visit] the Head of – [village] concerning the harvest evaluator.[17]

Later in the proceedings, two *jarḥ* witnesses were brought by the defense to disparage, literally, to "wound," this witness for the claimants. One of these *jarḥ* witnesses testified that this individual was a "false witness and a sorcerer (*sāḥir*) and [that] he eats [during the day] in Ramadan [the month of daytime fasting]." He further stated, "– [the claimant witness] enchanted (*saḥara*) the sons of – [another villager] and they lost their minds." The first accusation thus is elaborated and substantiated by reference to named parties, the "sons of –," and their alleged fate. A fragment of a story backed the second assertion, namely, that the targeted witness broke the fast of Ramadan: "The [*jarḥ*] witness stated that he arrived to buy *qāt* from – [the claimant witness] and he was eating lunch [i.e., during the day in Ramadan]. And he said to him, 'Why [are

15 What I have termed a "compound" as opposed to the doctrinally normative single-sided case. See Messick, "Evidence," 244.

16 Commonly worn by Muslim men.

17 Murder case, lines 238–243.

you doing] this?' And he excused himself that he had vomited [i.e., he was sick and so eating was permitted]." According to this *jarḥ* witness, the wife of the targeted witness was available to support this story of his breaking the fast.[18]

These accusations are meant to place in question the religious and moral integrity, and thus the veracity, of the targeted witness. What the sorcery accusation may refer to in actual activity on the part of the witness in question, or may index in terms of local practices and beliefs, is unknown. The usage here may be formulaic – as many accusations were – but from a doctrinal perspective such an accusation could have serious consequences.[19] In this case, however, the accusation remains simply that, a one-liner that is neither responded to by the claimants in a response-statement nor noticed by the judge in his ruling.

In the already mentioned marriage case, *jarḥ* comes up in the course of a litigant's statement, specifically, as part of the claimant's (the paternal uncle's) argument. Elsewhere in the case, the same litigant cited an imamic opinion of 1949 regarding the "content" (*jawhar*) of a judge's decision (*ḥukm*).[20] Such opinions, or "choices," were intended to guide judges in their case rulings, and this one requires the judge to ascertain the soundness of the substantive focus of his judgment. It states that "argument diversions (*taʿlīlāt*) which are of no benefit except to widen the conflict and the gulf between the disputants and the take-and-give, and [serve to] alienate the [possibility of] resolution by a judgment of God, are not to be decided," that is, they are not to be taken into consideration by the judge in his ruling.

In his statement, the claimant appropriates some language from the imam's opinion as he states that the defendant spoke at great length in his response and he extended remarks to that which is irrelevant. As is comprised in the

18 Murder case, lines 341–349.

19 The words for magician and for the practice of magic are common in spoken Arabic, figure in the Qur'an and the hadith, and also are taken up by the jurists. As a field of inquiry, magic entailed not only a developed written tradition but also important linkages to other literatures, such those concerned with divination, astrology, saintly miracles and also pharmacology and medicine. By the turn-of-the-twentieth century some of the key books on Islamic magic, by classical authors such as al-Buni, were available in printed editions (See T. Fahd, Art. "Sihr," *EI* 2, 9: 567–71, and references cited there). For the jurists, the magician takes his place in a list of special types who, under certain conditions pertaining to each, may be put to death according to special *ḥadd* rules. For the Zaydis, see Ahmad b. Qasim al-ʿAnsi, *Taj al-Mudhhab li-Ahkam al-Madhhab*, 4 vols. (Sanʿaʾ: Dar al-Hikma al-Yamaniyya, 1993 [rpt. 1936–47]), 4: 255–256; for other schools, see Joseph Schacht, Art. "katl," *EI* 2, 4: 770.

20 Listed in *Ikhtiyarat* of Imam Ahmad, ms. number 13.

claim of the claimant, the conflict involves the [marriage] contract, first and last, in each of two situations. The basic principle (*aṣl*) in the contracts of Muslims concerns the legality of the consensus-based shariʿa rule (*qāʿida*), and it is obligatory for the judge, may God protect him, that he consider the content (*jawhar*) of the judgment (*ḥukm*), according to the [imamic] opinion, without giving attention to other [issues brought up] in the take-and-give and thus like. He should interpret one matter (*qadiyya*), and that is that I have proven with witnesses the occurrence of the contract, and then the contract document.[21]

It was in the context of this argument about the focus of the case that the same litigant spoke in general terms about *jarḥ* witnessing:

> If shariʿa judges open to people the door of *jarḥ*, the scope of the litigated conflict will not be contained, and thus in this era false testimony occurs frequently. False witnessing today is the nearest of means and easiest of methods for falsifiers who lack any sense of manly honor (*muruʾa*).[22]

It may be observed, generally, that in a *jarḥ* accusation somebody is not telling the truth. Either an unjust witness is being justly discredited or, the opposite, a just witness is being unjustly disparaged.

Challenges

Unlike the situation in western courts, which relied either upon an interrogating judge or (and) on direct and cross questioning by attorneys or public prosecutors, shariʿa court witnesses of the period were not systematically questioned in formal litigation. While judges directed such proceedings, they were largely passive listeners to testimony, posing only the rare query for simple clarification. In this judicial system, witnesses were not directly confronted. They appeared, testified, and departed, and a transcript of what they said – in direct or indirect quotation, or in summary – was entered in the court record. Testimony could be challenged, but only at a later point in the proceedings, and not face-to-face. The two mechanisms available to the opposing party in the litigation were, 1) a "response" (*jawāb*), a recognized type of litigant party statement that was entered, often verbatim, in the record (illustrated above), or 2) the bringing of a critical *jarḥ* witness.

21 Marriage case, line 304.

22 Marriage case, 243–244.

Litigation parties also challenged their opponent's evidence without it being suggested that lying was involved. Thus there were cases with generally agreed-upon facts, but with differing arguments as to their significance, and lying tended not to play a role. I want to give some examples of the wider practices of challenge and contestation to provide a context for a more detailed view of the local culture of lying and forgery. I will start with the issues surrounding the authority of written documents.

Written documents were routinely presented as evidence and quoted or excerpted in the case record. In doctrinal terms, which I will simply mention here in passing, the main protections or guarantees the literary jurists proposed to support the authority of a written document involved (1) foregrounding the role of active memory of the legal act in question; (2) using the technique of oral reading of the text in court with accompanying witness testimony; and (3) connecting a recognized script to a well-reputed writer. For their part, archival records also speak to the status of written texts and to the problems of forgery and falsification related to those that worried the doctrinal jurists.

Contestation around writing also could focus on the integrity of the court record itself. In the marriage case, for example, the status of the minutes entered in the designated court register became an issue. At one point in this case the claimant requested and was provided a copy of the accumulated minutes. On the basis of what he learned from reading this text he then made an argument, presented in writing and, itself, entered in the minutes. Referring specifically to a section in the minutes that recorded the testimony of a set of his own witnesses and the immediately following procedural developments, he states, "We did not know at the time about any response to our witnesses from the aforementioned opponent ... until our reading of the minutes." He continues that, "We found in it [viz., the minutes text] a response from the opponent which we did not hear in the shariʿa [court] session, or after it." His main contention is that, upon reading the minutes and finding unknown entries of responses from the defendant, his opponent in the litigation, "there became apparent to us the assistance of the [court] secretary to the mentioned opponent to transcribe (*naql*) everything he [the defendant] wanted while denying us the possibility of defense, as is required in the shariʿa."[23] The writing in contention, again, was the minutes transcript prepared by the court secretary. The direct implication of the alleged injustice was that the judge would later use this written record, which the litigant argues was biased, or fraudulent in its construction, as the authoritative basis for his final decision in the case.

23 Marriage case, lines 166–168.

However, the judge did not take note of the claimant's assertion, either at this juncture in the proceedings or in his final ruling in the case.

Primary written instruments presented as evidence also could be contested in various ways. While most documents were the work of third party notarial writers, autograph documents were not uncommon. The treatment of one such autograph text in a family endowment and inheritance case engaged practical textual understandings at the archival level. The defendant, the elder brother, challenged a key document previously entered into evidence by the claimants, his younger siblings. The document in question, which had been written by their now deceased father, carried out his retraction of the endowment he had previously created for the exclusive financial benefit of the elder brother and this individual's line of descendants. Specifically, it was a private "recitation" endowment that involved a responsibility for regular readings from the Qur'an to the "soul" (*rūḥ*) of the father by the beneficiary (or beneficiaries). The reversal of the father's act of endowment through his written retraction proved to be momentous for the family and appeared to have been wrenching for the patriarch himself. For this act he assembled some consequential local personages as witnesses, inviting them for an afternoon of *qāt* in his family residence.

The patriarch's passionate written retraction is entered in the court minutes: "When I saw the hostility and hatred between my sons," he wrote, "and understood that it would be the cause of the ruin of my free estate, the endowment, and, possibly, some of my descendants, I made myself subservient to God and retracted it. I entrusted myself to God's mercy. I do not want recitation from any of them." He concluded this retraction with a warning: "He among my descendants who violates this, may God bring him adversity and upon him is the hatred of God."[24]

In the court case some years later, the elder brother, the defendant, sought to counter this key piece of evidence presented by his younger siblings. To do so he raised the issue of his father's legal capacity at the time of writing. This on the grounds of what is known technically as "the sickness of [i.e., leading to] death," an interval of diminished or of no capacity.[25] The elder brother argued that, due to his impaired capacity caused by the sickness that eventually led to his death, the father's script no longer carried his legal authority and, therefore, that his act of retraction of the recitation endowment was not valid. The unexpressed assumption was that, for an individual of full legal capacity,

---

24 Endowment case, lines 33–41.

25 Cf. Hiroyuki Yanagihashi, "The Doctrinal Development of "Maraḍ al-Mawt" in the Formative Period of Islamic Law," *Islamic Law and Society* 5, no. 2 (1998): 326–358.

handwriting is authoritative, that it directly conveys the presence, the intention, and thus the act of the autograph writer-subject.

The court record states,

> [The defendant, the elder brother] replied concerning this [the document presented in evidence by the claimants] that his father undertook this [retraction] in the sickness before his death. "He was not fully competent (*annahu fī ḥāla ghayri muʿtabara*) since he died at about the time of this [document]. He set down what he wrote in a script that is without authority (*lā ḥujjata fīhi*), because the right (*al-ḥaqq*) had commenced to adhere to his [the defendant's] descendants." What he wrote should not be considered a binding document for them, …[26]

In this argument, the handwriting in question is recognized as the father's, yet it is asserted to be without the active authority of the self. In this view, while the father was physically able to write, he was not able to act through his writing. Rather than a false instrument, it was asserted to be one lacking in evidential value.

As the case record continues, we read that the defendant lost the capacity argument, as a decisive added note on the document is quoted and evaluated. Written by another writer, this added note appeared underneath the main text of the father's retraction document and served to verify it. This note suggests that the assembled witnesses both observed the moment of composition, so that they were able to speak to the physical presence of the writer as he drafted his retraction, and also that they heard from him an accompanying oral expression of this act. This seeing and hearing also enabled the witnesses to affirm the patriarch's capacity to act.

On the basis of this appended note, the judge resolved the contended evidential point. The judge writes:

> In the document of retraction this line is written at the end, and the signatures of the witnesses are after it, [in] the expression of its writer: "This is in the handwriting and signature of al-Ḥājj – [name of the patriarch], and we have [also] heard this from him speaking in person with soundness of his mind and his body, on its date." Below are their signatures, and they are [five names], and others. This refutes the statement of [the defendant] that his father had entered into a state of severe illness.[27]

---

26 Endowment case, lines 42–46.

27 Endowment case, lines 46–51.

Forgery

Although much less common than accusations of false witnessing, allegations of forgery (*tazwīr*) by third party writers appear in these records. The marriage litigation provides an unusual instance in that the accusation of forgery later eventuates in an admission. At the beginning of the litigation, the claimant, the young woman's earlier mentioned paternal uncle, introduced a marriage contract document in evidence. The defendant in the case, and her supporter, her maternal uncle, was present when the contract was introduced in court, as is required. This man is quoted as responding to the documentary evidence by declaring that the writer of the contract is "well-known for forgery."[28] He then exercised his right to demand that his opponent, the claimant, produce the writer and the document witnesses. Summoned to court, the writer and the witnesses to the document testified to the authenticity of the contract.

After a few additional recorded words concerning the document witnesses' estimations of the ages of the boy and the girl in question at the time of the contract, the court transcript passage concludes "and they gave an oath (*ḥalafū*) about this," that is, about their just given testimony.[29] According to the Zaydi tradition evidence doctrine, judges have the option of asking witnesses to swear an additional oath "that what they testified to is true."[30] Why did the judge take this step of augmenting the regular formula of swearing by God that initiates the giving of testimony by requiring these witnesses to give a further oath after their testimony? Was he simply trying to affirm the crucial evidence presented in the written contract of marriage, or did he suspect they were lying?

With the marriage contract introduced by the claimant and authenticated by testimony from the notarial writer and the witnesses to the writing, the defense endeavored to undermine the status of this evidence. The following record of testimony mounted by the defendant exemplifies a stratagem that recurs in these court minutes. This involves witnesses from one side in a case who testify on the basis of a purported encounter, outside of court, with the opponent's witnesses. In this sort of testimony, the testifying witnesses report either having overheard incriminating statements by individuals who had previously testified for the opponent, or having engaged in brief but significant conversations with them. The pattern thus is one of witness testimony based on chance meetings with the opponent's witnesses including, in the marriage

28 Marriage case, line 47.

29 Marriage case, line 65.

30 al-ʿAnsi, *Taj*, 4: 71.

case, the contract document writer. This type of testimony focuses on alleged exchanges of words with other men who had earlier given evidence in court. Both the earlier evidential testimony and the later accusatory testimony appear at different points in the minutes transcript. Since the principals in this particular case were from a rural village west of Ibb, the encounters in question involved men who walked into town.

For the initial individual in a set of four such counter-witnesses appearing for the defense, the transcript uses indirect quotation to record

> that he entered [Ibb] on Saturday, the last day of the month of al-Ḥijja, 1376 [July, 1957], with the intention of going to the [town] market. Then he headed back to his house. They [he and some other named men] had arrived part way on the road [back to their village] when they met – [three named men, the claimant's witnesses to the marriage contract], and these individuals were saying that each of them had received four riyals for testimony from – [the claimant].

As this record continues, the next phrase, "the witness said," marks a shift to direct quotation which then embeds further reported words, also in direct quotation:

> and we said to them, "how could you have sold your responsibility (*dhimma*) and how [could you have given] this testimony of yours?" They said, "We testified that – [the deceased father of the girl] contracted for his daughter with the son of – [his brother, the claimant] in the year 1362 [1943]." And we said to them, "Were you present [at the contract]?" And they said, "No, we went in and testified for a fee as partisans for [the claimant], and each one of us received four riyals, and by God it was false, and the Judge additionally made us swear an oath. And [the claimant] brought in [as a witness] the writer of the document, [name], and he authenticated it and received ten riyals."[31]

After repeating the names of the three marriage-contract witnesses met on the road, the testimony of this defense witness concludes with his statement, "these [men] are among those for whom the proverb (*mathal*) on false witnessing applies."[32] The proverb referred to here is clarified by its citation in later defense testimony in this case, which I will discuss below. But before considering

31 Marriage case, lines 70–77.

32 Marriage case, line 77.

this passage, I want to briefly demonstrate that this sort of encounter between men who have been and will be witnesses in court is patterned, that the production of such testimony represented a known court stratagem. I will do so by giving two further examples. The first is from the same case, but with the situation reversed. In this testimony a claimant's witness responds in kind to the witnesses mounted by the defendant against the contract writer and the document witnesses. It is the same sort of testimony about conspiracy and bribery to obtain false testimony, but now the defendant and his witnesses are the alleged perpetrators:

> – [individual from the claimant side] bore witness to God that he entered [Ibb] Saturday the sixth, or the seventh, of the month of Muḥarram, in the year 1377, intending to go to the market, and – [the defendant] was in the Zihar [a location just west of Ibb town], he and six or seven individuals. They [these individuals] said to – [the defendant], "we will not testify for one *riyāl* for each of us to invalidate writers, witnesses and sharīʿa contracts." And – [the defendant] said to them, "What do you want from me?" And they said, "We will not testify unless it is for two *riyāl*s for each of us, with expenses, and, otherwise, no." And the witness stated that among these men he knew – [named individuals].[33]

A second example, which demonstrates the patterned nature of such testimony, is from a different type of case, a murder trial that also concerned villagers who lived west of Ibb town. At a stopping place named Mashwara, which is at the crest of a ridge, witnesses for the accused murderer, the defendant in the case, testified that they met witnesses for the claimants who were returning from testifying in court in Ibb. The relevant part of the testimony of the first of these defense witnesses is reported in the minutes as follows:

> The witness asked them [viz., the returning claimants' witnesses, numbers four through seven] about the murdered man [saying] he did not know who he was. They [the returning claimant's witnesses] responded, "We went in [to Ibb] to remove a disaster from over us in [the form of] expenses and soldiers [associated with disputes]. We testified against – [the accused defendant] that he murdered the son of – [the claimant, the father of the killed individual]." And the witness said to them, "How [could you], they will cut off his head based on your testimony!" They said, "He harmed us, he and his mother, for a long time." And he

33 Marriage case, lines 99–103.

> [the witness] stated that he returned to his house, and that this [occurred] next to the storehouse of Mashwara, and that this was the day of the return of the witnesses from [their appearance] before the Judge.[34]

The second of this set of three witnesses for the defendant is reported to have asked the returning witnesses for the claimants, "How could you testify and kill a man (*nafs*)," to which the reply was, "That's what we want." This witness stated, however, that this interchange occurred, not next to the storehouse, but in a coffeehouse where they were drinking coffee. The judge in the case later concluded that this set of defense witnesses had lied. He did so, he stated, on the basis of the small disparity in their testimonies as to the location of the encounter, i.e., storehouse versus coffeehouse.[35]

My aim in briefly pursing the issue of the patterned quality of such testimony is to underline the fact that evidential struggles around both testimony and written documents employed known practical techniques of wider import in litigation. To return now to the forgery accusation and the earlier mentioned "proverb," I want to cite the next passage in the minutes of the marriage case. Adding to the previous testimony about an encounter with the summoned witnesses to the contract (quoted above), the following defense witness reports on an equally incriminating conversation on the same day with the notarial writer of the contract, who, as noted, also had been summoned to testify. Embedded in this passage is an issue of fact about the ages of the boy and the girl. Given their estimated current ages (there were no birth certificates), neither would have been alive when the purported contract was written. There were various other textual complications in this case that I will not go into here, which include the writing of both an agency contract and a "renewal" (*tajdīd*) of the original contract.

I quote the record of this further testimony concerning the notarial writer to illustrate how practical conceptualizations were deployed in litigation. Unlike the sustained and elaborated formal arguments about textual and related evidential issues enshrined in doctrinal chapters and opinions, these conceptualizations take the humble form of passing bits of folk wisdom that appear scattered in the court records. Anthropologists have thought of common sense as a kind of "cultural system" that offers an "interpretation of the immediacies of experience," while linguistic anthropologists have examined metaphors and

34 Murder case, lines 220–225.

35 In the doctrine, "differences" in testimonies were grounds for rejecting their evidence value, see Messick, "Evidence," 244–248.

proverbs as essential reflexive materials for the study of speech.[36] What was the authority of such everyday knowledge in this setting? What work did its adages do? How did this common thought interact with related formal ideas about evidential texts? I suggest that such common talk about oral and written texts should be viewed as a complement, or counterpoint, to the jurists' academic models and arguments.

For the following "proverb" about lying, it is important to keep in mind that it was uttered in the context of agonistic court testimony, specifically, in testimony about the testimony of the opponent's witnesses. This miniature metatext illustrates the general phenomenon of existing everyday understandings concerning false testimony and, by extension, forgery. Within the frame of the earlier described type of patterned testimony that alleges an out-of-court encounter and that seeks to impugn the integrity of the opponent's witnesses, a local conception such as this took the concentrated form of a kernel of popular wisdom.

Actually, there are two such kernels in the following segment of the court record. This passage of reported testimony conveys two subtypes of these colloquial proof-texts: a phrase characterized as a "proverb" and a twisted rendition of an apparent hadith (the term is not used) from the prophet Muhammad.

> On Saturday, the last day of the month of Dhū al-Ḥijja, 1376 [July, 1957], he [the defense witness] met – [the document writer] in the marketplace of Ibb and he asked him why he had come in to Ibb. He said, "on account of a document we made for – [the father of the girl] in the contract for his daughter with the son of his brother – [the claimant]." And the witness said to him, "Have fear of God, whose prison is the Fire, how could you make a document [dating] from the year 1362 [1943], when now the age of the girl is approximately twelve years and the boy's age

36 Clifford Geertz, "Common Sense as a Cultural System," in *Local Knowledge. Further Essays in Interpretive Anthropology* (New York: Basic Books, 1983), 76; Peter Seitel, "Haya Metaphors for Speech," *Language in Society* 3, no. 1 (1974): 51–67. In his study of Jewish perspectives on the shari'a regime of the twentieth-century imamic period, Mark Wagner mobilizes a richly narrated corpus of memoirs, anecdotes and folkore. Mark S. Wagner, *Jews and Islamic Law in Early 20th Century Yemen* (Bloomington & Indianapolis: Indiana University Press, 2015). For their part, scholarly Yemeni Muslims, including one of the Ibb court secretaries in my day, were students of proverbs. Court secretary al-ʿIzzi Fahmi al-Sabahi, who I occasionally sat with in the late afternoons in his marketplace shop, kept a personal list of local proverbs in an unpublished notebook. In his characteristic humor, he referred to his explanatory commentary in stilted terms as his "*tafsīr*." Isma'il al-Akwa', who resided for a time in Ibb, published *al-Amthal al-Yamaniyya*, 2 vols. (San'a': Maktab Jil al-Jadid, 1984 [orig. 1968]).

> is approximately eight or ten years?" And he [the notarial writer] said, "Don't you know my son about what the Prophet of God said to our mother 'A'isha [the Prophet's wife], that if your livelihood (*rizq*) comes to you do not refuse it?" The witness said, "and I said to him, 'how [can you take] this livelihood in the name of falsification (*tazwīr*)? How much did you get?' He said, 'I got ten riyals and – [the claimant] paid – [the countersigner, a court secretary in the nearby town of Jibla] to authenticate the document, whereas the document had only been written the week before. And the judge additionally took the oath (*yamīn*) from us. The judge does not know among the proverbs of the Arabs that, 'He who fornicates swears, and he who steals swears.'"[37]

Judges of the period confronted dense thickets of back-and-forth testimony, some of it quite outrageous. Presiding over his court, this particular judge listened to bold but, as I have suggested, stereotyped witness testimony that in this instance included a reference to his purported personal ignorance of an Arab "proverb."[38] Later, in considering his decision in the case, the judge was likely to have consulted the just quoted passage of testimony from the written transcript. For our part, we may speculate about the veracity and likelihood of the above quoted passages of defense testimony. Would an individual who had just falsely testified and accepted money to that end so readily admit these facts to others, and in such precisely incriminating detail? How could the serendipitous interlocutor and future defense witness have had at his conversational disposal such relevant facts as the precise year of the purported contract and the approximate ages of the two children?

Given the fact that the defendant and his niece were in the right and, with the ruling, won the case, how should we understand their having mounted this seemingly fabricated testimony? Was this precisely targeted testimony presented on the defendant's behalf simply a necessary strategic and equivalently formulaic response to the dangerous weight of the claimant's systematic falsehoods? Had the proverb about lying been mobilized for sustaining the truth? If so, such a passage serves to highlight the "fictive," necessarily creative, and also locally scripted qualities shared by testimonies both true and false.

There was a late development in the case, however. The minutes state that the young woman, who had reached her majority (by reason of her first period)

---

37 Marriage case, lines 79–88.

38 This "proverb" is known in the northern highlands as well. Cf. Shelagh Weir, *A Tribal Order: Politics and Law in the Mountains of Yemen*, Modern Middle East Series (Austin: University of Texas Press, 2007), 206.

during the court process, "brought in a written document in the script and signature of – [name] and countersigned by its witnesses and by the District Officer of Jibla [the nearby town]." This document is quoted in full in the court transcript, in "its wording":

> There appeared before me the learned 'father' – [the writer of the contract], from Jibla, and he verified that he was responsible for fraud (*tadlīs*) and deception (*taghrīr*) in connection with the contract document that is in his script and [bears] his signature describing.... He had disavowed (*qad tabarra'a min*) this document in its era and ... he informed – [the claimant] of the non-legality of the contract and requested from him the return of the aforementioned document. He [the claimant] continued to promise him [the contract writer] that [i.e., the return of the document].... And when the news now reached him [the writer] that a dispute was underway on this matter under the auspices of the ... Judge of the Province, may God preserve him, the aforementioned 'father' – [name] hastened to me for the writing of this disavowal of his responsibility (*bara'a li-dhimmatihi*), and to this end it was written for its presentation to Our Master the Judge of the Province, may God protect him, for his view, on its date, Muḥarram, 1378 [July, 1958]. Witnessing this was the 'son' – [name] and the 'brother' – [name], and God is sufficient witness.[39]

With this document entered in the minutes, the young woman immediately "pressed for the writing [i.e., a judgment] of that which is required in the shari'a." The notarial writer's admission that the marriage contract had been falsified thus was made, in writing, in a text prepared by a third party on his behalf. Identified in this document as "the learned 'father,'" and throughout the case as the sermon-giver (*khatīb*) of Jibla, this was the same contract writer who had earlier testified in the proceedings in support of the instrument when it was challenged after being introduced into evidence.

Were notarial fraud and false testimony punished? Perhaps not so much by temporal authorities such as shari'a judges, who acted in this "world" (*al-dunyā*), as by God, in the "afterlife" (*al-ākhira*). The important caveat is that an individual's worldly reputation for probity (*'adāla*) could be damaged, and that his or her capacity to engage in undertakings and to give testimony could be altered. Thus the relevant evidence doctrine refers to the judge's knowledge of the probity of witnesses either "by experience or by reputation."[40] In some

39 Marriage case, lines 350–358.

40 al-'Ansi, *Taj*, 4: 70; cf. Messick, "Evidence," 239.

historical Muslim societies, following the doctrine of *tashhīr*, false witnesses were made known to their communities by public proclamation or by parading the offender.[41] The author of a local Yemeni treatise of model notarial documents (a *shurūṭ* work) recommended that the authorities bar unprincipled writers and publicize the names of the perpetrators of fraud in the market.[42]

Truth and falsehood often appear intertwined in this archive, as in the tit for tat testimonies I have cited. Verisimilitude and plausibility were characteristics of skilled and effective lying, and the same was true of successful forgery. Falsehood thus mimicked the truth, at least in language and form, if not always in substance. In the murder case, for example, defense witnesses testified, falsely according to the judge, to an alternative theory of who killed the deceased, so that the judge confronted distinct narratives of what had transpired. The parties to a lawsuit were responsible for bringing witnesses, even in period homicide cases. Testimony, both truthful and false, was sought out and had to be prepared in advance of the court appearance. The testimonies of false witnesses were the most "creative," of course, since they had to be created from whole cloth. However, such witnesses did not always succeed, as we say, in "keeping their story straight." Judges, meanwhile, endeavored to distinguish the true from the false for the purposes of arriving at their final judgments. If we are able to distinguish them, we may read both the true and the false as instructive, each in its own right. In its illicit effort to approximate a correct document even the fraudulent written contract in the marriage case (quoted in the case minutes) provides an informative "source" for local contract stipulations. Falsification thus may be interesting not only for the study of the deceitful stratagems it enables but also for the extent to which it articulates moral values or masquerades in the guise of standard correctness. This is to consider the false as an essential component of a "regime of truth."

What, finally, is the utility of comparative reference to Foucault's work? The positive potentials of comparison derive from associating new material with existing, already studied cases, showing similarities and differences, and, thereby, at least potentially, expanding or challenging the conceptual and substantive range of the phenomenon under study. This mainly is accomplished through working with and exploring the capacity of generalizing terminology. The countervailing imperative, of course, is that of adherence to historical

41 Christian Lange, *Justice, Punishment and the Medieval Muslim Imagination* (Cambridge: Cambridge University Press, 2008), 223–226.

42 Ali b. ʿAbd Allah al-Iryani, *Najah al-Talib fi Sifat mā Yaktubu al-Katib*, Ms. Dated 1343 AH. (Sanʿa', Great Mosque, Western Library, 64 Fiqh. The pagination of the manuscript is pp. 50–91), 54, 87.

specificity. One would not want to obscure the new material by entirely rephrasing its realities in comparative terms. It is clear, as Foucault notes and I mentioned earlier, that conceptions such as his "regime of truth" were the products of reflections specific to materials in western thought and institutions. Since highland Yemen in the period in question was non-colonial and pre-national, these western forms had not become relevant there by reason of their extension in the world. In addition, whereas Foucault was concerned with penal institutions, my interest is in courts.

Foucault's analytic language is of two basic types. One consists of indigenous terms, such as the Greek *parrhēsia*, which he presses into wider analytic service; the other is such evidently analytic usage as "truth-telling" and "truth-establishing." In studying Islamic materials, I think it is possible to make similar moves, that is, to appropriate Arabic categories for broader analytic application and to create closely related general terminology. From the point of view of historical specificity, however, a crux in thinking of Foucault's analyses is the key notion of "truth" itself. Does use of this western (French) word obscure the forms and institutions of, for example, the pursuit of *al-ḥaqq*? In a 'premodern' Islamic court, are we really studying a "regime of truth," or is it more precisely a "regime of *al-ḥaqq*?" Comparison, in short, also hinges on translation.

The wider implications of Foucault's work on "regimes of truth" are also instructive. In the course of his analyses, he moves in three interconnected contextual domains, all of which have suggestive implications for Islamic settings. The first of these concerns the relations of what he terms "governmentality," which in the Yemeni instance would lead one into the sphere of the ruling Imam, a qualified interpreter of the shari'a. The second concerns relevant conceptions of "knowledge." Here the implications range from the forms of knowledge acquired in madrasa training in jurisprudence (*fiqh*), among other disciplines, to what is known, in the court arena, as the "knowledge of the judge" (*'ilm al-qāḍī*). How do these differently constituted "knowledges" interact in court processes? The third concerns types of subject formation, which bears on such individual acts as "truth-telling." In the Islamic court context, the immediate focus would be on the witness role and the institutional act on which the entire litigation process depends, namely, the giving of testimony.

Bibliography

Ali b. 'Abd Allah al-Iryani. *Najah al-Talib fi Sifat ma yaktubu al-Katib*, Ms. Dated 1343 AH. San'a', Great Mosque, Western Library, 64 Fiqh. The pagination of the manuscript is pp. 50–91.

ʿAnsi, Ahmad b. Qasim al-. *Taj al-Mudhhab li-Ahkam al-Madhhab*, 4 vols. Sanʿaʾ: Dar al-Hikma al-Yamaniyya, 1993 [rpt. 1936–47].

Foucault, Michel. "Political Function of the Intellectual." *Radical Philosophy* 17 (1977): 12–14.

Foucault, Michel. *Discipline and Punish: The Birth of the Prison*. Translated by Alan Sheridan. New York: Vintage Books, 1979.

Foucault, Michel. "Truth and Juridical Forms." In *Power*, edited by James S. Faubion, 1–89. New York: New Press, 2001.

Foucault, Michel. *The Courage of Truth.* Translated by Graham Burchell. New York: Picador, 2011.

Foucault, Michel. *Lectures on the Will to Know*. Translated by Graham Burchell. New York: Picador, 2013.

Foucault, Michel. *Wrong-Doing and Truth-Telling: The Function of Avowal in Justice.* Translated by Stephen W. Sawyer. Chicago: University of Chicago Press, 2014.

Geertz, Clifford. *Local Knowledge. Further Essays in Interpretive Anthropology.* New York: Basic Books, 1983.

Lange, Christian. *Justice, Punishment and the Medieval Muslim Imagination*. Cambridge: Cambridge University Press, 2008.

Messick, Brinkley. "Textual Properties: Writing and Wealth in a Sharīʿa Case." *Anthropological Quarterly* 68, no. 3 (1995): 157–170.

Messick, Brinkley. "L'Écriture en Procès: Les récits d'un meurtre devant un tribunal *sharʿī*." *Droit et Société* 39 (1998): 237–256.

Messick, Brinkley. "Interpreting Tears: A Marriage Case from Imamic Yemen." In *The Islamic Marriage Contract: Studies in Islamic Family Law*, edited by Asifa Quraishi and Frank E. Vogel, 156–179. Cambridge: Harvard University Press, 2008.

Seitel, Peter. "Haya Metaphors for Speech." *Language in Society* 3, no.1 (1974): 51–67.

Wagner, Mark S. *Jews and Islamic Law in Early 20th Century Yemen*. Bloomington & Indianapolis: Indiana University Press, 2015.

Yanagihashi, Hiroyuki. "The Doctrinal Development of "Maraḍ al-Mawt" in the Formative Period of Islamic Law." *Islamic Law and Society* 5, no. 2 (1998): 326–358.

PART 3

Daily Life

CHAPTER 9

Waqf Documents on the Provision of Water in Mamluk Egypt

Maaike van Berkel

... and their Lord will slake their thirst ...[1]

This Quranic verse written on the *sabīl* (public water fountain/well) of the Mamluk sultan Faraj b. Barquq (r. 801/1400–815/1412) situated right outside the Soutern Gate (Bab Zuwayla) of Cairo is one out of many references to the provision of water as charity in both the Qur'an and the hadith. Water supply was in the Mamluk era, as it is now, one of the vital services cities had to provide. Waqf (charitable trust) documents – to which I was introduced as a student by Ruud Peters – are sources of paramount importance for the social history of the Mamluk era. More specifically, they contain a wealth of information on the organization of transport and distribution of water in the city of Cairo.

In this article I will analyse information on the supply of drinking water in Cairo on the basis of one specific waqf document from the Mamluk era, the foundation deed of the *sabīl* of sultan Faraj b. Barquq from the early fifteenth century. By examining in some detail the information on the water supply of Cairo which can be gleaned from this deed, I intend to demonstrate the great promise of waqf documents for the debate on the nature of "the Islamic city" and on the functioning of urban institutions. I will argue that the dichotomies of formal and informal or public and private – frequently used to contrast the "Islamic" and the European cities – lack analytical value when dealing with an institution as the waqf.

The Islamic City and its Institutions

For decades historians have discussed the concept of the Islamic city, an urban type that was considered to be essentially different from the European city.

1 Qur'an, 76.21. See also Saleh Lamei Mostafa, *Moschee des Farağ ibn Barquq in Kairo* (Glückstadt: Verlag J.J. Augustin, 1972), 39.

 | DOI 10.1163/9789004343733_011

Based on Weberian models and nourished by Orientalist notions of a dichotomy between the East and the West, the Islamic city has often been defined in terms of its deficiencies in comparison to the European pre-modern city, in particular its lack of formal urban institutions. Although area specialists argued otherwise,[2] until today the assumption of urban institutional weakness continues to inspire scholars to formulate essentialists theses of the East as an area of stagnation and economic backwardness.

Weber defined the cities of the non-European world in terms of what the West had and they lacked, a sociology of absence, as it is coined by Sami Zubaidi in his article on Max Weber and the Islamic City.[3] According to Weber the medieval European city was equipped with a fortification, a market, its own court of law and, at least in part, autonomous law, associations of inhabitants and (partial) self-governance.[4] Weber compared this prototypical city with cities of the Orient and concluded that cities in the Middle East might be considered cities in an economic sense, but do not fit the definition in other respects, because they lacked autonomous administration and associations of inhabitants, collectives of urban citizens, other than according to clan, and, sometimes occupation.[5]

This analysis of the city, with, on the one hand, the European medieval city and its institutions and, on the other hand, the absence of these institutions in cities in the rest of the world formed an essential element in his thesis on the development of economic rationality and modern capitalism in the West.[6] Weber ascribed differences between the European and Oriental city to cultural and religious factors; more precisely for the Middle East, he ascribed the differences to Islam. Given the crucial role that cities played in Weber's idea on the

2 See, for example, André Raymond, *Les grandes villes arabes a l'époque ottomane* (Paris: Sindbad, 1985). See also André Raymond, "Islamic City, Arab City: Orientalist Myths and Recent Views," *British Journal of Middle Eastern Studies* 21, no. 1 (1994): 8–12, which provides an overview of studies reconsidering and rejecting the traditional view of the Islamic city, among which its alleged "non-administration." Others emphasise the personal and informal relationships in, for example, the transmission of knowledge, but show the vitality and openness of this form of organisation instead of its stagnation: Jonathan Berkey, *The Transmission of Knowledge in Medieval Cairo: A Social History of Islamic Education* (Princeton: Princeton University Press, 1992).

3 Sami Zubaidi, "Max Weber's *The City* and the Islamic City," *Max Weber Studies* 6, no. 1 (2005): 111.

4 Max Weber, *Economy and Society* (Berkeley, Los Angeles, London: University of California Press, 1978), 1226.

5 Weber, *Economy and Society*, 1226–1236.

6 Zubaidi, "Max Weber," 112.

economic development of Europe, in his view Islam was, in short, the reason why societies in the Middle East stayed behind.

Weber's thesis on the institutional weakness of the Islamic city has and still continues to inspire orientalists, historians and social scientists. And still often his dichotomy of the European and non-European city is used to explain the rise of the West and the stagnation of the East in the late medieval, early modern period.[7]

Criticism of this concept appeared most prominently in the 1960s with Ira Lapidus' important book *Muslim Cities in the Later Middle Ages*. Lapidus concentrated on the urban society and urban organization. He still adhered to the dichotomy between the European and Islamic city, but in contrast to the previous generation of scholars he argued that the Muslim city was not without structure and organization. Whereas in Europe, according to Lapidus, "a highly divided society required formal agencies for the defence of special interests," in Muslim societies life was less segmented and the organization of urban life was informal and fluid.[8]

More as well as different kinds of criticism on the concept of the Islamic city appeared in the 1980s and 1990s. Authors such as Janet Abu-Lughod, André Raymond, Richard van Leeuwen, Nezar AlSayyad, and others criticized the essentialist approach and the very small number of cities on which the research had been based so far, mainly north African cities.[9] They pleaded for more geographical and historical differentiation and context. There were also differences in their approaches. While Abu-Lughod, for example, stuck to the idea of the influence of Islam on the city and its institutions, AlSayyad and Raymond argued for an approach more based on geographical and historical

7 For the standard Orientalists' account, see Gustave E. von Grunebaum, "The structure of the Muslim town," in *Islam. Essays in the Nature and Growth of a Cultural Tradition* (London: Routledge and Kegan Paul, 1955), 141–158. For a recent analysis see, for example, Aiden Southall, *The City in Time and Space* (Cambridge: Cambridge University Press, 1998), 207–209; 226–227.

8 Ira Lapidus, *Muslim Cities in the Later Middle Ages* (Cambridge, Mass.: Harvard University Press, 1967), 186–187.

9 See, for example, Janet Abu-Lughod, "The Islamic City. Historic Myth, Islamic Essence and Contemporary Relevance," *International Journal of Middle East Studies* 19 (1987): 155–176; Richard van Leeuwen, "The Quest for the 'Islamic City,'" in *Orientations. Changing Stories: Postmodernism and the Arab-Islamic World*, ed. Inge Boer, Annelies Moors and Toine van Teeffelen (Amsterdam: Rodopi B.V., 1995), 147–162; André Raymond, "Islamic City, Arab City: Orientalist Myths and Recent Views," *British Journal of Middle Eastern Studies* 21, no. 1 (1994): 3–18; Nezar AlSayyad, *Cities and Caliphs. On the Genesis of Arab Muslim Urbanism* (New York: Greenwood Press, 1991).

context and against a dichotomy between eastern and western cities.[10] That is why Raymond and AlSayyad speak about Arab cities rather than Islamic cities. Raymond further played an important role in the rejection of the idea of the Islamic city as economically backward. Studying the Ottoman era, he showed dynamic expansion and development of these cities.

Since then few general studies on the concept of the Islamic city have appeared. The few studies from area specialists that do use a more comparative approach and deal with the Islamic city as a concept often continue to stress the importance of Islam in the development of cities in this region.[11] However, most historians of the Middle East do not focus on the notion of the Islamic city as such, but on specific cities or specific urban institutions.[12]

This heated debate makes clear that if we want to understand the actual workings and organization of urban services in Middle-Eastern cities we should avoid Eurocentric or essentialist models. Therefore, it might be useful for the moment to move beyond the impulse to study Middle-Eastern cities in comparison with European ones. Instead much more can be gained from an analysis of the ways in which contemporaries from these cities describe their organizations, institutions and problems. We need to understand specific

10 See also Amira Bennison, "Introduction," in *Cities in the Pre-Modern Islamic World. The Urban Imoact of Religion, State and Society*, ed. Amira Bennison and Alison Gascoigne (London and New York: Routledge, 2007), 1–12.

11 See, for example, Paul Wheatley, *The Places Where Men Pray Together. Cities in the Islamic Lands, Seventh Through the Tenth Centuries* (Chicago: University of Chicago Press, 2000), 336–337, which argues that during the Early Islamic period Islamic values were less prominent, but that "by the 9th or 10th century [...] religion had come to contextualize virtually all perceptions and expectations of urban life, past present, and future".

12 On the institution of the *ḥisba* (supervision of moral behavior and, more particularly, the markets), see, for example, Ahmad Ghabin, *Hisba, Arts and Craft in Islam* (Wiesbaden: Harrassowitz Verlag, 2009) and Kristin Stilt, *Islamic Law in Action. Authority, Discretion, and Everyday Experiences in Mamluk Egypt* (Oxford: Oxford University Press, 2011); on charity, see, for example, Yaacov Lev, *Charity, Endowments and Charitable Institutions in Medieval Islam* (Gainesville: University Presss of Florida, 2005) and Adam Sabra, *Poverty and Charity in Medieval Islam. Mamluk Egypt, 1250–1517* (Cambridge: Cambridge University Press, 2000); on specific cities, there are numerous studies; see for example, Julien Loiseau, *Reconstruire la maison du sultan. Ruine et recomposition de l'ordre urbain au Caire (1350–1450)* (Cairo: IFAO, 2010); Alastair Northedge, *The Historical Topography of Samarra* (London: The British Institute for the Study of Iraq, 2007); André Raymond, *Le Caire* (Paris: Fayard, 1993); Chase F. Robinson (ed.), *A Medieval Islamic City Reconsidered. An Interdisciplinary Approach to Samarra* (Oxford: Oxford University Press, 2002); Jean Sauvaget, *Alep. Essai sur le développement d'une grande ville syrienne des origins au milieu du xix*[e] *siècle* (Paris: P. Guethner, 1941).

cases first before we can understand the Middle-Eastern or Muslim city as a concept and compare it to cities elsewhere in the world. In this article I will study a waqf document from Mamluk Egypt and analyse what it tells us about the organization of the water supply in Cairo. In the conclusion I will come back to the debate on the Islamic city and try to situate my findings on the *sabīl* of the sultan Faraj b. Barquq within the larger context of urban organization and urban services in Middle Eastern cities.

Waqf Deeds as Sources for the Organisation of Urban Life

Under the Mamluks in Egypt and Syria, city life flourished; cities were renovated and large building projects achieved. In Cairo, for example, numerous monumental buildings were erected both inside and outside the walls of the Fatimid city such as the Qalawun complex – including a madrasa, a hospital and a mausoleum – built over the ruins of the Fatimid palaces at the Bayn al-Qasrayn during the reign of the sultan al-Mansur Qalawun (r. 678/1279–689/1290).[13]

The waqf played a crucial role in the building activities of Mamluk sultans and amirs and their endowments contributed immensely to the provision of urban services such as medical care, education and provision of food and water. There are several reasons why the institution of the waqf played such a crucial role in the organization of urban services.

Whereas in the first four centuries of Islam, urban services had mainly been financed from the central treasury (*bayt al-māl*), which gained the bulk of its income from taxes, from the fourth/tenth century onwards some of the major tax-collecting structures disintegrated and caused urban services to be (partly) neglected or taken over by individuals or groups, generally rulers, high state officials and their relatives. In a recent study on charity, Stefan Heidemann argued that when the Seljuqs conquered large parts of the Middle East they could no longer rely on land-tax income for urban and other public services,

13 See for example, Doris Behrens-Abouseif, *Cairo of the Mamluks: A History of Architecture and Its Culture* (Cairo: The American University in Cairo Press, 2007), 132–142, and Linda S. Northrup, "Al-Bimaristan al-Mansuri – Explorations: The Interface between Medicine, Politics and Culture in Early Mamluk Egypt," in *History and Society during the Mamluk Period (1250–1517). Studies of the Annemarie Schimmel Research College I*, ed. Stephan Conermann (Bonn: Bonn University Press, 2014), 107–142; for other monumental buildings, see, for example, Nasser O. Rabbat, *The Citadel of Cairo. A New Interpretation of Royal Mamluk Architecture* (Leiden: Brill, 1995); for later periods, see, for example, Loiseau, *Reconstruire la maison du sultan*.

since those revenues were directly claimed by their military through the system of the *iqṭāʿ* (administrative grant). Instead they first financed urban services from taxes that were deemed illegal by Islamic scholars such as tolls on long distance trades (*mukūs*) and various dues on sales. However, in their search for legitimization they soon introduced new means of organizing urban life and providing urban and other public services. They adopted the already existing but only privately used Islamic institution of the waqf as their main instrument for the financing of public life. The first promotor of this policy seems to have been Nur al-Din Mahmud (r. 541/1146 – 65/1174). Especially from the middle of the sixth/twelfth century, the waqf became part of an extensive and deliberate policy to finance urban services. The waqf thus provided services that had hitherto been financed by tax revenues.[14]

Under the Mamluks this model of funding, the waqf policy, reached maturity.[15] However, at the same time the private and public financing of urban services became entangled as many of the monumental *awqāf* of the Mamluk sultans were funded by revenues from state lands. For the founders of a waqf this institution was a multifaceted and flexible instrument serving both charitable and family purposes. The waqf guaranteed the protection of one's property from confiscation, while the founder's descendants or freedmen profited from its revenues as designated beneficiaries. In addition, the establishment of a waqf was considered a charitable act to benefit certain public services. This work of piety provided legitimization for the ruling class and care for one's soul.[16]

When a founder established a waqf, his declaration, the revenues supporting the waqf, the beneficiaries and all conditions regarding the administration of the waqf were laid down in a deed, a *waqfiyya*. Hundreds of waqf deeds from the Mamluk period survive and those concerning endowments in Cairo are now mostly kept at the National Archives of Egypt and the Ministry of Awqāf.

14 Stefan Heidemann, "Charity and Piety for the Transformation of the Cities," in *Charity and Giving in Monotheistic Religions*, ed. Miriam Frenkel and Yaacov Lev (Berlin and New York: Walter de Gruyter, 2009), 159–169.

15 See also Sylvie Denoix, "A Mamluk Institution for Urbanization: The Waqf," in *The Cairo Heritage. Essays in Honor of Laila Ali Ibrahim*, ed. Doris Behrens-Abouseif (Cairo: The American University in Cairo Press, 2000), 191–192. Sylvie Denoix, "Pour une exploitation d'ensemble d'un corpus: les waqfs mamelouks du Caire," in *Le waqf dans l'espace islamique, outil de pouvoir socio-politique*, ed. Randi Deguilhem and André Raymond (Damascus: Institut français d'études arabes de Damas, 1995), 29–44.

16 See also Sabra, *Poverty*, 5–6 and 69–100 which provides a valuable overview and analysis of various types of urban services provided by the *waqf* in Mamluk Cairo.

These deeds are a tremendously valuable source of the legal, social, economic, cultural, political and architectural history of the era. For urban historians these deeds contain a wealth of information. So far they have been used quite frequently to study the architectural history of the city, but less extensively for its social organisations.[17]

Some of these deeds contain surprisingly detailed information on the schools, hospitals and libraries that were founded such as the number of clean sheets that should be provided to an ill person in a certain hospital.[18] Similarly rich are the documents on the water supply of Cairo. Both the description of the revenue producing estates of a waqf and the stipulations on the beneficiaries of the waqf can contain information on the provision of water. Conduits, cisterns and tanks used to transport water from the Nile to the suburbs of the city were sometimes designated to finance a certain waqf complex and as such described in great detail in the deed. On the other hand, drinking water facilities for people or animals often benefited from the waqf revenues, and their organisation and staff were similarly described in the deeds.

The most detailed study so far on water supply in medieval Cairo is an excellent article by Amalia Levanoni.[19] Levanoni's focus is on the technologies of directing water from the Nile to the city (Fustat, al-Qahira and the citadel). She collected detailed information on canals, aqueducts, artificial lakes, cisterns, tanks and wells and has a final section on the directing of the water from these wells to the houses, covering the history of water supply in Cairo from early Islam to the Mamluk era. Levanoni pays much less attention to the social practices surrounding the water supply such as questions on responsibility and daily organization and the mechanisms of distribution and division. And this is exactly the kind of information waqf documents provide.

---

17 Social historical studies that use waqf documents are, for example: Muhammad Muhammad Amin, *Al-Awqaf wa l-Hayat al-Ijttimaʿiyya fi Masr 648–923 H / 1250–1517 M. Dirasa Tarikhiyya Wathaʾiqiyya* (Cairo: Dar al-Nahda al-ʿArabiyya, 1980); Berkey, *Transmission*; Denoix, "Les waqfs Mamelouks"; Ulrich Haarmann, "Mamluk Endowment Deeds as a Source for the History of Education in Late Medieval Egypt," *al-Abhath* 28 (1980): 31–47; Yaacov Lev, *Charity, Endowments and Charitable Institutions in Medieval Islam* (Gainesville: University Press of Florida, 2005); Loiseau, *Reconstruire la maison du sultan*; Sabra, *Poverty*.

18 Amin, *Awqaf*, 155–177.

19 Amalia Levanoni, "Water Supply in Medieval Middle Eastern Cities. The Case of Cairo," *al-Masaq. Journal of the Medieval Mediterranean* 20, no. 2 (2008): 179–205.

The *sabīl* of Sultan Faraj b. Barquq

The waqf deed of the *sabīl* of sultan Faraj b. Barquq forms part of *ḥujja* 66 of the al-umara' wa-l-salatin collection of the National Archives of Egypt.[20] This *ḥujja* is the foundation deed of a complex including a mosque, a *maktab*[21] (Qur'anic/primary school) and the *sabīl* founded by the sultan Faraj b. Barquq. The inscription on the building dates it 811/1408; the date on the waqf document is 812/1409. The complex was moved back and restored in 1922/1923 when the street in front of it was widened. The most recent restorations finished in 2007.[22]

The goal of the *sabīl* of Faraj b. Barquq was to supply water to the neighbourhood. The waqf deed on this endowment contains quite some relevant information on how this should be organized. We should keep in mind though that the stipulations of the waqf were normative and the waqf deed does not provide us with information on whether the stipulations were carried out exactly as they were spelled out by the founder.

Levanoni emphasises that drinking water did not reach the suburbs through canals, lakes, conduits and cisterns, but was transported daily in water skins on camels and mules.[23] Our document seems to corroborate this view. Although the emphasis on daily transport is absent, it does mention continuous transport. It says:

> ... As for the aforementioned cistern (*ṣahrīj*), it was endowed for the purpose of collecting the potable water carried to it from the blessed Nile so that the water could be distributed to Muslims – as is done by similar cisterns. [...][24]
>
> [...] The [waqf] administrator (*nāẓir*) pays every year during the days of the flooding of the Nile whatever has to be spent to fill the above-mentioned cistern from the water of the blessed Nile, [and he pays] the cost of two camels and a number of waterskins (*rawāyā wa qirab*) and uten-

20 Dar al-Watha'iq al-Qawmiyya, al-umara' wa-l-salatin, no. 66, *waqf* of Sultan Faraj b. Barquq. A small part of the document edited and translated by Ulrich Haarmann and Saleh Lamei Mostafa, *Moschee*, 44–60 and also in Saleh Lamei Mostafa, "The Cairene Sabil. Form and Meaning," *Muqarnas* 6 (1989): 33–42.

21 Or *kuttāb*.

22 See Behrens-Abouseif, *Cairo*, 237–238; Saleh Lamei Mostafa, *Moschee*; Caroline Williams, *Islamic Monuments in Cairo. The Practical Guide* (Cairo and New York: The American University in Cairo Press, 2008; new revised edition), 106.

23 Levanoni, "Water Supply," 181, 191, 194.

24 Salah Lamei Mostafa, "Cairene Sabil," 40, lines 431–433, English transl., 41.

> sils (*ʿudad*) for transporting water to the aforementioned cistern from the aforementioned blessed Nile for the entire year without interruption; and [pays] for the expenses of the aforementioned camels and the charges for workers whatever he deems should be spent from the money of the aforementioned waqf. [All this is] so that work goes on continually and the transport of water from the Nile (*al-baḥr*) to the cistern is perennial without interruption.[25]

But perhaps more important is the additional information gleaned from the document on the organization of the transport and distribution of drinking water. Levanoni talks about the role of water vendors (*saqqāʾūn*) in the streets of Cairo. She cites Ibn Battuta, the Maghribi traveller who visited Cairo in the early fourteenth century, who said there were 12.000 water vendors in the city. She further pays attention to how and where these vendors had to fill their water skins. She also mentions inhabitants who went to the river themselves with their servants to collect their own drinking water, especially when prices were high. Levanoni thus far seems to emphasise private enterprises and one-man businesses in the collection and distribution of drinking water. The description of the waqf of Faraj b. Barquq, however, describes an additional way of organizing drinking water. The waqf deed stipulates the transportation of drinking water to a centrally located cistern in a residential neighbourhood from which it was subsequently distributed among a much larger number of inhabitants. The difference with the practices described by Levanoni are that the water supply of the *sabīl* serves the common good rather than the commercial interests of the trader or the private interests of the inhabitants who go to the river themselves. Further it organizes the transportation of water on a larger scale and on a permanent basis.

In addition, the waqf document has much to say on the practices of the distribution of water to inhabitants in the neighbourhood. Water was said to have been distributed "all day long – and all night long during the month of Ramadan," following the model of other *asbila*.[26] Additional information ranges from the structure of the building and how it facilitated the daily distribution to the types of vessels used and the tasks of the staff providing the water.

25 Salah Lamei Mostafa, "Cairene Sabil," 40, lines 612–616, English transl., 41.

26 Salah Lamei Mostafa, "Cairene Sabil," 40, lines 434–435, English transl., 41.

On the *sabīl*'s architectural layout the document says, for example:

> On the sides of the room already mentioned are two large windows with thick lattices (*sanābil ghilāẓ*) of gold-plated bronze. One of these windows overlooks the road coming from the southeast. The other overlooks the road in front of Bab Zuwayla. In the latter a small door is removed, and here water is distributed and the cupbearer (*al-saqqāʾ*) sits. In front of each of these two windows is the stone plate that is borne by the projecting corbels, intended for the placing of vessels.[27]

Similarly, the waterproof construction of the cistern underneath the *sabīl* is laid out in the document:

> Beneath this [*sabīl*] and that which is adjacent to it is the cistern (*al-ṣahrīj*), built deep into the earth with baked bricks and waterproof mortar (*mūna muḥkama*). [The cistern] is for storing water [...].[28]

On the utensils needed for the distribution it says:

> The *sabīl* room mentioned and described above was endowed for having deposited therein the vessels prepared for the distribution of water and for storing whatever is in it in the way of clay jars (*azyār*), mugs (*kīzān*), and the like.[29]

Finally, also on the task of the *sabīl*'s staff and thus the daily practices of water distribution the document is quite precise:

> It is incumbent upon the aforementioned cupbearer (*al-saqqāʾ*) to raise water from the cistern and put it into vessels to give to drink to the people;[30] to wash said vessels, clean them, and protect them from creeping reptiles (*al-dabīb*) vermin (*al- hawām*), and insects (*khishāsh al-arḍ*)

27 Salah Lamei Mostafa, "Cairene Sabil," 40, lines 114–116, English transl., 40; for a German translation see also Saleh Lamei Mostafa, *Moschee*, 55.

28 Salah Lamei Mostafa, "Cairene Sabil," 40, lines 119–120; English transl., 41; for a German translation see also Saleh Lamei Mostafa, *Moschee*, 55.

29 Salah Lamei Mostafa, "Cairene Sabil," 40, lines 433–434, English transl., 41.

30 Unfortunately, the document does not provide any information on the number of vessels a person was allowed to drink when passing by in the street. Nor whether people could take away water to their homes.

> by covering them; to clean the space mentioned, sweep it, wipe it, and [keep it] clear from dirt; to fill vessels and mugs (*kīzān*), put them in the places made for them, provide them to drinkers, and refill the empty ones from among them; and to facilitate drinking for the people, treating them with kindness and a pleasant manner and going as far as possible in making arriving persons feel at ease. For this [purpose] the cupbearer sits from forenoon to sunset every day, and during Ramadan from before the breaking of the fast to the last evening meal and from before dawn up until dawn, so that there be lasting charity and continual benefaction all day long.[31]

Especially this latter type of information, on the daily workings of the water distribution, the personal interaction between the cupbearer and the water drinker, the ideal of kindness which might have been intended as an extension of the sultan's generosity and practical rules of cleanliness, all seem absent in other types of sources such as chronicles.

Conclusions

Obviously, this single waqf document from the *sabīl* of Faraj b. Barquq is too small a sample to draw any final conclusions concerning the organization of water supply in Mamluk Cairo. However, it refers in several cases to how this is done in other *asbila* in a similar way. Moreover, comparison of the information found in the waqf deed to the data collected by Levanoni – who mainly based herself on the narrative sources of the Mamluk era such as al-Maqrizi, al-Qalqashandi and Ibn Iyas – shows the relevant additions these deeds might have to offer. These additions are mainly in the field of the everyday practice of the distribution of drinking water from the various *sabīl*s of the city.

More generally, we may conclude that the waqf forces us to rethink the so-called public-private or formal-informal divide in urban services. The organization of the water supply was partly carried out by the state. Some of the bigger water works, such as canals, aqueducts and lakes, were built with money from the *bayt al-māl*. At the same time the transport and distribution of water to the inhabitants is both a private enterprise (through street vendors) and an act of charity (the waqf). Moreover, the waqf is in itself an institution that does not allow for a clear public-private divide. It was built either on private assets,

31 Salah Lamei Mostafa, "Cairene Sabil," 40, lines 604–611, English transl., 41.

often granted for (public) military services that had been delivered, or on revenues from state lands. Sultans and important emirs who initiated a waqf organized both public services such as education, medical care and free food and a family income through it. They were motivated to found a waqf because it protected their property and functioned as an act of charity at the same time, thus taking care of their souls and the legitimization of their rule.

In this way the analysis of waqf documents will also contribute to the debates on the Islamic city and its institutions, a debate that has been coloured by the juxtaposition of the Islamic city with its alleged informal and private organizations versus the formal and public services of the European late-medieval city. The waqf and its wide range of goals, applications and intentions, both public and private and more or less formal, shows us that it is perhaps better to analyse the actual organization of urban services in their specific historical context instead of searching for the absence or presence of predefined urban institutions based on Eurocentric models. The understanding of the actual working of these urban services will be the best starting point for effective comparisons with services in cities elsewhere in the pre-modern world.

Bibliography

Abu-Lughod, Janet. "The Islamic City. Historic Myth, Islamic Essence and Contemporary Relevance." *International Journal of Middle East Studies* 19 (1987): 155–176

Amin, Muhammad Muhammad. *Al-Awqaf wa l-Hayat al-Ijttima'iyya fi Masr 648–923 H / 1250–1517 M. Dirasa Tarikhiyya Watha'iqiyya*. Cairo: Dar al-Nahda al-ʿArabiyya, 1980.

Behrens-Abouseif, Doris. *Cairo of the Mamluks: A History of Architecture and Its Culture*. Cairo: The American University in Cairo Press, 2007.

Bennison, Amira. "Introduction." In *Cities in the Pre-Modern Islamic World. The Urban Impact of Religion, State and Society*, edited by Amira Bennison and Alison Gascoigne, 1–12. London and New York: Routledge, 2007.

Berkey, Jonathan. *The Transmission of Knowledge in Medieval Cairo: A Social History of Islamic Education*. Princeton: Princeton University Press, 1992.

Denoix, Sylvie. "Pour une exploitation d'ensemble d'un corpus: les waqfs mamelouks du Caire." In *Le waqf dans l'espace islamique, outil de pouvoir socio-politique*, edited by Randi Deguilhem and André Raymond, 29–44. Damascus: Institut français d'études arabes de Damas, 1995.

Denoix, Sylvie. "A Mamluk Institution for Urbanization: The *Waqf*." In *The Cairo Heritage. Essays in Honor of Laila Ali Ibrahim*, edited by Doris Behrens-Abouseif, 191–202. Cairo: The American University in Cairo Press, 2000.

Ghabin, Ahmad. *Hisba, Arts and Craft in Islam*. Wiesbaden: Harrassowitz Verlag, 2009.

Grunebaum, Gustave E. von. "The structure of the Muslim town." In *Islam. Essays in the Nature and Growth of a Cultural Tradition*, 141–158. London: Routledge and Kegan Paul, 1955.

Haarmann, Ulrich. "Mamluk Endowment Deeds as a Source for the History of Education in Late Medieval Egypt." *Al-Abhath* 28 (1980): 31–47.

Heidemann, Stefan. "Charity and Piety for the Transformation of the Cities." In *Charity and Giving in Monotheistic Religions*, edited by Miriam Frenkel and Yaacov Lev, 159–169. Berlin and New York: Walter de Gruyter, 2009.

Lapidus, Ira. *Muslim Cities in the Later Middle Ages*. Cambridge, Mass.: Harvard University Press, 1967.

Leeuwen, Richard van. "The Quest for the 'Islamic City.'" In *Orientations. Changing Stories: Postmodernism and the Arab-Islamic World*, edited by Inge Boer, Annelies Moors and Toine van Teeffelen, 147–162. Amsterdam: Rodopi B.V., 1995.

Lev, Yaacov. *Charity, Endowments and Charitable Institutions in Medieval Islam*. Gainesville: University Presss of Florida, 2005.

Levanoni, Amalia. "Water Supply in Medieval Middle Eastern Cities. The Case of Cairo." *Al-Masaq. Journal of the Medieval* Mediterranean 20, no. 2 (2008): 179–205.

Loiseau, Julien. *Reconstruire la maison du sultan. Ruine et recomposition de l'ordre urbain au Caire (1350–1450)*. Cairo: IFAO, 2010.

Mostafa, Saleh Lamei. *Moschee des Farağ ibn Barquq in Kairo*. Glückstadt: Verlag J.J. Augustin, 1972.

Mostafa, Saleh Lamei. "The Cairene Sabil. Form and Meaning." *Muqarnas* 6 (1989): 33–42.

Northedge, Alastair. *The Historical Topography of Samarra*. London: The British Institute for the Study of Iraq, 2007.

Northrup, Linda S. "Al-Bimaristan al-Mansuri – Explorations: The Interface between Medicine, Politics and Culture in Early Mamluk Egypt." In *History and Society during the Mamluk Period (1250–1517). Studies of the Annemarie Schimmel Research College I*, edited by Stephan Conermann, 107–142. Bonn: Bonn University Press, 2014.

Rabbat, Nasser O. *The Citadel of Cairo. A New Interpretation of Royal Mamluk Architecture*. Leiden: Brill, 1995.

Raymond, André. *Les grandes villes arabes a l'époque ottoman*. Paris: Sindbad, 1985

Raymond, André. *Le Caire*. Paris: Fayard, 1993.

Raymond, André. "Islamic City, Arab City: Orientalist Myths and Recent Views." *British Journal of Middle Eastern Studies* 21, no. 1 (1994): 3–18.

Robinson, Chase F., ed. *A Medieval Islamic City Reconsidered. An Interdisciplinary Approach to Samarra*. Oxford: Oxford University Press, 2002.

Sabra, Adam. *Poverty and Charity in Medieval Islam. Mamluk Egypt, 1250–1517*. Cambridge: Cambridge University Press, 2000.

Sauvaget, Jean. *Alep. Essai sur le développement d'une grande ville syrienne des origins au milieu du xixe siècle*. Paris: P. Guethner, 1941.

AlSayyad, Nezar. *Cities and Caliphs. On the Genesis of Arab Muslim Urbanism*. New York: Greenwood Press, 1991.

Southall, Aiden. *The City in Time and Space*. Cambridge: Cambridge University Press, 1998.

Stilt, Kristin. *Islamic Law in Action. Authority, Discretion, and Everyday Experiences in Mamluk Egypt*. Oxford: Oxford University Press, 2011.

Weber, Max. *Economy and Society*. Berkeley, Los Angeles, London: University of California Press, 1978.

Wheatley, Paul. *The Places Where Men Pray Together. Cities in the Islamic Lands, Seventh Through the Tenth Centuries*. Chicago: University of Chicago Press, 2000.

Williams, Caroline. *Islamic Monuments in Cairo. The Practical Guide*. Cairo and New York: The American University in Cairo Press, 2008; new revised edition.

Zubaidi, Sami. "Max Weber's *The City* and the Islamic City." *Max Weber Studies* 6, no. 1 (2005): 111–118.

CHAPTER 10

Ottoman *Amān*

Western Ownership of Real Estate and the Politics of Law prior to the Land Code of 1876

Maurits H. van den Boogert

On 13 Ramaḍān 1194/21 January 1780, two members of the Shaykhbandar family, who belonged to the notables of Aleppo, sold one of the city's covered bazaars, which consisted of 14 workshops for the production of textiles, another for the sale of bread, two apartments (*buyūt*), and a guarded warehouse. The deed of sale recorded in Aleppo's legal court identifies the buyer as Raphael Picciotto ("Rafāʾīl Bījūt"), a Jewish Tuscan merchant. More than ten years later, in Rabīʿ I 1207/October-November 1792, the court was informed that, although the bazaar had been registered in Picciotto's name all this time, its actual owner was Matlub w. Murdakhay Rahamim, a Jewish protégé (*berātlı*) of the Dutch consulate in Aleppo. Neither of the two parties appeared in the court in person, both having appointed Nasrallah Dallal, a dragoman of the Habsburg consulate, as their legal representative (*wakīl*). About two months after Dallal had registered Matlub's ownership of the bazaar, the latter sold the property to two sons of Mustafa Efendi Jabiri, Aleppo's former *muftī* and *naqīb al-ashrāf*. Matlub recorded the transaction in a notary deed in court on 20 Jumādā I 1207/3 January 1793.[1]

There seems to be a consensus among students of Ottoman history that Western residents in the Levant were not allowed to own real property prior to 1876. It has also been suggested that "since foreign ownership of real estate was illegal [...] most foreign-owned property was held in the name of Ottoman citizens."[2] Even Western diplomats in the 1920s were convinced that

1 *Mahkama al-Sharʿiyya Halab* (hereafter MSH), Dar al-Wathaʾiq, Damascus, register 141:176, and 141/1:24 (first numbering). In the meantime, Picciotto had been appointed consul of Habsburg Empire in Aleppo in 1784, but this is not mentioned in the document. On the Picciotto family, see Abraham Marcus, "Picciotto Family," in *The Encyclopedia of Jews in the Islamic World*, ed. Norman A. Stillmann [hereafter referred to as *EJIW*] (Leiden and Boston: Brill, 2010), vol. 4: 57–60.

2 S. Rosenthal, "Urban Elites and the Foundation of Municipalities in Alexandria and Istanbul," *Middle Eastern Studies* 16, no. 2 (1980): 125–133, esp. 131. Cf. Abdul-Karim Rafeq, "Ownership of real property by foreigners in Syria, 1869 to 1873," in *New Perspectives on Property and Land in the Middle East*, ed. Roger Owen (Cambridge, MA: Center for Middle Eastern Studies of

 | DOI 10.1163/9789004343733_012

the Ottoman government only made "the concession of the right of foreigners to own real estate" around the mid-nineteenth century.[3] A recent study on the concept of extraterritoriality describes the Ottomans' ability to uphold the prohibition for so long as "the single success" in the Ottoman Empire's attempts to withstand Western imperialism.[4]

Is the abovementioned document from the records of Aleppo's qadi courts reconcilable with this notion? That depends on who the true owner of the real estate in question really was. If we accept the document at face value, then it seems that Piciotto may have attempted to conceal the fact that he owned an Aleppo bazaar while he was not allowed to. With Matlub's help, the transaction described above literally set the record straight in Picciotto's favour. But an alternative interpretation is possible too. Western observers of the eighteenth century have suggested that it was prudent for non-Muslims at this time to avoid "the ostentation of wealth" for "fear of drawing the attention of the rapacious governors."[5] This might explain the transaction in 1780, assuming that the properties had belonged to Matlub all along. Dutch sources, however, suggest that he did not so much fear extortions as incessant demands on his services as a banker.[6] Registering some of his real property in the name of a Western merchant may thus have served as a protective arrangement, because if anyone laid claim to the buildings involved, this would immediately escalate into

---

Harvard University [Distributed by Harvard University Press], 2000), 175–239, esp. 181, and 227, where the author notes that "before foreigners were granted the right to own real property in the Ottoman Empire, they were able to rent real property either on their own or in partnership with local people." Also see Nora Seni, "The Camondos and their Imprint on 19th-Century Istanbul," *International Journal of Middle East Studies* 26, no. 4 (1994): 663–675, esp. 665: "Foreigners did not have the right to own property in Turkey until Abdülaziz made it legal in 1867."

3 Philip Marshall Brown, "The Capitulations," *Foreign Affairs* 1, no. 4 (15 June 1923): 71–81, esp. 72–73. Brown was a former second secretary to the American legation in Istanbul and later Professor of International Law at Princeton; Eleanor H. Finch, "In Memoriam: Philip Marshall Brown (1875–1966)," *American Journal of International Law* 60, no. 3 (July 1966): 515–516.

4 Turan Kayaoğlu, *Legal Imperialism. Sovereignty and Extraterritoriality in Japan, the Ottoman Empire, and China* (Cambridge: Cambridge University Press, 2010), 104–148, esp. 128.

5 Alexander Russell, *The Natural History of Aleppo*, ed. Patrick Russell (London: G.G. and J. Robinson, 1794), vol. 1: 46.

6 The National Archives (The Hague), Legatiearchief Turkije (Archives of the Dutch Legation in Turkey) 752, 59–66, "no. 2: Alep," Ambassador Baron van Haeften to consul van Maseijk in Aleppo, 18 November 1781. The letter explicitly states that Matlub and other protégés of the consulate in Aleppo were "extending loans to the notables of this city, whereby they involve themselves in public affairs" ("zig bemoeyen met geld-leningen te doen aan de grooten van de stad, waardoor zij zig in de publyke zaken steeken").

a diplomatic conflict. In any case, the document begs the question of how unusual it was for Ottoman real property to be owned by, or officially registered in the name of, Westerners. If it was forbidden for foreigners to own real estate in the Ottoman Empire, why did the court in Aleppo seem to have had no objection against registering Picciotto as the (nominal?) owner of an entire bazaar?

This article explores the complicated nature of foreign ownership of real property in the Ottoman Empire prior to 1876. How common was this? Were the Ottoman authorities aware of it? And if so, what did they do to stop it? On the basis of eighteenth-century legal documents from Aleppo and decrees and surveys from the Ottoman state archives in Istanbul which shed light on the actual situation on the ground, this article will argue that Ottoman policies on this issue were far from black-and-white.

1876

The Ottoman law on the Acquisition of Property by Foreigners was issued at the end of Jumādā al-awwal 1284/20–29 September 1876. It was promulgated in order to

> remove difficulties, abuses, and doubts of all kind that arise by reason of foreign subjects becoming possessors of property (*emlāk*), and to place this important matter under a firm law, and to complete financial and civil security.

In itself, the regulations of 1867 are explicit and clear (see Appendix below), but the question remains whether this law allowed foreigners to own real estate in the Ottoman Empire *for the first time*, or "placed under a firm law" an already existing practice. Only two articles of the earlier Ottoman Land Code (*ārāḍi qānūnnāmesi* of 7 Ramaḍān 1274/21 April 1858) refer to foreigners, and both would seem to confirm the notion that they were not allowed to own real property until then. Article 110 states that

> the land of an Ottoman subject does not pass by inheritance to his children, father or mother who are foreign subjects, and a foreign subject cannot have the right to Tapu [i.e. title deed] in the land of an Ottoman subject.[7]

---

7 *The Ottoman Land Code*, translated from the Turkish by F. Ongley, of the Receiver-General's Office, Cyprus, revised, and the marginal notes and index added by Horace E. Miller (London, 1892), 59.

Article 111 adds that

> The land of a person who has abandoned the Ottoman nationality does not pass by inheritance to his children, father or mother who are Ottoman or foreign subjects. It becomes vacant by the act [...][8]

The latter article implies that land owners who had abandoned the Ottoman nationality did not thereby lose the right to own property in the Empire; article 111 specifically refers to the transfer of ownership through inheritance, which would be irrelevant if the change of nationality had annulled the right to own real property altogether.

Strictly speaking, the terms 'foreign' and 'nationality' are problematic for this period, because the law on Ottoman nationality was only passed on 6 Shawwāl 1285/19 January 1869. Until then, in theory the legal and fiscal status of Westerners in the Ottoman Empire was principally based on the Islamic legal concept of safe-conduct (Ar. *amān*). It is thus on everyone with the legal status of *müstemin* (i.e. those enjoying *amān*) that we should focus. Since the case that triggered our inquiry is from Aleppo, it is in that city that we will start looking for additional documentary evidence of historical practice. Subsequently, the net will be cast wider, first including the Syrian lands (Bilād al-Shām) and then the Ottoman capital too. Ottoman policy and legal theory will also be considered in an attempt to explain the contradictions between the literature and the archival evidence.

Practice

On 8 Jumāda II 1275/13 January 1859 the Ottoman government promulgated the Tapu Law, which covered the issuance of title-deeds. It was followed by Regulations regarding Tapu Seneds and Instructions regarding Tapu Seneds, issued on 7 and 15 Shaʿbān 1276/29 February and 8 March 1860, respectively. This new law and regulations introduced few changes in the registration of real estate transactions between individuals, which continued to conform to established Hanafi prescriptions. The core elements of the legal deeds (*ḥujja*) concerned consisted of the identification of the parties and of the property involved, a description of the transfer of ownership, assurances of its legality,

8 Ibid., 59–60.

and the registration of witnesses.[9] When non-Muslims were involved, the court's scribes invariably recorded whether they were Jewish or Christian, and if the latter, of which community (*ṭāʾifa*). The registration of the names of Westerners was based on their last name, e.g. "Mister (*khawāja*) Clark, son of Clark from the English community of *mustaʾminīn* in Aleppo,"[10] while the records of names of Western Jews combine elements from the normal procedure and the format for foreign names. While there is thus an indication of the foreigners' geographical origins in the court records, the legal concept of nationality as such did not yet exist in the Ottoman Empire at this time. The nationality of either party involved in any commercial transaction (and its registration in an Ottoman legal court) could therefore not have been legally significant before 1869, when the Ottoman passport was introduced.[11]

The records of the Islamic court in Aleppo contain ample evidence of Westerners owning real estate already in the eighteenth century. In the 1780s and 1790s, for example, a limited number of Jewish members of the Venetian community bought and sold real estate in Aleppo. Salomon, the son of Yitzhak Altaras (Salamun Ishaq Altaras); his son Moses (Musa); Aaron, the son of David Altaras (Harun David, or Dawud, Altaras); and Aaron's brother, Yantob (Yantub) all went to Aleppo's court of law (*maḥkama sharʿiyya*) several times to record transactions, where they were registered as "belonging to the Frankish merchants of Venice" (*min tujjār afranj al-Bunduqiyya*).[12] Salomon and Moses

---

9 These key elements are all listed, for example, in Tahawi's *Kitab al-Shurut al-Kabir*, where several additional clauses are described too. Jeanette A. Wakin (ed. and annot.), *The Function of Documents in Islamic Law. The Chapters on Sales from Tahawi's* Kitab al-Shurut al-Kabir (Albany: State University of New York Press, 1972), Introduction, esp. 49–70.

10 Rafeq, "Ownership of real property," 230, where he describes in detail the lease of the English consular house in Aleppo from 1141/1735 to 1298/1859. William Clark was the English consul in Aleppo from 1768 to 1770. Alfred C. Wood, *A History of the Levant Company* (London: Oxford University Press, 1935), Appendix II [p. 253].

11 Karpat has argued that "this law, which is often cited as having created a new and modern legal status for Ottoman subjects, was a mere technicality that legalized and clarified further an already established concept." It is true that the concept of Ottomanism already existed since 1839, but in a strictly legal sense the Ottoman nationality did not exist until 1869. Kemal H. Karpat, "Millets and Nationality: The Roots of the Incongruity of Nation and State in the Post-Ottoman Era," in *Christians and Jews in the Ottoman Empire. The Functioning of a Plural Society. Vol. 1: The Central Lands*, edited by Benjamin Braude and Bernard Lewis (New York and London: Holmes & Meier Publishers, 1982), 141–169, esp. 162–163.

12 E.g. MSH 126/30, 11 Ramaḍān 1197/10 August 1783. On the Altaras family, which is described in contemporary Venetian sources as "la più ricca e stabile casa mercantile veneziane residente ad Aleppo" (p. 165), see Vera Constantini, "Il commercia veneziano ad Aleppo net

Altaras appear to have lived in Khan al-Harir, but they owned property elsewhere in the city, including several houses in the predominantly Jewish quarter of Banqusa.[13]

Michel Germain, a French resident of Aleppo, owned a building (*dār*) in the quarter of al-Jallum al-Sughra. It consisted of three apartments (*buyūt*) with a staircase leading to them, and also had a balcony, a weighbridge (*qabbān*), a basement, a kitchen, a well, and an open courtyard. At the end of August 1792 he sold the property to a Christian named Nasri w. Antun Hawa for 1,400 *ghurūsh*.[14] Another Frenchman, Jean-François Pons, lived in Khan al-Nahhasin, near Aleppo's central markets, while he owned real estate elsewhere, both in the city and outside its walls.[15] To start with Pons' rural properties, two transactions were recorded in his name in Aleppo's court on 20 Ramaḍān 1208/21 April 1794, although both had in fact taken place two years and seven months earlier. The first document concerns the sale of a three-fourths (18 *qīrāṭ*s) share in four gardens in the *qaḍā* of Harim, which belonged to the province of Aleppo; the first was known as the garden of Kör ʿAjam, the second as "the small garden," the third as "the large garden," and the last as the Baraka garden. The transaction included a three-fourths share in the house known as *Dār al-ṣūbājī*, "the stoves' seller's (or maker's) house," which came with a stable and machinery used in the production of silk. Pons had purchased the properties on 30 Dhū l-Ḥijja 1205/30 August 1791 from the brothers ʿAbd al-Qadir Agha and Darwish Agha Shaykhbandar, registering the purchase before the qadi, *al-sayyid* Muhammad Amin Efendi Kalahi. The document also mentions that

settecento," *Studi Veneziani* N.S. 42 (2001): 143–211. According to Richard Ayyoun, "Altaras, Jacques Isaac," *EJIW* vol. 1: 191–192, the Altaras were originally "a family of Spanish rabbis that had settled in Venice in the seventeenth century and then in Aleppo […]." In 1805 one branch of the family moved to Marseilles (ibid.), but other descendants of the Altaras family still lived in Syria in the nineteenth century: Rafeq, "Ownership of real property," 217.

13 Their place of residence is mentioned in MSH 141–1/60, 1 Rajab 1208/2 February 1794. For an example of their transactions, see MSH 138/204, 28 Rabīʿ I 1206/25 November 1791. The transaction involved the sale of half of a building in Banqūsa to Shalom, the son of Shalom Yitzhak, a dragoman of the Russian consulate in Aleppo, for 250 *ghurūsh*. Cf. 136/253, 30 Rabīʿ II 1200/1 March 1786; 138/238, 5 Rabīʿ I [1207]/21 October 1792; 141–1/14, 3 Jumāda I 1207/17 December 1792.

14 MSH 141/147, undated [between 18 and 23 Dhū l-Ḥijja 1206/7–28 August 1792].

15 Khan al-Nahhasin was a waqf, so Pons must have rented a part of it. Heinz Gaube and Eugen Wirth, *Aleppo. Historische und geographische Beiträge zur baulichen Gestaltung, zur sozialen Organisation und zur wirtschaftlichen Dynamik einer vorderasiatischen Fernhandelsmetropole* (Wiesbaden: Dr. Ludwig Reichert, 1984), 357 (Cat. nr. 97).

the Shaykhbandar brothers had recorded having inherited the property from Yunus Agha Shaykhbandar, who was probably their uncle, in the court of qadi Mahmud Efendi on 7 Dhū l-Qaʿda 1203/30 July 1789. The French merchant sold his share in these properties for 1,890 *ghurūsh* to ʿAbd al-Qadir Efendi, the son of the former mufti and *naqīb al-ashrāf*, Mustafa Efendi Jabiri.[16] On 21 April 1794 Pons recorded having sold to ʿAbd al-Qadir Agha and Darwish Agha his three fourths share in an olive orchard for 750 *ghurūsh*. The property was located in the *qaḍā* of Harim too, in what was known as Wadi Biryat. The Frenchman had acquired this property from ʿAli Efendi Taha, a relative of Muhammad Taha "Çelebi Efendi," Aleppo's powerful *naqīb al-ashrāf*. This transaction had been recorded in Muhammad Kalahi's court too. Earlier Taha had purchased the orchard from the estate of Yunus Agha Shaykhbandar, registering his ownership before qadi Mahmud Efendi on 7 Dhu l-Qaʿda 1203/30 July 1789.[17]

In general, there was no legal obligation to record transactions involving real property in the qadi courts and many (possibly most) may only have been recorded on paper privately or been concluded orally in the presence of witnesses. Nevertheless, Ottoman courts in the eighteenth century increasingly favoured written evidence and the *ʿahdnāme*s even explicitly advised Western merchants to record their transactions officially for that reason.[18] The fact that many foreign traders took this advice to heart is noteworthy in itself. The most logical assumption is that Westerners registered these transactions in Ottoman courts in order to minimize risks, which in itself suggests that they were unaware of any legal restrictions on foreign ownership of Ottoman real property. It is also relevant that the courts registered these transactions without any evident reservations.

Aleppo's court records therefore suggest that Westerners frequently owned real estate in the city and its countryside at least 90 years before the Regulations of 1867 was promulgated. The foreigners' properties were not limited to any specific quarter of Aleppo, nor to any particular type of building. The Europeans bought property from and sold real estate to non-Muslims and Muslims alike, including members from notable ʿulamaʾ families, and they routinely registered these transactions in the local court. Aleppo had always attracted foreigners, principally because it was a terminus for the caravan routes which connected Syria with the areas further east. It is therefore imaginable that the city had a special position, and was not representative of Ottoman

16 MSH 141/77–78, 20 Ramaḍān 1208/21 April 1794.

17 *Idem.*

18 Maurits H. van den Boogert, *The Capitulations and the Ottoman Legal System. Consuls, Qadis and Beratlıs in the 18th Century* (Leiden: Brill, 2005), 44.

policies and attitudes towards Western ownership of real estate prior to the nineteenth century. To put Aleppo in context we need reliable information about other locations in the Ottoman Empire for the period under review, preferably from Ottoman sources.

The archives of the central administration in Istanbul hold a series of surveys of Western communities in the Ottoman Empire, which had been ordered by the office of the Grand Vizier in the autumn of 1759. Each document lists the name of each resident foreigner, the duration of his residence, his marital status, and whether or not he owned any real property. The reason for these surveys will be discussed below; first, let us see what they tell us about Ottoman property in Western hands in three ports in Bilad al-Sham: Sidon, Latakia, and Tripoli.

In the case of the Palestinian port of Sidon, the report lists the names of all ten foreign residents who possessed real estate (*emlāk muṣāhibleri olunur*), and those who had married local wives (*ehl ẓimmīden te'ehhul edenler*), recording how long they had resided in the port-city. The French names – no other Westerners appear to have lived in Sidon at the time of the report – are often difficult to decipher, but otherwise the document, drawn up by the adjunct-judge (*mūlā khilāfa*) of Sidon, Abu Bakr, is clear. It indicates, for example, that in 1759 the French consul in Sidon, Jean-Louis de Clairambault, a resident since 1167/1753–4, owned 1 garden (*bahçe*), sixteen shops (*dukkān*), a soap factory (*ṣābūn hāne*), and five other "khans."[19] Another Frenchman, whose name appears as "Baris" in the document, had resided in Sidon since 1153/1740–1; he owned a bath house and a warehouse.

The report on the Syrian port of Latakia informs us that the Western presence in the port of Damascus was more diverse. We learn that the former British consul, Daniel Boumeester (a Dutchman), had resided there for four years. He had owned a khan in a village outside Latakia, where he had also acquired a garden and some land planted with mulberry trees (*ṭūt ağāç*). After Boumeester had gone bankrupt and had left the city, his successor, Edward Purnell, a resident of Latakia of twelve years, took over Boumeester's property. The British community further consisted of "Giovanni," Purnell's scribe, and his wife, a Frenchwoman called Charlotte Jabertin, who had been born

19 Appointed provisionally French consul at Sidon on 17 May 1757, De Clairambault died there on 9 September 1768. Anne Mézin, *Les consuls de France au siècle des lumières* (Paris: Peter Lang Verlag: 1998), 732, 757. Başbankanlık Osmanlı Arşivi, Istanbul (Ottoman Archives of the Prime Minister's Office, hereafter BOA): A.DVN.DVE 101/50, 25 Jumāda I 1773/16 December 1759; BOA, Ecnebi Defteri (hereafter ED) 27/2, 114/484, 5 Ramaḍān 1170/23 May 1757.

in Istanbul. Two Frenchmen lived in Latakia, a ship's captain and a merchant. There was also a man called Hanna, who looked after the interests of any Maltese ships calling to port, and another Maltese, identified as "Bratu," whose wife was called Maryam. Purnell appears to have been the only foreigner who owned real estate in Latakia.[20]

For Tripoli there is evidence of Westerners also owning agricultural land or its usufruct. According to the survey, the French community there consisted of the consul, Jerome Gautier, with his French wife (*Françestāndan gelen zevcesi*) and two small children; four merchants; four scribes; and eight Jesuit priests. One of the merchants owned no less than twenty gardens spread over two villages, as well as 2,700 olive trees, which appear to have been planted in soil owned by (and therefore presumably rented from) the state (*mīrī*). Another merchant owned twelve gardens and 800 olive trees.[21] A French scribe named Bertrandon owned three gardens in the ʿAkka area, which he had purchased from someone called Abu ʿAli five years earlier. Even Christian missionaries turned out to own real estate, the Jesuits holding buildings (four khans in three quarters of the town), agricultural land (six gardens), and 66 olive trees.[22]

Sidon, Latakia, and Tripoli were all part of Bilad al-Sham, so maybe foreign ownership of real estate was common only in this region? Yet another report from the Ottoman archives in Istanbul indicates that this was not the case. This document focuses on the French community in Istanbul, which was divided into three administrative categories: 1) those married to local wives and having real estate "at their disposal" (*ehl ẓimmet-le muta'ahhul olup emlāk ve arāḍī taṣarruf edenlerin defteri*); 2) those without local wives, but with real estate at their disposal; 3) those without real estate, but only married to local wives. Thirteen Frenchmen in the Ottoman capital were married to Ottoman women, while fifteen owned real estate. The entries specify that we are indeed dealing with ownership. For example, one of the Frenchmen owned "one piece of private property in the Sultan Bayezid neighbourhood, and one piece of private property in the village of Belgrade" (*Sulṭān Bāyezīd mahallesinde bir qitʿa ve Belġrad*

20 BOA, A.DVN.DVE 101/51, *evāsiṭ* Jumāda I 1773/21–30 December 1759. The transfer of the consulate from Boumeester to Purnell is registered in BOA, ED 35/1, 112/368, 1 Dhū l-Qaʿda 1171/7 July 1758.

21 BOA, A.DVN.DVE 101/52, *evāsiṭ* Jumāda I 1773/21–30 December 1759. Gautier's first name is registered in BOA, ED 27/2, 115/490, 9 Jumāda I 1171/19 January 1758. He was in office from 1752 to 1761. Paul Masson, *Histoire du commerce français dans le Levant au XVIII*e *siècle* (Paris: Hachette, 1911), 514 n. 1.

22 Unlike nine other European priests who did not own any property (one of whom is explicitly identified as a Carmelite) the Jesuits are not listed individually.

qaryesinde bir qiṭʿa mulk menzilleri vardir). A surgeon (*cerrāḥ*) identified as Boniface, who had resided in the Ottoman Empire for fifteen years, owned a house in Beyoğlu. The merchant Magy, who had resided there just as long, was the owner of a "*mulk menzili*" in the Bayezid neighbourhood, while he also possessed part of an unidentified bazaar. A merchant named Maurice and his Ottoman wife lived in Beyoğlu next to the Austrian embassy, while they also had a property in the village of Therapia just outside the Ottoman capital. The document also lists two private properties used for the training of the French *jeunes de langues* (*diloğlanları içün*), one in Galata and another in the village of Belgrade, not far from the Ottoman capital. The document about the French community in Istanbul contains a stamp from the French embassy, which suggests that the French themselves may have supplied the information.[23]

Ottoman and European documents thus show that Europeans owned private property in Turkey and the Levant throughout the eighteenth century and that the Ottoman authorities were perfectly aware of this.

Ottoman *Amān*

Now that we have established that in practice it was fairly common for Europeans in the Ottoman Empire to own real estate there, we should return to legal theory, particularly to the concept of safe-conduct (*amān*). Although Joseph Schacht asserted that the capitulations "did not develop out of the Islamic concept of *amān*," the Ottomans explicitly invoked it as the legal basis for the capitulations.[24] There is no evidence that the Ottoman authorities considered this an obvious legal fiction, so we should assume that the basic theoretical conditions for the grant of *amān* were actually relevant for the legal status of Westerners in the Ottoman Empire. This is particularly true for the theoretically temporary nature of the arrangement; in theory, "a foreigner is granted the *amān* for a fixed period, usually one lunar year or less, except in the case of a truce, in which case the *amān* may be valid for up to ten years."[25] A clear indication that the Ottomans regarded the capitulations as a form of truce is found in the French capitulations of 1536, article 14 of which explicitly

23 BOA, A.DVN.DVE 101/48, 11 Ṣafar 1773/3 October 1759.

24 J. Schacht, "Amān," in *Encyclopaedia of Islam. New Edition*, ed. H.A.R. Gibb et al. (Leiden: Brill, 1960), vol. 1: 429–430.

25 Hasan S. Khalilieh, "Amān," in *Encyclopaedia of Islam – Three*, ed. Gudrun Krämer et al. (Leiden: Brill, 2007), 2007–3: 111.

TABLE 10.1 *The duration of stay of Westerners in Istanbul, Sidon, 'Akka, Latakia, and Tripoli in the late 1750s. The number of residents whose duration of stay was not recorded is marked with **

Place of residence	# persons	# owners of real property	Average duration of stay	High / low
Istanbul	19 (10*)	9	16.5 years	45 years / 4 years
Sidon	14 (2*)	4	4.28 years	20 years / 1 year
'Akka	8	0	4.75 years	9 years / 2 years
Latakia	6	2	5.25 years	12 years / 5 months
Tripoli	18	6	4.75 years	13 years / 6 months
Total	65 (12*)	21		

SOURCE: compiled by the author.

limits the duration of stay for individual merchants to ten consecutive years.[26] Although this limited period is stipulated in none of the later capitulations, it may serve as a hypothetical criterion to assess how many Westerners outstayed their theoretical welcome.

The above-mentioned Ottoman surveys from 1759 include information about how long each foreigner had resided in the Ottoman Empire. The documents are not entirely consistent, unfortunately; the one about the French community in Istanbul, for example, does not provide the duration of residence for 10 out of the 19 Frenchmen included in the survey. The document for Tripoli, by contrast, gives the number of years' residence for all 18 persons in the survey, sometimes including the months.

These records suggest that foreigners tended to reside the longest in the Ottoman capital. A French merchant identified as Milo (Mīlū) had lived in Istanbul for as long as 45 years, but he was clearly exceptional. If we correct our statistics by excluding him from the sample, the average drops to 13 years, six other Frenchmen having resided in Istanbul for ten years or longer too. For the

26 On the contested status of the 1536 capitulations, see Gilles Veinstein, "Les Capitulations Franco-Ottomanes de 1536 sont-elles encore controversables?", in *Living in the Ottoman Ecumenical Community. Essays in Honour of Suraiya Faroqhi*, ed. Vera Constantini and Markus Koller (Leiden: Brill, 2008), 71–88.

four Syrian ports (Sidon, ʿAkka, Latakia and Tripoli) the average is significantly lower, between 4.28 and 5.25. Fourteen (26.4 %) out of the 53 Westerners whose duration of residence is recorded in these documents had stayed in the Ottoman Empire for ten years or longer. We should be careful not to draw any far-reaching conclusions from this modest sample, but it does suggest that in many cases foreign residents remained well within the theoretical limitation on the period they were allowed to stay in the Levant.

The decree from the Grand Vizier's office which ordered the 1759 survey of various foreign communities in the Empire only obliquely refers to the temporary nature of their residence:

> [The fact that] the Sublime State makes treaties with the Christians, and [that] the *müstemin*s come and stay in the Abode of Islam, is only to promote trade and to maintain peace and as their stay is as a visitor, there is no sanction in shariʿa for their possession of land in the Abode of Islam by means of title deed or by lease. A fatwa has been issued [stating that *müstemins*'] possession of land and engaging in agriculture in the well-guarded dominions requires the implementation of the provisions of the People of the Book (*ehl-i zimmet*) on [these] *müstemins*. The *müstemin*s control and possess vineyards, orchards, fields and real property in Galata and in the large towns in the well-guarded dominions, but according to the shariʿa [they] are prohibited to possess land in Abode of Islam.[27]

Without elaborating further on legal considerations, the decree continues that

> moreover, if they are requested to pay the taxes on their real estate and lands they possess they refuse to pay arguing that they have capitulations (*ʿahidnāme*). It is apparent that this situation harms the order of the country and the treasury of the Muslims. It is written in their *ʿahidnāme*s that no *kharāj* should be demanded from the French, English, Dutch and Venetians residing in the well-guarded dominions whether they are married or single; no *cizye* and *tekâlīf* should be demanded from the Austrians, Swedes and Danes. [...] It would be good to settle this situation properly, to help the slaves of God and to prevent any loss for the treasury of the Muslims.

27 BOA, Sadaret Âmedi Kalemi, A.AMD 13/25. It is dated, in pencil, to 25-1-1173, corresponding to 17 September 1759. I am very grateful to Abraham Marcus for sending me this document.

By steering clear of juridical details and reframing the problem as a fiscal issue, the Sublime Porte diverted attention away from the legality of the capitulations in general. The reference to different privileges for different nations is incorrect; the principle of the most-favoured-nation, which the Ottomans applied from the start, ensured that all Western commercial communities had the same fiscal status. We can only guess whether this mistake was copied from the original petition which brought the matter to the Grand Vizier's attention, or this was a deliberate obfuscation to justify a formal inquiry. The end of the decree is almost certainly a verbatim copy of the original petition:

> For now, first of all the qadi and the voyvoda [Ottoman governor] of Galata should be advised and ordered that those possessing land and estates in and around Galata [should] be investigated by their ambassadors and dragomans and their names and the location of the land and estates they possess be reported in one register. And orders should be sent to the qadis and governors of the places where consuls reside, so that their names and the lands and properties they possess, are investigated by means of their consuls and reported [by the qadi]. Upon their arrival, the registers [should] be presented to your elevated presence [i.e. the Grand Vizier] and [your opinion] be asked. [Afterwards] the issue [should] be regulated in accordance with the requirements of the shariʿa and the *ʿahidnāme*s. For now your majesty's approval is requested for composing and dispatching the royal and Grand Vizierial orders whose copies are presented to your majesty's elevated threshold.[28]

We know that the investigation indeed took place, but little appears to have been done with the reports. It is also clear that all embassies were aware of the survey, because several of the documents contain embassy stamps. The Dutch ambassador in Istanbul also knew about the Grand Vizier's decree, but he did not seem to worry about its effects:

> People speculate whether the Jesuits or the marriages of Europeans with daughters of subjects of the Grand Signior gave rise to this; if the former, who own a large number of houses in Galata which they acquired from

28 I am very grateful to Ismail Hakkı Kadı for sending me his translation of the document. For references regarding decrees about Ottoman real property in foreign hands from concerning Izmir, Crete, Patras, Salonica, and Chios for the years 1791, 1792, 1814 and 1822, see Mübahat S. Kütükoğlu, *Tanzimat Devrinde Yabancıların İktisadi Faaliyetleri* (Ankara: Türk Tarih Kurum Basımevi, 1992), 112–113.

> Armenians of the Romish religion who are all rayas [T. *reaya*] or subjects of the Porte; this has invariably led to numerous disputes and conflicts and the public treasury may well have suffered from these transfers [of property].[29]

The Ottoman records do not list any property owned by the Jesuits in Istanbul,[30] but it is interesting that the Dutch ambassador evidently believed that this was little more than a – possibly justified – fiscal issue that hardly concerned his community. This is probably because the Imperial order to the Voyvoda of Galata to investigate the matter emphasizes the issue of intermarriages and says nothing about the presumed illegality of foreign ownership of real estate.[31] The European's surprise when they were later explicitly told that this was forbidden may therefore have been genuine.

On 7 Rabīʿ II 1206/3 December 1791, the Sublime Porte issued a *fermān* about the appointment of European consuls and vice-consuls in the Greek Archipelago, the contemporary French translation of which also contained the following clause:

> Comme la loi défend aux nations Franques d'acheter et de posséder des terres et des biens stables sur le pais Musulman et que pareillement se trouve d'être contraire aux articles de nos engagements politiques, il ne sera pas permit à l'avenir aux couvents et aux églises, appartenantes aux nations Franques, d'acheter des maisons, des boutiques ou bien d'autres possessions stables.[32]

The *fermān* contained several other clauses, but the impact of this one in particular is easy to detect in the European sources. For example, the Dutch authorities were not sure how to interpret the text, noting that "the decree forbidding Franks to own real estate … claims to be based on existing laws, and

29 Elbert de Hochepied aan Fagel, 1 October 1759 (in Dutch), published in: J.G. Nanninga (Ed.), *Bronnen tot de geschiedenis van den Levantschen handel, Derde deel: 1727–1765* (The Hague: Martinus Nijhoff, 1952), 393.

30 One would expect the Jesuits' properties to be listed under the French community (as was the case in ʿAkka), but BOA, A.DVN.DVE 101/48 is silent about them.

31 Nanninga (Ed.), *Bronnen … Derde deel: 1727–1765*, 394. This is a Dutch translation produced on the basis of the Italian translation.

32 "Commandement émané au sujet des consuls et vice-consuls sur l'Archipel, émané le 7 de rebiulahir 1206 à la Turque, communiqué aux ministres étrangers le commencement de Décembre 1791," in J.G. Nanninga (ed.), *Bronnen tot de geschiedenis van den Levantschen handel. Vierde deel: 1765–1826. Eerste stuk* (The Hague: Martinus Nijhoff, 1964), 480–482.

would therefore seem to be a restoration [of these laws]."[33] The consul in Izmir, Daniel Jean de Hochepied, pessimistically wrote to the ambassador in Istanbul that the order would affect several merchants, for example the houses of Fremeaux and Van Lennep, which owned private country houses and gardens near Izmir.[34] The Dutch ambassador, Baron Van Dedem, who explicitly called the prohibition an "innovation", was more optimistic. Writing almost eight months after the *fermān* was issued, he observed that

> until now [the Ottoman authorities] have been as accommodating as possible with its implementation, having forced nobody to sell [their possessions] so far. If the order is enforced at all, this would probably be less painful for the owners that it had appeared at first.[35]

Not much later De Hochepied confirmed that the effects of the order were much less severe than he had anticipated. The qadi of Izmir's implementation of the *fermān* was very favourable for the Europeans, who do not appear to have been forced to sell their properties at all. This was still the case at the beginning of the nineteenth century, when the Dutch government continued to own its embassy in Istanbul, as well as the Dutch hospital in Izmir.[36]

The *fermān* of 1791 reflected a genuine concern on the part of the Ottoman government about the rising numbers of Ottoman non-Muslims as vice-consuls. As the Ottoman measures to curb the extension of *berāt*s began to take effect, the Europeans increasingly exploited a loophole in the capitulations, which did not impose any limits on the number of vice-consuls they were allowed to appoint. To halt this development, the Porte had revoked quite a few vice-consular *berāt*s already in 1764, but as the vigilance of the government subsided in subsequent years the number of appointments increased again.[37] The decree of 1791 therefore represents little more than a temporary revival of this policy, even if the *fermān* was a more elaborate attempt to reign in the privileges of the vice-consuls.

---

33 The Directors of Levant Trade in Amsterdam to Ambassador Van Dedem in Istanbul, 6 July 1792, in *Idem*, 494.

34 De Hochepied to Van Dedem, 2 April 1792, in *Idem*, 488.

35 Van Dedem to the Directors of Levant Trade, 25 August 1792, in *Idem*, 501.

36 "Tafereel zo van de origine en inrichting der Directie....," 6 April 1807, in Nanninga (ed.), *Bronnen ... Vierde deel: 1765–1826. Eerste stuk*, 756. Interestingly, this document speaks of properties ("eygendommen") in the Levant – only the hospital at Izmir – and possessions ("possessiën") – the embassy, without spelling out the legal significance of the distinction.

37 Van den Boogert, *The Capitulations and the Ottoman Legal System*, 28.

It is also significant that the order was issued just before peace was concluded with Russia, the European power which was by far the most active in the Greek archipelago at the end of the eighteenth century. It is tempting therefore to interpret the *fermān* as a preventive measure, especially because the Russians were using the Treaty of Küçük Kaynarca (1774) to extend their patronage over the Greek orthodox Christians in the Ottoman Empire. This would explain why the decree so explicitly focuses on the ownership of real estate by churches, also prohibiting bequests to convents and churches in the Greek islands.[38] These political circumstances, and the fact that the *fermān* of 1791 explicitly addressed a situation peculiar to the archipelago, shed a new light on its non-implementation elsewhere in the Levant.

Conclusion

By the middle of the nineteenth century all European representatives in the Levant had become convinced that Westerners where not allowed to own real property in the Ottoman Empire. This was such an inconvenience for them that they were willing to concede that the Ottoman courts would have jurisdiction over all real estate, even that owned by foreigners, as long as the Ottoman government lifted the ban. The Ottoman Land Code of 1867 did just that. For the Ottoman authorities, this should be considered a major diplomatic victory. After all, they had taken away from the Europeans an informal privilege they had enjoyed for centuries, only to give it back to them a few decades later in return for a limitation of the extraterritorial status of Westerners in the Ottoman Empire.

At the same time, the provisions of 1867 should not be projected backwards. Europeans owned real property – houses, bazaars, garden, vineyards, etc. – throughout the Ottoman Empire throughout the eighteenth century and there is ample evidence that the same was true in earlier periods. Their acquisition of these properties was often recorded in the local qadi courts without any problem. In such cases, the court exercised its notarial function, so real estate transactions involving foreigners were merely recorded, not critically reviewed. This would suggest that, to all intents and purposes, their ownership of these properties was allowed. How should we understand this contradiction?

38 "Commandement émané au sujet des consuls et vice-consuls sur l'Archipel, émané le 7 de rebiulahir 1206 à la Turque,, 481: "... que l'on n'admet pas des legs en aucune façon que ce soit de la part de nos sujets tributaires en faveur des dits couvents et églises Franques."

The Ottoman form of legal pluralism included Islamic law, state law, customary law, and various other types of legal regulations specific to particular groups in Ottoman society. In theory Islamic law should rule supreme among these various kinds of law, but in practice the Ottomans decided which rules applied to any given situation. While always paying lip service to Islamic law – in this case by emphasizing the relevance of *amān* – the Ottoman state needed more manoeuvring space in its commercial and foreign policies than Islamic legal theory often allowed. The legal status of Europeans is a case in point. Not only had the specific temporal limitation of the validity of *amān* quietly been dropped, the collective nature of the capitulations granted to Westerners was also at odds with the formal conditions for *amān*. The issue of real estate ownership touched on both these issues. If Islamic law had been strictly applied, then this would have eroded the capitulations considerably, effectively reversing the collective arrangements to privileges for individuals; only then was it possible to establish properly whether or not an individual Westerner was in violation of the prescripts of *amān*. This was highly unpractical for both the Ottomans and the Europeans and it would have meant that the Sultan had to go back on his word. This would undoubtedly have damaged the Porte's relations with Western Europe and harmed its economic interests.

At the same time, towards the end of the eighteenth century it became politically expedient for the Ottoman government to curb the Europeans' privileges as best they could. This was not easily accomplished. In theory precarious, the legal status of Europeans had become firmly entrenched, the ambassadors in Istanbul tending to protest against any initiatives that were perceived as infringements of the capitulations. The Ottomans did have a few successes: for example, the Western practice of appointing local merchants as vice-consuls, particularly in the Greek archipelago, was temporarily halted at the end of the eighteenth century, when the Porte unilaterally cancelled the deeds of appointment of many of these vice-consuls. The discussion about real estate was another success from the Ottomans' perspective. The principal reason for this was that the Europeans were not familiar enough with the details and legal background of the privileges they enjoyed. The Dutch ambassador did not consider it unreasonable that the Porte should object to foreigners acquiring real estate in Istanbul and elsewhere, which suggests that the European representatives did not form a united front on this issue. The Ottomans capitalized on this by making it clear that owning real estate was technically not allowed, while at the same time neglecting to take measures against any violations. Although the Ottomans never actually seem to have disowned the real property of any Europeans, the uncertainty about its permissibility alone was enough to secure concessions from the Western ambassadors and to subtly redefine the nature of Ottoman *amān*.

Appendix

ACQUISITION OF PROPERTY BY FOREIGNERS [1867][39]

In order to extend the riches and prosperity of the Imperial Dominions, and to set aside the difficulties, abuses, and all kinds of doubts which arise from foreign subjects becoming possessors of property, and to put this important matter under a firm law and to complete the financial and administrative security, the law which has been decided on by Imperial Irade is made known as follows:

In the margin: Extension of law to aliens

1. The subjects of foreign Governments are allowed to take advantage of the rights to possess property within or without towns in every part of the Imperial Dominions, with the exception of the Hejaz, in the same way as Ottoman subjects, and without being under any other conditions, in the manner stated below, on complying with the laws that govern them in this case. Those who were originally Ottoman subjects and afterwards changed their nationality are excepted from this rule. Concerning them the provisions of the special law will be in force.

Note: *The procedure to be followed with regard to property (Emlak) and Land (Arazi) belonging to persons excepted from this 1st article is given in a Law approved by Imperial Iradé, dated 25. Rebi ul-Akhir, 1300 [4 February 1883].*

In the margin: Legal position of aliens as to property.

2. Foreigners who are owners of property within or without towns in accordance with the provisions of Art. 1, will be obliged to fulfill the conditions which Ottoman subjects are obliged to in all matters which concern their property. In order to give legal effect to this obligation: 1, he will comply with the laws which are at present and may be in the future in force concerning possession, inheritance, alienation, and mortgage (Istiglal) of property, and police and municipal; 2, he will pay all taxes which Ottoman subjects possessors of property are or may be assessed for, of whatever name or form, within or without cities; 3, they will have recourse to the Ottoman Tribunals in all matters concerning property, and in the event of an action affecting it, whether as plaintiff or

39 Extract from *The Ottoman Land Code*, tr. F. Ongley, revised, and the marginal notes and index added by Horace E. Miller (London, 1892), 168–171.

defendant or both sides [being] foreign subjects, which will be tried according to the system to which Ottoman subjects possessors of property are subject, the conditions to which they are obliged to conform, and the rights which they have acquired, without the interference of the actual quality of their nationality special to their persons, and having regard to the protection of the exemptions which belong to their persons and movable property in accordance with treaties.

In the margin: Bankruptcy of alien.

3. In the event of the bankruptcy of a foreigner possessing property, the syndics will apply to the Ottoman authorities and tribunals for the sale of the property possessed by the bankrupt, which by essence and law is permitted to be answerable for the debts of the owner, and if a foreigner has an action against a foreigner who is possessor of property for a matter other than property, and has gained his action by the decision of his Chancellerie, and the sale of the property which is valid to pay the debt of the foreigner who is condemned by this judgment is necessary, the matter will likewise be referred to the Ottoman authorities and tribunals, who will first inquire whether the property which the creditor claims to have sold is of the class permitted by law to be sold to satisfy debt, and afterwards carry out the decision.

In the margin: Testamentary power of alien.

4. A foreigner has the power to bequeath his property, the inheritance and donation of which by will is permitted; the Ottoman laws concerning Metruké will be carried out with regard to property which has not been given or bequeathed, or which the provisions of the Ottoman Laws do not allow to be given or bequeathed.

In the margin: Succession to alien's property.

NOTE. It has been notified by Vezirial letter, dated 24. July, 1291 [2 Rajab 1293 = 24 July 1876], *that in the event of the death of a foreign subject possessing property (Emlak), his property (Emlak) land (Arazi) will be inherited by his legal heirs.*

5. Every foreigner shall take advantage of the benefits of the provisions of this law as soon as acquiescence has been given by the Government to which he is subject to the mode prepared which is proposed by the Ottoman Government to be carried out concerning acquisition of property.

End of Jemazi ul evel, 1284 [20–29 September 1876]

Bibliography

Archives

- Başbankanlık Osmanlı Arşivi (Ottoman Archives of the Prime Minister's Office), Istanbul (BOA):
  - A.DVN.DVE 101/48, 101/50, 101/51, and 101/52
  - Ecnebi Defteri (ED) 27/2 and 35/1,
  - Sadaret Âmedi Kalemi, A.AMD 13/25.
  - Mahkama al-Shar'iyya Halab (MSH), Dar al-Watha'iq, Damascus, registers 126,136, 138, 141, 141–1.
- [Dutch] National Archives, The Hague: Legatiearchief Turkije (Archives of the Dutch Legation in Turkey) 752.

Secondary Literature and Published Sources

Ayyoun, Richard. "Altaras, Jacques Isaac." In *The Encyclopedia of Jews in the Islamic World*, edited by Norman A. Stillmann, vol. 1, 191–192. Leiden and Boston: Brill, 2010.

Boogert, Maurits H. van den. *The Capitulations and the Ottoman Legal System. Consuls, Qadis and Beratlıs in the 18th Century*. Leiden: Brill, 2005.

Brown, Philip Marshall. "The Capitulations." *Foreign Affairs* 1, no. 4 (15 June 1923): 71–81.

Constantini, Vera. "Il commercia veneziano ad Aleppo net settecent." *Studi Veneziani* N.S. 42 (2001): 143–211.

Finch, Eleanor H. "In Memoriam: Philip Marshall Brown (1875–1966)." *American Journal of International Law* 60, no. 3 (July 1966): 515–516.

Gaube, Heinz, and Eugen Wirth. *Aleppo. Historische und geographische Beiträge zur baulichen Gestaltung, zur sozialen Organisation und zur wirtschaftlichen Dynamik einer vorderasiatischen Fernhandelsmetropole*. Wiesbaden: Dr. Ludwig Reichert, 1984.

Karpat, Kemal H. "Millets and Nationality: The Roots of the Incongruity of Nation and State in the Post-Ottoman Era." In *Christians and Jews in the Ottoman Empire. The Functioning of a Plural Society. Vol. 1: The Central Lands*, edited by Benjamin Braude and Bernard Lewis, 141–169. New York and London: Holmes & Meier Publishers, 1982.

Kayaoğlu, Turan. *Legal Imperialism. Sovereignty and Extraterritoriality in Japan, the Ottoman Empire, and China*. Cambridge: Cambridge University Press, 2010.

Khalilieh, Hasan S., "Amān." In *Encyclopaedia of Islam*, edited by Gudrun Krämer et al., vol. 3, 111. Leiden: Brill, 2007.

Kütükoğlu, Mübahat S. *Tanzimat Devrinde Yabancıların İktisadi Faaliyetleri*. Ankara: Türk Tarih Kurumu Basımevi, 1992.

Marcus, Abraham. "Picciotto Family." In *The Encyclopedia of Jews in the Islamic World*, edited by Norman A. Stillmann, vol. 4, 57–60. Leiden and Boston: Brill, 2010.

Masson, Paul. *Histoire du commerce français dans le Levant au XVIIIe siècle*. Paris: Hachette, 1911.

Mézin, Anne. *Les consuls de France au siècles des lumières*. Paris: Peter Lang Verlag, 1998.

Nanninga, J.G., ed. *Bronnen tot de geschiedenis van den Levantschen handel, Derde deel: 1727–1765*. The Hague: Martinus Nijhoff, 1952.

Nanninga, J.G., ed. *Bronnen tot de geschiedenis van den Levantschen handel. Vierde deel: 1765–1826. Eerste stuk*. The Hague: Martinus Nijhoff, 1964.

Ongley, F. *The Ottoman Land Code*. Translated from the Turkish by F. Ongley of the Receiver-General's Office, Cyprus, revised, and the marginal notes and index added by Horace E. Miller. London, 1892.

Rafeq, Abdul-Karim. "Ownership of real property by foreigners in Syria, 1869 to 1873." In *New Perspectives on Property and Land in the Middle East*, edited by Roger Owen, 175–239. Cambridge, MA: Center for Middle Eastern Studies of Harvard University [Distributed by Harvard University Press], 2000.

Rosenthal, Steven. "Urban Elites and the Foundation of Municipalities in Alexandria and Istanbul." *Middle Eastern Studies* 16, no. 2 (1980): 125–133.

Russell, Alexander. *The Natural History of Aleppo*. Edited by Patrick Russell. London: G.G. and J. Robinson, 1794.

Schacht, Joseph. "Amān." In *Encyclopaedia of Islam. New Edition*, edited by H.A.R. Gibb *et al.*, vol. 1, 429–430. Leiden: Brill, 1960.

Seni, Nora. "The Camondos and their Imprint on 19th-Century Istanbul." *International Journal of Middle East Studies* 26, no. 4 (1994): 663–675.

Veinstein, Gilles. "Les Capitulations Franco-Ottomanes de 1536 sont-elles encore controversables?" In *Living in the Ottoman Ecumenical Community. Essays in Honour of Suraiya Faroqhi*, edited by Vera Constantini and Markus Koller, 71–88. Leiden: Brill, 2008.

Wakin, Jeanette A., ed. *The Function of Documents in Islamic Law. The Chapters on Sales from Tahawi's* Kitab al-shurut al-kabir. Albany: State University of New York Press, 1972.

Wood, Alfred C. *A History of the Levant Company*. London: Oxford University Press, 1935.

CHAPTER 11

A Comparative Study of Contract Documents

Ottoman Syria, Qajar Iran, Central Asia, Qing China and Tokugawa Japan

Toru Miura

Introduction

Although shariʿa court records in the Ottoman Empire have been used as socio-economic data for a long time, most recent studies of them focus on the role of shariʿa courts in local societies and the relation between legal practices and the legal theory written in legal treaties.[1] My earlier work on the Salihiyya court of Damascus in the latter half of the nineteenth century showed that it was there that ordinary people in the Salihiyya quarter recorded their contracts, especially transactions concerning immovable property and inheritance, their purpose being to confirm ownership and avoid future conflict. They acted according to the formalistic regulations of Islamic law, and yet utilised those regulations in looking out for their own interests. The court records thus reflect a dynamic relationship between formality and the reality within which people lived their daily lives.[2]

It has been a universal practice throughout the world, from ancient times down to the present, to keep records of contracts to certify ownership, but concepts of ownership and contract have differed according to time and place. In recent years, we have come to know details of shariʿa court records in Qajar Iran and nineteenth- and twentieth-century Central Asia (Uzbekistan)

1 Boğaç A. Ergene, *Local Court, Provincial Society and Justice in the Ottoman Empire: Legal Practice and Dispute Resolution in Çankırı and Kastamonu (1652–1744)* (Leiden: Brill, 2003); Zouhair Ghazzal, *The Grammars of Adjudication: The Economics of Judicial Decision Making in Fin-de-siècle Ottoman Beirut and Damascus* (Beirut: Institut Français du Proche-Orient, 2007). Recently Boğaç Ergene takes an analytical method of the Law and Economics scholarship to examine Ottoman legal practices in the seventeenth and eighteenth century Kastamonu court in collaboration with an economic historian, Metin Coşgel. See Metin Coşgel and Boğaç Ergene, *The Economics of Ottoman Justice: Settlement and Trial in the Sharia Courts* (Cambridge: Cambridge University Press, 2016).

2 Toru Miura, "Personal Networks surrounding the Ṣāliḥiyya Court in 19th-Century Damascus," in *Etudes sur les villes arabes du Proche-Orient, XVIe–XIXe siécle* (Damas: IFEAD, 2001), 113–150; Miura, "Formality and Reality in shariʿa Court Records: Socio-Economic Relations in the Ṣāliḥiyya Quarter of Nineteenth Century Damascus," *The Memoir of the Toyo Bunko* 59 (2002): 109–41; Miura, "Court Contracts and Agreements among Parties in the Islamic Middle East,"

 | DOI 10.1163/9789004343733_013

through a number of pioneering works;[3] beyond the Muslim world too, there exist abundant extant contract documents from Ming and Qing (seventeenth to twentieth century) China and from Tokugawa (seventeenth to nineteenth century) Japan. Their study tells us that neither ownership nor contract is defined simply by law; rather, their definitions have been generated, as well as altered, in accordance with the relationship between people and the state. The form in which the contract documents were written may therefore reflect social relations among the people and the relation of people to the state.

In this paper, I would like to discuss how and what we are able to read from court contract documents in terms of social history, by paying attention to formulary structures, that is, to how the contract documents were recorded, as well as to how they were used and preserved, in order to suit specific socio-economic needs. I will use here two types of comparison: between adjoining regions and proximate periods, and between widely separated regions and periods that could have had no direct influence on one other, as discussed by Marc Bloch.[4] I begin by examining the Salihiyya court registers of the eighteenth and nineteenth centuries to clarify historical changes within the same court, and then compare Ottoman, Qajar and Central Asian courts. I will conclude with a discussion of contracts in China and Japan in the early modern period in order to consider features of the shariʿa court from a comparative viewpoint.

Shariʿa Court Records of the Salihiyya Court in Ottoman Syria

The Centre for Historical Documents in Damascus (Markaz al-Watha'iq al-Tarikhiyya) has, for the Ottoman period, 2,361 registers from the shariʿa courts in Damascus, Aleppo, Hama and Homs, as well as documents called *ḥujja*, both of which recorded property transactions and provided proof of ownership. Ottoman Damascus had, until 1909–1910, a main court called the Mahkamat

Annals of Japan Association for Middle East Studies 19, no. 2 (2003): 45–74. See also Toru Miura, *Dynamism in the Urban Society of Damascus: The Ṣāliḥiyya Quarter from the Twelfth to the Twentieth Centuries* (Leiden: Brill, 2016), chapters 7 and 8.

3 Christoph Werner, "Formal Aspects of Qajar Deeds of Sale," in *Persian Documents: Social History of Iran and Turan in the Fifteenth-Nineteenth Centuries*, ed. Nobuaki Kondo (London: Routledge Curzon, 2003), 13–49; Nobuaki Kondo, "Shariʿa Court Registers from Tehran in the Second Half of the Nineteenth Century," *Toyoshi kenkyu* 70, no. 2 (2011): 1–32 (in Japanese); Toru Horikawa, "Islamic Court Documents as Historical Sources in Central Asia," in *History and Culture of Central Asia*, ed. Toru Horikawa (Tokyo: NIHU Program Islamic Area Studies, The University of Tokyo Unit, 2012), 73–84.

4 Marc Bloch, "Pour une histoire comparée des sociétés Européennes," *Revue de Synthese Historique*, (Dec. 1928); Bloch, "A Contribution towards a Comparative History of European

al-Bab, a special court for inheritance, Mahkamat al-Qassam, and five local courts located in the large quarters of the city, including the Salihiyya Court. The Damascus registers consist of 1,556 volumes covering the period 991 AH to 1343 AH, that is, 1583 to 1925 CE.[5]

The Salihiyya court was located in the Jarkasiyya Madrasa in the Salihiyya Quarter. This madrasa, founded at the beginning of the twelfth century, was quite small, with only three rooms. The following outline of the shariʿa court registers is based on those of the Salihiyya court.

Length of Documents

The Centre for Historical Documents has two registers of the Salihiyya court dating from the eighteenth century (Nos. 88 and 105) and six registers dating from the nineteenth century (Nos. 647, 660, 663, 669, 691 and 699). The volume and length of these registers differ according to the period. For the nineteenth century, Register 691 has 196 documents over 198 pages, covering 1290–95/1873–78, that is, 0.99 documents per page, and Register 669 has 248 documents over 276 pages covering 1291–94/1874–77, that is, 0.90 documents per page, while for the eighteenth century, Register 88 has 501 documents over 134 pages covering 1144–53/1733–40, that is, 3.63 documents per page, and Register 105 has 712 documents over 211 pages covering 1152–64/1741–51, that is, 3.37 documents per page. It is thus obvious that the average length of documents in the nineteenth century registers is about three times greater than those of the eighteenth century. The physical size of the registers, however, is almost the same in both the eighteenth and nineteenth centuries: Nos. 88, 105, 647, 660, 669, 691 and 699, for example, are 23×34 cm, but No. 663 is larger, 29×41 cm.

The relative length of the documents through the centuries is also reflected in the registers of the Midan court, located in the southern suburbs of Damascus, with about 1.92 documents per page in the nine registers from 1141 to 1164/1728–52, showing that the documents of the Salihiyya court are much shorter than those of the Midan court in the same period. The shortness of the documents in eighteenth century Salihiyya registers reflects the simplification of registration, as discussed below.

Societies," *Land and Work in Medieval Europe, Selected Papers by Marc Bloch*, trans. J.E. Anderson (Berkeley: University of California Press, 1967), 44–81.

5 Brigitte Marino and Tomoki Okawara, eds., *Catalogue des registres des tribunaux ottomans conservés au Centre des Archives de Damas* (Damas: Institut français d'études arabes de Damas, 1999).

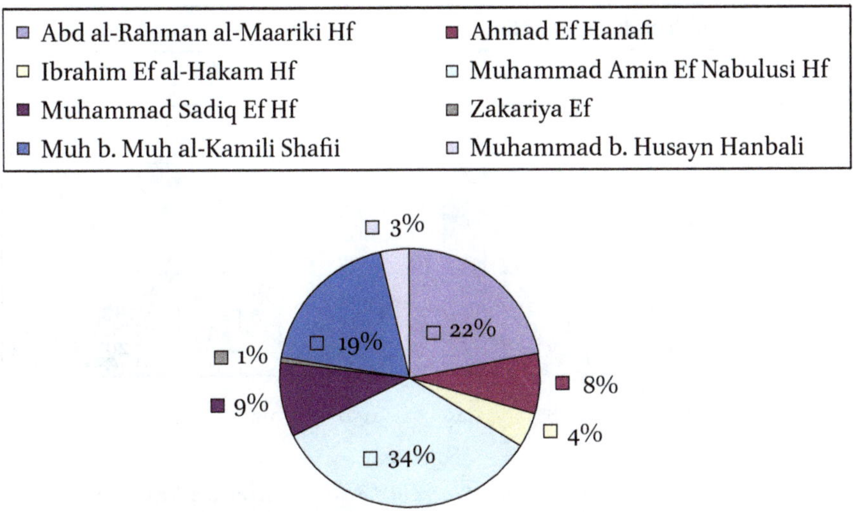

FIGURE 11.1 *Distribution of judges in the eighteenth century* (LCRD *88*).
SOURCE: COMPILED BY THE AUTHOR.

The Court and its Registration System

The courts were held by a judge (qadi) in the eighteenth century and by a deputy judge (*nā'ib*) in the nineteenth century. In Register 88 (eighteenth century), four Hanafi judges presided over about 78% of all the cases, with the Shafi'i taking 17.6 % and the Hanbali 3.3% (see Figure 11.1). Different judges held court at the same period. In the nineteenth century, six Hanafi judges presided over about 85% of the cases, the Shafi'i 14% and the Hanbali 1.3%. The Shafi'i and Hanbali judges often dealt with lease contracts for land and shops, because these two schools approved long-term lease contracts of nine years by renewing three-year contracts, whereas the Hanafi school restricted such contracts to only a single term of two or three years. The registers were recorded by scribes (*kātib, muqayyid*), whose names are written at the end of each document, and they acted as the witness (*shuhūd al-ḥāl*) who certified the deed.

The nineteenth century registers are not recorded in a precise chronological sequence, as each volume was written over a period of two to four years, and their periods overlapped. (Figure 11.2 shows the number of cases each year.) The legal documents were written according to a manual (*shurūṭ*) which shows the format and formula for each kind of transaction so that the scribe could make a deed merely by filling the blanks with individual information,

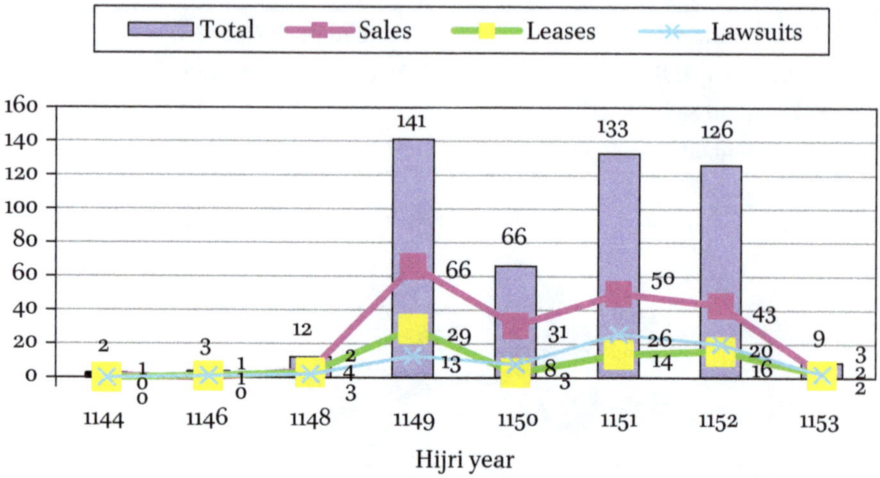

FIGURE 11.2A *Chronological distribution of cases in the eighteenth century (register 88).*
SOURCE: COMPILED BY THE AUTHOR.

such as the names of the parties and witnesses, and the location and composition of the properties being transacted. The scribes did not necessarily record the deeds (*ḥujja*) issued in the register in a chronological order, but registered those in the same category of transaction at a single time, based on notes classified according to the type of transaction or the individual/family concerned. The eighteenth-century registers, on the other hand, are recorded in a more chronological fashion: Register 88 ended in the year 1153/1740, and was followed by Register 105 which began in the year 1154, although it did include a very small number of documents from before 1153 AH (see Figure 11.2). The documents in them were not recorded strictly according to date, but nevertheless follow an almost chronological sequence.

The court dealt with 4.71 cases on average per month in the eighteenth-century according to Register 88 (there were about 10 cases per month in Register 105, with 712 cases over 60 months from 1154–64), and the number reached 11.8 cases per month in the year 1149/1736. In the nineteenth century, the Salihiyya court dealt with 12.2 cases per month, reaching 16.2 cases in the year 1291/1874–75 with a peak of 31 cases in the month of Muharram.

As may be surmised from the length of the documents, descriptions in the eighteenth-century registers are simpler than those in the nineteenth-century ones. Taking the example of the authentication process, in the nineteenth-century documents it was usual for two attestants (*muzakkī*) to attend the court

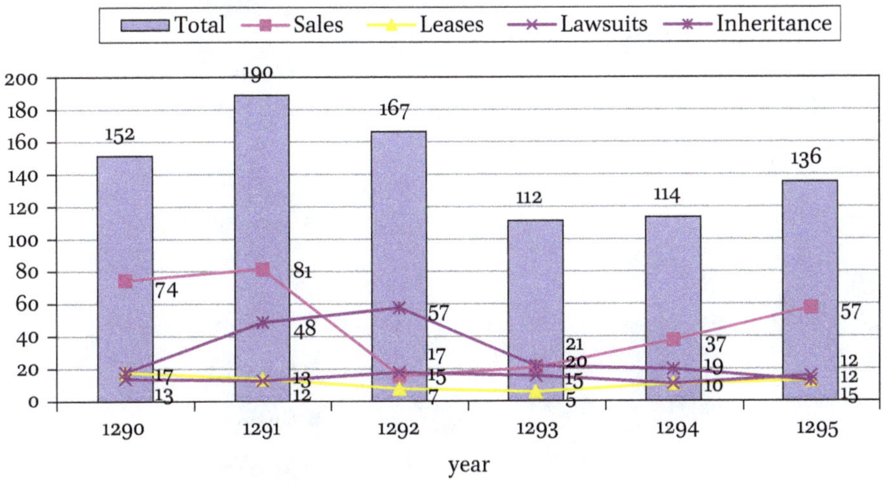

FIGURE 11.2B *Chronological distribution of cases in the nineteenth century.*
SOURCE: COMPILED BY THE AUTHOR.

to authenticate witnesses (*shāhid*), whereas it was rare for the eighteenth-century registers to record the attendance of such attestants.

Contents

Most of the shariʿa courts registers record transactions among residents such as the sale and lease of immovable property. The contents of the eighteenth-century Register 88 are shown in Figure 11.3A; the largest number of cases concern sales (42%), followed by property leases (14%) and lawsuits (14%). There are no records concerning inheritance, since there was a special court to deal with such matters. The contents of the nineteenth-century registers are shown in Figure 11.3B; again the largest number of cases concern sales (33%), but now inheritance (20%) and the guardianship of minors (14%) follow in terms of number, followed in turn by lawsuits (9%) and property leases (7%). It is notable that the major role of the Salihiyya court was to authenticate the transactions of people, especially those living in the quarter and in nearby villages, rather than to adjudicate lawsuits. When the transaction of a property was registered, reference was made to how the present owner obtained it, the date, and the court which registered it. Registering transactions of contracts in this way would have served to protect the owner's rights in case of any future conflict.

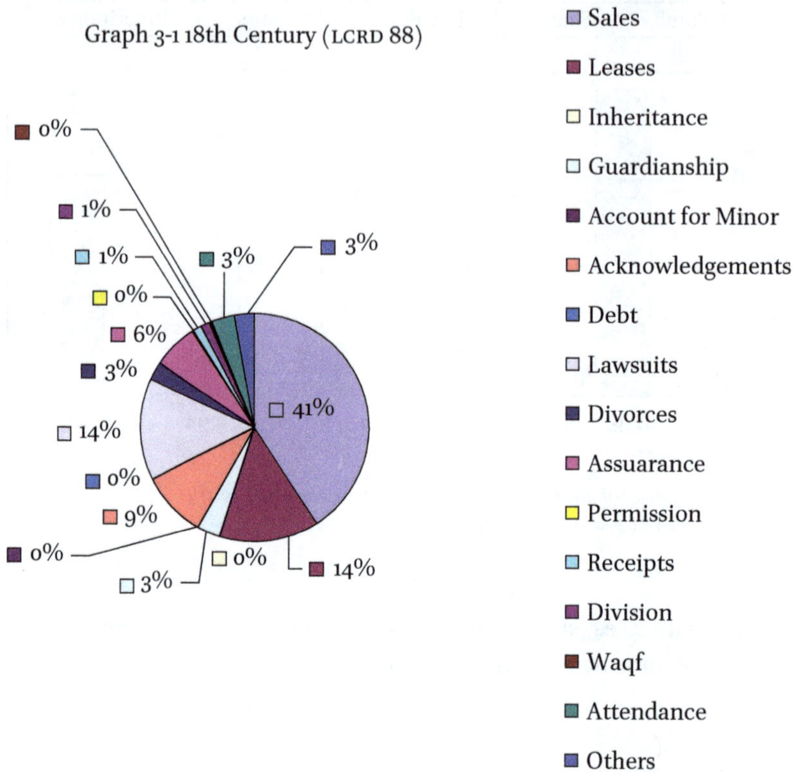

FIGURE 11.3A *Contents in the eighteenth century*
SOURCE: COMPILED BY THE AUTHOR.

In the nineteenth century, lawsuits primarily concerned debt (37%), followed by inheritance (24%) and sales (23%); criminal matters did not appear. Similarly, in the Çankırı and Kastamonu courts in Anatolia in the seventeenth and eighteenth centuries, disputes centred on civil matters such as inheritance, property and debt, though there were also cases involving theft, murder and rape.[6]

The descriptions in each document in the nineteenth century registers had to be exact copies of the original deed, while those in the eighteenth century appear to be summaries of the original deed, with some elements omitted. This will be discussed further below.

---

6 Ergene, *Local Court*, 58–59.

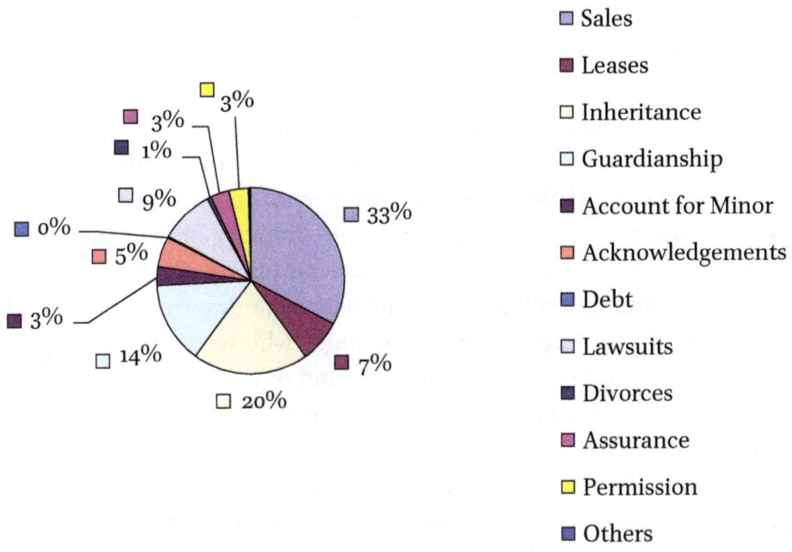

FIGURE 11.3B *Contents in the nineteenth century.*
SOURCE: COMPILED BY THE AUTHOR.

Parties

In cases involving sales and leases, a great number of sellers/buyers and lessors/lessees attended the court, for most immovable property was owned by more than one person. Figure 11.4 shows the number of transacting parties in the eighteenth and nineteenth centuries. Eighteenth-century sales documents show that there were 1.39 sellers and 1.20 buyers per case, and lease documents show 1.53 lessors and 1.69 lessees. The average number increased in the nineteenth century to 2.01 sellers and 1.29 buyers, and 2.81 lessors and 4.74 lessees. What was the reason for this increase? One assumption is that immovable property had been subdivided among descendants from generation to generation. The other possibility is that the eighteenth-century registers might not have recorded all the transacting parties, omitting some, such as minors and females.

The ratio of females and minors as transactors is different between the eighteenth and nineteenth centuries; both increased in the nineteenth century. In the eighteenth century, minors were 6.7% of all sellers, and 1.2% of all buyers, but 0% in cases of lease, while in the nineteenth they were 20.8% of all sellers and 14.1% of all buyers, and 11.7% of all lessors and 12.5% of all lessees. According to Islamic law, minors have the same rights of inheritance as adults and so can receive immovable property through inheritance. In fact, minors occupy 39.3% of all inheritors in the nineteenth century. The high ratio of minors in transactions concerning immovable property in the nineteenth century shows that minors did inherit and transact property, and were not unlawfully prevented from inheriting it by adults. Their shares were administered by guardians (*walī* or *waṣī*) appointed by the judge who were obliged to provide them with food, clothes etc. The guardian and other relatives received a loan from the minor's share, which they acknowledged in the registers. Reports of the accounts of the estates of minors recorded the balance between income such as interest earned from the loan and rent from any immovable property and the price of any property sold, and various expenses such as the daily costs incurred in the maintenance of the minors and repairs to immovable property. Since the cost of daily maintenance was relatively high, the minors' estates decreased year by year. This means that the minors' share of inheritance was nominal, being spent by their guardians and relatives.[7]

How then do we explain the low ratio of minors in the eighteenth century? It is strange that no minors at all were involved in lease contracts. We do not know whether they inherited their share according to the regulations of Islamic law, for the eighteenth century Salihiyya registers lack reference to any inheritance, nor do they contain reports of the accounts of minors. A possibility is that the inheritance by minors of immovable property was avoided to prevent further and smaller subdivision.[8] Alternatively, minors may not have been recorded in lease contracts, even if they were a lessor or lessee, since to record minors as transactors it was necessary to assign an agent (*wakīl* or *waṣī*) to authenticate the procuration contract itself. This complex procedure of agent authentication was done in the nineteenth century, but was very rare in the eighteenth.

7 Miura, "Formality and Reality," 120–122; Miura, *Dynamism in Urban Society of Damascus*, 268–271.

8 In sixteenth to nineteenth century Morocco, the *mukhāraja* partition was adopted where one property was allotted to one inheritor or a small number of inheritors in order to avoid subdivision among many sharers. See Toru Miura and Kentaro Sato, eds., *The Vellum Contracts Documents in Morocco in the Sixteenth to Nineteenth Centuries* (Tokyo: Toyo Bunko, 2015), 14.

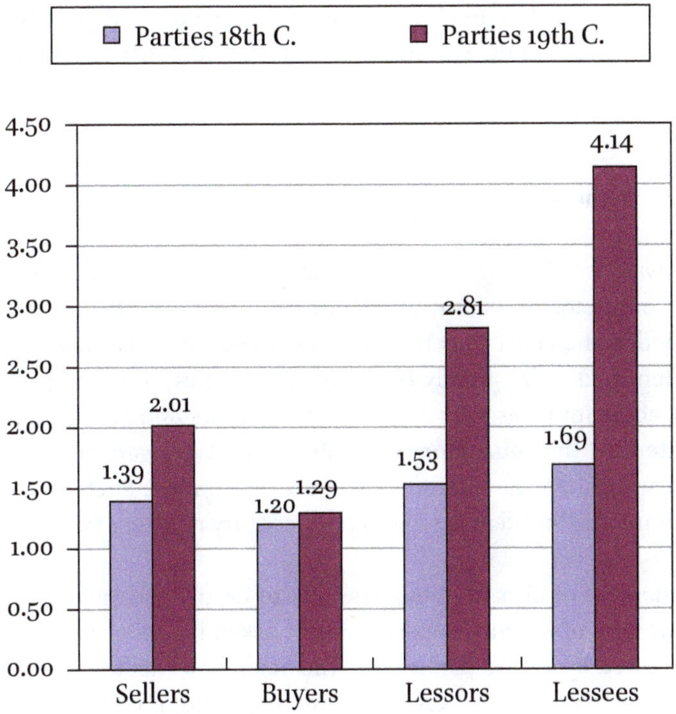

FIGURE 11.4 *Average number of parties in the eighteenth and nineteenth centuries.*
SOURCE: COMPILED BY THE AUTHOR.

In the eighteenth century, the ratio of females as transactors was 33.1% of all sellers and 7.4% of all buyers, and 19.6% of all lessors and 22.0% of all lessees. The ratio of females increased in the nineteenth century to 45.1% of all sellers and 28.1% of all buyers, and 31.1% of all lessors and 40.8% of all lessees. The high ratio of female sellers, approximately equal to males, shows that females exercised their rights of inheritance and owned immovable property, as they made up 51.7% of all heirs in the nineteenth century. However, the lower ratio of female buyers (28.1%) means that females tended to sell their property to get cash, rather than buying more property. What is the reason for the low ratio of females as transactors in the eighteenth century? Since female inheritees occupied about thirty percent of the total in Damascus during that time,[9] they

9 Colette Establet and Jean-Paul Pascual, *Familles et fortunes à Damas: 450 foyers damascaines en 1700* (Damas: IFEAD, 1994), 49.

must have possessed immovable property. Therefore, their names might have been omitted in order to avoid the complicated procedure for authenticating agents for female transactors.

Agents and Witnesses

An agent (*wakīl*) was usually assigned when females or minors transacted business, and in the nineteenth century, two witnesses, and two attesters for each witness, attended the court to certify this agent's contract. Twenty persons have been identified as frequently (more than ten times) attending the court as attestors, acquaintances (*ʿarrafa*), witnesses, agents and confirmers. Of them, seven attended the court more than fifty times. We regard them as professionals who were there to authenticate court registration. Such attendants at the courts are also found in the eighteenth-century registers, confirming the procedure.

Furthermore, there were also fictitious lawsuits to certify the validity of procuration. In this type of lawsuit, the seller/lessor asked his agent to claim payment of a debt owed by a third person, and the defendant (debtor) would acknowledge the debt, but deny the validity of the procuration contract between the seller/lessor and the agent. The agent would then ask the witnesses to confirm this procuration contract. Subsequently, the judge would evaluate the validity of the claim and order the debtor to pay the agent. As the amount of the debt was very small, the real purpose of this lawsuit was to recertify the procuration contract, in order to prevent the seller/lessor from bringing a lawsuit against the agent or the buyer/lessee that the agent had sold or leased property without his consent. The nineteenth-century registers carefully recorded such complex procedures. By contrast, in the eighteenth-century registers there can be found female parties without an agent, no attestors and no fictitious lawsuits to certify the procuration contract. The authentication procedure was simpler in the eighteenth century than in the nineteenth.

What is the reason for the strict and precise registration in the nineteenth century? The first is a change in economic conditions, due to the participation of Europeans in the Syrian market, especially in the latter half of the nineteenth century. Court registration was a safer way to protect one's rights than a deed without registration, as a British consular report testifies.[10] The second reason was a change in the court system, with the introduction of secular courts by

10 John Bowring, *Report on the Commercial Statistics of Syria* (London, 1840, repr: New York, 1973), 101.

the Ottoman government, which required a more speedy and precise registration by the shariʿa courts. The third was that unfair conduct such as bribery and false testimony at the shariʿa courts increased in the nineteenth century in Syria.[11] In such conditions, both court officials and the parties in the transaction might have felt the need to make court registration more precise and suited to Islamic law and the manuals (*shurūṭ*) for writing legal documents, either to protect their ownership from embezzlement or to attain ownership by fraud. Though the regulations regarding contracts in Islamic law are basically constant, the practice of issuing contracts and registering them differed greatly in the same Salihiyya court, depending on socio-economic conditions.

Qajar Iran

In contrast to the abundance of shariʿa court records in the Ottoman Empire, those of the Qajar period (1796–1925) in Iran have only recently become known, due to the growing accessibility of archival documents there. Legal deeds were endorsed and issued by a qadi (judge) or *mojtahed* at the courts, and then preserved at the houses of these judges. They have remained in private collections down to the present and have been used for study only since the end of the 1990s. Christoph Werner studied the development of deed formulae from pre-Mongol times to the Qajar period, and showed clearly that the textual formulary of sales deeds was settled in the later Qajar period in accordance with the establishment of the role and authority of the Iranian ʿulamaʾ independent from the state.[12] Nobuaki Kondo has published an article introducing and analysing three shariʿa court registers from Tehran in the latter half of the nineteenth century.[13] Here I will use his study to outline Qajar shariʿa court registers and compare them to those of Ottoman Syria.

The three registers were recorded and preserved by high-ranking ʿulamaʾ (*mojtahed*) who supervised the court outside government appointment in Qajar Iran. The registers should be regarded as the private archive of the judges. Between eleven and nineteen *mojtaheds* managed the court in Tehran, according to government yearbooks from the latter half of the nineteenth century. The individual documents written in the registers are summaries of the

11 Miura, "Personal Networks," 141–142; Miura, *Dynamism in the Urban Society of Damascus*, 245–246.

12 Werner, "Formal Aspects of Qajar Deeds."

13 Kondo, "Shariʿa Court Registers." See also his recent English book, Nobuaki Kondo, *Islamic Law and Society in Iran: A Social History of Qajar Tehran* (London: Routledge, 2017), chapters 3 and 5.

deeds endorsed and issued by the judge at the court. The main task of the court was to notarise the deeds presented to the court by registering them, and secondly to solve a dispute by issuing the judge's response (*ḥokm*) or by arranging a settlement (*muṣālaḥa*).

The contents of the documents are shown in Table 11.1. Of them, 23.9% were sales contracts, 14.3% were sales with optional stipulations, and 11.7% concerned debts. Most of the objects of sale concerned immovable property such as houses, villages, and land lots, the same as found in the Ottoman courts. However, a characteristic of the Qajar documents is that about 66% of the sales documents were written in the form of a mutual agreement (*muṣālaḥa*) contract, a type that has not been found in Ottoman Syria. It is not clear why a *muṣālaḥa* contract was concluded for a sale, but Werner has suggested that the *muṣālaḥa* contract allowed more flexibility for later cancellation or additional stipulations than did strict contracts.[14]

Another feature of the Qajar registers is the sales contract with stipulations (conditional sale): here, the seller was able to cancel the contract within the period declared in the contract, and he rented the property from the buyer, paying rent until he could cancel the contract by paying back the sales price to the buyer. This type of contract was eventually used so the seller could borrow cash from the buyer by pawning his property to the latter, and the rent was equivalent to interest. This was not found in the Ottoman Syrian registers.

Ḥokm (response) is a deed issued by the *mojtaḥed* in response to the party and includes the judgment on the litigation, while the *muṣālaḥa* contract served to register the contents of the mediation among the parties. The frequency of mediation, almost as often recorded as *muṣālaḥa* agreements, is the third feature of the Qajar records. There are a relatively small number of inheritance documents, though they were common in the Ottoman registers. The three major subjects treated in the Tehran court registers – the sale and lease of immovable property, debt and litigation responding to socio-economic needs in Tehran – are however similar to those in the Ottoman registers. The court was a place to record deeds in the registers for authentication, rather than being a place for deciding on litigation. The documents in the registers of Qajar Tehran and Ottoman Syria treated the contracting parties objectively, whether seller or buyer, lessor or lessee, using the grammatical third person; by contrast, contracts in Qing China and Japan were written in the first person, in a self-declaratory pronouncement.

14 Werner, "Formal Aspects of Qajar Deeds," 42–43.

TABLE 11.1 *Contents of the Tehran shari'a court registers.*

	Court S1	Court S2	Court N	Total	ratio
period	1867–68	1875–79	1886–89		
sales	194	1174	247	1615	23.6%
conditional sales	174	519	271	964	14.1%
debt	128	359	303	790	11.6%
ḥokm (response)	79	379	2	460	6.7%
muṣālaḥa	69	204	189	462	6.8%
proculation	66	266	47	379	5.5%
confirmation	60	419	7	486	7.1%
lease	47	198	130	375	5.5%
transcription	35	182	22	239	3.5%
ḥokm	32	122	5	160	2.3%
Total	993	4319	1524	6836	

SOURCE: compiled by the author based on Kondo "Shari'a Court Registers" and *Islamic Law and Society in Iran*, 279.

Central Asia in the Nineteenth Century

Toru Horikawa of the Kyoto University of Foreign Studies has been conducting a research project on Central Asian Archives since 1992,[15] when he purchased a collection containing about 1,700 shari'a court documents dating from the time of the Khiva Khanate in the nineteenth and twentieth centuries. He subsequently donated them to the al-Biruni Institute of Oriental Studies, Academy of Sciences of the Republic of Uzbekstan. In 1997, the Kyoto University of Foreign Studies concluded a memorandum with the al-Biruni Institute of Oriental Studies to edit a catalogue of these documents and to reproduce them photographically, and the first catalogue, in Russian, was published the same year. This project continues to collect and catalogue the court documents of Central Asia in cooperation with the al-Biruni Institute, the Ichan Qala Museum in Khiva, the National Museum in Samarqand, the Regional Museum in Ferghana, and the National Museum of Bukhara, through memoranda of joint research. It has held annual seminars in Kyoto since 2003 to contextualise

15 Horikawa, "Islamic Courts Documents."

and read the documents. Here I will give an outline of the shari'a court records in Central Asia based on the reports of these seminars.

Ken'ichi Isogai has outlined the documents collected in Khiva and Samarqand during 2001 to 2003.[16] There were 731 in total (Khiva 476, Samarqand 255), with 366 (50%) dating from the twentieth century and 19% from the latter half of the nineteenth century. Isogai classified the documents into four categories: administrative (12%), court contracts (51%), court litigation (23%), and others (14%). The majority of the contracts concern sales with an optional stipulation (*bayʿ-i jāʾiz*) to cancel within a limited period (40%), and sales in general (39%); third in number are declarations to abandon one's right. A sale with stipulations means selling a property with the stipulation that the seller can cancel the sale and take the property back by repaying the sales price to the buyer within a specified period. Its actual purpose was to borrow money from the buyer in the form of pawning the seller's property and renting it, paying a rent equivalent to the interest on the debt. It is similar to the contract with stipulations recorded in the Qajar registers in Tehran. Most of the documents are written as a form of acknowledgement (*iqrār*) in which one party acknowledged that he/she gives his/her right to the other party; this is then certified by witnesses (*shāhid*) and recorded by a scribe under the authority of the judge. Such registration might act as evidence when a conflict over rights occurred. Of particular interest are fatwa documents in the Samarqand collection where a mufti gave his opinion about a problem to the party (plaintiff or defendant) who requested his response in the litigation process.[17]

A few court registers, compiled under Russian governance (1867–1917) in the early twentieth century, were found in the provinces of Khoqand and Ferghana after 2006. Yoichi Yajima reported on a court register of the Khojund District in Khoqand Province dated 1908, recording 523 documents in the Uzbek language.[18] Their main concerns are sales (20%), sales with a stipulation (17%), and appointing an authorised proxy (*wakīl*) (14%). A court register of 1922 was found in Ferghana containing about 1,650 documents, recorded in

16 Ken'ichi Isogai, "Contract Documents in Central Asia: Format and Function," Paper presented at a seminar at the Institute of Languages and Cultures in Asia and Africa, Tokyo University for Foreign Studies 2003 (in Japanese).

17 Ken'ichi Isogai, "Seven Fatwa Documents from Early 20th Century Samarqand: The Function of Mufti in the Judicial Proceedings Adopted at the Central Asian Islamic Court," *Annals of Japan Association for Middle East Studies* 27, no. 1 (2009): 259–282.

18 Yoichi Yajima, "Court Records of the Khoqand Khanate under the Russian Rule," Paper presented at the Seminar for Central Asian Documents at the Kyoto University of Foreign Studies, 2006 (in Japanese).

Uzbek by several scribes in a chronological sequence. It should be noted that each document in these registers is recorded with a successive number, and the same successive numbers are written on the two individual documents which were collected by this Project. The description of each document in the register was a summary of the relevant case. Yajima assumes, drawing on Russian sources, that a numbering system with the same number written on the document and its copy in the register might have been brought into use under Russian governance.[19]

China in the Ming and Qing Periods

A great many contract documents remain in China from the third century CE, with most dating from the Ming and Qing periods (fourteenth to twentieth centuries). These contract documents were called 契 (*qi*) in the Ming-Qing period. Contracts were commonly used for an enormous variety of transactions, such as the division of households, betrothals, adoptions, the purchase of real property, conditional sales, the purchase of people, loan agreements, and bills of exchange.[20] The largest collection of documents from the Ming-Qing periods are from the province of Huizhou 徽州 and number more than one hundred thousand. There are also collections of contract documents from Taiwan 台湾, and contract documents from Guangzhou 広州, Fujian 福建, Zhejian 浙江 and other provinces have also been collected and published by Chinese scholars. There are in addition two thousand documents from Beijing 北京, Jiangsu 江蘇, Taiwan and other places in the collection of the Institute of Advanced Studies on Asia at the University of Tokyo.

I will introduce the content and formula of the contract documents based on studies of Chinese history.[21] Most of the contract documents relate to

19 Yoichi Yajima, "Court Records in Central Asia under the Russian Rule," Paper presented at the Seminar for Central Asian Documents at the Kyoto University of Foreign Studies, 2007 (in Japanese). There were a great number of legal documents in shariʿa courts as well as rulers' courts before and after Russian rule in Central Asia. See, Paolo Sartori, *Vision of Justice: Sharīʿa and Cultural Change in Russian Central Asia* (Leiden: Brill, 2017), in which he discusses how legal justice was conceived and attained in Central Asia.

20 Madeleine Zelin et al., eds. *Contract and Property in Early Modern China* (Stanford: Stanford University Press, 2004), 23–24.

21 Rosser H. Brockman, "Commercial Contract Law in Late Nineteenth-Century Taiwan," in *Essays on China's Legal Tradition*, ed. Jerome Alan Cohen et al. (Princeton: Princeton University Press. 1980), 77–136; Mio Kishimoto, "Contract Documents in the Ming and Qing Periods," in *Chinese Legal History*: Studies on Basic Source Materials, ed. Shuzo Shiga (Tokyo: The University of Tokyo Press, 1993), 759–805 (in Japanese); Kishimoto, "Property

transactions of immovable property, especially sales documents which were given by the seller to the buyer to certify the transfer of the property, similar to the contract documents in the shariʿa courts. Other sales items included movable property, water supply, usufruct of ovens and mills, government work such as taxation and the sale of salt, business rights for shops, and slaves.

There are two kinds of sales contract: an unconditional and perpetual sale called *juemai* 絶売, and a sale with the stipulation to reserve the right to redeem the property later, called *huomai* 活売. The latter means that the seller pawns his land to the buyer until the redemption deadline. Thus it was also called *dian* 典 (pawn). In principle, all land in China belonged to the emperor/king (or the state), but this notion did not prevent actual possession of the land by the people who cultivated it and transacted it by means of open and free contracts.

An unconditional sales document for agricultural land first states the name of the seller using the phrase "the one making the contract of unconditional sale is so-and-so." In general, the seller is the head of the family. Second, the seller states the reason and purpose of the sale. Third, the object of sale (e.g. agricultural land) is described. Fourth, the price of the land and its payment is certified by the names of the seller, the buyer and the middleman. Then follow certain prescribed sentences that the relatives have consented to the sale, that the buyer will pay the required tax, and that all has been done by the mutual agreement of the seller and the buyer. Finally, additional information such as the names of any lessee and the rent paid is recorded. Sometimes the seller attached to it the older documents which the seller received from the former owners. Where the seller has asked the government to certify the contract and has paid the contract fee, authorisation is given in the form of an official stamp by the government. This is called a 'red contract,' as opposed to a 'white contract,' one without an official stamp. The format hardly varied according to region and time during the Ming-Qing period.[22]

The Chinese contract documents have six features. (1) The contractor made the contract document himself and passed it to the other party through the mediation of a middleman. (2) The contract was certified by the middleman and authorised by the government with a stamp. (3) The main concern of the government was to record the name of the taxpayer. The government recorded

Rights, Land and Law in Imperial China," in *Law and Long-Term Economic Change: A Eurasian Perspective*, ed. Debin Ma and Jan Luiten van Zanden (Stanford: Stanford University Press, 2011), 68–90; Sachiko Usui, "Contract Documents between Individuals in the Ming and Qing Dynasties," in *The Multilateral Comparative Study on Documents from 9th to the 19th Centuries: Annual Report 2010* (Tokyo: National Institute of Japanese Literature, 2011), 91–99 (in Japanese).

22 Kishimoto, "Contract Documents in the Ming and Qing Periods."

the change of taxpayer when the sales document was submitted to it. However, since sales contracts were valid without being submitted to the government, many sales documents are without an official stamp. (4) There were two kinds of sale: unconditional, and conditional with a stipulation that the seller had the option to buy back the land within a limited time (usually three or five years, but possibly more), renting it from the buyer in the meantime. (5) Two kinds of right were connected with land: the right of ownership of the land itself, with the right to sell, inherit and donate it, and the right of its use as usufruct. The notion and custom of "two masters to a field" were widespread. The idea of multi-layered ownership is characteristic of China and similar to that found in Islamic law (*rakaba* and *manfa'a*). (6) There was not much positive law that regulated ownership and its transfer. Economic transactions were conducted based on social customs and relationships. When a conflict occurred, it was settled by means of mediation, arbitration, and adjudication.

In Korea, which was located between China and Japan in terms of geography, history and society, many kinds of contract documents were made in the Joseon period (fourteenth to nineteenth centuries). As in China, there were two kinds of sales contract, perpetual/unconditional sale and sale with a stipulation to repay the cost in ten years. After a sales contract was concluded and completed, it had to be submitted to the government, which then issued an authorizing document. Government authorisation was effective if a conflict occurred among the persons concerned, but all the same there seems to have been many contract documents that were not submitted to the government. The sales documents, with older ones certifying former transactions, were the most important evidence to certify ownership.[23]

Tokugawa Japan

A great many contract documents were produced and preserved in the Edo period (1603–1867) under the Tokugawa Shogunate. It should be noted that most of them were written by rural and urban notables, signed by those concerned and by third parties, and preserved at the houses of the owners of the transacted rights. The National Institute of Japanese Literature has been running a research project headed by Professor Koichi Watanabe from 2010 called

23 Sook-Ja Moon, "Contract Documents between Individuals in Joseon Korea," in *The Multilateral Comparative Study on Documents from the 9th to the 19th Centuries: Annual Report 2011* (Tokyo: National Institute of Japanese Literature, 2011), 133–143 (in Korean), 144–154 (in Japanese).

the Multilateral Comparative Study on Documents from the 9th to the 19th Centuries. International conferences have been held on topics such as contract documents, dispute resolution and authentication of private deeds in collaboration with scholars of European, Ottoman, Chinese and Korean history. I survey the features of contract documents in East Asia using the reports in this project.

There were two kinds of land sale documents in Japan in this period: one for the sale of rural land and the other for that of urban land. Peasants had a low-ranking ownership, that is, a usufruct right to cultivate the land and to take the harvest with the obligation of paying tax to their overlords. From the seventeenth century, they could sell this ownership to another with the stipulation that they could buy it back within ten years, though perpetual sale of land was in principle forbidden. This type of sale was in effect pawning the land in exchange for cash. The conditional sale document was titled "a written proof of the pawning of land" and gave basic information such as its location, size, and putative agricultural yield (*kokudaka*) affirmed by the official land register (*kenchichō*), as well as the reason for pawning it, the price of the pawned land, and the redemption deadline. It states that the pledgee was to pay land taxes while the land was in his possession and that the pledger could repay the cost of the pawned land no later than the redemption deadline, while the pledgee would become its owner if the pledger could not pay the amount back. The pledgee had the right to use the land during the period of pawning, either to cultivate himself or to lease it to the pledger. The pledgee received income from the harvest or rent, equivalent to the interest for the loan. The pawning document was authenticated by the head of relatives and the village chief, and the change of ownership was recorded in the land register. The authenticated document and the land register were the certificates of land ownership.[24] This contract of pawning land is very similar to the conditional sale of land in Central Asia and China. The deadline had to be declared in the contract in Qajar Iran and Central Asia, but in Japan and China it was based on social custom, and ambiguity of possession caused disputes between the seller and the buyer there.

Urban land could be sold in perpetuity. The sales document was written by the seller and given to the buyer, and certified/guaranteed by a member of the neighborhood organisation (*gonin-gumi* 五人組) and the head of the

24 Tatsuo Shirakawabe, "Customs of Land Sales in Early Modern Japan and Peasant Societies in East Asia," in *The Multilateral Comparative Study on Documents from the 9th to the 19th Centuries: Annual Report 2010* (Tokyo: National Institute of Japanese Literature, 2011), 108–115 (in Japanese), 123–132 (in English).

TABLE 11.2 *Common items of contract documents for immovable property.*

Items	Description		
Subject	individual person	family/ lineage	corporation/association
Object	land	house	shop
Transaction	sale	pawn	lease
Production	writer	format	phrase
Certification	middleman	government	court/witness, judge
Preservation	individual person	family	court/ registration
Regulations	law	customs	manual

SOURCE: compiled by the author.

quarter. The latter revised the several kinds of land register (*mizuchō* 水帳 and *kenchichō* 検地帳 etc.) that he kept.[25] It is characteristic of Tokugawa Japan that land ownership and its transfer should be certified and recorded by the heads and notables of the local community, in both rural villages and urban areas.

Concluding Remarks

I conclude my paper by presenting some comparative viewpoints regarding contracts for transactions concerning immovable property (sales, lease and pawn). A number of common items relating to the contract have been found in the five regions mentioned above (Ottoman Syria, Iran, Central Asia, China and Japan): (1) subject of contract (2) object of contract (3) kinds of transaction (4) production of contract (5) certification/authentication (6) preservation (7) regulations.

We may assume various types of contract based on the above-mentioned criteria. In a previous paper, I suggested, as the device used to bind different individuals beyond the three points of time (past, present and future), "the universality of law in Europe, a third party in the Islamic Middle East, and

25 Koichi Watanabe, "Contract Documents in the Early Modern Japanese Cities: The Case of Land Trades," in *The Multilateral Comparative Study on Documents from the 9th to the 19th Centuries: Annual Report 2010* (Tokyo: National Institute of Japanese Literature, 2011), 30–35 (in Japanese), 42–47 (in English).

complete agreement in China".[26] Here I present two different models of region/society concerning contracts: the East Asian/Chinese model (China, Korea and Japan), and the Islamic/Ottoman Syrian one.

The East Asian/Chinese model is characterised by four features. First, the subject of the contract was in effect the family, although an individual such as the household head represented the family in the document. In Islamic law, though, only an individual person could be the subject for owning and transacting a property.

Second, in China, the contract was certified by the attendance and signature of a middleman who knew the persons concerned (seller and buyer, etc.) and the object of the transaction. In Tokugawa Japan and Joseon Korea, middlemen were local notables. Land registers were revised when the contract was submitted to the government or the local community in China, Korea and Japan. By contrast, in Islamic regions, the contract was certified by professional witnesses who did not necessarily have a personal relationship with the persons concerned.

Third, the objects of transaction are common to both regional models: immovable property had multi-layered rights that were transacted separately in individual contracts in both China and in Islamic regions. However, conditional sales with the option of redeeming the object (land) within a limited time were often made in East Asia, whereas sales with any condition at all were in principle forbidden under Islamic law. Islamic law allows pledging a property as a surety for credit, but the pledged property could be used or leased only by the mutual agreement of the pledger and pledgee.[27] Nevertheless, it may be noted that conditional sales with a stipulation to buy back the object within a limited time are found in Central Asia (Uzbekistan) in the nineteenth century and in Qajar Iran. No such conditional sales documents to pawn the land have been found in Ottoman Syria, but a loan to waqf property when it needed repair, called *murṣad*, did exist and it was common in Damascus in the eighteenth and nineteenth centuries. In general, the creditor had the right to rent the waqf property, and the rent paid by the creditor/renter was to be allotted to repay the debt owed by the waqf.[28] It resembles a pawn contract in that the waqf property, or more precisely its superintendant, lends the immovable

---

26 Miura, "Court Contracts and Agreements," 66.

27 Joseph Schacht, *An Introduction to Islamic Law* (London: The Clarendon Press, 1964), 139–140; Hiroyuki Yanagihashi, *Islamic Property Law* (Tokyo: The University of Tokyo Press, 2012), 745–774 (in Japanese).

28 Miura, "Formality and Reality," 117–118; Miura, *Dynamism in the Urban Society of Damascus*, 263–265.

property to the creditor in exchange for a long-period loan, but the ownership does not change either in the present or the future.

The fourth point is the role of government. In East Asia/China, it was not necessary to submit a contract to the government, though it was authenticated by an official red stamp if submitted. The state's interest was confined to identifying and recording the tax payer. In reality there were a great number of sales documents in China that were without the red stamp. In Japan, the local community revised the land register according to the sales documents and these registers were used to certify ownership and identify who paid tax. Both in pre-modern China and Japan, when selling or donating an immovable property, it was the custom to give old documents to the new owner together with the contract document of the present transaction, in order to certify the ownership in the past and in the future. On the other hand, in Ottoman Syria and Qajar Iran, sales documents of immovable property were issued at the shariʿa court and authenticated by being recorded in the court registers. The court took the role of authentication. The Ottoman government compiled land survey registers for taxation until the sixteenth century. The Ottoman state left the registering and authenticating of contracts among the people to the courts, but organised the collection of taxes in another way, such as tax farming.

In summary, it seems that Ottoman Syria and Tokugawa Japan stand at opposite poles with regard to contract documents. The former model is individualistic: individual persons contracted with one another to transact ownership either by sale or lease, and the contract was certified and authorised by a third person. The intervention of the local community was minimum, but the role of the court to register the contracts as well as to judge the lawsuits was huge. By contrast, Tokugawa Japan was collective: collective bodies such as the family and regional and professional organisations possessed ownership and transacted it, and the contract was certified and authenticated by these regional/professional bodies. Regarding the judicial system, in the shariʿa court a civil lawsuit is in principle judged by the testimony of two witnesses, although written documents were submitted as corroborating evidence. In Tokugawa Japan, a civil lawsuit could be submitted to the court with the agreement of the headman of the local community, and mediation between the parties was recommended. The decision was made based on both written certificates and oral testimony.[29]

---

29 Reiko Sugimoto, "Justice in Early Modern Japan Revisited; Society and Justice," in *The Muslitateral Comparative Study on Documents from the 9th to the 19th Centuries; Annual Report 2012* (Tokyo: National Institute of Japanese Literature, 2011), 286–299. Reiji Iwabuchi, "Documents of Dispute Resolution in Early Modern Japanese Cities:

However, we should not regard these two models as being exclusively in opposition. As seen in Ottoman Syria, minors and females were flexible and changing actors subsumed in the body of the family (household). Female household heads and creditors did exist in Tokugawa Japan, though male household heads had gained great power. As Jonathan K. Ocko, a legal historian of China says, transactors in China should be understood "to be part of a multilateral web of relationships rather than as parties in a simple bilateral transaction."[30] In Qing China, the ultimate goal of the judicial system was the agreement of the parties under the authority and insight of the provincial governor by various means of investigation, persuasion and threat of punishment, rather than judgement according to a consistent law of universal validity.[31] The lawsuit ended by submitting a letter of consent to the judgement from the parties in Qing China and Tokugawa Japan. In Islamic regions, mediation between the parties was also done either inside or outside the shariʿa court.[32]

Although there were commonalities and differences in regard to the form of the contracts among the five regions, registering or making a copy of the contract was unique to the shariʿa court, which demanded enormous commitment by the parties and the court officials. Its spread and generalisation might be due to the division of the property ownership under Islamic law. Second, the individual, whether party, witness or judge, took a more formal role in the shariʿa court, rather than the more substantial one seen in China and Japan. A further question we should consider is how contract documents were produced and kept to certify the ownership of immovable property in regions under Islamic law without court registers, such as pre-modern Morocco.[33]

A Case Study on Litigation over Land Ownership" (Tokyo: National Institute of Japanese Literature, 2012), 123–129 (in Japanese), 137–145).

30 Jonathan Ocko, "The Missing Metaphor: Applying Western Legal Scholarship to the Study of Contract and Property in Early Modern China," in *Contract and Property in Early Modern China*, ed. Madeleine Zelin et al. (Stanford: Stanford University Press, 2004), 178–205.

31 Shuzo Shiga, *The Law and the Courts in Qing China* (Tokyo: Sobunsha, 1984) (in Japanese).

32 Miura, "Personal Newworks," 134–142; Miura, *Dynamism in the Urban Society of Damascus*, 244–245; Işik Tamdoğan, "Sulh and the 18th Century Ottoman Courts of Üsküdar and Adana," *Islamic Law and Society* 15 (2008): 55–83.

33 Toru Miura, "Introduction," in *The Vellum Contracts Documents in Morocco in the sixteenth to Nineteenth Centuries*, ed. Toru Miura and Kentaro Sato (Tokyo: Toyo Bunko, 2015), 6.

Bibliography

Bloch, Marc. "Pour une histoire comparée des sociétés Européennes." *Revue de Synthese Historique* 46 (1928): 15–50.

Bloch, Marc. "A Contribution towards a Comparative History of European Societies." In *Land and Work in Medieval Europe: Selected papers by Marc Bloch*, translated by J.E. Anderson, 44–81. Berkeley: University of California Press, 1967.

Bowring, John. *Report on the Commercial Statistics of Syria*. London: Clowes, 1840.

Brockman, Rosser H. "Commercial Contract Law in Late Nineteenth-Century Taiwan." In *Essays on China's Legal Tradition*, edited by Fu-mei C. Chen, Jerome A. Cohen, and Randle Edwards, 77–136. Princeton: Princeton University Press, 1980.

Coşgel, Metin and Boğaç Ergene. *The Economics of Ottoman Justice: Settlement and Trial in the Sharia Courts*. Cambridge: Cambridge University Press, 2016.

Ergene, Boğaç A. *Local Court, Provincial Society and Justice in the Ottoman Empire: Legal Practice and Dispute Resolution in Çankırı and Kastamonu (1652–1744)*. Leiden: Brill, 2003.

Establet, Colette, and Jean-Paul Pascual. *Familles et fortunes à Damas: 450 foyers damascaines en 1700*. Damas: IFEAD, 1994.

Ghazzal, Zouhair. *The Grammars of Adjudication: The Economics of Judicial Decision Making in fin-de-siècle Ottoman Beirut and Damascus*. Beirut: Institut Français du Proche-Orient, 2007.

Horikawa, Toru. "Islamic Court Documents as Historical Sources in Central Asia." In *History and Culture of Central Asia*, edited by Toru Horikawa, 73–84. Tokyo: NIHU Program Islamic Area Studies, The University of Tokyo Unit, 2012.

Isogai, Ken'ichi. "Contract Documents in Central Asia: Format and Function." Paper presented at a seminar at the Institute of Languages and Cultures in Asia and Africa, Tokyo University for Foreign Studies 2003 (in Japanese).

Isogai, Ken'ichi. "Seven Fatwa Documents from Early 20th Century Samarqand: The Function of Mufti in the Judicial Proceedings Adopted at the Central Asian Islamic Court." *Annals of Japan Association for Middle East Studies* 27, no. 1 (2009): 259–282.

Iwabuchi, Reiji. "Documents of Dispute Resolution in Early Modern Japanese Cities. A Case Study on Litigation over Land Ownership," 123–129 (in Japanese), 137–145. Tokyo: National Institute of Japanese Literature, 2012.

Kishimoto, Mio. "Contract Documents in the Ming and Qing Periods." In *Chinese Legal History: Studies on Basic Source Materials*, edited by Shuzo Shiga, 759–805. Tokyo: The University of Tokyo Press, 1993 (in Japanese).

Kishimoto, Mio. "Property Rights, Land and Law in Imperial China." In *Law and Long-Term Economic Change: A Eurasian Perspective*, edited by Debin Ma and Jan Luiten van Zanden, 68–90. Stanford: Stanford University Press, 2011.

Kondo, Nobuaki. "*Shari'a* Court Registers from Tehran in the Second Half of the Nineteenth Century." *Toyoshi kenkyu* 70, no. 2 (2011): 1–32 (in Japanese).

Kondo, Nobuaki. *Islamic Law and Society in Iran: A Social History of Qajar Tehran*. London: Routledge, 2017.

Marino, Brigitte, and Tomoki Okawara, eds. *Catalogue des registres des tribunaux ottomans conservés au Centre des Archives de Damas*. Damas: IFEAD, 1999.

Miura, Toru. "Personal Networks surrounding the Ṣāliḥiyya Court in 19th-Century Damascus." In *Etudes sur les villes arabes du Proche-Orient, XVIe–XIXe siécle*, edited by Brigitte Marino, 113–150. Damas: IFEAD, 2001.

Miura, Toru. "Formality and Reality in Shari'a Court Records: Socio-Economic Relations in the Ṣāliḥiyya Quarter of Nineteenth Century Damascus." *The Memoir of the Toyo Bunko* 59 (2002): 109–141.

Miura, Toru. "Court Contracts and Agreements among Parties in the Islamic Middle East." *Annals of Japan Association for Middle East Studies* 19, no. 2 (2003): 45–74.

Miura, Toru. "Introduction." In *The Vellum Contracts Documents in Morocco in the Sixteenth to Nineteenth Centuries*, edited by Toru Miura and Kentaro Sato, 1–7.Tokyo: Toyo Bunko, 2015.

Miura, Toru, and Kentaro Sato, eds. *The Vellum Contracts Documents in Morocco in the Sixteenth to Nineteenth Centuries*. Tokyo: Toyo Bunko, 2015.

Miura, Toru. *Dynamism in the Urban Society of Damascus: The Ṣāliḥiyya Quarter from the Twelfth to the Twentieth Centuries*. Leiden: Brill, 2016.

Moon, Sook-Ja. "Contract Documents between Individuals in Joseon Korea." In *The Multilateral Comparative Study on Documents from the 9th to the 19th Centuries: Annual Report 2011*, 133–154. Tokyo: National Institute of Japanese Literature, 2011.

Sartori, Paolo. *Vision of Justice: Sharīʿa and Cultural Change in Russian Central Asia*. Leiden: Brill, 2017.

Schacht, Joseph. *An Introduction to Islamic Law*. London: The Clarendon Press, 1964.

Shiga, Shuzo. *The Law and the Courts in Qing China*. Tokyo: Sobunsha, 1984.

Shirakawabe, Tatsuo. "Customs of Land Sales in Early Modern Japan and Peasant Societies in East Asia." In *The Multilateral Comparative Study on Documents from the 9th to the 19th Centuries: Annual Report 2010*, 108–132. Tokyo: National Institute of Japanese Literature, 2011.

Sugimoto, Reiko. "Justice in Early Modern Japan revisited; Society and Justice." In *The Multilateral Comparative Study on Documents from the 9th to the 19th Centuries; Annual Report 2012*, 286–299. Tokyo: National Institute of Japanese Literature, 2011.

Tamdoğan, Işik. "Sulh and the 18th Century Ottoman Courts of Üsküdar and Adana." *Islamic Law and Society* 15, no. 1 (2008): 55–83.

Usui, Sachiko. "Contract Documents between Individuals in the Ming and Qing Dynasties." In *The Multilateral Comparative Study on Documents from 9th to the 19th Centuries: Annual Report 2010*, 91–99. Tokyo: National Institute of Japanese Literature, 2011.

Watanabe, Koichi. "Contract Documents in the Early Modern Japanese Cities: The Case of Land Trades." In *The Multilateral Comparative Study on Documents from the 9th to the 19th Centuries: Annual Report 2010*, 30–47. Tokyo: National Institute of Japanese Literature, 2011.

Werner, Christoph. "Formal Aspects of Qajar Deeds of Sale." In *Persian Documents: Social History of Iran and Turan in the Fifteenth-Nineteenth Centuries*, edited by Nobuaki Kondo, 13–49. London: Routledge Curzon, 2003.

Yajima, Yoichi. "Court Records of the Khoqand Khanate under the Russian Rule." Paper presented at the Seminar for Central Asian Documents at the Kyoto University of Foreign Studies, 2006 (in Japanese).

Yajima, Yoichi. "Court Records in Central Asia under the Russian Rule." Paper presented at the Seminar for Central Asian Documents at the Kyoto University of Foreign Studies, 2007 (in Japanese).

Yajima, Yoichi. "Russian Supervision over Islamic Courts in Early Twentieth-Century Samarqand." *Annals of Japan Association for Middle East Studies* 32, no. 2 (2017): 21–32.

Yanagihashi, Hiroyuki. *Islamic Property Law*. Tokyo: The University of Tokyo Press, 2012.

Zelin, Madeleine, Robert Gardella, Chao Li, and Jonathan K. Ocko, eds. *Contract and Property in Early Modern China*. Stanford: Stanford University Press, 2004.

Index

Page numbers in bold refer to illustrations

www.ingramcontent.com/pod-product-compliance
Lightning Source LLC
Chambersburg PA
CBHW071249180926
51613CB00002B/177